ACTIVIST ARCHIVES

Youth Culture and the Political Past in Indonesia   DOREEN LEE

DUKE UNIVERSITY PRESS   DURHAM AND LONDON   2016

© 2016 Duke University Press
All rights reserved
Printed in the United States of America on acid-free paper ∞
Designed by Heather Hensley
Typeset in Minion Pro by Graphic Composition, Inc., Bogart, Georgia

Library of Congress Cataloging-in-Publication Data
Names: Lee, Doreen, [date] author.
Title: Activist archives : youth culture and the political past in
Indonesia / Doreen Lee.
Description: Durham : Duke University Press, 2016. | Includes
bibliographical references and index.
Identifiers: LCCN 2015044451
ISBN 9780822361527 (hardcover : alk. paper)
ISBN 9780822361718 (pbk. : alk. paper)
ISBN 9780822374091 (e-book)
Subjects: LCSH: College students—Political activity—
Indonesia. | Student movements—Indonesia. | Indonesia—Politics and
government—1998– | Nationalism—Indonesia.
Classification: LCC LA1273.7 .L443 2016 | DDC 378.1/98109598—dc23
LC record available at http://lccn.loc.gov/2015044451

Cover art: Daniel Rudi Haryanto, *Red Cafe*. Courtesy of the artist.

| For my parents.

CONTENTS

This book is about young people inhabiting a radical position in time and space, breaking up the malignant calm of an authoritarian regime in small and massive ways. It is mostly about university students, but other youth and social types are present as well. It takes place in Indonesia, an archipelago of more than nineteen thousand islands, the fourth largest country in the world, with the largest Muslim population. It takes place against Suharto's New Order regime, which lasted from 1966 to 1998. Most important, it takes place in the shadow of violence, structural, epistemological, and physical.

Indonesia's transition to democracy was marked by a series of unresolved acts of violence, martyrdoms, and popular push-back. These pages give the dates and events that formed the context of violence for activist lives and decisions during a particularly intense period of confrontation between the state and civilians. My book was never going to be an exhaustive history of Reformasi or of the various groups that composed the movement itself; others have done it better than I could. Nor do I take a hardboiled, whodunnit approach to confront the conspiracy theories that follow whenever violence occurs in Indonesia. Yet I think it important to show readers what regime change looks like, and how the cumulative effect of violence begets the traces of fear, memory, and adrenaline that lurk in the smallest spaces and in the most ordinary event.

The events in the list that follows serve as a historical primer for the violence that shaped the student movement's experience of the Indonesian state and gave youth a vocabulary to talk about injustice. The list is select, as most of these events occurred in the capital city, Jakarta. And it begins with a foundational violence that foreshadows the treatment of leftist students three decades later.

OCTOBER 1965–MARCH 1966:
THE BIRTH OF THE NEW ORDER AND ANTI-COMMUNISM IN INDONESIA

These dates correspond to the period of organized mass killings of an estimated 1 million alleged leftists in Indonesia, led by the army. It was also the period during which General Suharto came to power, stripping the nation's founding father, Soekarno, of his powers. The "New Order" state created the specter of communism as the nation's greatest enemy and maintained its anti-communist propaganda to the very end, effectively silencing dissidents and stamping out protest among the peasantry, workers, and urban intelligentsia.

JULY 27, 1996: THE JULY 27 INCIDENT

The forcible removal of Megawati from the chair position of the opposition Indonesian Democratic Party came to a head in a violent attack by troops and armed militias on the party's Jakarta headquarters. Hundreds were injured and arrested; more than twenty people disappeared. Students were among the attacked supporters of the party, yet they were accused by the state of being communists and of fomenting violence. Left-leaning activists and Megawati supporters fled Jakarta to avoid arrest.

1997–1998

Over the span of a year, twenty-three activists were kidnapped by the army, and thirteen were disappeared. At the same time, the Asian Financial Crisis swept through Southeast Asia, and Indonesia's currency, the rupiah, tanked. "Total Crisis" followed, and nationwide student demonstrations calling for Suharto's resignation increased rapidly from March 1998 onward.

MAY 12, 1998: THE TRISAKTI TRAGEDY

The first of the Reform-era tragedies, the killings of four students and two other civilians at Trisakti University, sparked major protests around the country.

MAY 13–14, 1998: THE MAY RIOTS

Jakarta became a city under siege following the Trisakti Tragedy. Angry mobs looted and burned Chinese-owned commercial areas and property. The most frightening acts of violence took place against women and girls of Chinese descent or Chinese appearance who were gang-raped, mutilated, and burned to death. More than a thousand residents of Jakarta, many of them looters from urban poor communities, died trapped in burning malls. Investigations by independent researchers and by the National Commission of Human Rights have strongly suggested that the riots were organized rather than spontaneous acts.

MAY 17–19, 1998

Students occupied the parliament building in a show of force, with tacit support from political leaders that they would have safe passage from the compound.

MAY 21, 1998

Suharto's resignation was read aloud on national television. Vice President B. J. Habibie succeeded Suharto to become the third president of Indonesia.

NOVEMBER 13, 1998: THE FIRST SEMANGGI TRAGEDY

Students amassed on the streets of Jakarta to protest the Extraordinary Parliamentary Session amid heavy security by the armed forces. Provocations by progovernment militia groups led to violence on the streets. The army opened fire, killing thirteen people, including four students.

SEPTEMBER 23–24, 1999: THE SECOND SEMANGGI TRAGEDY

As parliament moved to debate an emergency bill that would increase the powers of the army, demonstrators mobilized in Jakarta to protest the return of militarism. Six people were killed when the security forces opened fire.

| | |

It was a difficult thing to title this book. "We live in the roundness of life," as Gaston Bachelard wrote. It is this very quality of fullness, roundness, that I see in the political lives of activist youth in Indonesia and that seemed to reject each naming as flatly partial, not quite right. This book means to give you a sense of why that was so.

ACKNOWLEDGMENTS

This book encompassed three stages of my academic life: graduate school at Cornell University, my visiting post at Amherst College, and my present job at Northeastern University. As a result, I have many people to thank and intellectual debts to pay. It is my pleasure to thank the following for their contributions to this book.

Field research for this project was supported by a Fulbright-Hays grant, the Milton Barnett grant, with follow-up trips sponsored by the Dean's Office at Amherst College. I thank Benny Widyono for his help in locating Indonesian sponsorship for my research, and the CSDS at Atma Jaya Catholic University for hosting me. The Karl Lowenstein fellowship at Amherst College enabled me to work on chapter 2 and chapter 3 of this book. An IIAS fellowship at the International Institute for Asian Studies at the University of Leiden gave me the time and space to carry out archival research at the International Institute for Social History (IISG), and to write the introduction and chapter 1. At the IIAS I thank Philippe Peycam, Bernardo Brown, and Jenna Grant. At the IISG I thank Emile Schwidder, Eef Vermeij, and the staff at the circulation desk for their help. At the KITLV I thank Henk Schulte Nordholt and Gerry van Klinken for their indefatigable support for Indonesian studies. I thank Patsy Spyer for finding time for me in her busy schedule while I was in the Netherlands. I am forever grateful to Leonard Retel-Helmrich for being my extra-institutional host in Amsterdam.

I have presented chapters and ideas from this project at UC Santa Cruz, the University of Indonesia, the National University of Singapore, Cornell

University, Colgate University, Amherst College, Northwestern University, Yale University, Boston University, the IISG, the IISAS, the Inter-Asia Faculty Seminar at the Five Colleges, Harvard University, the University of Toronto, and ANU. Some ideas loosely connected to chapter 2 were first developed in a working paper series at the University of Sydney, and in an article in the *Journal of Urban History*. An earlier version of chapter 3 appeared as "Images of Youth: On the Iconography of Protest in Indonesia" in the journal *History and Anthropology*. I thank the journal for allowing me the use of that material. A small essay on the activist, the key figure in my book, appeared in a multi-authored volume edited by Joshua Barker, Johan Lindquist, and Erik Harms. I thank Joshua and Johan for their invitation to join the edited volume.

At Cornell University I learned from the anthropology department and the Southeast Asia Program, and consequently enjoyed the best of both worlds. Andrew Willford introduced me to the great anthropological debates about globalization and postcoloniality that were taking place in the discipline and taught by example how to be an anthropologist of grace, patience, and depth. Jim Siegel gave me a singular education and a powerful way to see the world. Eric Tagliacozzo encouraged my interest in history and trained me to be a committed Southeast Asianist. I was fortunate to take Ben Anderson's famed "Nationalisms" course, which shaped my scholarship irrevocably as it has so many scholars before me. Thak Chaloemtiarana and Nancy J. Loncto supported my research throughout graduate school and made the Southeast Asia Program a home to return to time and again. Ben Abel's immense knowledge about Indonesia enlivened my visits to the Kroch Asia Library. Keith Hjortshoj shared his fieldnotes with me and helped me write when I was stuck. I am thankful for my grad school comrades Dan Reichman, Tyrell Haberkorn, Nina Hien, Richard Ruth, Jane Ferguson, Aaron Moore, Sheetal Majithia, Allison Truitt, Erik Harms, Ivan Small, and Samson Lim. Chris Brown came to Cornell for a conference and fit right in. Tyrell Haberkorn has been my first reader and fast friend since the beginning and deserves credit for what is good in my early work.

From 2007 to 2010 I resided in the "Happy Valley" in western Massachussetts, where I taught in the Political Science Department at Amherst College and got to know the Five Colleges community. I cotaught with Amrita Basu, whose superior intellect, teaching skills, and warm friendship made our shared classroom a wonderful learning space. Across the college I thank Uday Mehta, Tom Dumm, Theresa Laizer, Chris Dole, Marisa Parham, and John Drabinski. Dale Hudson's friendship sustained me for the two years we shared a campus (and lunch). Sheetal Majithia's presence at Hampshire College for a year improved my life enormously. The Inter-Asia Faculty Seminar at the Five Colleges facilitated my frequent meetings with Kavita Datla, Amina Steinfels, Paula Chakravartty, Ruchi Chaturvedi, and Nerissa Balce. At UMASS Amherst, Jackie Urla's wit, conversation, and delicious dinners brought a deeper engagement with visual anthropology and comparative histories of struggle.

I arrived in Boston in the fall of 2010 and was warmly welcomed by friends and colleagues in the Northeastern University community and beyond. I would like to thank my colleagues in the Department of Sociology and Anthropology, especially Alan Klein, Steve Vallas, and Matt Hunt. Nina Sylvanus was a frequent writing and discussion partner in my mad rush to finish the book. I could not have done so without her genuine good faith and intellectual support. Mike Brown and Rob Weller read my book prospectus before it went out to the presses. Kate Luongo and Charissa Threat introduced me to the cultural and gustatory attractions of the South End. Kimberly Brown brought together an amazing group of women for the study of race and visual culture in the Dark Room. Friends in Cambridge remind me to cross the river more often. Kerry Chance, Clapperton Mavhunga, and JuYon Kim are among those friends. I am thankful to Mary Steedly at Harvard for including me in all things related to Indonesia and anthropology, and to Stefan Helmreich at MIT for his kindness and practical advice. In life and work Nicholas Harkness is always nearby.

Peter Agree is a gentleman of the first order, and renewed my confidence in this book. I thank Beth Drexler for introducing him to me, and for blazing a trail with her own work on violence in Indonesia. My utmost thanks go to my manuscript readers, whose theoretical insights, regional knowledge, and writerly instincts contributed to a better book. Ed Aspinall is the foremost authority on student movements and contentious politics in Indonesia, and I benefited from his swift and sharp review of my manuscript. Karen Strassler's groundbreaking work on documentation and visuality in Indonesia has stimulated my thinking over the years. I am grateful that she read my manuscript with a sympathetic eye and engaged deeply with its arguments. An anonymous reviewer at Duke University Press reminded me of the importance of history and paid me a compliment by attending to the small details of my ethnography. At Duke University Press I have been fortunate to work with Ken Wissoker and to be swept up in his enthusiasm for new ideas and the forms that they take. Jade Brooks led me through the entire process of submission and revisions. I thank Heather Hensley for her cover design, and Daniel Rudi Haryanto for allowing me the use of his artwork for the cover.

In Indonesia I have many people to thank, especially the men and women who are Generation 98. I can only mention some of them by name. I must thank Yasmin Purba, Simon, Reinhardt Sirait, Veronica Iswihnayu, Agnes Gurning, Seli Woyla, Rulas "Carlos" Lebardo, "Jemi" Irwansyah, Jopie "Red-Jopi" Peranginangin (alm.), Ady Mulyana, Savic Alielha, Wilson, Margiy-ono, Rahardjo Waluyo Djati, Nezar Patria, Mugiyanto, Daniel Hutagalung, Tri L. Astraatmadja, Yeri Wirawan, Zaenal Muttaqin, Daniel Rudi Haryanto, Nona Fatima Astuti, Alex Supartono, Dolorosa Sinaga, Ardjuna Hutagalung, Fadjroel Rachman, Eli Salomo, Ricky Tamba, Hidayat Wijaya Kusuma, Oka Dwi Candra, Irine Gayatri, Muridan Widjojo (alm.), Munir (alm.), Beka Ulung Hapsara, and Nelly Paliama. Sadly, Jopie Peranginangin was killed in the spring of 2015. His death is a great loss to the environmental and indige-nous rights movement in Indonesia.

Lastly, I thank my family in Indonesia. My father, Bobby Lee, is a dedicated reader and thinker. He has imparted to me the importance of doing work with a social conscience. I hope this book answers that call. My mother, Darmawaty Yioda, is the smartest and most resilient woman I know. She has supported this project endlessly. My sister Peggy Lee and her children Zara Lee Hassan and Noah Zein Hassan make every trip to the field a happy one.

A NOTE ABOUT NAMES

I refer to individuals by their nickname or first name, and in some cases their only name, as is common practice in Indonesia. I have also adhered to anthropological convention by using pseudonyms for most of the individuals in this book in order to protect their identities. However, in the instances where I rely upon archival sources, media sources, and select activist sources to discuss aspects of state violence and injustice, I refer to activists by their real name. Certain personalities from Generation 98 have achieved acclaim, status, and recognizability in Indonesia as a result of their activism and they too appear by name. My ethnography retains a contemporaneous relationship with work done in the fields of history, sociology, and political science, where the same individuals I discuss have already appeared in print as themselves. I consider the act of naming them a historicizing act of recognition for the efforts of individuals who continue to work in the public domain of Indonesian human rights, cultural politics, and democracy.

Introduction | **PEMUDA FEVER**

AN ACTIVIST'S DIARY

Today Jakarta is really terrifying following the "Trisakti Tragedy" that killed 6 university students and made them into Reformasi Heroes.[1] After-effects rippled, riots breaking out from crowds gone amok all over Jakarta. . . . I witnessed a tragedy, moving, saddening, [I was] understanding, angry, anxious, agitated, even afraid! From Sabang to Merauke, the archipelago grieves . . . Jakarta, 14 May 1998.

Jakarta is crippled. . . .

On the evening of the 15th at the Museum of Struggle '45 the Work Forum [Forum Kerja] held a press conference. Arby Sanit and some other intellectuals attended.[2] I was only there briefly, I didn't know what a Work Forum was. An Assembly of the People's Will has also been founded, and who knows what else with what name? Jakarta, 16 May 1998.

The political temperature is rising. . . . Jakarta, 19 May 1998.

Today launches a new history. At 9:05–9:06 AM this morning Soeharto resigned from his presidency . . . The Reform struggle will never end. The Reform struggle will always come and will always be. Today is a new history. And in the future we will still push back against all challenges. Jakarta, 21 May 1998.[3]

In May 1998, the events and efforts that unseated the dictator Suharto escalated very quickly. Student-led mass demonstrations across the nation, months
of economic instability since the Asian Economic Crisis had hit in 1997, elite
desertion, public backlash against state killings of students, and the violence
of the May Riots in Jakarta (May 13–14) shook the foundations of the once
undefeated New Order military regime (1966–1998). The movement that
toppled Suharto on May 21, 1998, was called "Reformasi" (Reformation). This
book is concerned with the role and repercussions of the Indonesian student
movement that claimed a special responsibility for Reformasi, becoming the
de facto representative and mediator of Indonesia's transition to democracy.

Students were at the forefront of Reformasi. Those killed in violent protests
became martyrs and Reform heroes (*pahlawan Reformasi*), and those who
survived became pioneers (*pelopor*) of Indonesian democracy. Over the course
of a decade, I met many youth who had participated in, witnessed, or were
inspired by the student movement that took over the streets of Indonesia in
1998, launching the movement that heralded Indonesia's entry into the "third
wave" of democracy. Some identified themselves as *mahasiswa*, university students, while others identified themselves as *pemuda*, youth. They were united
under the term *aktivis* (activist), a term made popular by Reformasi.[4] Before
1998, activists forged underground networks within and without the country,
communicating with sympathetic foreign groups, finding compatriots at other
university campuses, securing patrons, and becoming advocates for politically
sensitive environmental, peasant, labor, and indigenous rights movements that
often met with state-sponsored violence. After 1998, activists became adept at
being seen and heard, organizing media spectacles and large-scale demonstrations, and making use of the divergent careers of friends, former activists,
and sympathizers who now populated civil society and media structures. Activists were democracy's subjects par excellence. I was fascinated by the cultural creativity and political machinations of the loud and often fragmented
pro-dem (prodemocracy) groups who were marginal to power yet maintained
a disproportionate visibility in national politics. My anthropological interest
in street politics and student activism began in earnest in 2002, and in 2003–
2005 I carried out an eighteen-month stretch of fieldwork in Jakarta and other
major cities, walking and talking with former and present university students
and activists. Much of this ethnography centers on the capital city of Jakarta,
yet what I describe will resonate in some way or another with other university
towns and cities drawn into the street politics and mass movements of Reform.

Subsequent visits to the field each year allowed me to observe the long-term political involvement of Reformasi-era youth amid Indonesia's democratic growths and setbacks.

This book is about the lifeworld of the activist and the political implications of being young in Indonesia. It gestures toward youthful idealism at the same time that it describes the contradictions of "actually existing democracy" (Brenner and Theodore 2002). For sociological reasons of habitus, education, economy, and life-stage, youth have found a place in Indonesian politics and social movements. For historical and cultural reasons, youth pursue a populist claim on the nation, a claim that is strengthened by the "magic of the state"—the talismans, rituals, and elements of political efficacy that repeat and validate their claim (Taussig 1997). Unlike studies that have viewed democracy through the study of electoral politics, political institutions, mass organizations, and demonstrations in public space, thus overly emphasizing the demarcation between public and private, this book traces Indonesia's youthful culture of democracy through its concentrated, spatial, sensuous, ephemeral, and material forms. I present activism as lived experience to show how the intensity of political life bridges public and private domains, and individual and collective memories. The intertwining of history and memory plays a large part in fueling nationally inflected social movements in Indonesia. I name the invocation of youth spirit in the present age "pemuda fever" to describe how historical legacies infuse the present with urgency and legitimacy, naturalizing what often appear to be radical and disruptive thoughts and actions. However, activists are only one part of a broader set of political phenomena. Their creative and adaptive techniques of resistance world the world of the activist with lasting political outcomes, chief among which is the longevity of youth politics in Indonesia. In this book, I explore why and how social movements endure, how political identifications between individuals and the collective are achieved, and how contentious politics tap into rich veins of existing political tradition without veering into tradition for its own sake. As Asef Bayat argues in his study of youth "nonmovements" in the Middle East, revolutions are not planned; rather, they arise out of the alignment of youth resistance and already existing collective sentiment, often in urban centers (Bayat 2013a).

What produces and sustains youth activism? In what ways can our understanding of social movements be deepened by a turn to historical memory? Reformasi-style activism has been remarkably long lasting, despite the emergence of what Jessica Greenberg calls the "politics of disappointment" that often befall revolutionaries after the revolution is over (Greenberg 2014). I considered myself lucky that my research on the memories of 1998 took place in an unexpectedly lively time, among political actors who had not given up on Reformasi even after their main enemies, Suharto and the military, had formally retreated from politics. When I began my fieldwork, many activists were hopeful that the student movement, and by extension other politicized groups, would keep the tradition set by Reformasi politics alive, even in the transformed conditions of post-Reformasi Indonesia.

These activists' hopes had a strong foundation in everyday urban life. NGO and student-organized activities such as film screenings, discussions, and training sessions reminded students of their important historical and political role in Indonesian society. Off-campus and campus-based organizations at the local and national levels cemented the link between current students and their Reformasi-era seniors, as did campus commemorations and remembrance marches that recalled the student killings of 1998–1999. A feeling of closeness to the center arose from proximity to sympathetic politicians, intellectuals, and revered cultural figures in the capital city, such as former president Gus Dur (Abdurrahman Wahid) and the literary icon Pramoedya Ananta Toer, who in their final years still attended civil society events and charmed the young crowd with their cynical wit and insider view of Indonesia's epochal changes. On the streets, demonstrations persisted, while the visual culture of student activism transformed revolution into a youthful style that could be worn and circulated with ease. These informal and institutionalized linkages between youth and politics point to the public forms that Indonesia's culture of democracy and civic participation take—a cross between "the politics of fun" (Bayat 2013b) and more recognizable acts of political presencing. Youth activism in Indonesia aligns with the observations other scholars have made about the naturalized aspects of youth participation in politics, as a feature of political modernity, as a sign of generalized discontent, and as political subjects hardwired for change and self-empowerment (Bayat 2013b; Comaroff and Comaroff 2006; Greenberg 2014). Seen in this light, Indonesian youth are "natural" activists, granted a historical right to nationalist politics and a globalized claim to the transcendental logics of contemporary social movements.

Indonesia's well-established culture of demonstration contrasts with other social movements where mass demonstrations have emerged as transitive, climactic, and difficult-to-sustain elements of radical politics, from the networked, embodied, and transnational nature of Occupy (see Appel 2014; Juris 2012) to the crushed dreams of Egypt's short-lived revolution during the Arab Spring. Closer to the mark, but in a far more corrosive context, are the tendentious mass politics that define Thailand's post-Thaksin "ungovernability"

(Pavin 2014). Indonesian street politics in its post-Reform era serves as an important political institution that is accessible, thinkable, and imbued with populist immediacy. More worrisome are tendencies toward co-optation among former activists and the proliferation of undemocratic elements that mobilize mass demonstration tactics to assert their claim to public space.[5] The ongoing demonstrations during my own period of fieldwork in 2003–2005 had a distracting currency about them, for they spoke doublespeak about the place (and displacement) of activism in the present, in which Reformasi techniques adapted to a new and politically reactive context in fact worked to domesticate progressive activist politics. Under these compromised conditions, I had to find where activism was not only surviving but thriving. I followed activist praxis off the street, into places where subtle and profound changes were taking place, in youth domains where the memories and event-traces of 1998 had settled. These were not the institutions that we assume are fundamental to leftist and secular nationalist student movements, such as the school, the university, and the factory. Instead, my ethnography picks up from a point where the ideological transfer from ordinary youth to "activist youth" has already been made and secured, bypassing these foundational institutions. I bring to light those activist domains that enable social movements to linger, by reproducing student politics and imaginaries in everyday, exceptional, and seemingly apolitical ways, through their clothes, homes, and writings and even in the pleasure of friendship or the outbreak of violence. A recalibrated focus on the ordinary details of activist life shows most succinctly how resistance to the state endured and grew even in the worst of times. Most notably, in these lighter moments, activists would tell me stories, and in doing so, they *remembered*.

Memory is productive. It produces archives, spatial practices, bodies of writing, ways of talking and remembrance. These different sites and practices conjoin and overlap the past with the present, the eventful with the everyday. But Generation 98 did not indulge in unreliable nostalgic lament as a rule. Reformasi memories permeated everyday discourse as a readily available activist narrative of how much things had changed or stood still. They also served as important and authenticating eyewitness correctives to undemocratic attempts at repealing the changes wrought by the Reformasi movement. I became attuned to the presence of memory as an essential part of political discourse, and observed how memories tied to Reformasi, and an even longer-term collective memory about nationalist youth, marked a person's political location, legitimacy, and morality.

The supplemental excess of memory in post-Reformasi activism enacts what Diana Taylor calls the interplay between the archive and the repertoire, between fixed objects and embodied memory (2003: 19–20). Ironically, Taylor's analytic reverses the strengths of ethnography into a weakness. What I was lacking was not what Taylor considers the neglected domain of repertoire, observed in "scenarios" (demo settings), oral histories, and bodily performances (the act of demonstrating itself), for these filled my fieldnotes, photographs, and videos, but in fact what I lacked was the depth of the archive proper. The ethnographic burden of evidence for a genealogical project on youthful resistance exceeded my fieldnotes and entered a new archival field. Long after fieldwork ended, I found myself in the archives of the International Institute for Social History (IISG) in Amsterdam, poring over the photocopies and original papers of prominent leftist activists who had resisted the New Order state. Writing projects and fellowships (2008–2014) afforded me the chance to visit libraries in the United States and Europe that had diligently acquired the archival matter of the student movement.[6] I matched these documents with my personal collections, which included diaries, T-shirts, drawings, text messages, newspaper clippings, books, magazines, and numerous other fragments that activists shared with me and that until now had lain dormant as field research souvenirs rather than becoming a "site of knowledge production and concept formation, a repository of and generator of social relationships" (Verdery 2014: 5).[7] My research into activist material culture and knowledge production places acts of everyday activism in a synechdochal light. Youth activism is a mode of citation and documentation that strengthens and shapes the role of collective memory in nationalism and political resistance.[8] The activist is a historical-political subject who *feels* historical.

This book introduces the activist subject through the material and ideational elements that characterized everyday activist life in Indonesia. To reflect this classificatory approach to the everyday, the chapters are simply named "Archive," "Street," "Style," "Violence," "Home," and "Democracy." Each chapter showcases unique political amalgamations of Reformasi's globalized moments and older traditions of morality, masculinity, and nationalism. Paper ephemera, the public and political spaces of the street, activists' dwellings, activist style and appearance, as well as practices of violence and democracy come alive as sites and fields distinguished by the regnant activism that affected New Order youth before and after Reformasi. Each domain can be separately read as a cultural artifact, but taken together they form what the novelist Orhan Pamuk has aptly named the dynamic and revisited story of youth—a living "Museum of Innocence" founded in nonstate, ordinary spaces that counters the authoritative and instrumental character of the New Order's mausoleum for pemuda history (Pamuk 2010). The book ends with a calculated guess at the student movement's pending historical outcome. The most recent presidential election took place in 2014 amid great tension between resurgent conservative forces and new progressives in Indonesia; not surprisingly, the activists of 1998 have found roles to play there. What would Walter Benjamin's angel of history (1968c: 257–258) say now if he were facing the debris of Reform, piled high to rot in some places while other pieces are lodged like shrapnel in the present time? Which of those prodemocracy activists became weapons for the future, and how many more walked away or sank under the weight of disappointment or remembrance?

GENEALOGIES OF YOUTH

In many ways, Indonesia is a young country, with more than a third of its population classified as youth.[9] In Indonesian, the word for "youth," *pemuda*, has a strong political meaning beyond simply referring to age groups, owing to its distinct nationalist heritage. Pemuda nationalism has served an essential nation-building function since the revolution. It constitutes a distinct series (Foucault 1972: 7) in a twofold way; its genealogical function operates as a lineage system that is the bedrock of an "imagined community" for youth, while its seriality (Anderson 1998b), its very openness to the demands of the political present, authorizes and gives meaning to a range of political enunciations by youth. The influence of each generation lingers long after its time has passed, each becoming the illustrious predecessors to the next generation of youth. The official story of pemuda nationalism begins with the colonial-era Budi Utomo, founded in 1908 and credited as the first indigenous mass organization, followed by the 1928 generation, who declared the nationalist charter of the Sumpah Pemuda (Youth Pledge), crescendoing with the revolutionary youth of 1945, who fought for independence from Dutch colonialism, followed by the students of Generation 66, who allied with the military to overthrow Soekarno's Old Order, and finally, under the repressive management of Suharto's New Order, ends with the mass student protests of Generations 74 and 78.[10]

After 1978 there was a long break in pemuda nationalism's lineage, until it was revived again in 1998 with Reformasi. The pemuda generation of 1998 succeeded against the odds in deposing Suharto's thirty-two-year military dictatorship, given the measures the regime took to suppress its opponents and co-opt pemuda identity.[11] How should we interpret the long pause between the 1978 and 1998 generations? The time gap gives rise to at least two interpretations. First that the New Order state's measures to depoliticize students were wildly successful and that pemuda nationalism no longer provided an avenue for youth to participate in national politics in transformative ways— in which case the events of 1998 still need to be explained. Second, one could see the time gap as a period of *undocumented time*, with the events of the 1980s and 1990s still not widely known or integrated into pemuda history. If youth activism, and specifically student activism, continued during this neglected period, how should we understand such acts of resistance in a context of widespread repression? While the post-Reformasi era has brought new questions and doubts to bear upon the true extent of the New Order state's power and control,[12] there was no doubt that the militarized New Order state effectively controlled its population through systemic abuses of power, coercion, and consent.

How did the last generation of New Order youth gain the courage and the tools to rise up against the regime? Who were they before they became Generation 98? Activist youth were a mix of street, urban, rural, middle-class, cosmopolitan, provincial, and progressive men and women who were interpellated, obligated, inspired, and pushed by the demands of pemuda identity. The trajectory of the People's Democratic Party (PRD) activist Faisol Reza is a prime example of how a nationalist-leftist-populist orientation mingled with and eventually became the dominant framework for leftist activists raised in other intellectual and cultural formations. Reza attended an Islamic boarding school in Madura, where he was exposed to scholarly lectures by fellow *santri* (Islamic boarding school students) and developed a keen interest in theater. In high school, his growing "critical spirit" (*spirit kritis*) led him to stage a critical play about the school's administration, whereupon he was threatened with expulsion. When he arrived in Yogyakarta for university in 1992, he enrolled in two prominent institutions, one religious (IAIN Sunan Kaligaja—the State Islamic Institute at Sunan Kalijaga) and one secular (Gadjah Mada University), and became embroiled in city-wide student demonstrations. Reza cites two important books as his true inspiration to become a radical leftist activist, again one religious (Ahmad Wahib's *Revolutions in Islamic Thought*) and the other secular (Soe Hok Gie's *Diary of a Demonstrator*; see chapter 3 for a discussion of Gie).[13] If the middle-class and aspirational terms of university student life blurred the line between religious and secular divides, then pemuda nationalism, more broadly speaking, encompassed Muslim (majority) and non-Muslim (minority) interests, especially in providing a common advocative position toward the underclass *rakyat* (the People). My focus on leftist-secular-nationalist activism in this book acknowledges the popularity that these political configurations enjoyed in the immediate aftermath of Suharto's fall.[14] It was notable that several of my informants came from Islamic boarding schools and communities, or had grown up in observant Muslim or Christian families, but formed activist groups that were decidedly secular-nationalist and/or populist-leftist in thought and appearance. In part driven by the cosmopolitan environment of university campuses in large cities in Java, such secular-nationalist choices also revealed the New Order state's intrusion into religious domains. Prior to his public embrace of a more Muslim identity in the early nineties, which observers marked as a decided shift in New Order policy, Suharto had managed potential rivals from both traditional and modernist Islamic groups through a mix of suppression and accommodation. The secular emphasis of the New Order state disarmed the mobilizing capacity of religious groups critical of the regime in the years leading up to Reformasi. Similarly, the effacement of political Islam in the mainstream student movement reflects the minor role that Islamic organizations had on campus,[15] a picture that would change rapidly after 1998. With the identitarian and majoritarian path of religious solidarity closed off, the pro-rakyat and anti-authoritarian critiques of the development regime came from students and activists versed in the liberatory discourses of Marxist tradition. It bears reminding that the most politically risky aspect of the student movement remained the leftist tendencies of activists who knowingly took on "the pariah status of the left" (Aspinall 2005: 39), in contradistinction to a deeply anticommunist society where signs of "latent communism" were monitored, reviled, and punished by citizens themselves. Leftist and secular groups have received the most international media attention, state scrutiny, and scholarly interest, for they stood out so defiantly in the political landscape shaped by the gruesome history of the anticommunist pogroms of 1965–1966.[16] Max Lane, the translator of the banned novels of the imprisoned leftist writer Pramoedya, named the movement against Suharto a "movement without history," expressing the belief that Suharto had severed any ties that youth had to the nation's history of struggle (Lane 2008: 284). Pemuda nationalism was the remaining, albeit deeply compromised, history of struggle that functioned simultaneously as a New Order ideological state apparatus and a potential inspiration for youth.

Pemuda history provided the iconography and typology that informed the perception and appearance of contemporary youth's resistance against authority. There was never a need to question the nationalized identity of students or the nationalist intentions of activist youth, for such terrain was largely predetermined. There were distinct and recognizable ways that pemuda mobilized at times of political crisis or need. When new pemuda generations appeared, they were not dismissed as fake or inauthentic. Rather, they were continuing a thought rooted in the cultural assemblage of Indonesia's political modernity— an origin point that James Siegel has identified as the linguistic and domesticating forces by which national recognition was achieved (1997). In an argument that is important for chapter 3 of this book, Siegel describes how appearance and the idioms of nationalism became passwords that allowed Indonesians to switch identities and gain their rightful role as revolutionaries. "By the time of the revolution, one could be recognized as a nationalist. There were not only forms of dress and language and ideas to mark one, there were also inventions of nationalist leaders who verified one's national credentials" (10). The revolutionary pemuda of 1945 were especially good at ferreting out true and false nationalists, appropriating the language of appearance for themselves (Frederick 1997). Siegel's insight into how revolution sets new codes and authenticating gestures into motion unlocks the radical image transformation enacted by the largely middle-class university students and youth who shouted "Total Reform!" (Reformasi Total!) alongside the rakyat on the streets in 1998.

To go even further, we will need to explore how the highly reductive New Order vision of the sacrificial and nation-building role of youth, institutionalized and performed in various social domains, became a conduit for political action. Pemuda identity had its own memory capacity, its "archivable content" and its "relationship to the future" that could not be completely domesticated (Derrida 1998: 17). It was not mere historical repetition that tied youth to the last wave of mass politics, but the archivization of pemuda identity into a stable entity in Indonesian nationalism that became a supplementary source of activist power, specifically an activist power of representation: the power to mediate access to and from the rakyat. The simplicity of pemuda history's banal nationalism, its iterable and knowable qualities, created an unexpectedly fertile and stable foundation for dissident thought and a sense of alternative history to the New Order's official-speak and the gross social realities of the time. As early as the 1980s, student activists aimed their call to action at other students by declaring pemuda idealism and spirit (*idealisme dan semangat*) to be under threat by the New Order's hedonistic and selfish values; invoking a collective heritage, youth politics conveyed the need for a self-protective stance and an act of repair to sacred institutions (see chapter 1).[17] Finally, it was the familiar rendering of pemuda identity that gave such longevity and credence to the Indonesian student movement of 1998.

Indonesians know pemuda history backward and forward, and they know it primarily as a chain of nationalist, masculine, urban youth who banded together because of their indomitable youth spirit (*semangat pemuda*). *Semangat* denotes far more radical potential and willpower than the sanitized fervor of "teen spirit." As scholars of Indonesian politics have noted, pemuda generations are defined by their enthusiasm for their cause rather than the limits of their ages; hence the terrors carried out by the revolutionary pemuda of 1945 were legendary (Frederick 1989). During the New Order period (1966–1998), the well-known history of Indonesian nationalism was inscribed annually in ritualized displays of somber commemoration on days like Youth Pledge Day, October 28. Pemuda appeared in monuments, museum exhibits, and historical dioramas as exemplary youth, even though very few gained individual recognition the way older and highly ranked "national heroes" (*pahlawan bangsa*) did. Instead, their generational names served as their main calling card. Each of these named generations (1908, 1928, 1945, 1966) represented a specific and unique generational contribution to the evolution of pemuda nationalism, such that repeating the sequence only strengthened their associative frame and presumed to tax the present generation of youth with a question: What will be *your* lasting contribution to the nation?

After the fall of Suharto, a generational identity was conferred upon Generation 98, the Reformasi generation, which in turn codified personal and individual memories into a collective asset open to use and misuse. It was thus that Generation 98 understood their place in the world, as an extension of this nationalist history, as mandate, calling, and destiny (*takdir*). The romanticism of Generation 98 was thickly felt and described by the young Indonesians I encountered. Their descriptions layered national history onto their own biographies, laminating them into something thicker than the words "politics" or "resistance" convey. There were people who were moved to tears as they relived the magnitude of this feeling in the retelling of their Reformasi stories to me (see chapter 2). This feeling of a historically charged present was the kernel of what I call "pemuda fever," a contagious feeling of political belonging and identification that everybody in post-Suharto Indonesia recognized and that select youth experienced. Here I draw primarily on the work of Jacques Derrida in *Archive Fever* (1998) to theorize how the drive to document, consign, and assemble signs of pemuda nationalism became a fever, "a compulsive, repetitive, and nostalgic desire for the archive, an irrepressible desire to return to the origin" (91). In gathering together these signs of nationalist origin from within and without pemuda genealogy, activists call attention to the fact that "there is no archive without a place of consignation, without a technique of repetition, and without a certain exteriority. No archive without outside" (11). In other words, these signs, repertoires, and actions are exterior signs that become "the institution, in sum, of a *prosthesis of the inside*" (19). Pemuda fever becomes, in the hands of activists, a meaningful, emotive, and highly productive genre of nationalism that dynamically and practically reflects an interior state.

Yet the word "fever" can also seem problematic, associated in commonplace use with the abnormal, the irrational, the loss of self. When we are fevered, what the French call *en mal de* (in sickness from), we burn, we are in the consuming grip of something (Derrida 1998: 91). More the analytical problem that in talking about fever, Derrida claims, we repeat it, we intensify the object of analysis, we "raise the stakes" (91). Derrida's warning that analysis can become an act of reification and intensification gives me pause to reflect upon "pemuda fever" as a convenient label for youth politics. It is not the intention of this book to demystify or reduce activists' intentions to a single motif, nor is it my intention to appear an unwitting theorist of naturalizing youthful passions. We already know that pemuda identity was open to manipulation and that nationalism provides community in times of deep distress and change. Having proposed pemuda fever as an element of the student movement's mobilizing strengths, I must heed its cautionary tale, or else the study of radical youth politics risks becoming analytically *en mal de*, foiled by its own romanticism.

YOUTHFUL INTERVENTIONS IN NATIONAL TIME-SPACE

The words of D. Rudi Haryanto, an artist, aspiring filmmaker, and activist from Semarang who had moved to Jakarta in the midnineties give a strong taste of how pemuda fever formed the narrative backbone of youth politics. The handwritten journal and letters that he shared with me begin in 1997, a momentous year marked by the regional financial meltdown caused by the Asian Economic Crisis. The monetary crisis, dubbed *krismon* in Indonesia, and its ensuing total crisis (*krisis total*, or *kristal*) galvanized civil society groups, including students, into action. In 1997, Rudi was just nineteen years old, not yet a mahasiswa (university student), when he became involved in Jakarta's student movement politics. Rudi found it difficult to attain placement in a university because of his disciplinary record. He had been forced out of high school in Yogyakarta with an early diploma over a political act of resistance.

He later achieved his dream of becoming a student when he enrolled in the Jakarta Institute for the Arts, a bohemian arts enclave that was conveniently located in close proximity to other Reformasi campuses, such as the University of Indonesia-Salemba, Bung Karno University, Pancasila University, the Institute for Administration Indonesia, and various teaching and secretarial colleges. In Jakarta, he followed the footsteps of his older brother and other senior activists he admired by becoming active in an organization, Interaction Forum '66, founded by "Older Brothers of the 66 Generation" (Abang-Abang Angkatan 66), even though he joked that they were "disillusioned" (*sakit hati*) with the New Order regime. As committee secretary, he attended meetings and political events regularly. Each night, after a daily routine of film shoots, portfolio building, job seeking, political seminars and meetings, even a romance that suffered from his dedication to politics, he recorded and reflected on the changing tenor of Indonesian life. On the commemorative occasion of October 28, 1997, he wrote in the unmistakable tones of pemuda fever:

Today is Youth Pledge Day. Exactly 69 years ago Indonesian youth in groups of Jong Java, Jong Celebes, Jong Sumatra, Pemuda Betawi, pledged themselves to One Archipelago, Nation, and Language. Indonesia!!! The Youth Pledge of 28 October 1928 (before that Boedi Oetomo 1908) was the culmination of the role of youth in the independence struggle. *I imagine how boisterous the movement's atmosphere was during that time. How spirited the youth of Indonesia were at that time.* Once I saw documentary photographs in the Museum of the Youth Pledge. I saw the Spirit that lit up like sunlight the faces of the Indonesian youth activists of the time, faces pure and simply dressed. *1928 was the standard for Indonesian Nationalism. What about the youth of today?* The times have changed. . . . After 1966 in the thick of New Order conditions under Soeharto's power, Indonesian youth lost their essential character . . . today youth hang out in malls, skip school, get high on ecstasy, tout, fight, play arcade games, display themselves in malls, gossip at MacDonalds, meanwhile more than 300 of their brothers and sisters in Irian Jaya (Papua) die of hunger!!! Maybe the youth have forgotten that today is Youth Pledge Day. But there is still another event, still a small segment of youth who care about the fate of the nation and who commemorate the Youth Pledge, who reflect on current conditions and what is happening to the country that is being dragged far away from the values of the Youth Pledge. At the Proclamation Monument this afternoon some comrades were arrested while carrying out their remembrance of the Youth Pledge in an action [aksi]. Of course the arrests were expected but actually they are always puzzling and demand the question: Why does it occur? Such a question will only bring smiles and be answered with excuses, and will never be answered in the Soeharto era. *Indonesian Youth are very happy today!!! What you did, hail to you Youth of 1928, is recorded in Indonesia's history. The spirit of patriotism, nationalism, freedom and unity, intelligence, courage, have become a valuable legacy for us the youth generation who live in a time decades after you incised history with the 1928 Youth Pledge. Freedom!!!* (Emphasis added.)

I present Rudi's journal entry from Youth Pledge Day in its entirety to show how a self-referential pemuda history had become a means for critically minded New Order youth to express a political difference between themselves and mainstream youth. Pemuda fever moves Rudi's historical perspective forward and backward in a prophetic and nostalgic manner. It is consistent with what Agamben calls the defining quality of the contemporary actor, his sense that things are wrong in *his* time, betraying a "relationship with time that adheres to it through a disjunction and an anachronism" (2009: 41). Triggered by the memory of black-and-white photographs of Generation 1928 at the Youth Pledge museum, Rudi's imagination made their vivid scenes of nationalism unfold before his eyes. Disgusted by the westernized, capitalist, and frivolous pastimes that preoccupied contemporary urban youth, Rudi's thoughts immediately returned to the "spirited" and vibrant 1928 generation, whose purity shone in their faces (see fig. 1). Youth today, Rudi laments, are more apt to behave as *remaja* (teenagers) or ABG (the common abbreviation for spoilt and barely grown children known as *anak baru gede*) under the "New Order conditions" that had so corrupted the essence of youth that they are unable to muster a sense of solidarity toward their starving and marginalized "siblings." Yet, even while he disparages present-day youth, he brings to our attention the avant-garde actions of *other* youth, the activist minority who still care about and act on the values inculcated by Generation 1928. Those other youth with whom he identifies will not be recognized by the Suharto era. Their contributions can only be read in the light of history. And so, after recounting the arrests of his comrades on Youth Pledge Day in 1997, he addresses Generation 1928 directly. Thanks to *you*, he says to them, pemuda are happy, for Generation 1928 left the youth of today a lasting reserve of spirit (semangat) to draw on. "Merdeka!!!" (Freedom!!!), the final word in this entry, belongs more properly to the 1945 Generation, who fought for independence from the Dutch, but it is a fitting ending. Merdeka is coming. Many of Rudi's subsequent journal entries end in the same way, linking the feeling of Reformasi to the revolution's battle cry. Pemuda history's legacy is twofold—the nationalist values that belong especially to youth, and the fact of the radical break itself, since contemporary youth activism was only possible after Generation 1928 made what Rudi calls an *incision* (*torehan*, an Indonesian word that describes a surgical cut or an engraving in a hard surface) into history. The terrifying word "incision" describes the originating cut that created a new and permanent orifice in the body politic. More precisely, the incision made an opening no one thought to close.

Why is it important to isolate the drive to history in pemuda fever? And how might a focus on student movement practices of everyday life offer an antidote to pemuda fever's excesses? This book argues that both are necessary diagnostic tools to make visible the myriad practical, cultural, and affective ties that kept activists in the movement. As we have seen in the writing of D. Rudi Haryanto, historical linkages between one generation of pemuda and another are productive linkages that form part of a larger genealogical turn or, following Maurice Blanchot, an etymological seduction that translates everything in its wake into its own self-fulfilling terms:

> The other danger of etymology is not simply its implicit relation to an origin, and the marvelously improbable resources that it seductively uncovers. Rather, the danger is that etymology imposes, without being able to justify or even to explain it, a certain conception of history. This conception is far from clear: the necessity of some provenance, of successive continuity, the logic of homogeneity, the revelation of sheer chance as destiny and of words as the sacred depository of all lost or latent meanings whose recovery is thenceforth the task of him who writes in view of a last word or final rebuttal (fulfillment, realization). (Blanchot 1995: 97)

Pemuda history provides a structure of feeling and an abstract, idealized goal to which today's tasks are assigned. However, it masks how youth democratized Indonesian political culture by the very youthful and global interests and popular instincts that activists brought to their political work and behavior. Training sessions and demo planning meetings were opportunities to network, play, and potentially strike up friendships. Even small organizations maintained a busy schedule traveling to meetings in and out of town, going from *kost* (rented rooms in boardinghouses) to *kantor* (office), or from hotel ballrooms to NGO offices. With the mass demonstration under their belt, activists became confident experts at managing scale, "blowing up" an issue, or directing its information flow in media campaigns and press conferences. More important, an ethnographic study of the student movement's microp-

FIGURE I.1 "Soempah Pemuda" (Youth Pledge), drawing by D. Rudi Haryanto on the occasion of Youth Pledge Day, October 28, 1999. Top half: the ethnic youth leagues that first declared the Youth Pledge in 1928 hand in hand, appearing as equal partners. Below: the scattered New Order social types whose taste-based identities convey the fragmented, globalized, and exclusive qualities of contemporary youth. Reprinted with the permission of the artist.

olitics and everyday spaces is necessary because the literature on the actual personalities and practices of activism remains so sparse. While media coverage about Indonesia's economic and political crises were prevalent domestically and internationally in 1998–1999, and even though books, memoirs, and human rights reports poured out of Indonesia in subsequent years, scholars have tended to research and write around the student-shaped presence of Reformasi. Scholars have reproduced the dominant narrative of Reformasi as a given set of events that occurred in the center and heavily involved students but have not explored the post-Reform connection between student activists to larger national issues of decentralization, political and legal reforms, the rise of civil society, the role of the elites and the military, and so on. In the most uncritical and crude discourses about Reformasi, many of which continue to circulate to sharpen the distinction between elites and the People, the rakyat is no different from the floating masses of the Suharto era and the activist a misguided example of middle-class privilege. Mass mobilizations and mass politics, while being the purview of student activist efforts in the late 1990s through 2005, remained analytically estranged from a serious discussion of the middle-class politics and personality of studenthood and activism, except when middleclassness was diagnosed in cursory and disparaging terms by observers proclaiming the end of the movement (Heryanto, cited in Tauffiqur-rahman 2010). Thus, a glaring absence remains in our understanding of the institutions and structures of cultural politics that drove the changes of the Reform era and what survived and followed the wake of student activism as public culture. It is the same student activist–shaped hole, blown up.

THE FIELD: WHAT I DID WHEN I WAS THERE

What is the field of study? Where is the field? I have already described the archive as constituting a new and generative field of ethnographic inquiry that chapter 1 takes up to illuminate the affinities between New Order–style activism and post-Reformasi political pursuits. Now I turn to another site of cultural production, the city and its streets, to convey the temporal-spatial rhythms of activism. It is a truism that urban ethnographies differ from traditional ethnographies due to their multisited, socially complex, heterogeneous, and discontinuous spaces of research (see Gupta and Ferguson 1997). The communities found in the city are "global villages" made up of chains of uninhibited connections, while the field is more and more a constructed unity of the places and times the anthropologist chanced upon. Research challenges and dynamics in post–New Order Indonesia resonate with such descriptions of conceptual multiplicity, yet post-Reformasi Indonesia also provided me with what Indonesians call *benang merah*, a red and binding narrative thread. The thread that held my field site together was the continuing significance and memorialization of the Reformasi era, providing the narrative anchor and tonal break of "before" and "after" Suharto, before and after the student movement. Reformasi still comprised the underlying logic of comparison, commemoration, and aspiration for its direct participants and witnesses, even its indirect legatees. For instance, demonstrations in the present time instigated comparisons to past demonstrations, which in turn invited political memories, and it was not long before activists turned their talk to the Reformasi narratives of the end of the New Order in order to anchor present-day politics in the recent past. The activism of Generation 98 bore a tenuous relation to current debates about the future of national identity and Indonesian politics; it resembled a sticky residue, adhering to life after Reformasi yet subject to a new matrix of discipline, interests, and calculation.

My field site oscillated between the vast city of Jakarta and the more modest and ephemeral site of the demonstration. "Field" is translated as *lapangan* in Indonesian, the same word that is used for the demonstration site, the *lapangan demo*. A lapangan is a foursquare field of open space. Synonymously and metaphorically, Indonesian activists link the demo field to the more ambitious "field of struggle," *medan perjuangan*, indicating a projection of their political space and struggle onto the universally recognized franchises of freedom and sovereignty. Such scalar leaps between the local and the global, the everyday and the eventful, motivate a great deal of post-Reformasi political discourse. I had a hunch that "the true force of this history, or better, the sense of a certain age," was in "'a color, a tone of voice, a tactile choice of word, a simple vibration'" leaving the ineluctable trace of the "'unstable, incomplete, unsettled, irreducible to the word'" (Mrázek 2010: xiii).

I followed activists through the city and out of its bounds, paying attention to the sensory and practical realms that constituted the everyday life of politics but could not be reduced to a normative sense of the everyday. My movement through the city gave me a map of how political spaces and organizations formed constellations of memory and political practice. I rushed to attend events and lingered into the night, experiencing the micro and macro character of the field as demo site and city of struggle. I came to know the city differently too, on foot, and through public transportation, looking for markers that activists (many of whom could not drive or did not have cars) would name, and discovering green spaces and pleasant, hidden corners that were as close to public space as one could get in Jakarta. The learning curve of anthropological fieldwork involved learning mobility and communication: how to receive and respond to text messages in abbreviated Indonesian;[18] how to negotiate transport; how to arrive safely; how to be sent off by friends, and in what order; how to walk in the demo and on the streets; how to disembark a moving bus without falling flat on my face (as happened once); how to not laugh wildly every time the *bajaj* (auto-rickshaw) rattled me through to my bones; how to join up with the demo after speeding through the streets on a motorcycle taxi; how to spend hours as the lone young woman among young men. Fieldwork was, as anthropologist Saya Shiraishi describes it, an extended social ritual of *antar-jemput* (drop-off and pickup) (1997: 30). These sensory experiences of conducting research give a sense of how Jakarta's urban spaces were redeployed and occupied transiently by the city's youth.

How I came to this project is another story. My personal biography and interests put me near and distant from the political selves and lives of my informants. I am not Indonesian by birth or citizenship, but Jakarta was a place I was deeply familiar with growing up. In the 1980s I lived with my nuclear and extended family in an ethnically and religiously mixed neighborhood of tiny, one-story houses in North Jakarta. At the time the neighborhood and my family were fairly modest in income and appearance. Later, in the speculative boom years of the 1990s, we moved to an enormous planned city in North Jakarta—a suburb of large, two-story houses built on former naval landholdings and reclaimed paddy fields that accommodated international schools and cuisines, mansions and malls. I left for the United States in the summer of 1997, assured of an uneventful and privileged college life in New York. A few months later Indonesia's financial world collapsed, and not long afterward its political world overturned. My family fled the very real possibility of anti-Chinese violence in Indonesia following the May Riots in 1998. I had missed all the signs of these cataclysms. And so I came to learn Indonesian later in life at Cornell University during my graduate training through the Department of Anthropology and the famed Southeast Asia Program, referred to reverentially by visiting scholars as "the mecca of Southeast Asian Studies." My struggle with my American-sounding accent, my limited but correct and therefore inappropriate lexicon, my general inexperience with politics, all stood to brand me as foreign in class, race, and appearance. It was a long time before I could respond in a sensible way to the quick wit and rich political vocabulary of activist speech, with its serious bravado and its punny Jakarta slang. As Yuliana, a human rights activist I came to rely on, said, "You were quiet for the first six months! I thought there was something wrong with you." I "passed" as an upper-middle-class follower of the movement when I did not speak, and so I faithfully wore the activist uniform of faded jeans and a slogan T-shirt to all the meetings, seminars, and demos I attended. The ruse worked unpredictably. More than once, television news crews that were on the lookout for interviews with demonstrators in the field approached me, much to my alarm. My solidly upper middle-class background, in the populist context of the street-side movement, reared its head often. I must restate the stereotype here that "Chinese" are all seen as rich and their wealth is thought to result from exploiting indigenous Indonesians. My relationships with some informants became challenging when they assumed that I had access to financial resources and political connections by virtue of being from Amrik (America) and being ethnic Chinese.[19] In the student activist world of frequenting roadside vendors and walking in the heat, these were all things people who looked like me, *bersih putih* (clean and white [and rich]) did not do. This was a classed and gendered response to my presence, as few women activists ever questioned my choices to follow their lead. It was men who circulated derisive and cautionary stories about girlfriends who were so *borjuis* (bourgeois) they could not eat roadside food or stow away on the train. But these are surface stories about the anthropological encounter and difference that fell away the more time I spent in the company of Indonesian activists. In their present struggles against the neoliberal policies of an oligarchic state, leftist and progressive activists have to keep up with a fast-paced, mediatized state politics that exacts more national level organizing and internal solidarity on their part than ever. In 2016, the threats to democracy from well-organized oligarchic elements in the state and from less organized conservative forces in Indonesia augur yet another crisis in the making. The political map has changed since Reformasi. No matter. Generation 98 is equipped for it.

THE CHAPTERS IN SUMMARY

Chapter 1 provides a first look through previously unseen archival material to establish a paper trail for the student movement's "missing years" (1980s–1990s), locating material evidence of fragmented but vibrant student activism amid the inertia of the New Order's depoliticized campuses. The underground resistance movement depended on what I call the *techne* of paper to generate reams of counter-regime propaganda, internal communications, and legal documents in response to state charges of subversion. I unveil the epistemic tensions that animate the hopeful and moral gestures of student activism captured and circulated in paper form a full decade before Suharto fell from power. I theorize the relation between archives, documentation, and historicity to draw attention to the contradictory attributes of marginal student archives—from their fetish quality as invaluable souvenirs of the democracy movement to their tendency to reproduce, disappear, and reappear in new and unregulated contexts far from their point of origin.

Chapter 2 describes how student activists came to be at home on the street, asserting their transformational claim to the city through spectacular displays of political participation. The student-led mass demonstrations that overthrew Suharto in 1998 were emblematic of the intense spatial politics that formed the backbone of popular democracy in post-Suharto Indonesia. The street was a zone of strategic experimentation, student expertise, and efficacious nationalism that brought together middle-class university activists with rural and urban poor in an unevenly sutured political body, the rakyat (People). Throughout the chapter, I showcase the work of disappeared activist poet Wiji Thukul, whose poems about the dispossessed rakyat in the city operate as spoken anthems of resistance at demonstrations, reminding activists of the interplay between the spatial embeddedness of social injustice and the immanent revolution found in everyday urban life.

Chapter 3 argues that political movements are profoundly aesthetic frameworks that introduce new ways of looking, seeing, and being—turning style into the conduit and currency for political identity. I examine the singular importance of style to student movement politics as the terrain through which youth identities and affiliations were secured, and by which forbidden leftist references entered the mainstream. Student activist visual culture invested the activist body with a signature pemuda style that was iconic, historical-nationalist, and global in its orientation, and it did so through widely available objects of public culture such as film, photography, and clothing. I demonstrate how the production and consumption of political fashions in the activist movement became a popular access point to experiencing and desiring political youth identity. I conclude with a study of Reform's cinephilic infatuation with the 1960s activist Soe Hok Gie as an example of how pemuda style's saturated images of youth merged the political goals of the present with the pure nationalist intentions of the past.

Can heroes be moral *and* violent? Chapter 4 examines the ways that enduring perceptions of students as socially privileged and moral subjects have muted public and scholarly debates on student violence. I analyze activist narratives of state violence, trauma, and counterviolence over ten years of Reform politics to trace the intimacy of violence in activist narratives and political trajectories. As student movements evolved toward greater militancy and spectacular violence after the fall of Suharto, violent methods and experiences entered their agenda with increased frequency. I offer up controversial activist memories of retaliation against suspected state agents and symbols of the state as evidence of defensive and provocative student practices that have sparked state interventions. By asserting student experiences of state violence and counterviolence as linked discourses, I explicitly counter the silence obscuring student violence by drawing attention to the connections and tensions between civil society's framing of collective solidarity and the state's call for discipline and order.

Can revolutionaries ever settle down? Chapter 5 leads us "home" through the rarely seen domestic arrangements that provided spaces of rest, return, and belonging for student activists. It unlocks the spatial poetics and territorial logics of the *basekemp* (organizational headquarters), *posko* (command posts), and kost (rented rooms) as activist structures that housed extensive experimentation against New Order ideologies of family, home, and authority. I analyze how these shared spaces of work and play provided youth with the freedom to interact, mobilize, and socialize outside gendered social norms and hierarchies. However, the egalitarian dream of youthful community was also vulnerable to the movement's practical and logistical challenges. This chapter undoes the distinction between public and private spaces to show the reach of activism's territorializing potential—a project that makes political life as fully present in the makeshift homes of activists as in the demonstrations on the streets.

Chapter 6 shows Generation 98 in the grip of election fever during the 2004 elections, as activists sought to renew their representation of the People on the streets and from within the system. However, New Order rituals of "democracy festivals" (*pesta demokrasi*) and the monied politics of military and elite domination destabilized Generation 98's progressive vision of civic and public life. I argue that the transition to institutionalized democracy, the codification of Reformasi narratives, and the temporal distance from 1998 made activist futures more insecure than ever. By focusing on discourses of corruption, individuation, and social difference that emerged during the elections, I convey pemuda identity's uneven integration into post-Suharto Indonesia.

The book ends on a grace note of hope. At present, Indonesians are placing their hopes in Joko Widodo, popularly known as Jokowi, who won a very tight race in the July 2014 presidential elections. Generation 98 volunteered eagerly for his campaign against the former general Prabowo Subianto, a powerful elite figure thought to have been responsible for the kidnapping and disappearance of activists but never convicted. As one activist from Generation 98 described him, Jokowi is a previously unthinkable and entirely new breed of politician in post-Suharto Indonesia—one without tradition, ties, or capital, without *ormas* (mass organizations), religious networks, international affiliations or degrees, even without activism! The comment places activism as yet another Indonesian institution that Jokowi has surpassed, signaling the welcome end to Generation 98's long era of struggle in the pemuda spotlight.

Chapter 1 | ARCHIVE

Bambang "Beathor" Suryadi was an outspoken youth activist from Jakarta with a nickname that matched his feistiness: "Beathor the Trickster King" (Bitor si Raja Bandel).[1] A graduate of Pancasila University and a member of the radical organization Pijar, Beathor had been causing a stir since his student days in the 1980s. In January 1990 he was sentenced to four and a half years in prison for the subversive act of distributing *selebaran gelap* (lit. dark leaflets). The act of passing out two thousand leaflets in three neighborhoods in Jakarta turned Beathor into a political prisoner, proving that the charge of "insulting the head of state" (Pasal Makar) was a very effective tool to silence dissidents in New Order Indonesia (fig. 1.1). But Beathor the Trickster King did not stay quiet. Instead, after his arrest he switched from one activist form of paper, the newsprint *selebaran* (leaflet or pamphlet) to another form, and then another. A four-page bundle of materials at the IISG demonstrates his strategy of deploying paper to further his political agenda succinctly. These documents were collected by a fellow activist who was active at the same time as Beathor and donated as part of a student movement archive to the IISG. The materials consist of two resistance poems and one set of demands typewritten at three different police and military detention centers, two clippings from a newspaper detailing Beathor's trial proceedings, and a homemade flyer advertising his trial. A quick look at the longest of these documents, a poem dated November 20, 1989, suffices to give us a sense of student politics and their documentary output during the period often referred to as the height of the New Order.

Not content with passing out his subversive leaflet, which was titled "Kampus Perjuangan Bergema" (Campus of struggle reverberates),[2] no copies of which have surfaced in the archives, Beathor composed a statement while in police detention in the form of a prose poem directed at President Suharto. It addresses Suharto with the informal and lowering "you" (*kau*) and speaks on behalf of all the New Order's victims. Accordingly, the poem lists the ridiculous "crimes of subversion" that citizens were accused of committing, along with the real perpetrators (Suharto and his cronies) shameful deeds. Through the simple poetic structure of a litany, Beathor's poem marks the place and time of various acts of repression that colored the 1980s and which deeply concerned student activists, such as the death of three youths in Ujung Pandang, the expulsion of students in Bandung, the deaths of religious activists in Tanjung Priok, and the "Mysterious Shootings" (Penembakan Misterius, shortened to "Petrus") campaign, carried out by the military under Suharto's orders. The poem is simply titled "You, with Your Military Democracy."

You silence our campus, because you fear criticism
You massacre our friends, in Ujung Pandang just because of helmets
You arrest us, when we were in dialogue with people's representatives
   about electricity tariffs
You arrest and imprison our friends, in Yogya just because they were
   having a discussion
You arrest and expel our friends in ITB [Institute of Technology
   Bandung], only because they refused your Minister (entry)
And you let sweet Muslim girls be pushed out of your schools
You killed our young friends in Tanjung Priok and Lampung, because
   they didn't understand about Pancasila[3]
You mysteriously shot our young friends, because you were unable to
   provide work for them
You shot an officer, because you loved your daughter too much
And you have been unable to uphold the law in your 23 years in power
You let Corruptors and Manipulators rule with impunity in front of you
You let your children, your siblings, your friends have economic
   monopolies over the weak
And you let the people be oppressed and evicted, because of development
While your son, you let gamble in Macao, meanwhile our national debt
   grows higher
You say you are anti-totalitarianism and anti-militarism, but to the
   Military you give a greater share

You control all information until we are impotent
You are a dictator because you refuse an opposition
And you step on our feet, until who knows when, then you say this
   country is democratic! Are these actions of yours not insulting???
—BEATHOR SURYADI, FORMER COORDINATOR, STUDENT COMMITTEE
FOR THE REDUCTION OF ELECTRICITY TARIFFS[4]

Beathor was initially accused of engaging in *fitnah* (libel) through his pamphleteering, and from the harsh language of his "defense statement" above, we can see that he did not hold back in his moral condemnation of Suharto. Each "you" in the poem acts as a righteous finger pointed at Suharto.[5] In response to the prosecutor's charge that he had insulted the head of state, Beathor retaliates by asking rhetorically in the final line of the poem, "Are these actions of *yours* not insulting???" There is no attempt in any of his writings to defer to the status of "Bapak" (Father) Suharto or to plead for clemency. Instead he launches a cross-examination that exposes Suharto's many personal and associated weaknesses, using an argument similar to the one Hannah Arendt offers in her treatise *On Violence* (1970): that state violence reveals once and for all the evacuation of the state's claim to legitimate power rather than its tactical strength. In Beathor's eyes, the injustice against a youth activist such as himself delegitimized the dictatorship further.

Beathor was keen for an audience to lend support at his trial. Appended to the front of this stapled set of documents was a simple flyer, designed with a word processing program, that invited supporters to his trial on January 8, 1990 at the North Jakarta district courthouse. It began festively: "Attend! Freedom of Thought on Trial!" As expected, Beathor was found guilty by the judge and ended up serving time in Cipinang Prison in Jakarta, home to some of the New Order state's most targeted and disenfranchised political prisoners. Beathor was released after three years but was shortly after sent back to prison for daring to organize a free speech demonstration following the widely publicized publishing ban of the news magazines *Tempo, Detik,* and *Editor* in 1994.

Of those two thousand leaflets Beathor was convicted for, it is unlikely that any still exist, since such *selebaran* are often printed on cheap and small-sized newsprint. They wet and crumple easily. Thus, the very presence of these four documents beg questions of their survival and production, indeed, of activism as a kind of artisanal workshop for graphic forms and moral language. The legal facts preserved by Beathor's slim packet of papers can be verified by reading international human rights reports or by searching for additional news stories from the time. Such acts of verification are mandatory

FIGURE 1.1 Cartoon image from cover of student publication *Mimbar Demokrasi*, June 1989. The cover story, "Critical Youth on Trial: Critical = Subversive?" is about the subversion trials of two youth, Bambang Isti Nugroho and Bambang Subono, who, like Bambang "Beathor" Suryadi, were arrested in Yogyakarta on subversion charges. The cartoon balloon shows the presiding judge thinking about the choice between furthering his career or justice. The opposing counsels on either side of the judge argue the two sides of the case: "Subversive" and "Critical."

for historical fact-checking of the subversion trials and how they determined Beathor's fate, but I remain distracted by these four pieces of paper and their relationship to subversion and what Indonesians call "youth spirit" (semangat pemuda). Instead of trying to see Beathor the activist through the filter of an Indonesia Country Report on Political Prisoners, I can see more of Beathor the Trickster King in these taunting and disrespectful poems and flyers from an earlier era of student activism. I am therefore receptive to the duality of the student movement materials—they are both social things and things of extreme thinginess—paper-as-text and paper-as-artifact. Reading them becomes an act of graphology that employs a material attunement to the documentary details of the paper; engaging their textuality allows surprising biographical affects to course through; in Beathor's case and for many others, "I did this, because Suharto did that." The "social life of things," their circulation, their changing values and contexts over time, can begin to emerge (Appadurai 1986). Remember, it all started with an illegal leaflet Beathor wrote, printed, and distributed. Upon arrest, he used a manual typewriter. Likely, his friends outside helped him with the design and distribution of the trial flyer. Engaging Beathor's words and paying attention to the formats in which he presented them illuminates the contemporary pemuda stance inherent in his activism.

Pemuda fever suggests that Indonesian students had such an attachment to a historical understanding of their present-day selves that they sought to document each action, each gesture, at every turn, through every medium available. In her book *Refracted Visions* (2010), Karen Strassler provides the antecedents of this documentary and liberating turn by students, liberating because student acts of documentation counter statist narratives and claims to a single authority as a matter of course. Strassler argues that Indonesians value the importance of a "culture of documentation" as proof of a technologized modernity and value it all the more because they see themselves as lacking a culture of documentation that would firmly root national history within a te-leology of global progress. Because the New Order state so successfully affixed its seal of authority upon the idea of documents as "national resources" to be managed by the state, documents themselves became viewed as uniquely historical "material resources of the historical imagination" (2008: 217). Still, the historical awareness about this particular resource deficit and its supplemental need was a middle- and upper-class privilege that largely excluded the rakyat from having any claim to a historical imagination. Reformasi overturned the stability of New Order historical narratives, normalizing what Strassler calls the "documentary fetish" among students who assumed the role of "archon," or steward of history (219).

My research in this chapter pushes this timeline back, to show that pemuda fever was providing another powerful fetish that aligned with the desire for documentation long before Reformasi hit. Student activists like Beathor Suryadi deployed documents to produce and circulate critical discourse against Suharto in an act of counter-hegemonic imagining. However, student activists understood that the literature they produced was inherently fragile and disadvantaged. Their documentary work depicts the state as oppressor and the nation as the oppressed in matter-of-factly insurgent and romantic tones, blurring the line between propaganda and social analysis. The artifacts of the politics they dreamed of and sketched out are abundantly available yet largely decentralized and incidental to the movement's later development. The dispersed, but nonetheless fetishistic, quality of activist documents is well illustrated by the following example. At the end of my fieldwork in 2005, Nurdin, an older activist from Bandung who had been active since the 1980s, promised to share with me the unpublicized reports from the ad hoc National Human Rights Commission investigation on the May Riots and mass rapes of Indonesian-Chinese women in May 1998. He had been a member of the investigating team and had kept a full set of the reports before they were redacted or shelved. Because of the sensitive nature of the issue and continued government denials that the rapes took place, the documents were of paramount historical importance, of which Nurdin was well aware. I was surprised when he showed up for our meeting in a public place bearing an ordinary, transparent supermarket plastic bag stuffed to the brim with paper. The reports were copies with corrupted tones and faded pages. I took the heavy bag from him and promised to return it once I had photocopied the report. The return of the files was delayed for a few months as I finished up my fieldwork, during which time I received several insistent and pleading emails and text messages from the activist to please return his files, for they were very important to him. When I did return the documents, I presented them in a sturdier paper bag, in the order I had found them in. He made no remark on their condition.

Student and activist materials thus have a quality of disarray and assemblage, loss and contingency. Paper was their *techne* of choice. As Heidegger explains in "The Question Concerning Technology," *techne* is a mode of revealing that asks us to go beyond the instrumental notion of paper as form, idea, and content (1977). Instead, techne is a *bringing forth*, a way of knowing and a means of making essential truths known. Why focus on paper when there are other means of accessing history, such as oral histories, interviews, and other anthropological tools in trade? Why should scholars fetishize the very materiality of the thing they study? I call attention to the *techne* of paper to challenge the idea that paper is mere trace and supplement to the real, live witnesses of history and that there are certain preconditions to be met for naming the activist archive. As Foucault has famously described the archive, it is a system of laws that determines what can and cannot be said, it produces regularities and marks differences, it composes distinct formations and relations (1977: 128–129). The archive is none other than "the system of . . . enunciability," and activist paper's prolific reproduction, disarray, and dispersal begs to be seen as such a parallel system of political enunciations by youth. The technical aspect and technological contribution of paper is maintained in my usage of *techne*, but more important, thinking about paper as *techne* reveals the documentation practices of student activism to be social texts.[6] Paper as *techne* indicates the way of things, and paper itself is the thing that remains. By this understanding, every activist text is charged with the burden of awareness, of a strong sense of wrong happening *now* that Agamben has called the identifying mark of the contemporary.[7] Sifting through the paper record, this chapter uncovers the proto-history of the student movement in the archival assemblages and graphic forms that activists pioneered in their struggle against the repressive New Order state. Their archive is not a story of the state. It is a story of a type of communication and communicability thought to belong purely to students as the exemplary youth of the nation.[8] It is a story that continuously rewrites the morality clause into nationalism in times of crisis.

A SLOW SIMMER OF DISCONTENT

Did pemuda fever burn slowly? It would seem so if our vantage point began with a history of the present through the lens of Reformasi. In the introduction, we have been made aware of a missing sequence in pemuda history. Nationalist and official historiography records nothing between the pemuda generations of 1978 and 1998.[9] Thus there are twenty years of student absence from politics to account for. Was it true that those in-between years were in fact peaceful and prosperous, with university campuses churning out diplomas and factories producing goods dutifully? Just three years prior to Reformasi, Anders Uhlin, a political scientist reviewing the odds of continued authoritarianism versus grassroots democratization, concluded that "popular upsurge leading to the breakdown of the authoritarian regime" was "not a likely scenario for Indonesia. The authoritarian state is too strong and the popular movements too weak to make this a feasible alternative. Besides, there is little external support for such a path of democratization" (1995: 155). In a cautious caveat, Uhlin continued, "This scenario could, however, not be entirely ruled out. Some people compare the Indonesian society to a volcano that might erupt violently and unexpectedly" (155). The flawed analysis of "amok" resurgence notwithstanding, Uhlin's sense of the unexpected brewing within Indonesian society describes a general feeling of unrest without knowing its source.

Observations such as Uhlin's are partially accurate in that it took over a decade of "quiet" subversion and underground organizing for student-led resistance to appear on the national stage in 1998, when students mobilized in significant enough numbers to destabilize Suharto's crisis-stricken government. However, this commonly accepted narrative about the sudden eruption in 1998 commits two disservices to students and grassroots politics. First, it dismisses the continued nationwide interventions of students during the prior *zaman normal* (normal times). Second, it assumes that the Campus Normalization Act of 1978, which forced students "back to campus" and dismantled the organizational structures of student politics, successfully instilled a long period of dormancy for the most critical segment of Indonesian society. In fact, as Edward Aspinall's work reminds us, the "proto student movement" (a term I will use henceforth to refer to pre-Reformasi activism) was deeply critical of Suharto and hit the streets in protest, but their small numbers and sporadic protests accord them (at best) the status of handmaiden to the next, more eventful chapter of pemuda history. Many of the innovations that activists discovered during Reformasi, such as national-level networking, connecting to the grassroots in the urban poor, labor, and agrarian sectors, and the creative use of public space for political protest, existed in a smaller scale in the 1980s, yet these practices appear novel later on. The proto student movement looked "polite" and conservative in comparison to the radical street politics that emerged off campus in the mid-1990s and erupted during Reformasi.

Paper as *techne* had its drawbacks. The proto student movement's focus on analog documentary practices as a mode of political organizing (writing, teaching others to write, printing flyers, making zines and journals) was integral to the social reproduction of activism but had diminishing returns beyond their circles. Paper did not lead to a media war or a broad expansion of their political base. Activists innovated and produced popular graphic forms such as zines, newsletters, human rights reports, and position papers, but their readership was limited to students and their supporters. Activists themselves were on the whole increasingly drawn to direct action rather than being on the receiving end of dissident literature. They produced much writing that went unread, including the flyers that are passed out at demonstrations and are often disposed of immediately.[10] An intriguing outcome of activists' attachment to paper's imagined conductivity has been the unplanned archiving of New Order political norms, transactions, and expressions. The paper medium captured the geist of proto student movement politics and set the standard for communicative forms that activists continue to use in the present.

A closer look at the range and extent of student actions and communications in the period roughly between 1985 to 1997 proves that students engaged in open resistance against the state and suffered injury, expulsion, arrest, and imprisonment for it.[11] In the New Order–era archival material available to me, consisting mainly of three activist collections at the IISG, student literature kept at Cornell University's Kroch Asia Library, and personal documents activists shared with me in Indonesia, we can see a generation of youth crossing an ideological threshold that foreclosed the possibility of their collaborating with the army or the power-brokering elite. The court documents and defense statements (*pledoi* and *eksepsi*) from the high-profile subversion trials of youth in 1996 and 1997 that I discuss later in this chapter illuminate the connections between local student issues and national-level politics quite powerfully. The fortunes of the student press matched the pockets of political openness and unexpected repression that the media experienced. In other words, a sovereign notion of "freedom" (*merdeka*) was intimately tied to what concerned observers perceived as the struggle for academic freedom on university campuses across Indonesia.[12] I have mobilized the sum of these understudied Indonesian student materials to submit new sites of evidence for the regime's "decadence" and to highlight dissident possibilities practiced over a longer term than the abrupt revolutionary forms suggested by the more visible mass demonstrations of 1998. These materials illuminate the continuity of thought and practice between two eras that have tended to be treated as separate, that is, the "analog" years of the 1980s and the digitized and fast-moving years of the late 1990s. Such continuities are revelatory in light of the dominant narrative that gets ascribed to the Reform era that followed Suharto's fall and repeal the idea that student activism was a spontaneous act of collective effervescence, due to dissipate upon its ritualized expenditure.

AS REAL STUDENTS DO

For Indonesian youth, business as usual was tightly bound up in didactic messages from the state to be obedient and apolitical, whether they be middle-class privileged university students, or deployable lower-class pemuda.[13] Thus the loudest means of resistance was to speak in the language of politics, the natural language of the pemuda. The critical New Order youth who began to veer away from their claim to privilege under the developmental state broke ranks with mainstream youth, whose vision for a developed Indonesia mirrored the uplift promised by the popular youth film *Catatan Si Boy* (Boy's diary, 1987). In the film, Boy cruises through life driving a BMW, wearing name-brand clothes, and eventually embarking on study abroad in the United States (Sen 1991). He works out, dates girls, studies, and remains an observant Muslim. For all his "ideal boy" features, early on in the film we see a troubling scene of Boy's sense of impunity stemming from his class status and his family's connections to the state; Boy is driving his BMW and talking to his friend in the passenger seat, neither are paying attention, and they very nearly run over a poor sidewalk vendor, hitting and destroying his cart instead. After a moment of shock, Boy and his friend laugh and drive off. A group of students made their rejection of Boy's lifestyle explicit on the occasion of the National Youth Pledge Day (Hari Sumpah Pemuda) on October 28, 1989. In their statement, the student alliance reclaimed their identity as the nation's pemuda, not "Mas Boy" (Mr. Boy) hedonists.[14]

Mainstream students who were hardworking, earnest, and to some extent interpellated by the New Order's "mass ornaments" and pleasure palaces could be equally dismissive of their radical counterparts. Regular students were infuriated by the disruptions to campus normality that "whiny," "bratty," and "still nursing at the breast" activists caused with their antics, as an open letter written by a mainstream student makes clear. The letter I quote here is addressed to the "fake students" in the Bandung-Semarang student alliance and begins with a loud and scathing insult "Kalian Gombal!!!" (You're all phonies!!!) The letter clearly reached its intended recipient, as it was housed in the archives of a Semarang activist. The student writes:

> We do not need riots, blah-blah-blah, and the like. We are in the midst of studying for an acute result to catch up on our backwardness in comparison to other countries, so as to not be strangled by and dictated to by other nations. We are aware that the engineering world is developing in leaps and with a high rate of obsolescence, unlike (your, sorry) social sciences that are slow and almost stagnant. What we need is a good study atmosphere for the sciences, not one contaminated by blah-blah-blah issues of a bunch of fake students. Signed, A Real ITB Student, Bandung, November 22, 1989.

The letter is a three-page, dot matrix printout in blue ink on white paper. Written by an anonymous angry student at the elite Bandung Institute of Technology, it refers to a much-publicized on-campus protest against a visit by Rudini, Suharto's minister of the interior. The protest resulted in nine students expelled and thirty students suspended from the institution. A further six students, known as the Bandung Six, were singled out for trial and sentenced to three years in prison.[15] It is a telling document of what "normal" law-abiding citizens thought about troublemaking students, particularly in an elite institution such as the Bandung Institute of Technology, which served as a laboratory for the nation's technological and technocratic dreams. The tone of the letter serves as an exemplary cultural clash taking place among the student body between "pro-Indonesian" developmentalist, modernist values and the populist, leftist ideas held by a minority of students. It would seem that life on campus was riven with concerns about the role of youth. So how did youth get on with forbidden politics?

ORGANIZING UNDER THE CAMPUS NORMALIZATION ACT:
STUDY CLUBS AND CRITICAL WRITING

Beginning (again) in the mid-1980s and operating under the strictures of the Campus Normalization Act, students poured energy into building a platform for free speech and youth politics, organizing study clubs (*kelompok studi*), forging links with legal aid, human rights, and environmental NGOs, and writing manifestoes, statements, leaflets (selebaran) and position papers on the "national situation" (*sitnas*). Extracurricular activities, such as the Nature Lovers Club (Mahasiswa Pecinta Alam) and human rights or journalism training sessions, served as surrogate spaces for youth bonding and agency in the absence of autonomous student politics on campus (Tsing 2004). All of these activities comprised a self-study regime that suited the flexible lifestyles of students who valued their autodidacticism above the limited curriculum they learned on campus. The study clubs in Bandung, Jakarta, and Yogyakarta have been well documented as the first successful alliances that brought students from different faculties and institutions together (Arismunandar 2012; Aryono 2009; Supriyanto 1998). Study clubs were important forums where students were exposed to critical ideas and forbidden texts and trained in debate, comparison, and political analysis, which they used to good effect in their writings. Activists would translate texts from English and other languages into Bahasa Indonesia for discussion. Theories of political economy, dialectical materialism, historical revisionism, liberation theology, and dependency theory, which rarely showed up in classrooms—with the exception of the most critical lecturers, who were targeted and punished for being outspoken[16]—could be found in the essays written for internal circulation and in the student press. While the Campus Normalization Act introduced measures that ensured tight scrutiny of all writing produced on campus (Hill 2006: 116), student publications that enjoyed the support of their university administrations gained a reputation for the quality and courageousness of their journalism, often drawing on the same pool of politicized students as activist groups did. *Politika*, a student journal published by the private National University (UNAS) in Jakarta, summarized the establishment's patronizing mindset and the students' rebellious attitude against it in their inaugural issue in 1985: "The student press cannot be critical. [It] cannot talk politics, it has to lurk behind the campus walls. Says who? The flush of youth, their education as well as their sensitivity to social issues, demand that the student press 'appear different' from other mass media."[17] This type of self-referential language, of students as critical pemuda and obligated members of society, appears frequently in student writings, to remind their audience that activism bears a historical legacy from which it draws its moral legitimacy. Student activism is, as it were, prepolitics.

While there have been studies of the history of the Indonesian press and its important role in democratization (Hill 2006; Steele 2005), it remains necessary to remind ourselves why students' relationship to writing as a political activity was so richly developed, in part because their access to the street was cut off by the Campus Normalization Act of 1978. It would take some time for new student traditions to adapt to the strictures of the development aegis the technocracy promoted,[18] which positioned students as educated (therefore aligned with the state rather than the masses), disciplined (therefore distant from noneducational activities), and moral (therefore absent from the corrupting influence of politics). Student dissent in the 1980s was a development that corresponded to, but was not entirely dependent on, elite opposition from within the military and Suharto's former allies. Overall, the period of openness (*keterbukaan*) between 1989 and 1994 saw a softer stance from the regime regarding its critics and enabled a space for democratic politics and oppositional discourses to grow. Such experiments included efforts by elite factions in the military and other political traditions to push for alternative leadership to Suharto and for frank and public debates on succession, human rights violations, and democracy led by the media, intellectuals, and civil society groups.

The periodized timing of "openness" in Indonesian society (1989–1994) provides a context for the way the mass mobilizations of 1998 began to grow a decade before, yet it was also true that neither a continuous opposition nor a consolidated student network survived from the 1980s through to the 1990s. Rather, the shape of opposition was one that was extremely compromised and collaborative with the regime, organizationally weak and ad hoc (Aspinall 2005). However, "sporadic" student attempts at mobilization could not be so easily dismissed. The newspaper clippings that students kept and that I found in their archives show that hundreds of students mobilized on the streets, over student and nonstudent issues. The repression of students by the regime became more overt in the mid-1990s as the period of political openness ended.[19] Using a tried and true tactic, the state turned to familiar anticommunist propaganda to demonize left-leaning student groups, yet students only escalated their political experiments when the regime grew intolerant (Aspinall 2012).[20]

Students were concerned with issues that were *national* in character, including human rights, the constitution, the occupation of East Timor, various land struggles, religious freedom, militarism, and workers' rights. They organized demonstrations and "Long Marches" that involved activists from universities across Java, and beyond Java, through the telephone, clandestine meetings, and by post. Looking back, we must ask how so much student labor and passion for democracy, captured on paper and other media, could be so easily overshadowed and disciplined by the realpolitik of elite interests and the impressive mass movements of Reformasi.[21] Is it as simple as concluding that the gaps in the historical record are necessary to maintain the political expediency of dominant historical narratives? What would allow us to compose a new history of struggle that exonerates students from the charge of complicity and silence under the New Order? How might we redeem political meaning and engagement from "minor and uneventful" acts of resistance, when spectacular mass movements seem to be the "real" arbiter of grassroots democracy?[22]

CAN THERE BE HISTORY WITHOUT DOCUMENTS?

At the end of the New Order and during the transition to democracy, there was a strong need to "straighten out" (*meluruskan*) the nation's history and to create a more "complete" historical record. Concurrently, the ambiguity and anxiety over potentially illicit texts and unresolved arguments over historical controversies concerning state violence hampered the creation of a "people's history" of Indonesia (Adam 2005; McGregor 2009; Zinn 1980). Even the valorized "Reform heroes" (an honorific title the media bestowed on students) were not exempt from the ambivalent and reactionary cultural politics of post-Suharto Indonesia that sought to discipline youth by asking them to go back to school once again. To date, the well-trod history of democratic uplift wrought by Reformasi contains a few uncomfortable bits of "gravel in Jakarta's shoes," notably the lack of state accountability in the disappearances of activists in 1997–1998 and the shootings of students in 1998 and 1999.[23] Historian Asvi Warman Adam was among one of the most outspoken critics who pressed for an accounting of state violence against citizens through curricular reform and more open political dialogues about the past (2005, 2009, 2010). Activist-oriented NGOs attempted to revitalize Indonesian history by cultivating oral history projects involving victims of state violence (Roosa et al. 2004), focusing on the neglected stories of former communists and alleged sympathizers. The drive to document was a clear outcome of Reformasi consciousness about the role of pemuda. Activists were hopeful that their leftist ideas and populist programs would finally gain broader social acceptance, for "commodity Marxism" already existed in the marketplace (Kasian 2001). A wave of public interest in historical revisionism, driven in large part by press freedom and the pleasure and possibility of speaking out against the former master Suharto, cohered with the liberal cultural politics of then-president Abdurrahman Wahid, who in 2000 attempted to repeal the ban on the Communist Party of Indonesia and on Marxist literature. The response of the political elite was a resounding no, triggering a political crisis and calls for Wahid's impeachment.

Pemuda fever, perhaps tainted by its oppositional and leftist history, its unresolved cases of state violence, or more pragmatically by a lack of political will to pursue the matter of official recognition, has not yielded an officially sanctioned, publicly accepted monument or archive to serve as a cultural site for the memories of the student movement. Indeed, neither the private nor the public sector has succeeded in erecting a monument or a permanent archive to mark the inclusion of the student movement's role in the demise of the New Order (Kusno 2010). The objective fact of a few surviving student archives provides some relief from the opacity of the proto student movement.[24] I have had to search outside official institutions in Indonesia to borrow and copy much of the materials I collected. The bulk of student organizing and knowledge production from that time can be found in the counter-regime literature on newsprint, typescript, and paper, known collectively as *dokumentasi* (documentation). Many of these materials did not extend further back than Reformasi. It is thanks to a few committed individuals in Indonesia and abroad that there are so many materials to consult. Activists have addressed the archival gap by aiding researchers selflessly. They create "lending libraries" out of their own collections, lending personal memorabilia, such as diaries and drawings; giving interviews that become transcriptions of oral history; and sharing the documents they photocopied from others. In some cases they have shared rare, out-of-print books and photos. These personal archives were invaluable to me as a researcher. Each activist had a tale about why dokumentasi mattered, usually attached to a truth claim, and why most organizations lacked dokumentasi, despite its importance. Youth's follies were partially revealed in their stories: to lack dokumentasi was to lack discipline and stability, a perfect explanation for life on the go and under siege.

Robbie, once the leader of the National Student League for Democracy, told me the story of how in 1999 their secretariat in Benhil, South Jakarta, was raided by right-wing paramilitary groups who took their computers. All their hard drives that stored their written statements, meeting notes, and propaganda leaflets were gone. In 2002, during the great flood that hit Jakarta and surrounding areas, former PRD activist Wilson suffered a great loss. His mother's house in Bogor flooded, and all his books and papers, including many history books and much leftist literature that had been hard to procure during the New Order, had been stored in his room and were destroyed by the floodwaters. In 2004–2005, I met Wilson often at the demonstration sites. He was still collecting leaflets and activist material off the street. Some of these found objects and his handwritten letters from his imprisonment survived and were deposited in the IISG. Savic Alielha, an activist with a Nadhlatul Ulama background and prominent member of Generation 98, had been active since his college days in Yogyakarta in 1993. He had been a founding member of City Forum (Forum Kota: Forkot), the largest alliance of student groups in 1998, and then its splinter group Action Front for Students for Reformation and Democracy (Front Aksi Mahasiswa untuk Reformasi dan Demokrasi: Famred), before founding yet another organization, the Front for Indonesian Youth Struggles (Front Perjuangan Pemuda Indonesia: FPPI). He told me that he had once had a complete set of documents, rare photographs included, that traced the early history of the student movement. Alas, as he moved between cities and from one rented room (kost) to another, he left his papers with friends who were either as mobile as he was or simply careless with his belongings.

These authenticating and original documents were among a long list of lost and untraceable dokumentasi that activists talked about. Activists regretted their lost documents and hinted that missing archives contained secrets that would "complete" their history (Lee 2012). Their wistfulness for lost papers paralleled another common claim of authentication they made: a claim to a historical agency linked to their witnessing of a landmark historical moment, when they had forced Suharto to resign on May 21, 1998, a moment that had left its mark on their persons as memory-object, lodged deep. Both were irretrievable except through memory—a moment in time, a souvenir of that time. Okwui Enwezor expresses the tensions within unstable indices of history and memory as "archival returns [that] are often conjoined with the struggle against amnesia and anomie. A heightened sense of urgency surrounds the demand to remember and commemorate in societies where social codes of communication have been historically unstable or preempted by state repression" (2008: 37). In a supplementary act to the missing archive, Indonesian activists would narrate their own chronology of events perfectly; perfecting their narrative was a way to ward off anomie and amnesia. Still, the missing archives diverted attention from an obvious fact. If one paid attention to the actual political practices of student activists, it was clear that activism did not regard dokumentasi as a scarce resource. There was always more and more stuff to make, disseminate, and discard, in keeping with a productivity level required for activists to stay relevant in contemporary politics.[25]

As Karen Strassler has shown in her study of Reformasi photography's "culture of documentation," students' archival ideologies served various purposes: historical reflection, networking, information gathering, self-study, and antistate propaganda (2010). Activist materials are souvenirs, fetishized as secrets and keepsakes (204–205; Stewart 1993: 135) or used and discarded as mere media. These twin poles of value that oscillate between disposable commodity and fetishized remnant (reminiscent of how fragments of the Berlin Wall could serve as historical monuments and be sold in the marketplace) determine the afterlife of activist materials and present a conundrum: what are the connections between memory work that privileges authentic and lost dokumentasi and a pemuda fever that is remarkably self-replenishing and not subject to scarcity? I take up this issue of reproducibility and material culture again in chapter 3 to show how activist messages have expanded their circulatory power by migrating onto other sites beyond paper, notably the body and visual media. One of the main thrusts in this book is to recuperate what I call the "trash of democracy" (the print, material, and electronic matter of activism) as a repository and resource for public and political culture. During my fieldwork in 2003–2005, Indonesian youth activism had adopted a multiplatform approach to the technologies of demonstrating, networking, and archiving, using social media, text messaging, mobile phones, video, film (documentary and feature), Internet press releases, websites, spanduk (banners), posters, and T-shirts printed on demand. Post-Reformasi activism's technological approaches reflect global trends of crowdsourcing, smart mobbing, and "swivel chair activism" that signal the new "Internet age" of politics (Hill and Sen 2005; Rheingold 2003).

On the surface, the digital methods of propagation and organizing seem radically different from those of the New Order past, promising transparency and quick results. In the analog era, activism required face-to-face connection, secrecy and lies, and protection from state surveillance. As the analog methods of the proto student movement became anachronistic, in many ways a style of expressing political commitment bound to paper also exited the movement.[26] Argumentation and clever rhetorical flourishes in student writings gave way to more formulaic slogans and pragmatic instructions on how to be a demonstrator. Sly satire gave way to crude insult. But the changes were not only formal nor completely driven by content. As I looked at the vast quantities of material activists generated in the Suharto years and in the post-Suharto era, I became aware that the student movement archive functioned as a trove or, spelled differently, a trough of communicative forms that revealed student attitudes and youth interests in resisting the state. "To analytically restore the visibility of documents, to look *at* rather than *through* them" (Hull 2012: 13), would mean a *longue durée* analysis of the graphic artefacts of student activism and a reading method that would not hesitate to "tickle" straightforward dokumentasi until it yielded its secrets (Mrázek 2002: xvi). And to do so, one needed to start doing participant-observation with that old-fashioned bureaucratic medium, paper.

LOOKING AT THE ARCHIVE

In what ways can the student protest materials be enlivened by new insights? How far would an empiricist attitude to the student archives take us? Reading the student protest materials, an analytical problem similar to Philip Abrams's problematic in studying the state arises: that is, the state is everything and everywhere and therefore nowhere, leaving us no clearer than in the beginning of our study (1977). In the same vein, it is tempting to track rather than analyze student resistance by "looking through" the student archive for instances of declarative resistance, compelled by the recurring nationalistic moral claims or orthodox Marxist claims made by students to justify their political arguments and actions. If we were to read every single piece of literature or pamphlet to determine just how radical Indonesian students were in the 1980s or 1990s, or how close they were to actually overthrowing the regime, we would not get very far at all.[27] Moreover, sifting through student materials is a task that requires foregoing the archive story as detective story (Burton 2006). It is beyond the scope of my research to trace the alliances and group names and identities scattered across the various materials.[28] A far more intriguing set of analyses emerges when one pays attention to the relationship between what lies within and outside the archives, to the documentary forms activists turned to, and to the affinities between different collections—in literary terms, reading for the "social etymologies" (Stoler 2009: 35) of themes and tropes that signal activist alliances, sympathies, and longings. One such happy coincidence emerged when I saw the phrase "Hanya ada satu Kata: Lawan!" (For there is only one word: Resist!), by the underground poet Wiji Thukul repeated over and over again in the documents spanning almost two decades, beginning in the mid-1980s (see fig. 1.2). Such coincidences in the archives are, in historian Arlette Farge's words, everything and nothing. "Everything, because they can be astonishing and defy reason. Nothing, because they are just raw traces, which on their own can draw attention only to themselves" (2013: 12). Let the force of the coincidence speak to the nationalist question then.

"There is only one word: Resist!" appears as the epilogue to secret reports, in closing statements on leaflets, in demonstrations as a rallying cry. In this version from 1989, an activist has inserted the phrase into the triplet formula of the nationalist student oath, the Sumpah Pemuda: "There is only one word . . . Resist. There is only one goal . . . Seize. There is only one hope . . . Justice."[29] We can see the resemblance to the 1938 version of the Sumpah Pemuda: "We have one homeland, that is, the Indonesian nation. We are one nation, that is, the Indonesian nation. We have one language, that is, the Indonesian language" (see Foulcher 2000: 403). Keith Foulcher notes that the symmetry of the formulation has been maintained in all Sumpah Pemuda variations since its first declaration in 1928 and has been adapted to suit anticolonial, antiimperial, and Old and New Order needs. In its essential form, the Sumpah Pemuda stresses unity: *One* homeland, *One* nation, *One* language. The activist addition of "One Word: Resist!" adds the final word. Following the publications boom that revived discussions about the Sumpah Pemuda in the 1980s, subversive distortions and plays on the standard nationalist formula would have been unmistakable to its sensitized audience (Foulcher 2000). Both the Sumpah Pemuda and Wiji Thukul's dissident poetry continue to punctuate demonstrations today, long after Thukul's disappearance by the state (see chapter 2). Seeing Thukul's singular phrase scattered across the materials produced by different groups in different cities draws a line of communication between Thukul's radical populist formation and other more traditional activists. A composite view emerges of the underground activist economy during the New Order: how widespread illicit texts and ideas were;[30] how student politics took place on and off campus; and how political ideas counter to the regime were being distributed and circulated across the country by an ad hoc, decentralized movement.

Despite fomenting civil disobedience against the state, students attempted to assert legitimacy by reproducing familiar authorizing gestures that were common to bureaucracy and the professional white-collar world they were rebelling against. Notably, they did so by replicating the formality of communication and documentation technologies used by state and institutional bureaucracies, in the form of writing memos and cover letters on printed letterhead, using rubber stamps with their organizations' logos (Solidaritas Mahasiswa Semarang, a student group from Central Java used an image of a dove, striking in blue ink), even using stamp-duty (*meterai*) and notarized signatures on their documents.[31] Following such conventions allowed students to appear organized and exhibited their educated backgrounds even if the language they used was subversive. Open letters would open with the greeting "Salam Solidaritas" (Solidarity Greetings) or "Salam Demokrasi" (Democracy Greetings) and sign off with "Merdeka!" (Freedom!) or "Demokrasi atau Mati!" (Democracy or Die!). On the backs of flyers and petitions, on envelopes used to distribute dissenting materials in the regular mail service, there are tiny postage stamps decorated with the smiling face of Suharto. The unevenness of the archive demands a slower reading in the absence of chronology as reading guide. Entire years do not appear in the student archives at all. Understandably so. Papers were often lost, purposely burnt, or damaged by time and the tropics.[32]

With the speed of reading adjusted to account for the broken links, we might begin to see how history plays in "three keys" that correspond to "event, experience and myth" (Cohen 1998). The schoolroom practice of collecting clippings from newspapers served as an important means of documentation and fact-gathering about student "events" in a local, national, and occasionally international frame (as seen in English-, Dutch-, and occasionally German-language media).[33] Student methods of writing provide a wealth of information about two of these key representational modes: experience and myth. Student propaganda could be vague, deploying nationalist platitudes or orthodox Marxism-Leninism that rewrote Indonesia's political economy into a damning formula of capitalist oppression. But when they left the format of the propaganda statement and *spanduk* (banner) and turned to investigative human rights reports and chronologies, they amassed a great deal of factual information on how abuses of power were actually carried out. Student press publications named names of officers they recognized in the field and named students who were injured or detained by the military, as well as listing the destruction of property incurred by state violence against student and worker demonstrations. Student press activists addressed their supporters and detractors directly in editorials, claiming to present diverse perspectives from students, demonstrators, and even the common man on the street and at times explaining their reasons for sustaining dialogue and coverage of controversial issues such as state violence over several editions. The editors of the journal *Pijar* held an emergency meeting after "Bloody Kusumanegara," named after the street in Bandung where violence by the army against students took place; they decided that producing a special issue was necessary because "*witnessing has to be given* to this event" (*Pijar Edisi Khusus September* 1989; emphasis in original).

PUBLIC SECRETS

Complicating the archive is the activist's insistence on performing secrecy, on writing things down only to halt their distribution and escape. For whose eyes only are these materials? Is the organization leak proof? Who is reading whom? Much of the literature on archives features the making of the state and bureaucracy—that state archives reflect in principle the consignation of the functions and the secrets of the state (Gupta 2012). State archives are bound to institutionalized practice and form in ways that keep out dissenting voices and invisible subjects, mainly women and children, and in the case of colonial archives, the colonized (Cooper 2005). Dissidents may appear by name if they are the target of legal and illegal state operations, but even so, the politics of the state archives cannot fully accommodate other experiences and rationalities, particularly of those designated as the "floating masses." It is, as Jim Scott tells us in *Seeing Like a State* (1999), the logic of statecraft to turn individuals into populations, at once countable and anonymous. The state archives are reserves of information, capturing and counting every thing and event thought to matter now and in the future. The mark of secrecy in the archive, as Ann Stoler explains, is often the state's attempt to limit the circulation of nonsecret knowledge to its own proper channels (2009).[34] The shadow archive that is made up of dissident dokumentasi is assembled as a politically motivated project to disrupt, rather than complete, the narrative of state archives.[35] In these *other* archives, keeping illicit thoughts, ideas, and objects out of circulation is more obviously a protective measure against state surveillance and an attempt at material preservation; yet how secrecy was practiced cast doubt on the ways secrecy worked.

"BURN AFTER READING!"

In a typed report by activist groups detailing the divisional tasks of a nationwide protest in July 1989, the following notes emphasize the need for vigilance.

> The transcriber of this note is Daniel.
> This transcription is then handed over to the general coordinators: Nuka and Stanley.
> After [the document] coding by the General Coordinators, *then this transcription must be burnt*. And proof (the General Coordinators' signatures) that this transcription has been burnt is in Daniel's hands.
> The General Coordinator must explain to each department *only that which pertains* to the work of their department.[36]

The first three points name the people in the room and state their positions and tasks. The steps must be followed in administrative order. First transcription, then coding, then burning, and finally proof of burning. The paper economy of the proto student movement paints a picture of discipline, regimentation, and risk. Planning meetings require *notulensi* (transcription) to provide accurate records of statements and commitments from the parties involved, but as the note makes clear, the information must be kept hidden in the form of a code. Cultivating opacity is another way to take information out of circulation, as demonstrated by points 3 and 4. To commit fully to the group project of the demonstration, individuals had to remain separated from each other so that they could not reveal the whole if they were arrested, having been told only the part. Was it a slip-up of their careful rules of secrecy that this document still existed in the IISG archives, or was it a record of another record that had been burnt? Has Daniel already transcribed the notes? Has he handed them over yet to Nuka and Stanley? Has the coding taken place off-page, and so the directive comes at *this* interjectory moment to remind the students that it now has to be burnt, and is this document then the final proof of the burning? Given the absence of tenses in Indonesian, all translations, and indeed all reading out of context, produce an interpretive quandary that Henk Maier (2005) points to in his analysis of Malay and Indonesian literature. My translation of the Indonesian reproduces the aforementioned sense of temporal and contextual uncertainty, such that the imperative "burn after reading" has not (yet) been carried out and, coupled with the document's lonely appearance in the archive, has left the document insecure. The researcher begging for a sign that the message was heeded ("please sign here as proof of burning") is stymied by the document's loss of anchor to a foundational and broader semiotic context.

"Burn after reading" was a rule concurrent with "Meet after dark" or in secret. A report by a Java-based activist who traveled to Ujung Pandang, Sulawesi, in 1989 to meet with students is ostentatiously marked with the word *Rahasia* (Secret) underlined across the top left corner of each page.[37] Although taking place on university campuses, the meetings themselves were clandestine. The road trip was a preparatory exercise intended to extend the Java-wide student network to the possibly fifty thousand politicized students in Ujung Pandang, whose militant attitude toward Suharto could be summed up thus: "The Ruler of this Dynasty must be 'DESTROYED.'" In order to convince the skeptical students in Ujung Pandang of what the "hegemons" in the Java-based student movement were doing, the activist had to make the same presentation over and over, on "The National Political Constellation; Student Movement—Obstacles and Aspirations."

Each meeting was convened as a *diskusi* (discussion) that followed a formalized format known to students who had joined study clubs: a presentation on a theoretical subject would take place, and debates and questions by the participants would last for hours, often well into the night. On the first night, the activist ran one discussion from 8 to 10 PM before resuming a second discussion from 10:30 until 2:30 AM. The next day, he held a discussion on another campus from 10 PM to 1 AM. The secret report is thorough. It is organized as a scientific report with a prologue, summary evidence, and summary conclusions of the objective conditions, goals, and achieved realities from the activist's tour of three universities. While it is careful to exclude all names of students involved, it identifies the different faculties from which the curious groups are drawn to show the strength of youth spirit in overcoming petty campus rivalries.[38] In the conclusion, the author calls for a return to nationalist ideas encased in the Sumpah Pemuda and the Proclamation of Independence to overcome "misunderstandings" and "errant perceptions" of other (non-Java) students toward activists in Java. The nationalist framework was especially important in those years to bridge status and ethnic differences between Java and the rest. Campuses on Java were considered more prestigious than fledgling campuses in the outer islands of the archipelago, but it was those students from outside Java whose political weight was needed to make the student movement truly national. Perhaps the most subversive element of the document was not its surprising mention of interethnic tensions between students but the ordinariness of student activism as a domain embedded in campus life despite the Campus Normalization Act; the report records that a meeting on campus at the group's secretariat had to be rescheduled because the host students were busy overseeing a state-mandated orientation and indoctrination session (P4) for incoming students that day.

Certain practices of maintaining secrecy worked more as a form of ritual appeasement. State power can leak into the most private spaces of everyday life, controlling how citizens view what they think of as "unspeakable things."[39] In the conclusion to her book, Strassler describes how an Indonesian widow reads about the mass killings of communists in 1965 from materials found on the Internet in an effort to confront her past. At the center of her life's mystery is the husband who disappeared in 1967. To enact reading, she must hold the printed-out articles in her hands. She reads the dangerous papers in the dark, alone at night after the household is asleep. Finally, she burns her copy of information that is already in circulation to hide the evidence that she knows what the state disavows. But then the next day, she asks her family to find her more information (Strassler 2010: 296–297). To possess papers and then to burn them after follows a clandestine logic of self-discipline rather than paranoia. Conflicting desires of wanting to possess illicit (yet public) information and wanting to save oneself from stigma from the neighborhood community (a societal formation already linked administratively to the state) brings risk into the fold. Citizens betted on the likelihood that it might be all right to possess and perhaps save banned books as souvenirs. Activists recalled finding rare leftist materials in university libraries and feeling compelled to steal, no, save them. After all, anecdotal evidence by Indonesians who lived through the censorship years depicts the state's lack of reading; there was no consistency in the ways censorship was practiced, and often texts that had been produced by the government or prominent establishment figures were singled out by low-level officials as "bad" texts. Yet because of this indeterminacy, one can be seized by (state) terror. It is no comfort, or indeed it is unlikely, to imagine a floating public out there who might know what to do with the release of dangerous secrets. It is just as well that the state does not seem to read closely, for in doing so it masks its ignorance by exhibiting a contempt of the general masses who do not or cannot read. As Ben Anderson describes, it is not commodity Marxism's proliferation of leftist books and ideas in print capitalism that the state truly fears but the undeniable pull of television images on the uneducated masses that must be policed (Anderson 2014).

State propaganda shows quite a different image of students, as politically manipulated and vulnerable subjects who have foolishly forgotten their place.[40] Students kept evidence of how the state saw them, in police documents and court documents related to their arrests and trials. It is from these texts that we must learn to read *with* the form, as well as *against* its grain. In the next section, I develop an argument for reading the "rightful politics" of activist statements of appeal as an enduring form of critical citizenship and historical awareness that does double duty, disrupting and revitalizing authorized ideas about youth identity. The increasingly polarized language of the archive pitted civil society against the state and students against all forms of authority as a matter of manifest destiny.

DEFENDING THEMSELVES: ACTIVIST PLEDOI AND EKSEPSI

Reading against the archival grain, as Stoler suggests, becomes a productive enterprise when dealing with the amount of material generated by and around activist trials for subversion, in 1989 and later in 1997. From the 1989 trials, we have already seen the case of Bambang Beathor Suryadi at the beginning of this chapter as one of the youth the state made into an example. The Bandung Six, who had been sentenced to three years in prison for protesting the interior minister's visit to Bandung Technology Institute, also fall into this category. While the subversion trials in 1989 were straightforward attempts to silence student speech and repress campus politics, the trials in 1996 and 1997 were the repercussive shocks of national-level politics on grassroots supporters. The state's targeting of radical student groups followed a violent siege by progovernment supporters against the oppositional faction of the only viable opposition party at the time, the PDI under Megawati Soekarnoputri's leadership. The storming of the PDI headquarters in Jakarta on July 27, 1996, was used

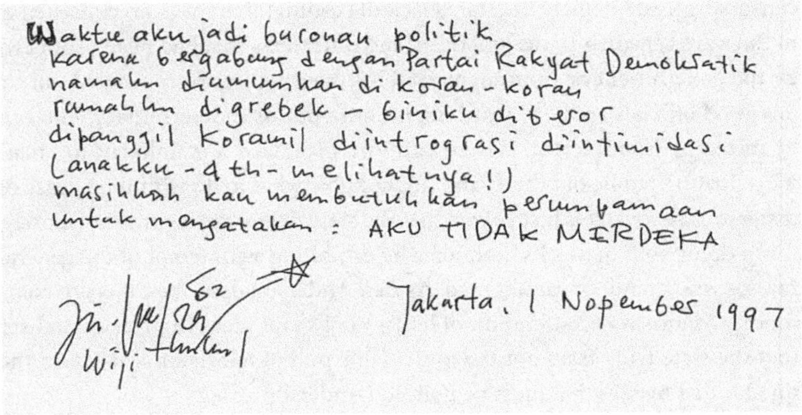

*Waktu aku jadi buronan politik
Karena bergabung dengan Partai Rakyat Demokratik
namaku diumumkan di koran-koran
rumahku digrebek — biniku diteror
dipanggil koramil diinterogasi diintimidasi
(anakku - 4 th - melihatnya!)
masihkah kau membutuhkan perumpamaan
untuk mengatakan : AKU TIDAK MERDEKA*

Jakarta, 1 Nopember 1997

Wiji Thukul

FIGURE 1.2 Excerpt from a handwritten letter by Wiji Thukul, poet and People's Democratic Party activist, disappeared while on the run, November 1, 1997:

When I was a political fugitive
because I joined the Democratic People's Party
my name was publicized in the papers
my house torn up—my wife terrorized
summoned by the military command interrogated intimidated
(my child—4 years old—witnessed this!)
Do you still need allegories
To say: I AM NOT FREE

JAAP ERKELENS COLLECTION, INTERNATIONAL INSTITUTE FOR SOCIAL HISTORY, AMSTERDAM. AUTHOR'S TRANSLATION.

by the government as a pretext to accuse the PRD student group of fomenting violence. Other activist groups were also impacted by the nationwide hunt for activists on the run. Hendrik Sirait, a UNAS student whose traumatic experience I discuss in chapter 4, was one of the victims taken and tortured by the military. The July 27 Incident set off a period of exile and disappearance for many leftist activists. A couple of Jakarta activists I knew who had organized rural communities outside Bogor, West Java, hid with their constituents, hoping that the cover of village life would shield them from the army's tightening net. Wilson, the PRD activist whose archive contains a volume three inches thick of state documents regarding his arrest and trial, got as far as Semarang. According to a wonderfully banal and incongruent (and perhaps unreliable?) detail in his police report, Wilson was caught in a comrade's kost while "in front of the TV."[41] His defense statement (pledoi), more than thirty pages long, was brave and defiant. "The number of years in our sentencing is a badge of honor for us. The heavier the sentence dropped on our struggle, the heavier the sins borne by the ruler and the court in the eyes of the Indonesian People."

The pledoi and eksepsi are rich rhetorical modes that activists adapted into an activist platform for free speech, a formalized extension of the spontaneous, unscripted *mimbar bebas* (free speech rally) speeches. Youth who were charged with subversion argued their cases passionately before the judges and, whenever possible, committed to the performative act of defending their honor by reading their statements out loud instead of having their lawyers read them on their behalf.[42] There are legal differences between the pledoi and the eksepsi. In the legal proceedings, the eksepsi (or refutation / challenge, from the Dutch *exceptie*) comes first. It is the first stage at which the defendant can protest the charges against him, based on procedural grounds such as incorrect charges, incorrect arrest or notification procedures, and inaccuracies in the context of the arrest. As I will show, activists interpreted this procedural frame broadly to insert their arguments about the *national* political context of the charges against them. The pledoi (from the Dutch *pledooi*, plea) is the last stage before sentencing in which the defendant can argue against the charges against him and moreover must provide a "logical argumentation" for disputation of guilt. The pledoi is often the more impressive statement because it summarizes and re-presents the entire defense from the defendant's perspective to the court. Pledoi became "white papers" (*buku putih*) that exposed the truth of an event, as in the case of the Bandung activists in 1989, or manifestoes about labor unionism and capitalism, as in Wilson's case in 1996. Pledoi ranged from dozens of pages to book-length statements. Because activists often wished to read the pledoi as a last-ditch attempt to sway the courts, judges were known to refuse a defendant's defense statement in court, with the ruling that the pledoi was "irrelevant" to the charges at hand.[43] Sometimes the defendant would only have read two pages for the judge to rule its irrelevance. Defense teams, often those affiliated with progressive legal aid NGOs, were ready for this possibility and would release the defendant's statements to the public in the form of student or alternative publications. This was what happened in the case of Oka Dwi Candra, a student activist from UNAS in Jakarta.

OKA'S EKSEPSI

Oka Dwi Candra was arrested on July 21, 1996, just a few days before the July 27 Incident. He was arrested in Bandung at a free speech rally that his group, Aldera, organized to support the opposition figure Megawati Soekarnoputri. Most of the grassroots supporters of Megawati were galvanized in

FIGURE 1.3 Wilson sifting through his archival documents, including arrest and release papers. Jakarta, May 2014. PHOTO BY AUTHOR.

those tense days, as it became more and more evident that the Suharto regime was preparing to shut down the opposition with force. The Aldera rally was one of several student reactions to the deepening repression. The police and military responded in heavy-handed ways, targeting known activist students. Oka had allegedly assaulted a police officer while resisting arrest at an Aldera rally, so he was charged, under Laws 170 and 351 of the Criminal Code, with assault and torture. According to Oka, it was a natural act of self-defense. He was getting pummeled by several officers as they held him down to arrest him, and his flailing fist just happened to make contact with a security officer. At the first trial, Oka shocked the court when he answered the question "Do you understand the charges that have been brought against you?" in the negative.

At the third trial, he produced a six-page eksepsi to read. However, the presiding judge rejected his eksepsi for referring to matters outside the case. At this point the courthouse full of students and Oka supporters jeered loudly. The eksepsi was then circulated by his defense team in a public statement and in a special journal titled *Suara Demokrasi* (Voice of Democracy) that covered the trial.[44] These details emerge from the personal copies Oka kept, which I photocopied in 2004. His collection contained the aforementioned *Suara Demokrasi*, his eksepsi, his legal aid team's eksepsi, photos of himself in prison with his fist raised high in solidarity, handwritten letters from his friends (complete with macho jokes, jibes, and slang), newspaper articles about his trial, and activist campaign materials publicizing his case.

The eksepsi itself is a long, narrow column of angular computer script. I have translated the following excerpts from the eksepsi's beginning points and endnotes to show how Oka built his case on the moral grounds of pemuda identity and love of nation. It begins in respectful tones.

To the Judges whom I respect,

On the 22nd of July 1996, in the North parking lot of the Padjajaran University campus, Bandung, I and my comrades from the Alliance of the People's Democracy (Aldera), for the umpteenth time, held a free speech rally. The free speech action that was held at 15.00 hours was meant as an open show of support for Megawati Soekarnoputri. As we all know, at that moment, there were attempts to topple Megawati Soekarnoputri from her seat as the head of the PDI council of representatives. And, there was a lot of evidence that the government, through the Interior Ministry and the commander of the military (ABRI), gave its full support to Soerjadi to take the PDI leadership from Megawati Soekarnoputri's hands. What happened in the PDI corps has touched my sense of justice and my comrades in Aldera, and forced us to hold a free speech rally to give moral support to Megawati Soekarnoputri, and at the same time function as a correction to the government.

Farther down the first page, Oka provides the rationale for his opening statements, as if anticipating the judge's reaction to refuse the eksepsi on grounds of irrelevance.

I deliberately narrated briefly the events of July 22nd 1996 above so that the judges can know the truth of what happened. This is important as in the charges put forth by the prosecutor, what happened on July 22nd was not clearly explained. The prosecutor has charged me with conducting torture against a police officer without referring to the events that formed the background of the incident. By not referring to the context of the incident, the prosecutor wishes to place me as a criminal defendant. Of course I state my objection to the charges. There are two things I want to foreground here. First, I am not a criminal who likes to torture without reason. What I did was an act of self-defense that emerged spontaneously. Second, I see the prosecutor's attempt to remove the physical struggle between me and the police officers from its context of the [July 27] incident as an effort to simplify the problem. Because of that, in this defense I wish to show the honorable judges that the case we are confronting together is not a purely criminal case, but rather a political case. To prove that this is a political case, I am going to re-attach the incident charged by the prosecutor to the context of the struggle for democracy.[45]

The activist's argumentation is orderly and logical, showing traces of a study club education in debate and analysis. Oka is respectful but not cowed by the majesty of the court. The state prosecutor is plainly wrong in his view. Oka saves his most powerful defense, his pemuda identity and sense of moral obligation, for the eksepsi's long conclusion. These are the sections he did not get to read to the court.

Honored judges,

In truth, it is in that context that I am in front of this court. As a young man who from his childhood was instilled with the values of Pancasila, it is natural that my conscience was moved at the sight of all this. I am really concerned that so many officials who speak about sacred values, do the exact opposite in their daily actions. *Is it wrong of me and my fellow youth* if we hold the sacred values of Pancasila sincerely and use them to criticize the existing institutions and political practices that deviate from those values? *Is it wrong of me and my fellow youth if we protest* the deviations that happened in the cases of Kedung Ombo, Marsinah, Tempo, Tanjung Priok, Dili, Golden Key, and lastly—what brought me to this court—that is the PDI case?

Without a doubt I will say that what I and Aldera are fighting for is truth. Easily I would say "Stating the truth is not a crime!" What I am doing is a realization of the sacred values of Pancasila.

As a closing I will say with certainty that I am not the first or last person who will be faced with the risk of imprisonment in wanting to return the running of the state to the ideals of nationalism. And, I also believe that *there will always be citizens who are willing to sacrifice their lives for the aspirations of the nation.* Freedom!!!

Rutan Kebon Waru, 30 September 1996[46]

Oka was a former member of Pijar, the same organization that had housed Beathor the Trickster King.[47] Recall how Beathor's poem composed a litany of the New Order's crimes, a rhetorical act that Oka has repeated in his eksepsi in order to link his arrest to a chain of national events that he could not ignore. His eksepsi describes the journey of politicization that a New Order youth could and did experience under military dictatorship. He was certainly not the first or the last person the New Order imprisoned for political reasons. Yet the irregularities of his arrest and the processing of the charges were too great to ignore. The bruises on the security officer did not match Oka's story, nor the claim of "assault and torture" leveled by the state. He was sentenced to only nine months in prison, with time remanded for the months he had already spent in detention while awaiting his trial. By the time Reformasi happened, he was with the crowds on the street.

ARCHIVAL CURIOS

The 1997 subversion trials were complicated affairs, especially when the state was dealing with intransigent activists who were becoming media celebrities in their own right. At Wilson's trial twenty-two witnesses were called. In Dita Indah Sari's trial and Budiman Sudjatmiko's trials, the witness lists were just as long and often consisted of fellow activists whose testimonies were used to place actors in certain times and places, to "frame" them as it were, and to provide indisputable proof of what the state's expert witness, a political science professor from East Nusa Tenggara, called their "un-Indonesian" thoughts and actions. (Even so, the expert witness refused to definitively state that the students were communists. Instead he made the careful delineation that the jargon they used was leftist, but that there was no evidence to suggest that the authors of such language were communists, thus saving the students from the serious accusation of "communist" treachery.) In any case, the testimonies proved the state's suspicion of and lack of evidence of the group's close ties. Witnesses spoke in their testimonies as if they did not know each other or, if they did, did not know each other well. All downplayed their organizational roles. Dita said derisively of her boyfriend Wignyo that he could never had made political speeches (*orasi*) at demonstrations because he was simply terrible at public speaking. In her witness statement for Wilson's trial, she spoke as if all directives came from a central party directive that remained vague and unnamed. They were simply "following orders" (instruksi). The same people would write passionate letters to each other in prison, letters that revealed how enmeshed they were in each other's lives—including Wilson's parents, Budiman's parents, Dita's parents, and siblings and friends who became their support network and even honorary PRD members outside the prison.

Lest we think that trials killed their youth spirit, the archive contains some curiosities that tell us otherwise. Like the odd sock or the lone button that appear to serve no function, paper curios are bits of extraneous detail that the archon preserves on principle. From the same PRD subversion trials of 1997, there is a charming interlude in "Wilson, box 3," in the form of one sheet of paper folded into four. On the front is an official-looking protest statement about the trial by the PRD leadership. The back of the page has the time, place, and signatures of the accused on trial:

Jakarta, 21 April 1997

PARTAI RAKYAT DEMOKRATIK

Budiman Sujatmiko (Chair/Ketua)
Petrus Hariyanto (Secretary General/Sekretaris Jenderal)

On the back are handwritten notes the defendants or witnesses passed to each other during one of the trials. Details are lacking, but we can parse out a few. Two PRD activists who were called on to testify at their comrades' trials, and who were themselves likely charged with subversion, passed these notes back and forth on the back of the official and courageous PRD solidarity statement. One of the activists is possibly Wignyo (or "No" as written in the first line); the other remains nameless. I have thus rendered them A and B here. They are listening to fellow activist Ndaru (Ken Budha Ndarukusuma) testify. Most likely Ndaru is reading his noble eksepsi, whose length is making their eyes glaze over. Their joking and insulting notes convey the undercurrent of youthful nonchalance and puerile lightheartedness even during the gravity of the subversion trial. It is not clear that the written notes follow a linear conversation after the first few lines. Here is my attempt at a translation that sutures their colloquial talk into youthful chatter:

> A: No . . . Look at that pisshead Ary laughing at us. After Ndaru finishes reading, it's your turn. So . . . you should ask the judge for a lunch break because it's already 1 PM.
>
> He just got to page 10, still 5 more pages to go.

B: It's making me sleepy.

A: Hey, I'm telling you to talk to the Judge No!

Hey, you're hungry aren't you? [sexually suggestive "hungry"] No wonder you're being chatted up by the judge.

B: (smug) I've known all along.

A: Go to hell you!

Judge has got it coming.

Emile Schwidder, the former archivist of the Asia collections at the IISG, had this to say about the challenges of constituting an archive of the Indonesian student movement. Specifically, Emile's response emphasized the difference between a formal, state-sanctioned archive and the disorganized and personalized scatter he had to track down in Indonesia, activist by activist, copy by copy. The original no longer existed in many cases. I asked Emile how important notions of authenticity and originality were to an archive like the student movement archives and whether the scattershot quality of the materials impacted his view of them. What he wrote in his email reply proved to be an intellectual and activist response:

> With the widely [*sic*] introduction of the photocopiers people began to make and to use more and more photocopies. It seems simple, but I think this is true. Sometimes in an organization staff made copies of the most important documents and brought the copies to their homes. Sometimes the originals did not exist anymore. When I am asking where the original archives of an organization were, people told me that there were only photocopies with the various staff members. So you could collect the copies from the staff members and then have an "archive."

> In general it is not so easy to acquire the material I am looking for.

> Why?: the feeling of losing the material; political distrust; indifference to "unimportant" paper; nobody takes the responsibility of the materials; papers are already burnt or thrown away. It is very important to keep this kind of material (written or oral documents) for the recent social history of Indonesia. *If you do not have the sources, you cannot write the social history of Indonesia.*[48]

In short, if there is no archive, make it yourself. Make it out of what we recognize as the material evidence of the socius. At the IISG in 2008 and 2009, I saw the evidence of Schwidder's labors of domiciliation. The Indonesian student movement archive had been carefully ordered into large files, with sheets of archival paper separating and protecting the bundles. But of course, on inspection, one could see the haphazard organization of the material that preserved the original chaos of the personal archives. The IISG had not yet been able to break up the archive and chronologically arrange the material. Rather, the archivists had seemingly given in to and preserved the activists' own illegible system of memory, which was likely the result of organizations breaking up and activists taking what they could before dissolution, the result also of multiple moves from one shabby room to another, deposits with unreliable friends and kin, and the remnants that had survived the periodic culling of possessions. From these and other papers, a protohistory of the proto student movement takes its tentative shape, coalescing in a crisscrossing of patterns, coincidences, and enlivened memories. The archon is holding onto as many papers as he can grab. There are inevitably too many to save. Pemuda fever keeps making more.

Pemuda Sever: leftist, youth spirit, radical + disruptive actions
Eksepi: court documents
Medoi = pleas, white papers that expose the truth
Bambang Beektho, Surgedi:: Student example of New Order's punishment
Bandung Six: 3yrs imprisonment
Burn after reading / Melt after dark / Vigilance
State archives tell different stories / Amnesia
"There is only one word: resist"
Study Clubs as education
Pro-Indonesian developmentalists vs populist left ideas students
A written document: Culture of documentation

HISTORY'S REFUSE AND THE TRASH OF DEMOCRACY

The demo site resembled a fairground. The ground was littered with trash and the sky overcast. Even though the demonstration was over, the policemen who had been deployed to secure the demonstration site were still standing in a relaxed row in front of the gates of parliament. A man in a bright orange cap and jumpsuit swept the entrance to the Indonesian parliamentary compound with slow, even strokes, wielding a long-handled broom (see fig. 2.1). Among the debris were piles of paper, remnants of the pamphlets and flyers (selebaran) that activist groups had been handing out a few hours ago to their fellow demonstrators. The cheap paper had pulped with rain. Lying about in abundance were empty plastic cups that had once contained a single serving of water, commonly known by their brand name, *aqua gelas* (a glass of water). Water provisions were always calculated into the cost of a demonstration.[1] On hot days aqua gelas passed from hand to hand when demonstrators were doing their sit-ins. These plastic cups were good findings for the scavengers who had waited for the demonstration's end to begin their harvest. Paper wrappings and empty cardboard and styrofoam lunch boxes were also strewn about, evidence of the appetites and menus of today's demonstration. Added to these were the occasional leavings of cigarette butts and boxed teas generated by the journalists, photographers, drink vendors, even *intel* (undercover officers) who trailed the demonstrators.[2] The common refrain of the establishment that such disorder was evidence of the political immaturity of those challenging the state

FIGURE 2.1 After the demo, a uniformed groundskeeper at work in front of the parliament compound, Jakarta. PHOTO BY AUTHOR.

echoed in my mind, as I stacked the plastic cups into neat towers before tossing them into the woven raffia sacks of the scavengers, who were hard at work.[3]

In Indonesia people burn their trash daily.[4] The scraps of today's demonstration join the informal piles of other rubbish almost straightaway. Wilson, the activist who remained in this fading demo space with me, was a historian by training; his archivist's scruples prevented him from leaving historical matter to decompose in the trash heap.[5] Picking up the activist flyers and pamphlets one by one, he smoothed them out from their crumpled wads, dried them, and placed them in his backpack. Wilson was a father, a husband, and an NGO worker in his midthirties, but he still insisted on wearing his customary political T-shirts and student backpack, a bag that came in useful now. This was how activist archives were compiled, and Wilson had a particularly good one that he had donated to the IISG (see chapter 1). His tall, bent figure resembled Walter Benjamin's *chiffonnier*, picking up the "refuse of history" (Wolfarth 1986). I learned from his behavior that these ragpicking tactics were necessary to save the underreported and uneventful demonstrations, or *demos* as they are more commonly known in Indonesia, from becoming part of the city's disposable debris, quickly put out of sight and mind. I thought that no one had read the flyers that the activists had written, full of prorakyat and prodemocracy polemics that they repeated in their speeches. The trash of democracy (as I came to think of those fragments of paper, cloth, plastic, photographs, and media clips) was not a "durable good" (Thompson 1979) but the ephemeral raw material of Indonesia's new public and political culture. It only made sense and retained value in its immediate zone of production and consumption, that is, in the newly formed public space tethered to the demonstration, a zone that activists depended on to justify their presence and their political work.

The demo has become an important institution in Indonesian political culture. This is a sharp change from the days of the New Order's ban on public assembly and collective organizing. The scene I began with conveys the festive character and routine end of the demonstration and draws attention to an obvious fact that, like most things taken for granted, appears almost as an afterthought; that one of the most important political achievements in post-Reformasi Indonesia has been the normalization of the demonstration's continued public presence. In this chapter, I focus on the production, assemblage, and sensory experience of the demonstration to show how demos are integral to public and political life in Jakarta. Where there is a demo, there are the People; enacting the former recursively enacts the latter. I show how contestations over political space and rights take place within the space of the demo, and how these claims articulate radical and moral discourses about the rakyat's power, legitimacy, and truth. Yet demos are also temporally and spatially contingent ritual events that need the skilled (and even instinctive) hands and bodies of experienced activists to come alive. They are fraught with the possibility of failure as well as success. As I observed the weekly and sometimes daily schedule of routinized demonstrations held by activists, students, and other groups, I learned to recognize the contours of a vulnerable and irregular public sphere founded on the street. This chapter contains ethnographic scenes from past demos (remembrances of a mythologized Reformasi era) and more recent demos to show how Indonesians create public space in an inhospitable city that marginalizes the rakyat; it shows how demos evoke historical breaks and continuities; it pays attention to the fine details of how demos become naturalized in an urban context such as Jakarta. When put together, this chapter provides a blueprint for understanding what Indonesian demonstrations are all about.

POLITICS AND THE CITY

Ever since the student movement (*gerakan mahasiswa*) took to the streets in 1998 and forced President Suharto to resign, the demonstration has become symbolic of Indonesia's transformation into a democracy. Knotted into the skein of representations of democracy are the various components of Reformasi student politics: mass demonstrations, violence, the People, radicalized youth, and the street as the site for protest—in short, the "romance of resistance" (Abu-Lughod 1990). What this formulation reveals is a dependency— in many ways student politics cannot exist without the aforementioned public space that hosts the demonstration. Public space has become coeval with political space. As John Berger explains, "a mass demonstration distinguishes itself from other mass crowds because it congregates in public *to create its function*. . . . Demonstrations are essentially urban in character. . . . It can be interpreted as the symbolic capturing of a city or capital" (Berger 2001: 247– 248). This symbiotic and dialectical pact between the public and the political, instantiated through a performative capture of the city, is repeated in the narratives and actions of my interlocutors, but rather than naturalizing the conflation between the public and the political, I mark the limits of a rhetorical claim to publicity. This chapter challenges the conclusion that mass mobilizations stimulate and reproduce the politics of resistance and democracy in straightforward ways. To that end, I seek a different illumination of politics in the city and how it came to be. I pay special attention to the temporality of the demonstration, both in its narrative center in the precedent-setting demonstrations of Reformasi and in its fragile sensory claim on the habituated political landscape of today. Lingering on the asphalt of the street and made momentarily legible through activist discourse about the People's place in the city, the presence of the political in the public arena forces us to rethink the formulation of public space as bourgeois achievement and stable "outside"; rather, the staging of popular politics in the city is a contingent stage that the demonstration attempts to institutionalize with various degrees of success. In order to understand the impact of activism on post-Suharto politics, we need to recognize that rather than an emerging "culture of democracy," Indonesian politics has created an increasingly developed culture of demonstration, or demo culture for short.[6] The former asserts a contextual shift toward discourses of rights within citizenship claims; the latter puts the praxis of the demonstration, what Michel de Certeau (1988) calls "strategy and tactic," front and center. The poetics of urban movement, the waxing and waning of the demonstration itself, becomes a diagnostic for the political conditions that produce public space in Indonesia.[7]

In the post-Suharto years, especially after the ascent of President Megawati Soekarnoputri and President Susilo Bambang Yudhoyono,[8] the Indonesian media and Indonesian state have characterized the disruptive tactics of the student movement as momentary and ill-considered flares of resistance, as if its purposeful occupation of the street, its composition, and its conflicts were accidental expressions by "angry young men" and spoiled students (*mahasiswa manja*). My fieldwork with activists of various political stripes refutes such cursory dismissals of demo culture. A later section of this chapter describes the complexity of activist expertise in organizing demonstrations, termed "action management" (*manajemen aksi*). Manajemen aksi is an integral part of demo culture which activists deploy to mobilize a shrinking political movement and to maintain an increasingly threatened moral and media foothold. Their expertise codifies the practices of song, performance, and visual and aural spectacle into a formula that ensures a successful demo, even if the ritual spectacle of success (*sukses*) encompasses the futility of "nothing happens" (Pemberton 1994).[9] Other activist methods that rejuvenate and transform urban spaces into politicized sites form part of the repertoire of haptic technologies that emplace public space within the zone of the demonstration. Walking, marching, assembling, remembering conflict and victory, running away from police, and being outside in the heat are all spatial practices that, following de Certeau's formulation of space as "a practiced place," orient and world the world of the activist (Lee 2011). These spatial practices gain conceptual clarity and political salience against the background of postcolonial and authoritarian notions of the city and political behavior in Indonesia, for these legacies trouble the idea of the street as politicized battleground and as always present and waiting public space.

DISPLACEMENT

For a brief period at the beginning of the twentieth century, a time historian Takashi Shiraishi calls "an age in motion," Indonesians experimented with mass politics and mass organizations, socialism, nationalism, and religious modernism. But the golden age ended with a failed Communist uprising in 1926 that resulted in the exile of an entire generation of Indonesian intellectuals, the quashing of indigenous mass politics, and a return to peace and order as the late colonial Indies became a surveillance state (Bloembergen 2007, 2011; Kusno 2010: 181). From the 1930s until independence in 1945, the urban *kampung* (native settlement), home of Indonesians and breeding ground of unrest, became a social engineering project for colonial architects to establish *zaman normal* (normal times) through heightened visibility, rationality, and consequently security. The cleanliness and order of zaman normal has had profound influence on the architectural ideology of the New Order state, which Abidin Kusno describes as similarly "born from the crushing of radical movements and the implementation of surveillance by an apparatus of suppression" (2010: 200). Accounts of military and state intrusions by the New Order regime in civic and associational life, from the rigging of elections in the smallest neighborhood unit to the patrolling of the university and the factory, reinforce the notion of a society of control. By disallowing freedom of assembly and instituting peer surveillance in the kampung, the streets were kept clear. In the 1980s, an overt attempt to instill fear in the urban population took place. Suharto executed the brutal campaign Petrus (short for Penembakan Misterius, Mysterious Shootings), in which the military assassinated petty criminals and tattooed men and left their bodies on the streets for civilians to find. From afar, the New Order practices of depoliticization and militarized surveillance appeared to have neutralized and terrorized the population sufficiently to prevent disorder; so it was with pride that activists, the poet Wiji Thukul included, envisioned the rebellious coupling of the different social strata of the urban kampung and the new town, a coming together that disrupted the normalcy of New Order times and profoundly altered the relationships between the state and citizen and between citizens themselves. In his poem "Songs of the Grassroots" (Nyanyian akar rumput), Wiji Thukul tells us how displacement and symbolic violence transform the urban kampung into a politicized zone of radicalism: "the roads are widened, we are displaced, building the kampung, evicted, we move and move, sticking onto walls, uprooted, thrown out; we grasses need land, listen! Join us, let's become the president's nightmare!" (2000b: 6). Displacement itself becomes a form of motion that fuels the grassroots. Even without the base material resources of land, space, or territory, the rakyat are the stuff of elite nightmares.

REJECTED BY THE CITY

The physical landscape of the city, and its concentration of political, cultural, and capitalist power, has provided fertile ground for dissident critiques against New Order hegemony for decades. One of the most popular protest poems to emerge from New Order critique is Wiji Thukul's "Sajak Kota" (Urban poem). In songs and in short stories, epic and short poems, the city figures as a prominent character that enacts brutality on the People. Popular writer and urbanist Seno Gumira Ajidarma describes the consequences that befall Jakarta's inhabitants, a species he calls *homo jakartensis*, if they do not achieve the status symbols and modes of distinction that New Order professionals and the urban middle classes enjoy, such as expensive cars and "lasagna that tasted like soap": "People who are not successful will not be visited, hands will not be shaken, they will not be greeted, looked at, let alone remembered. . . . Reformasi changed the government, but has it changed mental attitudes?"[10] In a similar vein, Wiji Thukul's poems serve as a vivid reminder of how the capital city (*ibukota*) physically and spatially expresses inequalities. The disappeared radical leftist poet wrote lyrical poetry about the dispossessed rakyat and the illegitimacy of the New Order dictatorship that became an inspirational soundtrack to student demonstrations. Thukul was the son of a trishaw driver, a street performer himself, and already a well-known poet-activist in underground circles by the early 1990s.[11] In his poems, the city is never far from the imagination of resistance. "Sajak Kota" paints the city's lights as captivating but inhumane:

> Lights
> Lights
> Cleave the roads
> The roads are smoothed
> With asphalt from the people's pocket
> Motorbikes smoothly gliding
> Brands on billboards
> Brands on billboards
> On top of buildings

Lit
Side-by-side with
Bakeries
Shoe stores
Side-by-side with
Beauty salons
Who is planning
The people's future?[12]

Thukul's poems identify the city's development as a driving force for the alienation and suffering of the rakyat, who become the matter out of place in the modernist dreams of the postcolonial city. The poem continues: "What kind of city are we building; Whose dream is being planted in the minds of the people; Who is planning this" (1994). His fierce questions place the dispossessed rakyat back into the New Order state's dubious blueprint for Indonesian urban modernity, as dupe, potential collaborator, and increasingly a critical voice, while making it clear that power is personified and traceable. It is a "he" who paves over the city with lights and asphalt paid for by the rakyat. In response, "We, the People," reject "your" dreams. We can see how Thukul's poetry renews the script for political dissent, as the *massa* (masses) in the demonstration chant from memory the climactic final line of his poem "Lawan" (Fight back): "For there is only one word: Resist!"

OCCUPYING PUBLIC SPACE

In the post-Reformasi era, the chaos of the Indonesian public sphere, which sees Islamic, militant, interfaith, leftist, conservative, radical, pacifist, and nationalist groups sharing the same demo spaces, can seem excitingly plural or perplexingly incoherent. In the absence of official monuments and venues for "urban popular radicalism," demonstrations do not necessarily happen in the most central, convenient, or rational locations.[13] The culture of demonstration presumes a relationship to the city built on an intimate knowledge of how streets function and what effects of traffic, media, sound, and visibility they facilitate. The colonial grounds of Koningsplein in Batavia, later the site of the national monument Monas, is a prime example of a centrally located "public space" that the state kept clean of unwanted elements. The central square was never intended for occupation. Under the auspices of Jakarta's governor Sutiyoso (1997–2007), Monas underwent a makeover into a manicured public garden with tall fences, gates, and a continuous security presence, thereby eliminating access by street vendors and the urban poor to the park. Sutiyoso was also responsible for the multimillion-dollar renovation of the Hotel Indonesia Roundabout Fountain, replacing the flat 1960s architecture with a slippery, angled granite base that was hard to stand on.

The gating of the national monument and the renovation of the fountain, both favored demo locations in 1998, also proved to be the state's attempt to rid the city of demonstrators (Sastramidjaja 2006: 278–279). When demonstrators wish to utilize the desirable location of Monas to begin their march, they are forced to gather outside the monument's parking lot, right next to the long line of parked tour buses and out of the sightline of urban traffic. The chartered buses that the organizers use to ferry demonstrators to the demonstration park are there too. From there they can march quickly to the tony address of the Presidential Palace, just a few minutes away on tree-lined Jalan Medan Merdeka Barat. The Hotel Indonesia fountain in the center of Jalan Sudirman also remains occupied; activists simply climb into the fountain and get their feet wet. The picturesque backdrop of the fountain's lights and the lit-up skyscrapers surrounding the fountain make it especially effective as a rallying space for nighttime demonstrations. Before the Sampoerna corporation rebranded the twin Sudirman towers located on a spacious corner lot on the prestigious Jalan Sudirman (Sudirman Street) as "Sampoerna Strategic Square" (boasting a beautiful but private garden that can be rented for events), activists used the conveniently located square, which was near bus stops and an overhead pass, to assemble for demonstrations. A well-executed demonstration that promises political efficacy thus requires a finely honed sense of where and when such political spaces can exist. In turn, each dramatic step of the Long March revisits Reformasi heroes and movement memories that the demonstrator seeks to commemorate.[14] Such perspectival knowledge of the city and its streets scores the motions that constitute the demonstration, its creative practices, and its sensory limits. As the "fourth wave" of social movements and People Power in Asia and in the Middle East increase our expectations of achieving democracy and social justice through cultures of demonstration, the demonstration and the street require examination as formal objects and sites of analysis.

The universal model for the well-planned modern city assumes the need and desire for the public gathering function of the plaza, the boulevards, and the street;[15] whereas there are many different political, commercial, and transit functions for the Indonesian street.[16] Public space in Jakarta, even those spaces that bear the designation of sacred national space, are the outcome of unstable and capitalized arrangements. The market forces of neoliberal privatization and suspect land conversion deals have contributed to the appropriation of rare greenbelts and parks in Jakarta, such that even the protected greenbelt of

Senayan, South Jakarta, with its prestigious athletes' parks and sports facilities built under the first president, Sukarno, has been repurposed as an exclusive commercial area that keeps the lower classes out. Formerly accessible mixed-use spaces, once open to food vendors, office workers, and urban poor pass-ersby, such as the privately owned yet publicly used open spaces in the Central Business District, have also been enclosed and policed through a variety of beautification schemes and fencing.

Urban space in Jakarta is subject to land speculation, privatization, and takeover. Roads, sidewalks, and green spaces can disappear through encroachment. Still, the student movement achieved spatial forms that changed the way residents saw the city. One such political effect that the student movement deserves credit for is the resuscitation of the Long March, a mobilization technique that had not been seen in Indonesia for decades. A major component of student movements in the 1960s and 1970s, it disappeared following state reprisals over the last big demos against the Campus Normalization Act in 1980 (Sastramidjaja 2006). As Reformasi approached, student groups emboldened themselves and took to the streets. By early March 1998 in the city of Yogyakarta, thousands of students from various campuses were breaking the laws forbidding public assembly and pushing through the barriers of the campus gates that held them inside. To put this scale into perspective, the PRD's anti-Suharto and antimilitary demonstrations in the early 1990s only drew about thirty students. By considering public space to be one of the important effects of the movement, this study makes evident the ideological interventions against New Order social and class hierarchies that social movements made in placing new populist subjects on the street. The first leading figure of the street was the university student as present-day pemuda; the second was the massa (masses) in a new revolutionary guise. Once denigrated as the manipulated, bought, and mindless masses, the urban poor emerged from the urban kampung to become the rakyat (People) of the demonstration.

THE RAKYAT AND STUDENTS DESCEND ON THE STREET

A former activist told me of his experiences of the Long March that began on November 13, 1998, that later became known as the First Semanggi Tragedy:

> There was a moment. Semanggi I.
>
> The first starting point was at Jayabaya [University]. There was the massa, which was apart from the student body, and even if the students denied there were differences, there were.

The beginning of Semanggi I. With a long march to Matraman, the ABA-ABI campus to Salemba, from there to Diponegoro, [we] marched to Jalan Manggarai, and Kampung Melayu areas. In front were students with banners, but behind them were already thousands of massa. . . .

And then we were blockaded by the army.

We had an emergency meeting, should we go forth, or retreat? We decided to go forward so as to not disappoint the massa who were so enthusiastic. We passed through Sudirman and Thamrin, and for the whole length of the road there were no cars. The government had already spread the news that the situation called for high alert. The armed forces were also on alert. All activities were quiet in Jakarta.

Our high school brothers also readied themselves. They said, Older Brother [Kak], we're ready.

Oh, I'm moved just remembering this. [He wipes his eyes.]

We got through the police lines, all four layers of men. By hitting, by all kinds of means. Right at the Semanggi bridge, in front of Atmajaya University, we were stopped by at least eight to ten rows of army troops. We made speeches until 9 PM. Still energetic, and still supported by the masses. Businessmen, professors sent medicines, food, drinks, so that we could stand our ground for at least quite a while there. After two hours, we moved forward to parliament. And the troops were ready, with tanks, water cannons, weapons, lethal bullets [peluru tajam]. At 10 PM we clashed with them in front of Atmajaya. . . .

We ran to Atmajaya, some ran to the Jakarta hospital, and to the naval hospital. The students were busy defending themselves, the massa were resisting also. They threw stones, made Molotovs, we filled empty bottles and cans with fuel, and launched them. That was three in the morning. We rested. Worn out. . . .

Sudirman was overtaken by the army again. That was early Friday morning. Friday morning, we all hid in the small alleys [gang kecil]. Friday night, there was movement again at Atmajaya. We made speeches. Because of the print media, the press, the coverage [of the violence] roused the anger of the public, and we gathered momentum again.

Saturday morning [November 14], the massa gathered, people from the NGOs, bringing flowers, moving like a tidal wave, they took over the streets again. We moved toward parliament.

There was another obstacle. We negotiated with the commander of the marines. They said, "We are not your enemies, but please let's not have a repeat of what happened last night." We negotiated to pass their barricade, and at last they agreed, with one condition: the students had to be nonviolent, [we agreed] so they would open the streets.

We walked until Taman Ria Senayan, and there we met the land forces, and the police. We negotiated between those two bodies. But there was a conflict between the navy who supported the massa, and the army loyal to the government. They ended up fighting hard, until the army lost to the navy.

But it was Saturday, and parliament was not in session, so we dissolved ourselves [membubarkan diri]. We agreed to demonstrate again next Monday. On Monday, all the campuses were open, but no students went to class. Instead they joined us on the streets. The death of our friends became a hot political issue.

A former student activist from a private university in North Jakarta whom I will call Sony, told me in great detail the chronology of the mass demonstrations and the ensuing acts of state violence on November 13–14, 1998, when five demonstrators were shot and killed, which quickly became known as the First Semanggi Tragedy (Tragedi Semanggi I). Sony's narrative functions as a map of urban politics as well as a historical timeline, fusing together the sequence of events and the spatial story of the massa's march through the city. The advance and retreat of the Long March reveals a coded map with a social key; Manggarai and Kampung Melayu are densely populated working-class and urban poor kampung; Matraman and Salemba are main streets with a mixed working-class and heavy university and high school presence; while Diponegoro, Sudirman, and Thamrin streets are elite areas that the armed forces sought to defend from activist occupation. Atma Jaya Catholic University, located at one end of the prestigious Semanggi "clover leaf" bridge off Sudirman Street, became the contested site of student and army clashes. Sony's chronology depicts rakyat solidarity as a visual and spatial fact. In the foregoing excerpt, his description muddles the social segregation of the urban middle and lower classes—already the masses are everywhere, a presence in the thousands; meanwhile the middle-class students seek refuge in the alleyways of the lower-class kampung at particularly dangerous times. The image of the massa is softened as they stand with middle-class NGO workers and students, bearing flowers of grief and peace, buoying the students onward so that the demonstration gathers force "like a tidal wave" to swallow the streets. Sony's story conveys the surge of victory and strength that the students felt in looking back and seeing the massa behind them, propelling them forward with revolutionary force. There is a spectacular quality to what Liisa Malkki has described as images of "the sea of humanity," where the image of human beings as mass presence transmits a universal message and overrides the possibility of representing individual interests and histories (1996). The "tidal wave" of change presents an image of the moment activists remember as the grassroots rising from the kampung to change the nation's future. Instead of invoking the middle-class fear of the crowd, the massa are valorized as the revolutionary "body" connected to the students' heroic "head."

Displaced, evicted, and always threatening to return, the slums of Jakarta persist and grow, from the colonial to the postcolonial era.[17] Recent attempts by the Jokowi-Ahok city government (2012–2015) to resettle slum populations and cleanse public areas of graffiti, unruly sidewalk vendors, and other tenets of Jakarta's urban informality have met with applause from the middle classes and resistance from below.[18] During Reformasi, the urban kampung was seen as the place where student activists could enter ethnically and socially diverse communities and cultivate the rakyat's dissatisfaction into organized political will and action. Activists lived in these slums for extended periods of time to teach courses on Marxist concepts and vocabulary (*kursus politik* or *kurpol*), organize communities, encourage alternative publications and small enterprises, and gain lived experience of urban poverty, often through the kindness (and expense) of kampung-dwellers. As previous research on student-led movements in Thailand (Haberkorn 2011), South Korea (Lee 2007), and the Philippines (Abinales 2012) has shown, the cross-class alliances built through "live in" was remembered as a profoundly transformative time for both student activists and the communities involved. Indonesian student activists who gained proximity to the rakyat in the kampung worked to embed themselves in the crucial days and nights before mass demonstrations were scheduled to happen, ensuring that the massa could be mobilized in synchrony.

In the early Reformasi years (1998–2000), the demo's success depended upon harnessing the energy of the disaffected young men and urban poor who felt stuck in the kampung. Abirahman, a student activist from the UNAS campus, did so by reaching out to the pemuda in his own neighborhood of Palmerah, an urban slum area famous for its criminal activities. Abirahman's network of fellow activists included students who gained nicknames such as "General," in recognition of their ability to mobilize and lead lower-class youth outside the university walls. "Turun ke jalan!" (Descend to the streets!) was the rallying cry activists used to mobilize their troops onto the streets. "Turun ke jalan" was especially effective at conveying students' descent (*menurun*) from the ivory tower (*menara gading*) of the university, which had become a privileged and depoliticized zone for furthering New Order technocratic aims (Weiss and Aspinall 2012). The phrase reminds us of the central role that public space played in Reformasi-era activist discourse. The street was where the rakyat appeared in Durkheimian fashion as a collective apparition and where individuals recognized themselves and others as political subjects rather than as a crowd of manipulated massa.[19] Student movement discourse described space as medan perjuangan, the field of struggle where the rakyat and the massa gathered, or as *jalan*, the streets student activists laid claim to beginning with the mass demonstrations of 1998. In a student publication, the PRD referred to the enormous crowds that had gathered during Semanggi I (November 13–15, 1998), the same demonstration Sony remembered so vividly, as a model for organizing the next wave of ambitious mass demonstrations. The student party's leaders issued an injunction that was simultaneously demo management and traffic management: "Occupy the lanes of strategic roads — main streets with many alleys [gang] that lead to well-populated neighbor-hoods — in the parade / action to enable the People to get involved / participate in student-led action. The experience of our struggle in the month of No-vember has confirmed this!"[20] The enthusiasm with which student movement leaders commanded their fellow activists to lead the rakyat out of the urban kampung reveals how publics materialize by assemblage. With the right con-ditions of preparation and political will, activists could ignite key collection points in densely populated kampung and draw out the rakyat hidden in the *gang* (alleys). In the enthusiastic language of student activists, bridging the ideological distance between the gang and the main streets was thus a matter of navigating the streets like a Pied Piper and controlling the crowd, in con-trast with their often-stated Marxist goals of securing the grassroots by first raising class consciousness and political awareness (*kesadaran*).[21] Read differ-ently, student activists' confidence that people would join them on the streets reflected the "moral" and unsettled mood of Reformasi but did not necessarily prove a widespread cross-class political consciousness beyond already politi-cized and networked communities. In fact, the urban violence linked to Refor-masi heightened middle-class fears of the street, such that everyday practices of work and leisure ensured that most middle-class Indonesians never came into contact with the street.[22]

In the post-Reformasi era, rumors about crime and lurking violence circu-lated through talk, text message, and news reports to cement the association between street and crime, invoking the otherness of those who belong on the streets: namely, the migrant, the mad, and the criminal. Well-to-do residents of Jakarta attempted to assert control over uncertain conditions, especially in the wake of the May 13–14 riots, by investing in technologies of class and ethnic separation, surveillance, and security (Nas and Pratiwo 2003: 275–294). They retained in their daily practice a mental map of possible escape routes. Urban residents connected with each other to obtain information via remote technologies (cell phones, radio, and for a time, high-frequency walkie-talkies capable of receiving police frequencies) as a means to overcome their sense of imminent danger. Rumors of mass riots and theft fed these paranoid visions of the city, creating new urban myths and material changes to the built environment, with gates and "pointy fences" demarcating more sharply the line between street and nonstreet spaces (Brown 2010; Simone 2014).[23]

THE EFFICACY OF DEMONSTRATIONS

Viewed from different class and political perspectives, the demo is both a political necessity and an urban nuisance. From the perspective of the movement, the mass demonstrations of 1998 "worked" to radically transform Indonesian politics and therefore set a historical precedent for the politics of the future. Yet most observers and longtime activists would agree that a decade later, demos fail to shock the political system. The answer to the quandary lies somewhere between the unfulfilled promises of Reformasi as a revolution in the making and the instrumentality of a broad-based political culture (of demonstration) rooted in performative acts of resistance. The work of David Harvey (2012), Don Mitchell (2003), and James Holston (2009) argues that insurgent citizenship tactics that claim a "right to the city" constitute an important element of political dissidence by seeking to transform political and social relations through specifically urban modes of occupation and appropriation. Interventions made by the growing body of literature on insurgent citizenship rely on a politics of illumination, where contradictions come to light and move us closer to moral or social action in a politicized domain. Yet such an approach that valorizes "contentious politics" in everyday life (Tilly and Tarrow 2006) does not get us any closer to understanding the interplay between domination and resistance inherent in the material and discursive conditions of sovereignty, publics, and space (Sassen 2008); in other words, in what ways the demo "works" to secure public and political space for dissident practices, and what enables or sustains power in the face of unruly practices.

In postcolonial democracies, as Dipesh Chakrabarty has noted, there is a tension between the moral legitimacy of "the People" and the state's disavowal of the disorderly and unseemly (read: unmodern) politics of the masses (2007). On the one hand strikes and demonstrations were once deemed necessary to draw attention to the immorality of existing colonial, apartheid, or authoritarian regimes; on the other hand the same actions of civil disobedience were tolerated for only a brief transitional period before formal democratic institutions took their place. As Chakrabarty argues, postcolonial democracies are hybrid systems that require and foster unruly mass politics as a way of maintaining the myth of direct democracy and as a politics of appeasement. In the following passage, Chakrabarty's analysis reveals how an uprising operates and disappears in lockstep with the disciplinary mechanisms of the Indian state.

> This power of the multitude, however, is not a programmatic one. It spends itself in its execution. It is not oriented to a future; nor is it the vehicle of any dialectic of history. Yet, at the moment when a crowd unleashes its power in a situation where the memory of repression has become remote, it creates a vision, however fleeting, of direct and popular control of governance. Not only that: by forcing otherwise anonymous officials to come and speak to them, the crowd forces the state to represent itself in a concrete manner. The logic of abstract representation of the people is thus defeated. The democratization and dissemination of this kind of popular power—something that stands in for "people's power"—suggests that one perhaps needs to see this very form of power and its associated pleasures as constituting a "good" that Indian democracy makes available to the people. (53)

Here, the multitude is a political presence only by the fact of its contemporaneity, as an authorized presence (by virtue of the state's restraint) and a permanent substitute for enacting alternative political relations between the state and the People. Yet it is precisely the predictability of the demonstration by which nothing changes that enables a wide range of oppositional groups in Indonesian civil society to safely express their views. Sumit Mandal observed a similar dynamic of democratized civil society in tandem with good governance in a remarkably "friendly" demonstration that progressive Muslim groups held on October 8, 2002, outside the US embassy in Jakarta on the eve of the Iraq War. Mandal reported:

> The demonstration *enjoyed* a police escort throughout the journey of some forty minutes through some of Jakarta's busiest districts. More than 200 people came together as the marchers approached the U.S. Embassy, they were funneled through a line of police officers on one side and journalists and onlookers on the other.
>
> The U.S. Embassy was heavily guarded. Traffic was diverted to some 20 meters away from its front gates while police officers and armored vehicles

were placed in strategic locations. Throughout the initial stages of the protest, the police maintained a tight defensive line. The police nevertheless handled the demonstrators *with professionalism and even curiosity if not friendliness*, a clear product of the democratization processes at work since 1998. (Mandal 2004; emphasis added)

With some violent exceptions, where the state actively oppresses peaceful demonstrations, as in the military-dominated and restive province of Papua, the slow and controlled deradicalization of the mass demonstration in urban Indonesia can be seen in the permissive attitude of the post-Reformasi state, which has accommodated mass assemblies through expanded security and legal measures.[24] Demonstrations showcase urban techniques of insurgent citizenship that utilize and temporarily secure the public sphere on and of the street. The space of the demo materially enacts the effects of transformative collective action, yet its ephemeral qualities and its purpose as a staging ground for a futurist vision of politics also limits its potency. Indonesian street politics provides keen examples of the political efficacy of the demo during Reformasi as well as the limits of direct action in the post-Reformasi era, as increasingly civil disobedience is narratively lumped together by the media and by the state with street justice and extralegal violence. The state's disavowal of the legitimacy of civil disobedience allows the state greater flexibility to selectively suppress student politics as inappropriate and "anarchic" (*anarkis*) behavior (see chapter 4) while remaining silent on the tendentious actions of right-wing and paramilitary groups who assert a majoritarian foothold through urban spatial politics (Wilson 2006, 2011). Politicized youth who appear unmoored from institutions and class loyalties are especially suspect under new regimes that view the forces of popular rebellion as troubling remainders of the past. This was true in the postindependence period in 1945 and was true for the 1966 generation that supported the rise of the New Order, as well as for the "moral heroes" of Reformasi. The conflict between activist youth and the political establishment was already apparent in 1998, as political reforms unseated the ruling party / civil service / military configuration of power, yet not quickly enough nor to everyone's tastes. Moderate activists posed this question that expressed the extent of their political hopes: "Revolution or Reformation?" (Revolusi atau Reformasi?), while more militant activists sang the lyric "Revolution Unto Death!" (Revolusi sampai Mati!). With Reform as the historical outcome of Suharto's fall, the next decade saw activists investing in maintaining the culture of demonstration among new recruits and turning toward more flexible platforms and global issues, while the state retaliated by becoming in turn indulgent or indifferent to the voices on the street.

DEMO CULTURE: MANAGING TECHNIQUES OF THE BODY

Unjuk rasa is the Indonesian term for a protest or demonstration. It means "to make a show of one's feelings." As a rebuttal to the state and media's depiction of mass demonstrations as unruly and anachronistic political behavior on the part of students and demonstrators, I argue that the demonstration is a site of expertise, strategy, and discipline, as well as a cultivated sphere of political and sensory experience (Mauss [1935] 2006). The culture of demonstration that activists perfected and trained themselves in emplaces the demonstration into Indonesia's political landscape in a dynamic fashion that points to the technical needs of oppositional politics as well as the contingency of the demonstration site. Demo culture stitches together various activist techniques of the body into a repertoire of style and sense. These range from engaging in clashes with the state security forces, the nonviolent and passive sit-in, and speechmaking (orasi) to the historically significant and commemorative Long March, so that even when the demo appears uneventful or falls into violence and the destruction of property, activist reactions correspond to a knowledge system based on activist techniques of the body, an expertise disguised as adrenaline and intuition.

A seasoned activist prognosticates by reading the signs at the demo site, divining from the mood of the massa, the issue at hand, the opposing forces, the number of journalists, the heat in the air that "Oh, this will be a violent one, look at their formation. Oh, an ambulance car parked over there, the police are ready for *bentrok* [physical clashes with the massa]." The activist who made the remark spoke with quiet enthusiasm, for the formal elements that he had identified as the preconditions for violence could, in the hands of skilled and prepared organizers, work to their advantage. If the police were ready to clash with the activists, the demonstrators would also push back and provoke the police, through taunts, songs, and incendiary props. With a good turnout of journalists present, a sensational few seconds of bentrok could make the evening news. When the right elements combine in the encounter between power and the people, the demo is a successful synthesis of media spectacle, political speech, palpable emotion, and organized style. The acquisition of the right look and the right sentiment to participate in unjuk rasa, demonstrating feelings, cannot be reduced to aptitude or performance. It is a matter of fusing those elements Marcel Mauss describes as psychological, physiological, and sociological into learned techniques of the body that, once gained, are never lost. Foster describes how the activist body transmits political intent and agency through these acquired techniques: "Over the time that they are practiced, they acquire increasing influence over corporeal and also individual identity. Not a script that the protestor learns to execute, these are, rather, actions that both require and provide strong commitment and, once practiced, slowly change the world in which they occur" (2003: 408). Demo culture visibly reminds its participants and spectators where political spaces can exist, a stance that requires continuous labor. The work is extensive: organizing massa, forming and maintaining diverse constituencies in different neighborhoods; producing leaflets and periodicals; going to seminars; providing *logistik* (packaged food and water for hundreds of massa); maintaining media contacts; giving press conferences, documenting each and every step of the organization's process through sound and video recordings, photography, and writing; tactical field operations; physical training in boot camps; and finding new recruits. The labor of activism becomes most apparent in the field, where "action management" (manajeman aksi) produces the demonstration as an elaborate and interactive event.

Once activists hit the streets, a militaristic formation takes hold (see fig. 2.2). Visually arresting flag-bearers lead the demo, followed by "happening art"[25] performance artists and then the *mobil komando* (command car, usually an open truck), which forms the tallest peak of the demo, with its stacks of rented sound equipment and precariously balanced activists on top. The mobil komando aurally directs the demo through a loudspeaker system, while the *korlap* (*koordinator lapangan*, field coordinator), the jenlap (*jendral lapangan*, field general), the *barisan* (the troops), and other strategic "ranked" positions position themselves in the field. The militarized taxonomy of the student movement mirrors that of their enemy, the "real" army, but also reflects activists' training and volition to encounter the physical danger the state security apparatus poses on the frontlines. The careful delegation of these roles during planning meetings demonstrates activist principles of shared governance and responsibility in controlling the demo site but, more important, emphasizes the centrality of technical knowledge in fostering revolution and revolutionary consciousness.

In actual practice, the demo is riddled with moments of bored silence and heightened emotions. Both extremes are constitutive of the life cycle of the demo, which approximates a regulated routine of work, replenishment, activity, and inactivity. These internal rhythms of the demo are left out of activist discourse, which commits to a narrative of the demo as event-history, whereas actual behavior by demonstrators exposes a more fluid interaction with the street, composed of the bodily techniques of walking, sitting, eating, and spectating. Organizers worry about their massa for the duration of the demo, wondering if disinterested demonstrators have wandered off, or if other rival groups have poached their massa and led them to another demonstration, unfairly claiming credit for their numbers. Fiercely protective over group boundaries and mindful of the synecdochic relation between the way demonstrators are perceived and the reputation of the organization, activists guard their massa with the attention and worry of a protective parent, particularly when it comes to the demo's underbelly: the technical and expensive issue of logistik. Activists' anxiety over providing sufficient logistik (food, water, and transportation costs) for the demo underlines the potential cost of neglecting demonstrators by not recognizing their worth in material and symbolic terms. Relatively poor activist groups could lose politicized and technically proficient activists and massa to mainstream political parties during election season, a move that has in the past damaged the reputation of Generation 98 when they have been seen as mercenaries brokering their expertise and their massa for social mobility and monetary gain.

These fears arise from the fact that large elite-sponsored demonstrations and political party rallies generate paid work for the urban and periurban poor, bringing back the image of the floating mass from the Suharto era and the civilian militias (Pam Swakarsa) of early Reformasi.[26] Such a monetized understanding of the crowd's power erases the question of political consciousness and returns political action to the pragmatic domain Indonesians refer to as *money politics* (using the English words), raising the possibility that street politics is cloaking the continuation of fundamentally undemocratic past practices with the rhetoric of democracy. I remember distinctly an experience one evening when I was asked by a taxi driver if I was a paid demonstrator. We had just dropped off two male activists who had genially tried to engage the taxi driver in political conversation, casting him as the "ordinary man" of the streets, or as de Certeau puts it, the oracle "whose voice is almost indistinguishable from the rumble of history,"[27] but they had misjudged their ability to overcome the driver's cynicism. The driver steadfastly refused to provide the generic and topical grassroots critique against the government that student activists had fostered among their urban poor constituents and that lazy ethnography would then recycle for popular opinion. Once they left the car, the driver revealed his suspicions about political talk in his brief query "Dari partai?" (From a party?) I informed him that they were still student activists (a status they maintained despite their age and appearance, for they were both in their early thirties). The next few questions he asked me were illuminating:

FIGURE 2.2 Oversight of a labor demonstration at Bundaran Hotel Indonesia. The banner creates a boundary for the demonstration, and the demo leader (wearing red) at the outer edge of the line keeps watch over the massa. PHOTO BY AUTHOR.

"Have you ever been to a demo? How much were you paid?" I said "What?" in confusion twice before realizing his insinuation that I was paid massa. The summary conclusions the taxi driver came to about his three passengers present an unflattering portrait of the student activist's political trajectory in the post-Reformasi era, from hero to mercenary. Despite her foreign accent and middle-class appearance, it was feasible that the anthropologist had been paid to attend a demo, since individual circumstances of desire or disadvantage were not reliable indicators of corruption, but rather, corruption was proof of the field of opportunities generated by the febrile site of popular politics. Student activists who achieved expertise in manajemen aksi were contributing to the longevity of grassroots politics, institutionalizing hard-won skills patented by Generation 98, but the activist ability to control the field and the massa as a *jenlap* (short for *jeneral lapangan*, field general) through tactical and optical strategies is also eerily reminiscent of the Overseer, whom Nicholas Mirzoeff describes as a troubling figure endowed with powers of surveillance who collaborates in overseeing exploitation (2011).

At this juncture, a revisit to the limits of oversight and crowd control is necessary, for in many ways, the perfect demonstration promised by the technical knowledge of manajemen aksi remains an aspiration. An ideal close to the demo's arc is brought with the cooling evening air and the sound of the evening call to prayers—two welcome signs to begin sending demonstrators home in disciplined busloads, in step with the planned design of the demo. Yet there are times when the activist sensorium leaks at the perimeter, broken by the contingency of violence in the field, corrupted channels of communication, and placid demonstrators. The activist body's response techniques to the sensory conditions of the street causes the massa to become what organizers fear, that is, a liquid state (*cair*) of dissolution rather than a solid (*kompak*) militant formation ready to deploy and strike at will.

CHALLENGES TO THE DEMONSTRATION: ESCAPING HEAT AND SOUND

In Jakarta, the streets can be overwhelmingly hot. Except for the elite residential areas of the city, most city streets and urban kampung are brown and dusty. Saya Shiraishi describes the street as a dangerous place for middle-class subjects, where "exposure to the sun's heat on the street is a sign of impending calamity" (1997: 26). Feeling cool and shaded in the tropics implies security and protection, so that one's social status is reinforced by the rules of having someone do antar-jemput (send-off and pickup). As Shiraishi describes it, those who walk the streets of Jakarta betray their marginality or exclusion by the very fact of being outdoors and outside a network of antar-jemput. The discomfort caused by the scorching heat is entangled with the fear of urban crime. Before their first bus ride, middle-class Jakartans are warned by their families of pickpockets, purse snatchers, and other threatening lower-class figures who will emerge, tempted by the displaced subject waiting alone on the side of the road. These ideologized prescriptions against encountering heat in public places add to the practical challenges of the demonstration, corrupting the scripted route of the demo by adding an additional rhythm of rest and unrest as bodies adjust to the demands of being outside. At the time of this research, the literature in sensory ethnography was on the rise, mapping the body in social space through touch, sight, and sound. But apart from Eric Klinenberg's *Heat Wave: A Social Autopsy of Disaster in Chicago* (2002), a sensory ethnography of heat has yet to be written. Klinenberg describes a setting much like Jakarta: "Chicago felt tropical, like Fiji or Guam but with an added layer of polluted city air trapping the heat" (see "Dying Alone in the Heat Wave" 2002).

Where is the heat in ethnography, anthropologist Michael Taussig complains. Taussig's brief chapter "Heat" in *My Cocaine Museum* (2004) provides the only anthology I know of that speaks of the torturous, altering otherness of heat, a heat so powerful it fragments our sense of well-being and wholeness. Heat is too often disavowed and distanced as nonagent and noncultural force, as "nature" rather then "culture." Most often it is simply absent in the literature on social movements. Yet it affects us physically and cognitively; it produces mirages; it weakens the strong; it introduces new techniques of the body to adapt to it.

In a 1983 study of human evolutionary adaptation to heat, Hanna and Brown state that "there is a single simple rule for humid tropical clothing—the least amount possible. Given the high humidity . . . it is desirable to leave most of the skin uncovered" (1983: 271). For reasons of modesty and political identity, nakedness is impossible. Then what if the cheap demo T-shirt you wear contains a high polyester content? Heat saturates the demonstrator, reflecting off the asphalt and one's clothes and hair. In accordance with pemuda style (chapter 3), women come prepared with scarves to cover their heads and wear long sleeves under their demo T-shirts; men wear hats, bandanas, and sunglasses. The anthropologist soon discovers the lingering effects of sunstroke, thirst, and cheap fashion after a Long March. In the commemoration of the May 12 Trisakti Tragedy, the Long March begins at 9 AM and ends at 6 PM, leading you through a historical trail of several kilometers of asphalt. The Trisakti Tragedy is the original event that galvanized public support for Reformasi, and so the massa are extremely motivated. Bereaved relatives of the dead have turned up to lead the march. The march is slow, and heat stroke settles in to tint everything you see a weird kodak yellow the next day. Under the hot sun, activists scream themselves hoarse about the injustice of the state and the political aspirations of the army: "Fight tyranny! Fight militarism! Fight neoliberalism!" The crowd repeats these chants. Sound sculpts the demo space, most concentrated at the demonstration's center, and radiating out to touch neighboring houses, businesses, and disinterested bystanders. You should be able to hear the demo coming from far away. Put together, heat and sound permeate and demarcate demo experiences, layering both sensory affects into the aesthetic qualities of the demonstration. Heat and sound remain omnipresent sensory facts that modulate the demonstrator's expression of political commitment.[28]

At the outer edges of the demo, participation is weak. Heat drives people apart like a centrifugal force, for it becomes hard to sustain unity after a few hours of baking outside. The crowd thins out to sit in the shade waiting to be called, their posture lax (the antithesis of the disciplined, strong, and upright soldier). Or they trail off to buy a drink and chat under the awnings of surrounding businesses, leaning against parked vehicles. The demonstrators are now at the outer fringes of the demo's soundscape, where speeches are faintly audible, so that the massa are not close enough to the command truck to repeat the yells or to respond to the orator's cues. From this resting post, they may listen to the protest songs but do not sing. Aware of the dissipating energy, the korlap (field coordinator) attempts to rectify the situation. First he yells "Rapatkan Barisan!" (Straighten the ranks!) over and over again into a *toa* (handheld speaker) as a command. When the massa do not respond, his tone changes and increasingly becomes a patient plea. At some point the masses decide to respond to his call and regroup, for by this point they are aware that the demo cannot go on for much longer. I found myself at the perimeter of the demo in exactly this mode of sluggish waiting, where the sound of the demo was the only quality that managed to puncture the haze.

GETTING THE DEMONSTRATION BACK ON TRACK

January 20, 2004. I was wilting in the heat of high noon. The demo site was located in the hot and inhospitable streets of old Kota, a commercial district that had once housed the social and commercial center of Batavia. This was likely the sixtieth demo I had attended, but I had never before experienced such a strong physical reaction to the heat. It enervated me so much that I completely lost interest in the otherwise gripping court case and lively demonstration taking place outside the courthouse. Instead I watched the proceedings from a distance, leaning against a row of parked motorcycles. The damage to my reputation as a *perempuan tangguh*—a tough chick who liked to walk long distances—was done. Simon laughed at me but bought me a Samaritan's icy *teh botol* from the ubiquitous drink stand nearby, which I sucked down in one long gulp.[29]

It was the afternoon of the *Tempo* magazine trial verdict, and two demonstrations were happening outside the district courthouse on Jalan Gajah Mada. One featured the real estate mogul Tomy Winata's quick-tempered massa against that of the *Tempo*'s crowd of prodemocracy activists and journalists outside the courthouse. This was a case of the ant versus the elephant. The "elephant," Tomy Winata, TW for short, was one of Indonesia's richest men, his business empire had flourished during the New Order.[30] He could well afford ruthless business tactics.[31] The "ants" in question were the editors of *Tempo*, one of the most widely read and nationally respected weekly publications, well-known for its daring investigative journalism. *Tempo* had often run afoul of powerful elite even before Reformasi, and this time Tomy was suing *Tempo* for libel over a news story that implied his involvement in the arson of Tanah Abang's huge textile market and its subsequent redevelopment.[32] The power difference between the plaintiff and the defendants propelled one of the largest solidarity actions of the year, bringing various student groups together with NGO activists. The front gates of the beautiful, cream-colored courthouse were

FIGURE 2.3 Activists atop a mobil komando (command car). Note the activist's finger pointing to the sky, a pose similar to that of independence-era pemuda Bung Tomo, popular in nationalist iconography. PHOTO BY AUTHOR.

packed with reporters and foreign journalists. The judge would rule in favor of *Tempo* in a triumph for press freedom, but we did not yet know that.

At first I sat with the other demonstrators outside on the street, but the asphalt had absorbed the heat of the sun. I made my way over to the shophouse (*ruko*) next door, where I could still see and hear the demo but was outside its zone of influence. No one would harass me there to get me to show enthusiasm or raise my fist in solidarity. I clambered onto a parked motorcycle in the shade, where rows and rows of parked motorcycles took up pedestrian space. Three activists from the labor group the Workers' People Party joined me in the shade. Someone from "our" demo was reciting Wiji Thukul's poem "Bunga & Tembok" (Flower and wall) loudly and badly into a loudspeaker. I stirred from my malaise and listened. And began to giggle. Hasan, a poet-activist from Solo, also got the giggles. And so we were off, hysterically doubled over, stifling these laughs. Our counter-demonstration of mirth was a far cry from the earnest and belabored screams that traveled from the mobil komando (see fig. 2.3). No one could see or hear us demo dropouts on the side.

The orasi (speech) from the central command of the mobil komando ought to be stirring, since it occupies the symbolic and physical center of the demonstration. This particular truck, with an un-self-consciously expressive orator, was circled by a large student group and NGO flags of various sizes. The Aliansi Jurnalis Independen (Alliance of Independent Journalists) union flag looked small, white, and forlorn amid the great red, yellow, black, and green flags of the student groups. The journalists had been outclassed at their own demo, a fact given stark relief by the arrival of Kesatuan Aksi Mahasiswa Muslim Indonesia (United Action of Indonesian Muslim Students). Their troop of flag-bearers was waving enormous green-and-white flags twice the size of everybody else's, even though they had fewer demonstrators than other groups. This low ratio of massa to flag-bearers violates demo rules, as the organizer is supposed to deliver on his or her promised massa to guarantee the demo's success. The flags are meant to be token symbols of the origins of the troops (*pasukan*) rather than a material replacement for the bodies that should be but are not there. And yet, in a media trial about the media, demo space had created a fierce competition for photographic and visual dominance. The colorful and overscaled flags crowded the landscape. Then we heard Wiji Thukul's familiar words originating from the central command truck:

Warning
If the People leave
While the rulers are speaking
We must beware
Perhaps they are desperate

If the People hide
And whisper
When talking about their troubles
The rulers must be alert and learn to listen

If the People dare to complain
That means it's terminal

And if the rulers' speech
Cannot be challenged
The truth must be in jeopardy

If suggestions are refused without consideration
Voices silenced criticism outlawed without reason
Accused of subversion and disturbing the peace
Then there is only one word: Resist![33]

"Peringatan" (Warning) is every leftist activist's favorite Wiji Thukul poem. It is also Thukul's most famous poem, as it simultaneously captures the spirit of resistance against the New Order and the despotic character of the ruling class. The poem starts with a warning about the rakyat's brewing desperation and ends with a crescendo of inevitable resistance. The rhythm of the poem builds anticipation for the climactic conclusion. During the demonstration, all demonstrators are expected to say these words in chorus, ending with the powerful final line: "Maka hanya ada satu kata: Lawan!" As it happened, Simon was standing next to me, mouthing the words. I tried to subdue my face, but Simon caught my amusement. The shrieking, arrhythmic, and over-the-top rendition of "Peringatan" that the enthusiastic orator bellowed through a megaphone had killed the beauty of the words. Indeed, the orator was shrieking so much that he had lost his voice, and all we heard was a hoarse, cracked echo of an adolescent's breaking voice. The discordant sound overpowered the music of the words and broke the ritual effect of the poem, which was meant to lead the demonstrators into chorus, united into one assured voice of the People.

This broken voice had happened before to men and women who climbed onto the stage of the mobil komando. At first I had chalked it up to the affectation of individual activists, but after seeing seasoned activists with years of experience get nervous before they took their turn on the mobil komando, I heard such dissonance differently. The mediated voice that the toa (handheld speaker) broadcasted was of a different quality altogether, a louder, emphatic, and more political voice that engaged the massa but also dominated it with orders and cues to move, stand, raise their arms, or sing.[34] The first president of Indonesia, Soekarno, was a famous orator who called himself *penyambung lidah rakyat*, an extension of the People's tongue. Bung Tomo, the nationalist pemuda figure who ruled the airwaves from Surabaya, was perhaps an even more rousing speaker. A famous photograph of Bung Tomo shows him from an angle, his finger raised, cutting dynamically across the frame. Activists changed their body language the minute they climbed onto the command truck or clutched a microphone to make a speech. They pitched their bodies at a forward-leaning angle to shout into the crowd, raising their arms and jabbing their fingers in the air performatively (see fig. 2.3). In this soundscape of leadership resonating from the mobil komando, the broken, harsh, and high-pitched screams of orators represented a climax. They were signs that one was overcome with emotion, that an everyday voice could not carry their *emosi* (emotions, anger), which was so physical that sometimes people swooned and had to be helped off the truck.

This was happening to the impassioned activist on the command truck, who had gone so far off the script of demo culture that he was no longer legible. Listening to the butchering of Thukul's poem "Peringatan," Hasan, who like any other street-trained poet could recite his own work lyrically, could not resist. He began to cruelly mimic the sounds from the megaphone in non-sensical syllables and guttural sounds. The more he did this, rocking his body forward and back, in tempo and tone remarkably similar to the overzealous activist on stage, the more hysterical we got. Even the polite and neatly dressed Sjaiful, a model of Javanese propriety, couldn't help but smile with us.

Ulin, a journalist and activist, decided to intervene at the end of the failed recitation and climbed up on the command truck to repeat the poem in a calmer tone. He produced an ordered chant that wove the demonstration back together, initiating the masses to repeat alongside. By the time he reached the last line, we were all back up on our feet and chanting along. His voice rose with a crescendo flourish to conclude the recitation, and then he gave a mock public service announcement. "If you are dissatisfied with today's protest, or have any further questions, my cell phone number is 081 . . ." We laughed at his audacity, given the movement's history of surveillance and subterfuge. In the past, undercover police (intel) would try to obtain key activists' phone numbers to initiate contact or to intimidate them, and now Ulin acted as though he could freely broadcast his number in public. Ulin's public service announcement was tantamount to proclaiming his reading of the poem a public service for collective catharsis and was a ritually satisfying end to the demonstration; so too did he wittily imply that the performativity of the demo had itself become a political commodity. Ulin's rectification of the failing situation, by repeating the poem in a recognizable and slogan-like form, brought the dispersed demonstrators together again in an act of interpellation. All the demonstrators, young and seasoned alike, knew which script to follow to appear united, strong, and resistant, like the rakyat, right until the final moment of dissolution.

← Displacement of people led the people to mobilise which helped fuel the grassroots, Slums grow
- Demonstrators must know the city they are demonstrating in p64
- Students + Masses
- Kampungs provided places to cultivate the rakyat's dissatisfaction into organized political will + action.
- Demonstrations linked crime to the street
- Unjuk rasa (Demonstration) takes careful planning + skill
- Heat dissipates energy + crowds
- Mass convergence of song/poems/slogans continued the marches despite the heat.

"A Frenchwoman climbs on top of the University of Indonesia campus gates. One foot on a pillar, one on the bars. In her hand, a camera becomes a weapon. . . ."[1] These opening lines of an article published in *Bergerak* (Motion), a UI student daily, on March 25, 1998, capture the power of images in Reformasi's student movement. They remind us of what Robert Capa, the iconic photographer of twentieth-century wars, once said about the importance of proximity to action: "If your pictures aren't good enough, you're not close enough." The title of the article, "Mereka Pun Meliput Kita" (They too cover us), projects an image of the French photographer, standing in for an interested international news audience, angled precariously on top of the gates in the stance of a war photographer, "shooting" the Indonesian students amassed below her. There appears to be a convergence of foreign and national perspectives at the scene of the demonstration. Specifically, something visually interesting has caught the foreign eye, and the local actors know what it is. Student demonstrations are enhanced by the monocolored blazers issued by their institutions, called "campus jackets" (*jaket kampus*). These jackets are ordinary, modernizing, and aspirational garments that prepare students for a lifetime of wearing Western professional attire, yet they are in this context quite exotic. "To the photographer, UI students are interesting artistic and meaningful targets. Their yellow campus jackets give a very dramatic impression. On top of forming a contradiction to the yellow jackets of Golkar (the country's ruling party), UI's yellow jackets stand out amid the green, brick red, and blue colors that dominate the Depok campus environment. Moreover, it is only at UI that alma mater jackets are worn by all demonstrators on a massive scale. . . . And this is what the foreign photographers want."[2] The article paints an image of UI students standing out in a color spectrum. Their yellow jackets are the brightest on the scene.

Bergerak understandably bears a bias borne out of campus pride regarding the true colors of Reformasi. In fact, the yellow jackets were not the dominant color of student activism but were latecomers to the scene. Intercampus and off-campus groups purposely cultivated a more informal and democratic style of political T-shirts, bandanas, and flags that drew primarily on the color red, to symbolize nationalist sentiments (a Sukarnoist red for the Indonesian flag and the colors of the opposition party, the Indonesian Democratic Party of Struggle [PDI-P]) and leftist and populist sympathies. The Marxist color palette included red, yellow, and black backgrounds and symbols. What the author of the article successfully depicts is the thrill of seeing student activist style as a political dress code for the Reformasi era, a sight that foreign journalists recognized and coveted and would put themselves at risk to get. The article's comparison of student aksi to the energy and dangerous conditions that drive award-winning war photography is deliberate. By March 1998, Japanese, German, American, and French crews had arrived on the University of Indonesia (UI) campus to shoot the historic scene of Indonesian Reform. The article reveals that the foreign press are veterans of political volatility as significant as Tiananmen and as violent as Cambodia, and when a local journalist acknowledges that "these are no ordinary reporters," it cements the belief that student aksi are extraordinary events. Student activist appearances in Indonesia yield visible truths about social changes that both outsiders and insiders can see.[3] The globalized visual dynamic that combines local meanings of style with broad, universalizing effects of the body's political appearance gives rise to the demonstration's compelling visual qualities. As the camera seeks, reproduces, and weaponizes the image of the demonstrator dressed in his or her patented clothing, the developing image becomes a powerful icon with the capacity to prophesy national political changes and evoke external democratic tides. In a time of Reformasi, student images are efficacious signs for democracy-to-come.

In the post-Reformasi era, activist visual culture expanded its visual domain into areas perceived as public space and public culture. Thus far I have provided glimpses of a specific activist aesthetic in the print culture of activist propaganda and publications (chapter 1), the publicity of demonstrations in public spaces (chapter 2) and in what will form the primary concern of this chapter, the cinematic and reproducible qualities of pemuda style through the activist body. For example, the activist-as-hero became the locus of desire in film and popular media representations after the fall of Suharto.[4] Documentary films about student participation in Suharto's fall were sold in major bookstores and music stores across the country, and activists themselves were inspired to bear witness to their experience by making their own amateur documentaries. The most common sign of political transformation was the ubiquity of leftist political T-shirts sold openly at independent outlets, at street market stands, and in shopping malls and worn openly on the streets. In chapter 2, I showed how student activist demonstrations disrupt disciplinary and territorial understandings of the urban by commandeering public space as temporalized sites for oppositional politics. It follows that the circulation of demonstrators through the city becomes a *sight*, if not a spectacle, enhanced by the visual paraphernalia of banners (spanduk), flags, posters, flyers, graffiti, happening art performances, campus jackets, and T-shirts. Most important, the presence of activists in public spaces promotes the broadcast function of individual activist bodies as blank canvases—that is, pemuda as historically significant icons attached to contemporary and ever-changing political messages.

In this chapter, I turn to the significance of activist visual culture in staging youth politics as nationalist interventions and in forging relations between student groups and the rakyat through nostalgic references to student and pemuda history. I pay close attention to the body of the student activist as it circulates throughout the city, concentrating on the significance of a carefully cultivated pemuda style as the dominant vehicle for propagating the visual iconography of radical youth politics. Student activists successfully circulated subversive symbols of the left by fusing them to activist identity and style. But none of the changes of Reformasi and the cultural impact of popular protest make sense without considering the long history of New Order ideological repression and anticommunist propaganda, rooted deep in its own origin myth—the coup known as G30S, the September 30th Movement. Even now, signs of communism can still draw political censure for their fundamentally un-Indonesian and threatening qualities;[5] yet in the post-Reform era, pemuda style blatantly displayed its political and chromatic redness. To measure the changes caused by the tidal wave of red T-shirts, the hammer-and-sickle's subversive appearance, and the spectrum of campus jackets, a quick look at the suppressed history of the left is necessary, to contextualize the contradictory messages surrounding Generation 98's appearance.[6]

SUPPRESSED IMAGES: THE MISSING HISTORY OF THE LEFT AFTER 1965

The September 30th Movement was a failed coup attempt on September 30, 1965, headed by a few low-ranking military officers and allegedly involving members of the Indonesian Communist Party (PKI) and their small group of supporters from within and without the party and the army. The botched coup culminated in the kidnapping and execution of six right-wing generals, an act that the last remaining general, Suharto, took as the "pretext" for enacting emergency measures, exacting a swift crackdown on the coup members, and beginning a strategic nationwide extermination of the left (Roosa 2006). This violent extinction of the left had severe cultural repercussions in the country that had once been the seat of the largest communist party in Southeast Asia. A generation of left-leaning intellectuals, artists, workers, teachers, soldiers, and ordinary peasants were imprisoned without trial or disappeared into mass graves. By extension, all things "left" were demonized as part of the military-led propaganda against the PKI, including trade unions, farmers' groups, socialist and Marxist ideas, socially conscious art, music, and literature, even the populist notions of the country's first president, Soekarno.[7] The 1966 Generation of student activists were vociferously anticommunist and allied with the military to overturn Soekarno's "Old Order." In the 1980s and 1990s, the trope of the treacherous communist remained a powerful political tool to silence dissidents and shame citizens who deviated from New Order practices and thought (Havelaar 1991). Student activists who were critical of the New Order regime were often criminalized as communist elements, even politically tame groups whose politics avoided references to anything that could be construed of as leftism. The activists who had spearheaded the 1998 student movement experienced PKI accusations and their violent repercussions firsthand; on top of academic expulsion and punishment, they were arrested, kidnapped, disappeared, and scapegoated for outbreaks of political violence, such as the PDI affair in 1996.[8] Aktivis identity was synonymous with being rebellious troublemakers, and on university campuses, activists were self-consciously marginal—in general, they lacked the elevated social status normally attributed to university students (mahasiswa), even though most activists were well-educated university students from middle-class backgrounds. The more outspoken and radical activists, such as the PRD activists who hewed to Marxist ideas, or those who were politicized through study groups and the student press, persisted in organizing against Suharto and his cronies despite the dangers of doing so.

During Reformasi, the New Order depiction of activists as a communist threat to society was replaced by a mainstream youth identity that appealed to young people who had grown up believing New Order versions of history. Moreover, the student movement was loudly dismantling the New Order using leftist ideas, images, and rhetoric. How did the student movement's unmistakable references to nationalist and leftist history bypass the deeply embedded fear and stigmatization of any kind of leftist discourse or image? What impulses, political or other, summoned youth to mobilize in such large numbers across Indonesia, and why was that will to politics expressed through appearances? As an answer to these questions, I analyze the connections between the visual culture and practices of the student movement and the historicizing effects that activists produce when they identify with pemuda history. I argue that the success of activist images lies in their imminent reproducibility; at once ephemeral, easily forgotten, and remade the next day, the production and reception of photographs, slogans, signs, and T-shirts resembled already widespread consumption practices belonging to urban youth culture. As Carla Jones's research on the concurrent rise in pious consumption among Indonesian Muslim women shows, fashion is an embodiment of ethics, self-proclaimed figurations of identity, and the more ideologically vexing "pleasure of consumption" (2010: 622). Far from defusing Reformasi images, the circuits of consumption for pemuda style created new hybrid combinations of rakyat-activist alliances and avenues for the political participation of youth. Even when these representations featured banned "leftist" colors and symbols (a combination of red, yellow, variations of the hammer and sickle, images of protesting workers and peasants) that would have aroused suspicion and guaranteed arrest during the New Order, the symbolic inclusion of the popular into the political order in the post-Suharto era meant that these images could find a place in everyday life without necessarily being assimilated. The final portion of this chapter explores the linkages between youth generations articulated through popular representations of Soe Hok Gie, an activist from the 1966 Generation whose story became a part of Generation 98's own struggles to redeem their historical legacy. I end by reframing nostalgia as an effective politics of memory, one that pays attention to the ways that historical consciousness becomes embedded in political consciousness through the cultural politics of youth.

VISUALIZING POLITICS

Michel-Rolph Trouillot has argued in his book on the history of Haiti and the Americas, *Silencing the Past: Power and the Production of History*, that silences illuminate power far more than what is known and spoken, repeated and commonsensical (1995). Silences are constitutive of official narratives; they are that which enable the naturalization and construction of select truths. Under Suharto's New Order, the most audible silence that reconfigured the nation was that of the disappearance of the PKI, but other silences where civilians disappeared in mass graves or were killed in military operations also haunted the nation's consciousness. Instead of tracking *silence*, which implies suppressed speech as the core issue of representation, I consider visibility the grounds for my analysis, for "the ultimate mark of power may be its invisibility; the ultimate challenge, the exposition of its roots" (Trouillot 1995: xix). Political secrets were neither heard nor seen.[9] In Indonesia, silencing the past was made possible through the conditions of invisibility demanded by the New Order state's narrative of development and progress. In keeping with Trouillot's insight that hidden things reveal the broader contours of power, this article locates the sites and times where the iconography of the 1998 student movement appeared, transformed, and resignified the present with its historical signature, returning long-suppressed leftist and populist ideas and images to the political domain in Indonesia.

How meaningful are the acts of seeing and making visible that which power kept invisible? The answer I give here is that both acts are potentially very meaningful indeed. My research suggests that the archive of political representations that the 1998 student movement created, which I term the "images of youth," were as effective a political strategy for the student movement in creating new political relations and subjectivities as the mass demonstrations and organizing that Generation 98 became known for (see figs. 3.1 and 3.2). Since Reformasi began in 1998, there has been a shift toward greater visibility of resistance politics in the public sphere that must be theorized in terms of its material and political effects. Formerly invisible and taboo subjects of the left, and resistance politics in general, have provided inspiration for the visual culture of the student movement. Dissident movements, such as the Free Papua Movement, and groups, such as the survivors of state violence, have also become more daring in their calls for justice and representation, staging demonstrations and petitions in public. However, I caution against privileging visibility as the primary measure of democratization without taking into account the power structures that have merged the symbolic nature of the demonstration's struggle for recognition with the fact of its appearance in public space. Changing the signs and symbols of the image world of politics may appear as a radical or even revolutionary declaration against past regimes, but the presence of potent visual symbols such as the communist hammer and sickle in the student movement does not signify the resurgence of a much-feared Indonesian left. Instead, the power of the state is being countered elsewhere, in the radical potential of individual youths who seek a nationalist, global, and cross-class identification and who are among the first generation of New Order children whose distant relationship to the left is marked by curiosity, ambivalence, and objectification rather than outright rejection and fear.[10] Without undertaking a serious consideration and contextualization of the student movement's iconography, its visual turn which formed the constitutive grounds for political expression, inclusion, and transformation, we would not be able to see the extent to which the substance of political life changed or, in some cases, remained unchanged.

The visual culture of the student movement attests to the materiality and visibility of political life and activity in Indonesia, which has, since Reformasi, extended the domain of politics into the realm of public culture, that "zone of cultural debate" and broad appeal (Appadurai and Breckenridge 1988: 6). Public culture, following Appadurai and Breckenridge's meaning, was the sphere in which the images of youth came to live and gain currency. Activist images had a long lineage of past pemuda in nationalist history to refer to, but they also made use of a globalized visual economy that declared the youthful Indonesian citizen a modern world citizen. Through their performative appearances, the visual techniques of their protest, and the engaging and repeatable textures and surfaces of their bodies, the student activists of 1998 created a new model of citizenship for Indonesian youth by making political participation desirable and accessible. Going out into urban spaces, turning up on television and even in feature films, the activist had become a recognizable character that reminded ordinary Indonesians that pemuda were once again active in their midst. In forging the links between public culture and political culture, I draw on Kajri Jain's ethnography on the "social life" of sacred images in the Indian marketplace (2007). For Jain, images are not simply two-dimensional representations—the pictures, posters, graffiti, and other material we expect to see in any student movement's propaganda arsenal. Rather, the arc of an image's social life reveals how images animate, touch, absorb, materialize, and inhere in social meaning. Repetition (in production and consumption) of these images enhances the dialectic effect between the "formal and symbolic work of an image" and its transposition onto "forms of bodily performance [that] come to manifest themselves in images" (316). Thus, the effects of seeing activist bodies and activist images are intermingled; to see one would be to imply the other. As activist bodies became increasingly stylized and recognizable as an image through activists' bodily performance (their look and their

FIGURE 3.1 The Demonstrator. Drawing by Daniel Rudi Haryanto, Jakarta 1999.
REPRINTED WITH THE PERMISSION OF THE ARTIST.

FIGURE 3.2 "Use if necessary." Drawing of a Molotov cocktail by Daniel Rudi Haryanto, Jakarta 2000. REPRINTED WITH THE PERMISSION OF THE ARTIST.

gestures in the demonstration field), the meanings of student movement iconography conformed to the ideological spectrum of the middle-class, urban, and educated worldviews of the activists themselves.

Nowhere was the dialectic between activist bodies and images more apparent than in the student movement's style of protest. Urban protest culture in Jakarta in 1998 generated a series of images that linked rebellion, New Order depictions of Indonesian leftist history, and style that spoke to global youth culture. The student movement's discourse and mass demonstrations privileged representations that were mobile and succinct, providing a shorthand for their politics. Protest culture had to be instantly recognizable, visually arresting, and communicable. The body of the activist most often stood for all of those needs. Student activists circulated a self-image that condensed the best of their political qualities and their revolutionary capacity into easily recognized visual markers. Subversive T-shirts, torn jeans, long hair, and colorful campus blazers[11] became the uniform of awakened youth, papering over their various degrees of commitment to activism (see fig. 3.1). In theory, anyone with this look could participate in street politics. Their slogans were truncated yells, mixing English and Bahasa Indonesia, acknowledging through their "globalish" language the scope of their audience.[12] Equipped with no other weapons than their provocative words and appearance, activists spread the message of historical awakening: Indonesian youth (especially students!) were meant to lead Reformasi! Admittedly, in the years since Reformasi began in 1998, this exuberant claim has gone a bit flat. As anthropologist Patricia Spyer has noted in her work on postreligious conflict in Maluku, there is a certain banality to the juxtaposition of shocking images and everyday advertising that permeates public space in Indonesia (2008). Nonetheless, losing the political charge that characterized Reformasi's early years did not diminish the circulation of some of these images and representational techniques. Even today, the tactics of the student movement linger on, taken up by new youth organizations, political parties, trade unions, and nonpolitical assemblies.[13] The look of protest, and indeed the style of street politics in general, benefited from the highly developed protest culture of the student movement.

As a counterweight to the student movement's glorified history, critics have lamented the demise of student politics in recent years, citing the political disillusionment and opportunism of former activists as symptoms of a failed movement (Taufiqurrahman 2010). Such criticism exposes an underlying instrumentality in political discourse that identifies the capture of state power as the ultimate aim and measure of success for political mobilization. In further developments of street politics, politically aggressive ethnic and religious groups now outnumber and out-demonstrate student activist groups, allowing political elites and state actors to dismiss what remains of student movement demonstrations today as anachronistic and "anarchic" behavior (see chapter 4). These characterizations of the student movement's failures neglect to see change in other febrile sites of political participation and engagement, particularly in the realm of public culture, which the remnants of Generation 98 have influenced in important ways. Youth activism provided the locus where globalized forms of mass mobilization could be grafted onto older, national-ist forms of identification. The student activist was "a bearer of signs" (Siegel 1997), a surface that disseminated political messages making universal claims to human rights and democracy, while also awakening in other Indonesian youth the desire to participate in national politics. Student activists' messianic call to defend the nation naturalized the desire to challenge authority in favor of the rakyat in post–New Order Indonesia.[14]

CONNECTING TO THE PAST: NEW HISTORIES IN MOTION

"Invented tradition" is taken to mean a set of practices, normally governed by overtly or tac-itly accepted rules and of a ritual or symbolic nature, which seek to inculcate certain values and norms of behavior by repetition, which automatically implies continuity with the past.
—ERIC HOBSBAWM, "INTRODUCTION: INVENTING TRADITIONS" (2003)

October 28 is Hari Sumpah Pemuda (Youth Pledge Day), a day that commem-orates the signing of the Sumpah Pemuda (Youth Pledge) by the youth gener-ation of 1928, who proclaimed the nationalist struggle for "one language, one people, one nation." The reenactment of the Sumpah Pemuda is important for activists in the post-Suharto context to produce a sense of locality (Appadu-rai 1996) by ritually contextualizing the demonstration and the activists in an Indonesian nationalist landscape, even as their causes and protest styles ap-pear to roam the globe. Many of the demonstrations I observed (from 2003 until 2009) ended with the Youth Pledge: the massa snapped into formation, raised their fists forward toward the sky (see the posture of fig. 3.1) and lust-ily recited the oath they knew by heart. The mostly male and young demon-strators around me would notice my reticence in those moments and nudge me to raise my fist, sometimes aggressively insistent that I get in line with the others, ignoring my discomfort as an anthropologist who had already donned the T-shirt but could not quite mimic the heartfelt declaration of pledging the self to the nation.

The populist identification between students, youth, and the People was remade and renewed at several points throughout Indonesia's nationalist his-tory. Anticolonial nationalism began in the *ethici* (ethical) period of colonial reforms in the late nineteenth century, as more Indonesians gained access to higher education and formed the first indigenous identity-based organiza-tions. Nationalism grew significantly in the 1920s, as leftist, Islamist, and na-tionalist mass organizations became powerful vehicles for native political as-pirations, and finally found its violent expression in the pemuda militias of the Indonesian Revolution of 1945. From this nationalist lineage, Generation 98 derived two distinct pemuda styles—one based on their elite student identity and the other on a primordial self that explained the more violent and militant aspects of their seizure of the demonstration field. The titles and contents of Reformasi books frequently describe youth rising, awakening, and transforming the nation in a tidal wave of nationalist spirit. The metaphors of light and movement, as well as their similar educational and cultural backgrounds, would seem to render Generation 98 most similar to the westernized elite of Generation 28, yet "the Indonesian dandy," to use Rudolf Mrázek's term, was not the dominant model for pemuda style. Instead students turned to the physical attributes of the revolutionary 1945 Generation for visual inspiration. Generation 45 were culturally distinct in their emphasis on semangat, the nationalist spirit of youth, as the quality that defined them, not their age or rank.[15] The image of daring youth who defied their elders in the service of the nation was most famously fixed in the story of the declaration of independence: pemuda had kidnapped the nationalist leaders Soekarno and Hatta to force them to declare independence on August 17, 1945, while Indonesia was still under Japanese occupation. New Order narratives consequently valorized the 1945 generation for what the state considered to be their most important contribution, the birth of the nation's armed forces. It was this New Order propaganda image of pemuda that youth were most familiar with; a barefoot, bare-chested man, with a bandana tied around his forehead, armed with a primitive weapon, the *bambu runcing* (sharpened bamboo stake). Generation 98's student activists took on Generation 45's revolutionary look by growing their hair long and accessorizing their campus blazers with red bandanas tied prominently around their foreheads.[16]

The student activists who dominated Generation 98 assumed their affinity to the pemuda category, although it led to uncomfortable encounters with urban poor youth, or rural youth who were also called *pemuda* but whose lower-class origins bestowed upon them a threatening masculinity and potential criminality.[17] Student activists thus came up with creative rhetoric to exercise their claim to pemuda identity, eliding the social distance between middle- and lower-class youth. In an interview with BOMB in 1998, Yosef, a student activist and founder of the student group City Front (Front Kota), insisted on being called a *pejuang muda*—a young freedom fighter or revolutionary—a term that conveniently becomes in shortened form *pe-muda*—the word *pemuda*. The reporter's description lends heroism to Yosef's credentials. "As a young fighter (Yosef rejects the title student activist), he cannot stand in silence with all the problems the nation is facing."[18] Yosef had initially enrolled as a student at the private institute Bina Sarana Informasi but soon transferred to the more politically active Bung Karno University. He then left the large Jakarta-based intercampus alliance City Forum (Forkot) to found a new splinter group, City Front (Fronkot), with membership from fourteen campuses. Even though his activities appeared no different from those of other student movement intercampus alliances, from the similarity in name to the style of organizing, Yosef was emphatic that his activism arose from a nationalist spring instead of from a narrow student agenda.

The need to justify their claim to an expansive pemuda identity resonated with students who pondered the complexity of their elevated status in society and their proximity to the street. In an on-campus interview with me, Felix, a bespectacled UNAS student who wore a green army jacket over his T-shirt, suddenly gave an impassioned barrage of reasons why the differences between pemuda and mahasiswa (university student) had to disappear. Articulating the divisive and yet surmountable nature of these differences, Felix stated that the dissolution of difference could only be carried out if the students rejected a sumptuary law that had long shaped student identity—that is, if they stopped wearing the brightly colored campus jackets that served to distinguish one campus from another. Campus jackets acted as long-range visual markers of political presence—at a glance, you perceived the demonstration's composition through its color pixels, with different blocks of color informing you which campus had contributed the most troops, which campus was the most militant, and so on. Moreover, the image of students en masse *looked* cool to students, reinforcing the images of themselves as agents of history. But through the circulation of Reformasi's populist rhetoric and leftist aesthetics, an exchange of student style for pemuda style was now possible. "We are all pemuda," Felix spoke with the finality of a logical conclusion he had arrived at from experience. His declaration of the unity of socially distinct youth under the species pemuda sounded inspired, but it was also a premature claim. Immediately afterward, Felix said, "Yes, we *should* remove our student jackets, just get rid of them, and become pemuda. All of us." It was unmistakable that Felix meant students when he referred to "us" in his speech. He followed this thought with an afterthought that deserves notice—that students would still be students even if they didn't wear their campus jackets. Students dressed in pemuda style on the streets could effectively enhance rather than contaminate their student essence. The visual dominance of the mediatized activist image in the public sphere and its transposition onto an older pemuda image ensured that the student body could never be truly stripped naked of its politicized identity. Felix's admission that students could maintain their social rank even when they adopted the appearance of other (underclass) youth assumes a stable indexical relation between a student's outward appearance and its owner's unperturbed political self, a self-referential assumption to middle-class hegemony that has remained remarkably fixed in contemporary Indonesian politics.

If student identity was not about dress, but rather an interior essence that could not be duplicated or faked, then students were safe to adopt other appearances and styles at will. In Simmel's essay "The Problem of Style," he writes that "style is the man himself" and, conversely, "the man is the style" (1997b: 65). We can extrapolate from Felix's statement that "we are all pemuda" a resonant symmetry. Of course the student belief that pemuda were really students and that students were really pemuda, and above all, that pemuda were the chosen nationalist citizens to lead the revolution, is contestable on historical and sociological grounds. Yet the visual craft of activist style subsumed the differences between the pemuda identity categories of student and (underclass) youth, specifically through the student movement's increased control over a generalized aktivis image and through the reproduction of the urban aktivis uniform: the protest T-shirt and jeans. Both fashionable and timeless in its spare ingredients, the student activist look successfully conveyed what Simmel has identified as the crux of a style felt to be both expressive of individual character and representative of a generation: "that style is a principle of generality which either mixes with the principle of generality, displaces it or replaces it" (65).

Indonesian student activists were not merely "inventing tradition" when they linked themselves to a nationalist lineage, as Hobsbawm would dismiss the self-legitimating acts of cultural hegemony that nationalist elites indulge in (1983).[19] One of Hobsbawm's most important contributions is his paired insight into tradition's appeal in a rapidly changing modern age (the age of nationalism) with the accompanying observation that "where the old ways are alive, traditions need be neither revived nor invented" (2003: 8). Hence invented tradition gives and recedes authority in the same breath: in claiming symbolic power from antiquity, one must repeat the invariant forms culled from history; yet the need for invention acknowledges the death of the once living thing, the source of organically derived traditions. The pemuda narrative could indeed be read in those negative terms—that the generational appearance of pemuda signals an absence in the political that can only be filled through a revival of "tradition" (Pemberton 1994). However, the efficacy of large-scale and frequent "democratic" protests in Indonesia suggests that the pemuda mythology is neither a purely volk-based myth that fosters popular resistance nor an inauthentic manipulation of history, as its resilience in shaping the different iterations of nationalist youth attests. The pemuda narrative provided a ready-made vehicle for present-day youth's assumption of a powerful and revolutionary "new" identity that was already naturalized and politically situated to its time and place—crisis and transformation in Indonesia.

ENEMIES OF THE STATE, FRIENDS OF THE PEOPLE

From Reformasi's early days in the first half of 1998, when student activists wore the boxy campus jackets to show their exclusive affiliation to their universities, to just a few months later, when group alliances and membership had become far more fluid and national in scope, pemuda style evolved to reflect the mainstreaming of the student movement. The premier activist image that cast global and political nuances most effectively onto seemingly neutral and pop-cultural surfaces was also the most common style of attire for student activists: the humble T-shirt and jeans. At first sight, activist style appears identical to what all youth wear. But the "stylization of the self" imbues this style with a political meaning and historical references (Nutall 2003). It is pertinent to make the obvious point that protest culture does not end with the close of the demonstration event. The messages of the demonstration travel alongside the circulation of activist bodies, particularly those adorned with political T-shirts. In the next section I describe the T-shirt cottage industry that plays a central role in the economy of student activist protest culture. But first I will concentrate on the identity effects and implications of activist style, given that the demand that activists have for such shirts is not simply retro-nostalgia for political kitsch (Bach 2002) but forms a distinct part of identity production and resignification of leftist iconography.

In crosscultural references to popular political leaders, and in the subversive display of leftist symbols, activists linked themselves to a greater history of youth struggles nationally and across borders (see fig. 3.3). Insisting on the fit of outside symbols brought in (Marx, Lenin, Mao, Che Guevara, Subcomandante Marcos), student activists renewed the pemuda narrative with references to heroic masculine struggles elsewhere. In a particularly ubiquitous example in the Indonesian context, the popularization of Che Guevara's image (on T-shirts, flags, banners, murals) was initially linked to the introduction of liberation theology and dependency theory in the 1980s. Similar to the spread of what Namhee Lee has called "pamphlet Marxism" in her study of the democracy movements in 1980s South Korea, a patchwork library of translated works on the global history of revolutions, Latin American populism, and recent case studies of urban-based left movements became study guides for activists who spoke of politicizing the rakyat (see Lee 2007). The romantic

FIGURE 3.3 Che Guevara and Lenin at a demonstration in Jakarta, 2004. The Lenin T-shirt names one of the largest student activist alliances in 1998, the City Forum (Forkot). The slogan below Lenin's image reproduces a popular demonstration yel (shout) and song lyric, "Revolution to the Death." PHOTO BY AUTHOR.

image of Che as a young, handsome, masculine revolutionary attracted both men and women, and over time the need for deep knowledge of Che Guevara's intellectual and ideological past fell away. While other male icons of the left, like Marx and Lenin, were also represented in the pantheon, Che was by far the most popular.[20] A former PRD activist fondly recalled being given a Che T-shirt by an Australian activist in the early 1990s. It was the first of its kind in Indonesia, he claimed. No one else in the student circles of Yogyakarta or Jakarta had them, and he took pride in its uniqueness. His friends were always wheedling him to give it to them. As images of Che proliferated, the use of the icon triggered other local responses. Activists were fond of telling a joke, an urban myth revealing the provinciality of the police who arrested them. "Hey, you young fools—what are you doing worshipping Iwan Fals?" groused the policeman, mistaking Che for another moustache-sporting, wavy-haired Indonesian icon. Iwan Fals was an immensely popular Indonesian folksinger in the Bob Dylan genre whose socially aware lyrics about the common people made him a counterculture hero. Indeed, Iwan Fals had released an album in 1999 entitled *Salam Reformasi* (Hello Reformasi) that consisted of his well-known protest songs. Yet in the early days of Reformasi, it would have been regarded as provincial to have Bang (Brother) Iwan's face stenciled onto one's protest shirt.[21] Iwan Fals's songs may have indicated solidarity with the little people, but the faces of Che and Lenin, like their signs in English, made the intentions of Indonesian activists more obviously political, more communicable and legible to the globalized world of democracy struggles and social movements that they considered themselves a part of.

The generic body of the activist had as its chief desirability the quality of a blank canvas in motion. Worn by almost all youth across the country, the T-shirt was the most effective technique of representation for the student movement, bearing the changing slogans of their protest (see fig. 3.4). Student activist style made one stand out from the crowd, but the difference did not merely convey an expression of individual personality. One was not just a local troublemaker arrested by the police; being an activist implied belonging to a group that shared this outlook. The political T-shirt allowed activists to identify one other and to stand apart from youth who were not yet politicized and for whom clothes were merely a consumerist expression of individuality rather than proof of a political identity. Yet the chosen mode of dress, the T-shirt and jeans, also places activists into a larger consumer culture. Student activists wear political T-shirts for demonstrations, to go to class, and even to events such as weddings, seminars, and workshops that call for more formal wear. It is expected that youth wear T-shirts in the same way that factory workers and professionals wear collared shirts as their uniforms. Youth appear most natural in T-shirts. How do activist investments in the visual culture of the student movement create subversions and emit radical political messages from images that are already entangled in popular culture and consumer fashions? The ambiguity of wearing the cloak of "resistance" is underscored in moments such as the one when the police outsider mistakenly mocks the activist, substituting local singer Iwan Fals for Che Guevara, appearing to cancel out the disturbing intent of the image. Or perhaps the police officer's confusion signals the success of the chosen medium—masked by the T-shirt's ubiquitous nature, T-shirt wearing activists become "young fools" worshipping harmless pop idols rather than dangerous leftists threatening the state of things in a nation haunted by its anticommunist past.

The slippage between local youth culture and a globalized leftist image repertoire exemplifies the zone of uncertainty that the student movement occupies in the post-Reformasi era. Are "leftist" students really enemies of the state or not? If activists with leftist inclinations deny or demote leftism in favor of nationalism's dominant rhetoric, an ideological position that includes more centrist or conservative groups, how should we interpret the continued use and circulation of highly charged leftist images and discourses? On the one hand

FIGURE 3.4 May Day demonstration with activists and workers, 2005. Their T-shirts read "Socialism: The True Path for the Liberation of the Workers."

the legitimacy granted by pemuda history glorifies the role of youth in politics; on the other hand, if the political practices of Generation 98 are taken seriously, the problem remains: how does one unlearn the internalized structures of fear that govern the visibility and circulation of "communist" ideas and symbols?[22] The remaining sections shed light on how activist images inhabit the uncomfortable terrain of being nationalist and leftist by "commodifying" leftism and repackaging activism as a youth tradition already present in Indonesian history (Kasian 2001). The anxieties about the left that still permeate Indonesian politics are thus pacified to some degree by the resettlement of activist images into the realm of public culture, where youthful transgressions appear as culturally appropriate avant-garde actions by urban, cosmopolitan, and ideologically hegemonic middle-class subjects. Disarticulating leftist meanings from their signifiers promotes a similar depoliticizing stance that the state, or any cynical observer, can take against "compromised" student activists; that is, activists may stem from the most educated, modern, and indulged social groups but have little impact, since they are not recognized as representative or dominant elites. A more nuanced interpretation of the cultural practices of youth is therefore necessary in order to maintain focus on how the activist body remains political even as it participates in a world of middle-class and modernizing desires.

THE T-SHIRT FACTORY: IMAGE-MAKING AND REPRODUCTION

The small-scale and limited-edition production of protest T-shirts that I discuss here enables a direct means of reproducing and consolidating group identity, which in the competitive political space of the demonstration provides a valued technique of distinction.[23] Slight nuances of activist style, achieved by varying the slogans and the symbols on the T-shirt, have allowed activists to be fashionably hip and politically current; at times grounded in local issues and at other times fashionably global (for example, Che Guevara and World Social Forum). The activist body in its T-shirt reinforced the role that activists envisioned themselves playing in the mediascape of national politics (Appadurai 1996): as belonging to a visible and concrete presence made up of individual Indonesian citizens occupying the political space of the street and at the same time a continuation of democratic forces elsewhere. In my interactions with activists from across the political spectrum, I was often asked a question that bore the assumption that their counterparts, the youth in other countries, shared common knowledge about the heroic role Indonesian students and youth played during Reformasi: "What do *they* (youth in the US, the West) think about us?"—a question that was then followed by stories of their attempts to network with foreign activists and NGOs. Images of youth provide partial representations of the political imaginary that "looks like us," a resemblance that allies urban middle-class modernity in Jakarta with sympathetic activist projects both in Indonesia and beyond its borders in a global populist network of politicized youth.

Nico, a good-looking young UI student, had started a business with a few of his activist friends. Aptly calling it "Turn Left production" (*sic*), they had decided to harness what artistic abilities they had to the avid demand for tight black, red, and white T-shirts with leftist symbols and slogans. They bought cheap T-shirts wholesale from textile vendors at the famous Tanah Abang Textile Market, built wooden and glass frames for screening the images, and bought images of Che, Lenin, or popular slogans that were of the moment. The slogans mostly were a kind of shortened demo *yel* (shout); "Socialism yes! . . . No!" Fill in the blanks yourself. They took special orders in these cases. The earliest series of T-shirts were rather limited in production and style, and ordering a shirt was a bit like ordering a meal (see fig. 3.5). You specified size and color, and they made you one on the spot, delivered the next day after the thick acrylic paint had dried. The first few had wobbly outlines where a beginner's technique on the glass-plate *sablon* (silkscreen) frames showed.

FIGURE 3.5 The order form for Turn Left products. The upper right corner contains the instructions: "These resistance T-shirts are for sale for Rp. 50,000 per piece. For comrades who are interested, just call [the following phone numbers]." AUTHOR'S COLLECTION.

Owing to the prepurchased templates that were screened onto the T-shirts, the same Lenin image—his thoughtful bald, shining head left blank, the moustache, beard, and eyes dark and eloquent—could be found on a T-shirt as well as graffitied onto the underpasses of bridges and the walls of the river embankments alongside Jalan Sultan Agung. Some images were less familiar than Lenin; slogans and symbols were lifted directly out of the World Social Forum website: "Another World Is Possible" with a picture of the globe, and perhaps even "La Luta Continua!" a phrase already well known in activist circles. On Turn Left's T-shirt menu, Chairman Mao shared space with an anti–George W. Bush image and an MTV logo. Other youth groups produced similar images, often with English-language slogans, on their T-shirts.[24]

Out of community loyalty, everyone in Nico's circle of friends, including myself, bought T-shirts. Cash up-front, about US$5 (50,000 rupiah) a shirt.[25] The women activists especially, who ranged from their early twenties to early thirties in age, were keen on buying their next demonstration T-shirt. Like many other collective business efforts that piggybacked onto the student movement, the apparel economy was one of patronage. If you knew the producer, and your peers were already buying the product, you were practically obliged to do so. "Wear it now!" People were often urged to put on their purchases immediately, so that the next activist who wandered onto the grounds would spot you and be enfolded in the collective excitement for the thing in question. The words "Lucu! Dapat dari mana?" (Cute! Where did you get it?) were often heard at demo sites. It was not just the T-shirt and its ever-changing slogan but the total image that you purchased. You paid slightly more than cost for a shirt and wore it at the next demo as both advertisement and a way to fit into the crowd. In the cacophony of demo cries, whether protesting the removal of fuel subsidies ("Tolak Kenaikan BBM!" Reject High Fuel Prices!) or calling for a free and fair election, these multiple demands and uniform outfits appealed to a sense of continuity between the act of looking the part and voicing the part.

I ordered several shirts as gifts in anticipation of the trip back to the United States at the end of my fieldwork, and was told that I would have to wait for a few days for production to commence. I wandered into the dark headquarters of Berantas (Fight, Eradicate), an urban-poor advocacy group that had been active in advocating for the rights of slum communities on the verge of eviction by the city authorities. Now the room, dark, with a computer in the corner playing constant rock music, or being cleaned of viruses secreted in the internet porn sites that no one would ever acknowledge visiting, was overtaken by the T-shirt factory. A system of learning-by-doing was taking place.

FIGURE 3.6 The raw materials for T-shirt production: a Lenin image template, a homemade screen, a plain black cotton T-shirt, and some paint. PHOTO BY AUTHOR.

One of the young men, who clearly had more experience in this line of work, was carefully explaining the importance of keeping the frame and image-template absolutely still, pinned in the same place, for one had to reapply the layers of paint several times to make the thick, almost embossed images on the shirts. He talked as he did this, standing over the tables in the center of the small room, a cigarette dangling from his lips. Another young man, Fami, stood at attention with a small red hair dryer in his hand. This was his task, to properly dry the image before the next layer of acrylic was applied. The personable and chatty demonstrator of the technique explained that on his university campus, he had done this sort of thing all the time. T-shirts, span-duk (banners), you name it. I grinned and snapped a photograph of Fami, the longhaired boy now intently blow-drying the finished T-shirt. It was Lenin again, this time in thick white acrylic paint on a black cotton-polyester surface (see fig. 3.6). Fami's long wavy hair looked ungroomed, and his punk-rock aesthetic of a child-sized black T-shirt and chain jewelry was incongruous with the feminine and domestic object he was utilizing so carefully. Suddenly he looked domestic, at home with this unremarkable tool of production. Where earlier generations of activists in the 1980s and early 1990s had given much care to the art of producing meaningful political theater on the streets, the practices of newer generations of activists alluded to the mall and the middle classes in their consumption of political images (see Young 1999). The self-fashioning of an activist look bled into their leisure time and their consumer habits. University cities like Jakarta, Yogyakarta, Depok, and Bandung saw the rise of "distribution outlets" or *distro* (Luvaas 2010): stores set up by enterprising youngsters like Nico to sell homemade alternative wear such as punk paraphernalia or political T-shirts. Politics had become casual wear in very effective ways.

In his essay "Consumption, Duration, and History," Arjun Appadurai links the production of a cultural economy based on repetition and consumption to the techniques of the body (1996). The body is "an intimate arena for the practices of reproduction," a privileged site that takes on the task of social reproduction by the force of repetition, which I have so far depicted in the predictable uniformity of activist style and personae. Appadurai's insight into the extent to which consumption (and class) practices reconfigure our relation to history creates a compelling analysis of why even the most radical political youth identities can never be far from a predisposition to overt displays of nostalgia. According to Appadurai, consumption in late capitalist and globalized societies has become a repetitive practice that creates a sense of "ersatz nostalgia" for the "authentic," which further drives the economy of consumption by equating the purchase of consumer goods with an authentic experience of past traditions in the present time. Thus, in his penultimate example, a Sears holiday catalogue replete with glowing images of the American Family, surrounded by traditional household goods, returns the experience of Christmas to us. Ersatz nostalgia completes the transaction by replacing individual, ambivalent, and heterogeneous pasts with a sanctioned and commodified experience. But here I depart from Appadurai's somber conclusion that our sense of temporality is "ersatz," fake, and a priori mediated by consumption. Appadurai's critique illuminates how ersatz nostalgia essentializes experience, to the extent that Generation 98's individual struggles and tragedies did conform quite closely to a master narrative of victimization by the state, and why ersatz nostalgia has a central place in our affection for certain products and images over others, such that Generation 98 renewed its pemuda status via a politics of consumption. Yet the revelation that certain political practices of activism were enhanced by repetitive acts of consumption that provided a short cut to political identity does not detract from the efficacy of such "commodified" political experiences. In the context of post-Suharto Indonesia, the desire of activists to wear the right T-shirt and jeans to demonstrations fit a growing concern among youth to publicly and performatively express their role in the moral economy of Reformasi politics.

The pemuda-as-activist image anchors the site of youth's political consciousness, one that depends on a nostalgic fetish and cultural consistency for its potency. Living vicariously through the consumption of pemuda histories and activist images allowed youth to reaffirm their connection to the pemuda legacy that fed their political identity. Pemuda mythology survived and was even enhanced by the New Order regime's claim on youth spirit (semangat pemuda), staged in annual rituals of state pomp, and through Suharto's visible support of the pemuda groups that acted as his henchmen. Yet these cultural constraints on youth identity, which in its worst form displayed a conservative, militaristic, and reactionary nationalism, also provide an unexpected venue for political solidarity across generations (Ryter 1998; Wilson 2006). Activist practices of image-making and reproduction widen the political imaginary, drawing the previously unimaginable past suddenly close by moving back and forth between 1998 and other experiences, placing the activist in other sites and times of political struggle. The blurring of time or, more accurately, the coming of the past to the present, was especially poignant in attempts by Indonesian artists, intellectuals, former communists, and victims of state violence to represent their own version of history. The merging of nostalgia and change in the zone of public culture came to life in the figure of Soe Hok Gie, a deceased activist of the 1966 generation whose story suddenly came to matter very much.

THE IDEAL PEMUDA: SOE HOK GIE THEN AND NOW

One of the most important signs of how activism had entered the public imagination since 1998 occurred during the period of my fieldwork in 2003–2005. Apart from the founding fathers of Indonesian nationalism, the pemuda who received the greatest admiration among activists was a young, ethnic Chinese activist who belonged to the youth generation of 1966, whose demonstrations had played a large part in legitimating the overthrow of the first president, Soekarno.[26] Soe Hok Gie's fame among the 1998 generation of activists marked an important loosening in the parameters of nationalist identity that had begun to surface in the post-Suharto era. Several contradictory and extraordinary elements coexist in the "Gie as pemuda" phenomenon. The first was Gie's popularity, despite his ethnic name and minority status as an ethnic Chinese, an identity that was often suppressed or ignored by Indonesians when discussing his writing or his politics. Gie was one of the most well-known *tionghoa* (the politically correct term for Chinese) who did not have the reputation of being "Chinese," that is, insular, selfish, and a greedy comprador.[27] Avoiding talk of Gie's ethnicity by claiming that Gie was unflinchingly loyal to the country he was born to was a coded way to avoid SARA (*SUKU AGAMA RAS*

FIGURE 3.7 Image of actor Nicholas Saputra, as Soe Hok Gie, in publicity still from the film *Gie*. The same image appears on the covers of reprints of Gie's published journal, *Diary of a Demonstrator*, often bearing the sponsorship logos of a prominent cigarette company. IMAGE BY MILES FILMS.

ANTAR GOLONGAN), the acronym that stood for sensitive issues of ethnicity, religion, and race.[28] Moreover, the suppression of Gie's Chineseness allowed other pemuda qualities to surface as essential to his being; namely his uncompromising criticism of the state, his concern for the rakyat, and his participation in the street politics of the 1960s. Given the uneven efforts in the post-Reformasi period to recuperate the role of other forgotten ethnic Chinese nationalists, it was all the more extraordinary that Gie became so popular that top-billed Indonesian actors would star in *Gie*, the film about his life. To gain mainstream popularity, Gie had to enter the public sphere in a recognizable fashion, sponsored by MTV and A-Mild cigarette ads. Increasingly, the primary focus on Soe Hok Gie shifted from his political ideas and writings to the reproducibility of his image in commodity form.

Soe Hok Gie was a campus activist at UI who became a respected public intellectual and a well-known critic of the PKI and the Soekarno administration in the 1960s. Unlike Che or Subcomandante Marcos, Soe Hok Gie was a home-grown icon from Indonesia's most elite university. His early death in 1969 added an element of tragedy to his reputation. Gie died without witnessing the steady abuse of power the New Order state would carry out in its thirty-two years in power and was therefore exempt from the taint of political corruption that would brand activists from the 1966 generation as right-wing collaborators and supporters of the New Order. As he was neither a declared rightist nor leftist, Gie's moral "purity" made him an Indonesian nationalist first and foremost. In fact, Gie denounced the PKI leadership as much as he supported the overthrow of Soekarno's "decadent, bourgeois" government. That he was adopted by left-leaning student groups in the 1990s attests to the strength of his populist ideas. Gie was best known for his posthumously published journal, *Catatan Seorang Demonstran* (Diary of a demonstrator). Students who had no way of experiencing firsthand the possibility of mass mobilization in the repressive 1980s and early 1990s read Gie's vivid passages about the left- and right-wing masses who filled the streets in the 1960s. His descriptive writing recorded the demo yells and confrontational politics youth had engaged in on behalf of the nation. The resuscitation of critical activist voices such as Soe Hok Gie's in the 1990s gave the pemuda narrative an intellectual foundation. When reprints of *Catatan Seorang Demonstran* were difficult to find after the last reprint in 1993, dog-eared photocopies circulated among student activists. Gie's reputation soared after 1998, when "the role of youth in establishing democracy" became a favorite discussion and seminar topic on university campuses. Activists went so far as to train new activists through the manual Gie's life and diary provided.

Soe Hok Gie did not care for clothes. The one attachment to his name describing his appearance was *lusuh*—tired, worn.[29] Like a crumpled old garment. The force of his personality was to be found in his writing, his clarion voice balanced by his diminished appearance. Gie was one of the original members of a nature lovers' group at the UI, and his nature hikes on the steepest slopes of Java (where his life would ultimately end) attested to his distaste for the bourgeois and decadent society he associated with then-president Sukarno. Gie's appearance was plain and therefore honorable, as a student should be, bookish but fiery in his outspokenness against political injustice and dictatorship. But the popularity of Soe Hok Gie as a touchstone for emergent activist identities on university campuses was soon replaced in 2005 by images of another sort. Gie's persona was overtaken in a film version of his life by the popularity of the handsome Eurasian actor Nicholas Saputra, who portrayed him. The young director of *Gie*, Riri Reza (only thirty-three years old at the time and a peer to Generation 98), stated his long-term investment in the project. It was, he said in an interview, a serious attempt to bring the politics of the 1966 pemuda generation to the screen and a testimony to the ongoing fascination with pemuda by which all things, including the once taboo history of 1965–1966, could be inserted into a framework of meanings created by the events of 1998. One regime change (the fall of Soekarno in 1966) substituted for another (the fall of Suharto in 1998). Reprints of *Catatan Seorang Demonstran* now featured a new cover—a black-and-white image of Nicholas Saputra as Gie, which was plastered all over Jakarta as part of the film and an A-Mild cigarette ad campaign ("*Gie* meminjam wajah Nicholas" 2005; see fig. 3.7). The image of Saputra shows him squinting, his indirect gaze fixed on something beyond us, accented by his thick black eyebrows and a tender young mouth. His wavy dark hair is blown by a gust of historical passion. The fact that Saputra did not resemble Gie did not deter the circulation of the romanticized images. Often the same image appeared with contrary messages, with Gie's own quotations from his journal about the need for youth to challenge the hypocrisy of the moment, along with the A-Mild cigarette logo, or in some cases, MTV's youth brand as well. The filmmakers acknowledged the necessity of merging "Nico's" popularity with a young, female audience, with the character (*sosok*) of Gie to generate renewed interest in Soe Hok Gie's politics as well as in the film, but the marketing ploy clearly leaned heavily on selling Nico's attractive teen image rather than raising the political consciousness of the audience.[30]

The film opened to warm but cautious reviews, owing to the volatile politics of the 1960s (especially 1965–1966) that the film had to include in realist good faith. Among those were historical facts that were potentially troubling in the current context, reminding the public that right-wing high school and university student groups had collaborated with the military in removing Soekarno from power and were implicated in Suharto's rise and the PKI's downfall. The more explosive issue of the organized massacre of an estimated one million alleged communists that began with the military crackdown and continued with civilian involvement following the 30th September Movement was barely alluded to in the film. All through 2004, the anticipation was building among youth eager to see a teen heartthrob in the role of Gie, but the student activists

I worked with were especially eager to see how one of their most important local role models had been portrayed. Several of them had attended UI, Gie's alma mater and Indonesia's flagship university, and had had firsthand involvement in the 1998 student movement. Would the fiercely honorable politics of Soe Hok Gie make the cut? Furthermore, how would the Indonesian left be portrayed on the screen for the first time in the post-Suharto era? Would leftist symbols and characters be demonized, as was standard New Order practice under Suharto? What had the director, Riri Reza, dared to show about this dark time? The excitement over the film revealed the contours of anticommunist feeling that decades of New Order propaganda had created and amplified. The New Order state's preoccupation with denouncing the undying, "latent" political disease that was communism-Marxism had created a powerful proxy enemy of the nation that many Indonesians continued to fear even after the fall of Suharto. The name "PKI," in words and images, still stirred powerful fear and hatred among Indonesians, dehumanizing those individuals, events, or organizations that were accused of being communist by right-wing groups and militias.[31] By 2005, mass demonstrations and political T-shirts were permissible and even expected, but a mainstream film representation of the PKI without the directive of New Order propaganda, no matter how fleeting a sight, was another proposition altogether.

On July 15, 2005, five demonstrators and one anthropologist watched the film *Gie* on its opening night. In the film, Jakarta was transformed into its nostalgic postcolonial self, featuring dusky lamplight and showy vintage cars on the streets. All the young men playing the student activists of the 1966 generation were clean-cut and handsome. The sets were pristine and the dress designs quaint in their 1960s detail. Only the urban poor (workers and demonstrators), who were destined in the film to be the communist masses, fit the descriptor *lusuh* (worn, tired) that had once described Gie or bore any resemblance to the everyman aesthetic of current student activists. Yet there were moments where images seemed to leap off the screen into the present. In shots of demonstrations set in the past, the *massa* (crowd) strode through the streets decorated in shades of communist red, with shirts, bandanas, and flags sporting the hammer and sickle. The activists I was with whistled and cheered as these scenes came on, joking with each other that they were the "invisible hand" behind those demos, the puppet masters behind the political curtain.[32] As the political situation in the film grew increasingly tense, the film showed slogans denouncing the PKI in graffiti on the walls. The oncoming slaughter of the Indonesian left was only hinted at on-screen rather than graphically depicted, with the ugliness of the political conflict underscored by the dramatic music of the film, but there was a feeling that these were contemporary acts. The outcome of one historical instance—the 1965–1966 massacre of the PKI and its alleged sympathizers—and the political ambiguities surrounding the left in the present time seemed to share a split screen because of the familiarity of the scenes going by: the look of the film and the mass demonstrations (red youth on the streets), and the act of writing on the walls. Here was protest as sign of the passage of man, the "cry of need or protest, (the) cry without words and without silence, an ignoble cry—or if need be, the written cry, graffiti on the walls" (Blanchot 1993: 262). The temporality of the present, belonging to the 1998 activists, was reflected in a film about 1965. The scene of the crowd of demonstrators marching to their known fate brought out traces of the 1998 activists' anger at the Suharto regime, and the violence they had experienced in 1998 and 1999 appeared transhistorical. An inherited trauma that remained unseen (1965), for the film had not dared depict the slaughter of the communists on screen, broke the "fourth wall" and touched the audience by evoking a remembered trauma that they had witnessed (1998), opening a wound that threatened to cry out (Caruth 1996).

In an interview with *Gatra*, the director, Riri Reza, recounted the reluctance of his extras to shout the slogan "Hidup PKI" (Long Live the Communist Party of Indonesia!) in the demonstration scene, and his ensuing terror when, once begun, they *would not stop* ("Wawancara: Riri Riza: Saya Dulu Makan Nasi Golkar" 2005). Shedding their initial fear of the taboo against any and all signs of communism, the extras channeled 1965 in the only way possible. They reenacted it through what they knew of present-day protest culture; that is to say, it was only logical that as demonstrators they yelled and kept yelling their slogan "Long Live the PKI!" wherein the import of their actions was lost in their angry shouts. And imagine the director running around the set yelling "STOP! STOP!" to his crew members, as if this counterfeit protest could indeed trigger the violence of 1965 all over again ("Wawancara: Riri Riza: Saya Dulu Makan Nasi Golkar" 2005). The extras were not activists, but in that instance they became like activists, and even the unimaginable—they became like what they imagined communists to be. One might say, an indeterminate haunting between memory and history took place (Brown 2001: 153). The story of the making of the film *Gie* was itself historically significant, a story of the "new left" embedded in a story about Soe Hok Gie's life and times. Even though Gie himself was sharply critical of the communists, the phantom relation that Gie had to the left was enough to imbue the film *Gie* with the present's fears and anxieties about the left. After we watched the film, my activist friends debated the authenticity of what the film portrayed. They recalled from news items in film magazines that the director had done five years of painstaking research, culling material from journals, personal effects, and oral history.[33] There was a consensus that the film had been largely faithful to Gie's biography, albeit overly indulgent in focusing on his romantic life. But perhaps the most authentic moment remained the scene of protest. The sight of the masses on the street clothed in red and bearing flags was one that they, as witnesses to history and political actors themselves, implicitly recognized. The impending violence on the screen belonged to their story of injustice and an unequal fight between state and citizen as well. And the young director's need to show the public a history with leftist elements, based on the pemuda narrative, brought another realization; none of *this* could have been possible without the youth of 1998.

THE END IN SIGHT

To return to a set of questions that I posed much earlier, how do we as scholars elect to see the patterns of change in political life? Is there a logical and sensical place where we look for signs of the political? Is there a natural boundary we do not look beyond? In Indonesia, as in many other societies, sight is increasingly construed as the space and the sense of the modern, a sentiment that naturalizes situated practices of cultural production, citizenship, and statecraft (Strassler 2010). Almost two decades after Reformasi, making the machinations and abuses of state power visible continues to be risky, exhilarating, and an important component of activist practice. The oral history and documentary projects and the greater body of youth images that began with Reformasi in 1998 suggest the interdependency that ideas about outward expression and democracy have in transitional periods of conflict and regime change. The recent interest generated in Indonesia and abroad by Joshua Oppenheimer's internationally acclaimed documentary film *The Act of Killing* (2012) and its sequel *The Look of Silence* (2014) has been unexpectedly productive for provoking national conversations about justice for the victims of 1965–1966. These films visually repackage human rights critiques that concerned activists and scholars in and of Indonesia have long argued: that Indonesia's communist past has left unsightly and traumatic traces on perpetrators and victims. But the transgressions of new ways of seeing and new sights to be seen are not the subject of this book; otherwise my use of Trouillot's argument about historical silences would be a gross misreading of justice; voicing is not reparation for silence, just as visibility in itself does not replace the conditions that produce invisibility. There is a danger today in paying *too much* attention to icons, symbols, and signs in politics, as if the aesthetic function had overtaken the political negotiations of modern life—as if these visual signs were proof of political change itself rather than the necessary and increasingly banal ingredients in a complex staging of the political. Visibility and public presence remain allegorical, elusive tracking devices of an even more elusive shift in power as the time of Reformasi is replaced by formal "democracy." We do not lack signs as much as we lack the ability to contain their contradictory logics, where bodies have become images and images have become signs of the political.

As Generation 98 gets enfolded into nationalist history as one more wave of youth politics, appropriate for the past but not the present, where there are more pressing and practical concerns than reconciliation and accountability for past injustices, Indonesians are impatient for the student movement to please leave already. Only when the pemuda leave will a new era be marked. In the aftermath of social and political experimentation, in the wake of the demonstration, we are left with the politics of memory, that uncertain terrain where interests, motives, actions, and radical ideas are debated, glorified, and forgotten. Such ephemera live on only in the happenstance archives that we as researchers are lucky enough to be exposed to. I have researched the most obvious and popular representations in the visual world of the student movement and public culture in order to craft an argument that shows the meeting point of the political, the popular, and the historical. The image world of politics, glossed as aesthetics or style, is not merely an accessory to political action; as I have argued here, in the increasingly globalized and mediatized state of contemporary urban politics in Jakarta, images have the power to constitute new identifications and alter political consciousness. Images of youth have enabled disturbing histories to "talk back" to the center, as their re-presentation overloads the nervous system of politics with their mimetic excess, causing meaning to tremble, to vibrate nervously with other possible meanings (Stewart 1996). Witness the fleeting "communist" scenes in the film *Gie* and the ease with which activists inhabit contemporary pemuda identity by sporting the insignia of the global left on their bodies. But such tremors in meaning, particularly the connections that Generation 98 has built to Indonesia's silenced histories, are frequently disciplined before they are fully resolved. The politics of consumption as well as the self-historicizing acts of contemporary youth speak out of pemuda nostalgia's forked tongue; they remind us that commodified experiences are productive, crude, and troubling affects for scholars of politics to consider. If we as scholars wish to analyze the pact between cultural practice, historiography, and ideology, the task is nothing less than learning to examine the fractures within the cultural objects of everyday life that render that pact visible.

Style

Red, yellow, black
ᴴnationalist sentiments

Activists = rebellious troublemakers

Activist success relies on reproducibility that
could be marketed to consumption culture

Reformasi began in 1998 ⇒ greater visibility in
resistance politics

Political life was ~~ready~~ material & visible

T-shirts, jeans, bandanas, bamboo stalks

Pemuda identity: elevated status in society & relation to
the street

Yellow Uni jackets good for photos

T-shirts with Che, Marx, Lenin, political t-shirt

The Street is a political space

Consumption of the revolution

Gie, Chinese revolutionary; campus activist, well known
critic of PRI & Soekarno administration in the 1960s

Chapter 4 | VIOLENCE

Galuh, the activist who told me the following story, might have been trying to impress me with his bold plan to strike at the heart of Jakarta.[1]

> I will tell you a story that you won't believe. It is just a story, if you choose to believe it. The most unimaginable thing that I did [with X] that unknowingly the PRD were doing too![2] At one point we formed the B-52 parabombers [sic], because we had reached a point of desperation. What could we do? This was at a time when the state was really coming down hard on us. So we decided to broaden our networks and we were serious about learning "terrorist" techniques. We contacted the IRA—and an IRA member flew here to train us—how to organize, how to set up targets, how to make bombs. At that time *this* building [Plaza Senayan][3] was one of the targets. We were going to set it up there, in that corner [of the second floor]. We had even selected our main target, the Jakarta Stock Exchange. After all that feverish planning, without our knowledge, the PRD had the same idea. Except they had accidentally set off the bomb when they were in their planning stage. This was in a hotel room.[4] And that was it, that was the end. We immediately packed up and abandoned all plans. We knew it was over. But we were ready to have brought down the symbols of capitalism and the government institutions. So the documents we had from that time are gone, on purpose, or were seized. But then, May happened, and that changed everything.

This was by far the most spectacularly violent story about student militancy that Galuh told me. On another occasion he had proudly recounted how he organized a surge of thousands of rakyat demonstrators to overwhelm and attack the unwitting police at a demo site. We were at a fancy mall in South Jakarta, surrounded by upper- and middle-class mall visitors, and I was as usual buying him a coffee. Galuh had a reputation among his friends as a shrewd political strategist, and he liked to talk about his personal highlights from his student movement days. I had heard other activists claim that they had received training from leftist and dissident comrades in nearby conflict zones, such as the Southern Philippines, but Galuh was reaching for the stars with the startling detail about the Irish Republican Army representative. It was an account so fantastical that it could very well have been true. Fortunately for him, nothing happened. His plan was marred by a series of coincidences and near misses (the Tanah Tinggi incident) that stopped him in his tracks.

As an activist of the 1990s, Galuh had experienced the full spectrum of late New Order repression, from arrest, trial, and imprisonment to beatings on the street, but as his story reveals, such repression did not quash the movement. Student activists in the late 1990s were eager, even desperate, to learn new political techniques modeled on the romanticism of other student uprisings, armed movements, and rebel forces. The mass demonstrations of 1998–2000 became a laboratory for developing demo techniques that stayed in use for a decade. As activists became more adept at demonstrations, they learned to protect themselves better. They concealed sticks and stones and made crude weapons such as Molotov cocktails; they brought water and toothpaste to keep out the teargas; they designated medics for each demo; they discouraged the army from making the first hit by putting strong men and daring women in the front lines; and they engaged frequently in verbal provocations and bentrok (physical clashes with the police and army). As I shall show, such techniques promoted self-defense among students, but they also encouraged an unprecedented level of commitment to experiencing and partaking in violence. Scholars have identified this shift as the reactive radicalization of student groups in an antimilitary and antiauthoritarian climate (Wimhofer 2001) but have not explained how moral subjects such as activists came to understand violence as a path toward justice and identity-formation. For student activists in Indonesia, violence always took place in a political and state context, but violence also enabled self-rationalizing acts. The student movement's complex relationship to violence forces us to reconsider the accepted societal discourse of students as beacons of nationalist, middle-class morality, an image that is reified by the self-description of the movement as a "moral movement" (gerakan moral) and students as a "moral force" (Aspinall 2005). How do we situate student techniques of violent resistance within the dominant framework of the nonviolent and moral student movement? When is violence ever not violence?

Galuh's boastful stories affirm violence to be an essential part of the student movement's imagination and internal history, yet counterviolence is one of the least studied and most often denied aspects of Indonesian activism, due to the pervasiveness of the "moral force" argument. In my analysis of the visual culture of the movement (see chapter 3), I found small reminders of how violence bound together memories of the movement; the iconography and memorabilia of Reformasi featured images of student-thrown Molotov cocktails as well as of students felled by the army. Student movement literature (including memoirs, media reports, and human rights reports), as well as scholarly work, tends to emphasize the illegitimate state repression students suffered and the "moral" and nonviolent character of student groups, which extends more generally to the ethical landscape of civil society (see Aspinall 2012; Hadikoemoro 1999; Human Rights Watch 2003a; Sulistyo 2002; Widjojo et al. 1999). However, comprehensive accounts of student resistance contain the thorny problem of "spontaneous" counterviolence and the destruction of property, which continues to mark inflammatory demonstrations today. In the eighteen months of fieldwork that I conducted between 2003 and 2005, student counterviolence appeared on the news regularly as a political sideshow to larger issues such as fuel price hikes or the sale of national assets, yet the phenomenon did not elicit concern as a sign of political conflict or of a social rift between students and others. Rather, student counterviolence appeared and disappeared quickly in news cycles without provoking analysis or comment. The practice of summarily showcasing and dismissing student protest violence over the course of a decade since Reformasi has naturalized student counterviolence into a predictable and risible feature of the democratic political landscape. Before I move on to a discussion of student counterviolence, I must emphasize at this point that counterviolence is not simply institutionalized cultural notions of "disproportionate revenge" (Hinton 2004). Counterviolence arose in response to what students perceived as the unpleasant repercussions and impressions made by national politics upon the grassroots. Counterviolence was the accumulation of individual responses to the student movement's need for consolidating group identity, self-defense, and moral recalibration.

In one of the few published studies of Indonesian student movement violence, Georgia Wimhofer writes uneasily about the lack of public discussion in Indonesia about the differences between "self-defense, counter-violence or active violent action" by students. Without providing any detail about whether differences exist between those three categories, Wimhofer attributes the growing tendency toward violence in the Reform era as a "weakness" and sign of New Order machinations generating internal conflict within the movement (2001: 178–179). The most common views of student counterviolence are to frame it as apolitical and natural reactions of pure feeling (emosi); the vestiges of *tawuran* practices;[5] a stand-in for elite intervention; or other undefined and imprecise causes. Such explanations summarize the extent to which Indonesian studies is dominated by two registers of violence: either "horizontal violence"—that is, violence with racial, ethnic, or religious dimensions conducted by the grassroots "independently" of the state—or top-down structural violence, focused on state interventions and elite interests (Munir 2001; Slater 2010; Winters 2011; van Klinken et al 2009). I find a more productive avenue of thought in scholarship that begins with the premise of inherently diverse "cultures of democracy" in the global South (Appadurai 2007; Chakrabarty 2007; Gaonkar 2007; Lomnitz 2007), and with studies of vigilante justice and spectacular violence in Latin America (Goldstein 2004; Han 2012). The Latin American cases yield insights into how new democracies that arose from "People Power" deal with the unevenness of social worlds that have been broken and remade in neoliberalized, postcrisis, and postdictatorship contexts; taken as a whole, these authors propose a framework for viewing the moral economy of violence in democracies as founding, constitutive, and maintaining structures of democracy for the grassroots. It is not my view that student violence deserves special attention because it is any more violent or concerning than other forms of violence. In fact, my fieldwork experience was heavily weighed toward encountering stories about students and rakyat as victims of state violence. Still, there are dissident stories from a range of activist groups about their victories in the battlefield—about the aura of defiance, suspicion, and encounter that defined the times and that were displayed as proof of how student activism and national politics were mutually imbricated.

We should ask here: what does student counterviolence operationalize? Student counterviolence must be examined for its functions as an extrainstitutional mechanism of popular democracy and moral responsiveness to suffering generated by the failures of the state. It must also be examined as the point of intervention by the state upon its unruly subjects. In order to once again surround violence with context, I propose that we take seriously the naming of counterviolence as such. The prefix transforms the meaning of counterviolence into a dynamic and reactive thing that belongs properly to the Reformasi era; for it breaks down the totality of state violence and pairs it with the micropolitics of student insurgency. Counterviolence is the narrowed effort by activists and demonstrators to respond to structural state violence with a comparable political vocabulary of force, disruption, and power, while solidifying the moral differences between the state and its victims.

I take up the problem of violence by and against students in this chapter to answer the following questions: How and why were students violent? Why is student counterviolence so troubling to think about? How did Indonesia's transition to democracy create generalized conditions of violence that implicated activists? My purpose in this chapter is to retrieve the meaningful and strategic dimensions of student violence, to enliven their political context once again. It is to offer a historical corrective so that student narratives about violence and counterviolence achieve the political symmetry that activists attempt when they "fight back" against the state. It is to count the epistemological violence discounted by activists and scholars alike when they dismiss students as authors of political violence. And last, it is to show that the politics of morality that inform such intensely identitarian movements such as student movements are complex and contingent moralities that draw on vernacular and temporally fragile understandings of justice and right. Pandey offers such a possibility of reframing violence when he describes the "routinization of violence" as "not only in the unashamed display of spectacular and brutal acts of aggression, nor yet in the mundane, banal, everyday exercise of power over women and children, politically disadvantaged communities, and the poor . . . [but] also in the construction and naturalization of particular categories of thought, in history and in politics" (2006: 15). At the end of the New Order, state violence was an overwhelmingly "continuous" category (Wessel 2001) that prevailed over other narratives of violence. Because student counterviolence could not be defined as political violence in Indonesia, the political repercussions of that limitation can be felt even today.

Galuh said, "May changed everything." May 1998 was the month of deadly riots, the shooting of students, and the fall of Suharto. May 1998 turned routine violence into a series of events and tragedies that transformed how student movement history was told. There was only before May and after May. Galuh's statement is common among student activists, but it elides the steady leaps of violent confrontation and demonstration by activists against the regime even before the regime ended. Most students in the mid-1990s used nonviolent methods such as hunger strikes and peaceful assemblies to protest the Suharto regime, but once demonstrations gained momentum in late 1997, student groups became increasingly vested in techniques of self-defense and militancy (Lee 2011). In 1997, 154 aksi were noted, with an increased rate of bentrok and arrests per demonstration. Police were increasingly prone to injury in these clashes with student activists. By 1998, the rate of demonstrations numbered in the hundreds for each month, with 530 aksi in May alone.[6] Direct action had become the standard for most student groups. With the almost daily occurrence of demonstrations by late 1997 and throughout 1998, it seemed highly likely that incidents of violence involving student activists would take place. Outbursts of physical violence between police and students (*bentrokan*, the noun form of *bentrok*, to clash) appeared as the natural outcome of the emosi (emotions) of the massa.[7] When clashes happened, sympathetic observers and demonstrators insisted that it was the work of an agent provocateur, a state agent in disguise who had infiltrated the demonstration to induce violence.[8] Student activists believed that provocateurs were provoking the massa, but student activists were also strengthening their ranks by installing the most daring students in the front lines to face off with the police. When students were killed or beaten in action, these "tragedies" (*tragedi*) would spur the next set of solidarity demonstrations in other cities, other campuses.[9]

KORBAN, THE VICTIM

When violence is narrativized by activists, they participate in a wider discourse that positions the rakyat as victims. The student movement's own narrative of violence is anchored by stories of student sacrifice and martyrdom in the various Reformasi-era "Tragedies" spawned by state violence. According to activists, the New Order state has time and again unleashed violence against the rakyat to achieve its own ends. Such violence designates the victim (*korban*) as a special person, a hero and a bodily representative of the people's suffering. *Korban* is the Indonesian word for "victim" and is etymologically linked to *qurban* or *qorban*, the Urdu-Persian, Arabic, and Hebrew words for a ritual offering and divine sacrifice. The everyday use of the word korban does not necessarily convey those religious roots, for a korban is not automatically a martyr or a vehicle for divine appeasement. Instead, a korban in the Indonesian context is an innocent who becomes collateral damage and maintains a direct causal link to the originating accident, fraud, disaster, or violence. The Reformasi korban became a politically expedient category for reminding others of the origin of injustice. As Danny Hoffman has written of the presentation of maimed survivors of political violence in Sierra Leone, the bodily existence of the victim becomes a physical remainder of political violence and a form of currency (2011). The korban circulates in the aftermath of political violence as survivor *and* victim. In post-Suharto Indonesia, korban became an expansive political category that included all innocents touched by, refracted, and brought together by state violence. Katherine McGregor's (2009) study of

Reformasi-driven reconciliation efforts between the progressive youth wing of the Islamic organization Nadhlatul Ulama and the stigmatized "communist" victims of 1965–1966 shows how challenging political projects mobilized korban rhetoric to emphasize the humanity of victims. Survivors of past incidents of state violence formed victims' groups, or *kelompok korban*, whose political agendas concerned retributive justice for the state violence committed against them. Mothers and fathers of victims became activist korban themselves, seeking accountability from the authorities until their own deaths precluded justice. And students who witnessed violence or felt the brush of violence against their friends and comrades contracted an understanding of victimhood as a collective suffering, especially in the wake of the Tragedi Trisakti (May 12, 1998), Tragedi Semanggi I and II (November 13, 1998; September 24, 1999), as well as the kidnappings and forced disappearance of activists (late 1997 to mid-1998) that claimed student lives. *Those* events happened to them, and *similar* things had happened to others. Hence they identified with past victims of state violence, such as those known collectively as the Korban 65 and the Korban Tanjung Priok, even though the torture, killings, and continued disenfranchisement of the alleged communists of 1965–1966 and the Muslim activists of Tanjung Priok in 1987 expressed very different scales of national and ideological victimization.

However, McGregor's work reminds us that the fluidity of the korban category can also lead to unexpected results, as in the case of older Nadhlatul Ulama members claiming absolution for their past by stating that under the New Order, "we are all victims" (2009: 216). What follows is an exposition of how victimhood became an inclusive political category, based on the narratives of violence that I collected from activists themselves, and from various electronic and print media that repeated the testimonies of victims, their families, and the surviving comrades who continue to advocate for investigations into human rights abuses by the Indonesian state. In the next section, which highlights student experiences of state violence, my analysis provides a way to reconcile the irreproachable figure of the korban created by Reformasi testimonies of victimhood with the more militant and retaliatory ends to which the activists of Generation 98 asserted their fight back against the state. The first steps toward creating an inclusive pattern of state violence that incorporates victims into a network of victims begin with a process that Dominick La Capra (cited in Drexler 2008: 11) calls working through trauma, transforming it from a violation of innocence into a political awakening of the dissident against the state. It is only then that violence begets a politics of "self-determination" (de Vries and Weber 1997).

Student activists cite their first severe beatings as their moments of radicalization.[10] At first, many student activists from middle-class and urban backgrounds had only an intellectual understanding of the rakyat's suffering, but being beaten and violated by state security forces at demonstrations created another means for identification. Mass arrests were often bloody and violent, as riot police deployed rubber bullets, truncheons, and water cannons and routinely gave out beatings. Women were not precluded from such violence. Women activists suffered sexual assault, rubber bullets fired at close range, and physical beatings in the demo field.[11] Young men and women learned to anticipate becoming targets of the security forces in the demo field rather than being spared physical assault because of their social status as university students. Their physical suffering gave access to another kind of consciousness—an experiential, bodily awareness of how the rakyat felt and suffered. A feeling of commonality arose between student and rakyat based on moral and sympathetic terms—from the state of victimhood, of being korban. As the rakyat suffered, so too did students. The image of student victims of state violence received attention in art, film, photography, and other venues of Reformasi-era public culture, as emblematic images of New Order brutality and student perseverance (Strassler 2005).

The mark of violence became an imprinting of an invaluable and essential knowledge about the activist self and the corrupt state. The human-rights-inflected terms of victim (*korban*) and perpetrator (*pelaku*) ascribe different moral positions to these two relational positions, which map neatly onto the relation between the rakyat and the state. Students learned that suffering created solidarity. It radicalized people. While the violence itself was arbitrarily dispensed, the young victims knew why they were experiencing violence. The grotesque physical assaults and traumas were meant to awaken their revolutionary spirit and identification with the rakyat. Their initial reaction of pain and bewilderment turned into an energizing hatred against the police and the military and emboldened students to resist more aggressively in the coming days. They became even more determined to fight injustice, through physical means if necessary. The encompassing perspective of solidarity with the rakyat enabled activists to incorporate the experiences of others into their own experiences of injustice and victimhood. I watched them sing in English the words "We shall overcome." With one important exception, in the case of the kidnapped activist Iblis, whose trauma narrative remained too visceral to be incorporated, these consciousness [kesadaran] tales positioned students as victims able to utilize victimhood and wield a moral violence in pursuit of justice, while maintaining that the state was always the true perpetrator of violence.

ABDUCTION AND DISAPPEARANCE: STUDENT EXPERIENCES OF VICTIMHOOD

Under Suharto, student activists suffered two major periods of increased surveillance and arbitrary detention, between 1996 and 1998.[12] In the aftermath of the PDI incident of July 27, 1996, and the Tanah Tinggi bomb explosion in January 1998, students were made scapegoats over an outbreak of social unrest in Jakarta, and many were forced to go underground. The New Order regime relied again on the charge of "latent communism" to demonize student activists, naming them as un-Indonesian agents and mindless proxies for elite interests. Activists fled Jakarta and sought sanctuary among workers and villagers with whom they had developed strong bonds in their advocacy work. In other towns and cities, sympathetic individuals from civil society and religious institutions provided shelter to those on the run.[13] The army indicated that there would be no mercy for the activists once they were hunted down. Often using one activist to gain information on the whereabouts of another, the army kidnapped and tortured activists to force them to confess to the bogus charge of their communist associations. The military's use of abduction, detention, and disappearance expanded in March 1998, in the restive months leading up to Suharto's resignation. Tim Mawar, the infamous special forces' "Rose Team," under the command of Suharto's son-in-law Prabowo, was in charge of the abduction of dozens of activists in Jakarta and other cities in that time period. To this day, the bodies of thirteen of the abducted activists have never been found.[14] Nezar Patria, a survivor of abduction and torture in March 1998 by the Rose Team, experienced all of the aforementioned techniques of intimidation and torture. Despite not knowing the precise address of Location "X," where he and other activists were held and "processed," Nezar guessed from the distance he was made to walk, the sounds of boots and vehicles and the yelling of male voices that he was at a well-maintained military facility. From the proximity of his cell, he could hear and recognize the voices and screams of his friends undergoing similar cycles of combined torture and interrogation. In between sessions, Nezar was chained to a camp bed and occasionally allowed to eat and go to the bathroom. Like the other activists, Nezar was interrogated about the whereabouts of his comrades at large, his own political activities, and alleged connections to elite figures. Of the torture itself, he wrote:

> All night long until dawn, we were electrocuted and terrorized with very shrill alarm sounds (that sounded like car alarms). The air conditioning was on high, until my half-naked body shook. Then an officer came to inspect my body closely (he seemed like a medic) and in low tones I could

hear him forbid them from electrocuting my stomach and chest area. Then my comrades and I were dressed again in our long pants. We were unable to sleep until the morning, when the guards changed shifts. Because our eyes were blindfolded we lost all sense of time. The new officer on duty repeated the same questions as the previous team. We experienced continuous torture all day.[15]

The activists were held from one to six weeks at Location X and then transferred to or dumped at local and out-of-town police stations. A few activists were further detained by the police for up to three months on subversion charges. On their release from Location X, the activists were warned by their abductors to keep silent. By June 1998 Suharto had fallen, and a few of the activists broke the silence and released lengthy statements to the National Commission for Human Rights detailing the torture the Rose Team had inflicted upon them, including murder threats, beatings, electrocution, verbal abuse, prolonged submersion under water, and being forced to lie naked on blocks of ice.[16] The aftermath of the orchestrated May Riots, the exposure of the Rose Team's brutality, and the various cases of korban that came to light shocked the nation into turning against the military. Forced disappearances of students were especially haunting, given the moral status of students. Students generated feelings of protectiveness and pride over their youthful idealism and inexperience, and Generation 98 appeared simultaneously to be "young heroes," as Saya Shiraishi referred to elementary school children, and Reformasi heroes. The catalytic experience of *korban penculikan* (kidnap victims) and the inclusiveness of the category of korban (victim) drew together supporters and survivors across generations and politics into a constellation of victimhood that positioned the rakyat as repeated recipients of state violence.

IBLIS: A VICTIM'S TESTIMONY

I met most of the activists I came to know at a viewing of the film *Imagining Argentina* held by the National Commission for Human Rights on March 26, 2004.[17] *Imagining Argentina* is a fictionalized treatment of Argentina's dirty war in the late 1970s to early 1980s, during which tens of thousands of men and women who resisted Jorge Rafael Videla's military dictatorship were tortured and disappeared. The film was a touching tribute to the sacrifice and victimhood of disappeared Argentinian youth, who, like the Indonesian youth of Reformasi, were university students whose lives took an irrevocable turn when they found themselves at the mercy of the state. The story line of the film provided a narrative model for the origins of Indonesia's postdictatorship democracy, borne out of a similarly cruel military regime and waves of youthful sacrifice.

More than one hundred former activists crowded the theater at the Haji Usmar Ismail Film Center in Kuningan, South Jakarta. Many had personal knowledge of kidnapped, tortured, and disappeared activists. Maruf, a journalist who met me at the door, introduced me to Raharjo Waluyo Djati, one of the PRD activists who was kidnapped by the Rose Team in 1998. He said, "Here's my boss at the Voice of Human Rights Radio. He was kidnapped too." The casual way this information was imparted was discordant, yet utterly normal. Activists who had been victims of political violence appeared to brush off their past experiences as something that had happened long ago, an act that belonged to a different epoch entirely. When they talked about being kidnapped or arrested, fear was barely present in their stories. Fear barely changed the timbre of their voices as they narrated terror. The strangeness of this distant quality emerged only in hindsight, when I thought about the ambivalence and trauma that former kidnap and torture victims could experience upon watching filmed scenes of systematic torture and brutality. Was it possible to witness such violence as merely fictional, historical, without in some way identifying with the torture victim or reliving the other's trauma as one's own? If violence was a binding experience, held in common by other victims of the state, then the odds were even greater that a traumatic reaction to violence would linger. Yet the only person who evinced an expected and visible response was a journalist named Iblis, who shook his head and said the film had given him the shivers. Iblis, whose name means "the Devil," was a Jakarta activist who had twice been kidnapped by the police in the 1990s.[18] Iblis's full name is Hendrik Dickson Sirait; he acquired his nickname during his student activist years in the left-wing organization Pijar (c. 1993–1997). While I never asked him directly why he had such a fearsome name, I heard varying explanations from older activists who had known him since the early 1990s. They claimed it was because of his long hair and fierce behavior, which made him look "like the devil." The description of his appearance did not sound unusual for most anti-Suharto activists inspired by antiestablishment pemuda styles. When I met Iblis during my fieldwork, there was nothing fearsome about him. In fact, he was a friendly and soft-spoken reporter who still covered student movement news for a radio program.

After the film screening of *Imagining Argentina*, he told me quietly that the film had made him break out into cold sweat. He said it had brought him back to his own scene of torture. For Iblis, his torture by intel (intelligence officers) was still traumatic to recall, and he was reluctant to speak to me about his kidnapping. Or perhaps I perceived his reaction this way because it stood in contrast to the lively manner with which other activists of Iblis's generation bracketed their past. I had seen other activists talk about their torture, tell me that they had been traumatized, and then return safely to the present moment. Unlike other former activists and kidnap victims, such as Andi Arief, Pius Lustrilanang,[19] Raharjo Waluyo Djati, Nezar Patria, Aan Rusdianto, or Mugi-yanto, who had mobilized their experiences of torture into a political narrative of state violence in documentaries, human rights activism, and NGO publications, Iblis lived with a much more bitter, and insurmountable, truth about suffering political violence. Val Daniel names the former a "therapeutic terror," where terror has been worked through, emitted, sequenced, and deindividu-ated, whereas Iblis showed signs of the "hyperindividuation" of terror: a terror that could not be shared no matter how many times one spoke about it (1996: 143–144). He was a korban whose victimhood remained too vivid in recollection, whose torture had not hardened into a political weapon that others could take up. I finally heard his story in a public discussion with kelompok korban at the National Commission for Human Rights where he was invited to speak as a victim of the New Order regime. His speech presents an exception to the student movement's recuperation of violence as the impetus for solidarity and political consciousness.

On June 28, 2004, the National Commission for Human Rights convened a discussion panel and film screening to commemorate the International Day of Solidarity for Victims of Torture (June 26). The invited police representative had not bothered to show up at the panel and was hastily replaced by a young filmmaker and a radio-journalist from the independent radio station 68H. Three films were screened for the event: *S21 La Machine de Mort Khmer Rouge* (S21 The Khmer Rouge's death machine), *Marsinah*, and *Djejak Darah* (Traces of blood). I arrived late to the cold, air-conditioned room on the ground floor of the National Commission for Human Rights building. An LCD projector projected the image of the Khmer Rouge's Tuol Sleng prison onto the bare cream walls. Things ran smoothly until the second film. Unfortunately, no one knew how to turn up the sound on the LCD player, and for a while we watched the muted film trailers for a gory horror flick and a historical drama about the anticolonial Acehnese heroine Cut Nya Dien. Finally the film *Marsinah* began, and the sound came alive again. Marsinah was a factory worker and union organizer from East Java who was murdered in 1993 by the army because of her labor activism. The director had opted to show the miscarriage of justice all the way through, from the initial discovery of Marsinah's mutilated body to the show trials and imprisonment of the eight factory personnel who had confessed under police torture to Marsinah's murder. The dark and dank of the detention cells resonated with the audience, who had survived their own stretch of unlawful detention and torture in the anticommunist purge of 1965–1966. The Korban 65 who were present threw out scathing comments at the film, offering correctives, as when a woman under interrogation refused to answer questions. "You'd be dead already," an old man behind me declared, addressing the film's protagonist directly.

After the film screening, the floor passed to Iblis, who was introduced as the survivor of two kidnappings. His name, "Devil," caused a wave of giggles from the audience, some of whom were university students who were too young to be familiar with his reputation as an activist from the 1990s. Iblis, in his halting, quiet way, said that he felt undeserving to be speaking, especially when there were so many elders in the audience whose experiences in 1965 had been far worse than his. He said:

> If I could speak, in the way of a testimonial, this is what I would say. About the atmosphere of pain and suffering experienced under the New Order regime. [His hands and voice shook.] I was in the student movement [gerakan mahasiswa] in the early 1990s. At that time, I was still acting out of solidarity and empathy, to join in the aksi because of Marsinah. *I had not experienced it directly.* At that time, Jakarta students, about fifty of us, had a demonstration (unjuk rasa) for Marsinah. When we had another demo in December 1993, there were two hundred of us from Java and Bali protesting against the Kedung Ombo case in front of parliament. Because of that aksi, twenty-one students were arrested and taken. We spent ten months in Salemba [jail]. That detention was officially registered [tercatat].
>
> After that, there was the 27 July Incident, where at the PDI-P headquarters, the party and its supporters were attacked, and there were riots where the masses were provoked [terjadi amuk massa]. The regime needed a scapegoat [kambing hitam]; this was where I came in. (Emphasis added.)

In the beginning, Iblis's voice and body betrayed his fear, even when he was recounting an impersonal chronology of abuses against others, namely Marsinah's murder, the displacement of Kedung Ombo villagers who resisted the dam project, and the PDI-P massa who were attacked by state security forces in the violent takeover of the party's headquarters in 1996. He only fully enters the story as a subject when he is chosen by the regime to be an innocent "scapegoat." Even though he was present as a demonstrator at the pro-Megawati rallies with other student activists, he had not, in his reckoning, committed a political action that called for punishment. Activists in the 1990s expected the state to mete out quick punishment on the streets or heavy-handed punishment in the courts using colonial-era *haatzaai artikelen* laws against them, not to terrorize them selectively.[20] As Iblis began to speak about his abduction and torture, his voice stopped trembling. The "enhanced interrogation techniques" he describes were plainly unlawful, inflicted by plainclothes security agents who did not bother to carry out an actual interrogation. As he described the conditions of his torture, his story took a turn toward the irrecuperable.

> On August 1, 1996, I was taken by three men in plainclothes, I was beaten, put in a car, and hooded. I didn't know where I was going, where I was being taken. I was afraid. I was thrown into a cell, and five unknown men came in and started beating me senseless, without saying anything or questioning me. I think that was a form of *shock therapy* [English in original] so that I would not resist. And after that I did relent.
>
> The torture was brutal, I was treated like an animal. I still feel it. What was the most outside of the limits of sanity for me, when it became surreal, was when at the height of the torture, I was in a room where next door, they were watching the Olympics badminton game, where Mia Audina [the Indonesian women's singles finalist] was playing Greece. I remember this so clearly, because I was being left alone then, and then when the break came on, a group of intel who had no authority to interrogate me came in to torture me in the eleven minutes of free time between sets. They did this for fun. One of their colleagues came to get them to say, "Hey, the match is starting again." They left the room, and I became aware of the brutality and the pleasure they got from torturing me.[21]

That was how he ended it, on a note of bleak awareness. "Torture perverts all dialogic" (Daniel 1996: 143). Iblis's reticence to speak was a rare exception to the general consensus among victims that they would work to transform the story of human rights abuse into a political resource for the student movement. Iblis deferred to the Korban 65, whose collective experience of execution, detention, torture, and continued deprivation under the New Order conveyed the magnitude of their political deviation, because he was aware that his story only highlighted the play of violence. As a scapegoat, Iblis was a replaceable unit. The intel (intelligence agents) he describes were equally captivated by two kinds of fun—torturing him and Indonesia's performance at the Olympic Games. Torture and entertainment were inseparable from one another and revealed the madness of a regime where national representations and everyday realities about "routine violence" openly contradicted each other. The torturer liked normal things like televised sports and might even turn out to be an avuncular figure whose normality appeared grotesque in the context of the torture chamber.[22] Iblis understood that as a sacrificial scapegoat for the Suharto regime, the violence he suffered had no relation to his individual politics. His function was to experience the wordless beatings until he submitted to power, or became *kapok*, the Indonesian word for submission and humbling by physical blows. Beyond that bodily capitulation, he admits to feeling traumatized and dehumanized. He does not testify about words exchanged or other lessons learned during the interrogation. Violence draws him to the past, instead of pushing him toward a future resolution.

Writing in the broader context of the Truth and Reconciliation project in South Africa, Nadine Gordimer describes the process of testimony as making common the history of political prisoners under the apartheid regime, which ultimately "creates the conditions for reflection" (1995a: 29). Gordimer's views on testimony merge the aims of the individual and the collective toward a transformative witnessing, and toward a nationalization and assimilation of the suffering of others. Testimonies and subsequent reflections on them allow the speakers to re-appear the conditions of their experiences of violence, in order to bridge the gap between victims and their listeners, who lack this crucial knowledge. "This is not so much an alternative history as a gathering-in of what was missing in South Africans' *perception* of their country, the actual context of their lives" (Gordimer 1995b: 22). The black holes in national perceptions are filled and made into public goods, achieved by the distribution of what once was the individual victim's injustice but had always belonged to the collective without their knowing it. Gordimer's optimism suggests that we cannot unsee or unfeel narratives of violence, once we find our national identities completed by them. Such accumulations of experience concretize the idea that a shared national history is an incomplete chronicle without the articulation of state violence, and indeed, the foundational pains of the people. As for Iblis, what national narrative and moral economy did he find for himself?

Iblis was candid about his fear, about his eventual submission to torture. As he critiqued the violence of the state and deferred to other "truer" victims, such as the Korban 65, Iblis did not attempt to narrate his experience as a triumphant rite of passage from ordinary student to enlightened activist. His story was not a testimony the way Gordimer destines such retellings and refashionings; in fact, he says at the beginning, "If I could speak . . . I would say this," and proceeds to reveal the arbitrariness of state violence, such that the torture of students could not be justified through the production of martyr or victim.

The inassimilable qualities of Iblis's experience gives hope to the idea that testimonies of violence can be disassociated from political strategy. Human rights groups working toward conflict resolution and state accountability through an examination of past state abuses begin from the same binary premise of perpetrator and victim but arrive at very different conclusions from those of the model of victimhood espoused by the student movement. The former model pushes for legal redress and acknowledgment of the suffering of the victims; the latter model effectively mobilized victimhood toward retaliation or preemptive violence. Student counterviolence worked effectively to publicize student issues for a few years, on the grounds of their moral standing as victims of the state and pioneers of democracy. Once the New Order began to fade from political discourse and competing explanations became available for students' proclivity for street violence and property destruction, students lost their claim to the legacy of counterviolence as political strategy.

STUDENT COUNTERVIOLENCE: SWEEPING OUT AGENTS OF THE STATE

A discourse of planned violence grew common in the student movement, splitting and uniting activist groups who were polarized by the issue of deploying violence. Groups that argued for more aggressive tactics felt justified by their revolutionary aims to strike while the iron was hot; nonviolent groups were adamant that their opposition to the military regime's violence would be voided if they also used violence. In the broader context of national politics, student violence was explained away as another sign of how "horizontal violence" really revealed elite conspiracies, thereby stripping students of agentive and autonomous thought. The unresolved Tanah Tinggi bomb is a case in point. In the tense months before Suharto's resignation on May 21, 1998, a homemade bomb accidentally detonated in a working-class apartment building in Tanah Tinggi, Jakarta (Human Rights Watch and Amnesty International 1998). On the grounds of possibly falsified "documents" found at the scene of the explosion, the police claimed that the Tanah Tinggi bomb explosion was linked to the PRD. The PRD leadership, already imprisoned by then for their alleged provocations in the July 27 Incident,[23] issued a statement from Cipinang Prison challenging these claims, even going so far as to allege that such incidents were common tactics the army used to frame its opponents. The head of the armed forces' Center for Information (Kepala Pusat Penerangan), Brigadier General A. Wahab Mokodongan, could neither confirm nor deny the PRD's absolute guilt. But he denied the charges that the army was behind the explosion in order to gain emergency powers ("Meledak di Kandang Sendiri" 1998). The Tanah Tinggi case provided the state with the convenient pretext to conduct an intense search-and-kidnap operation directed at activists driven underground. The special forces (Komando Pasukan Khusus), under the command of Suharto's son-in-law Prabowo, formed the secret Rose Team (Tim Mawar) to kidnap and torture dozens of activists, most of them young college students and PRD activists, into revealing their leaders' whereabouts and admitting to a prefabricated relationship to the outlawed PKI.

With such high-profile incidents, such as the PDI violence of the July 27 Incident of 1996 and the Tanah Tinggi bomb case, being used to persecute student activists, activists grew even more vigilant toward and convinced of the presence of infiltrators (intel or provokator) in their midst. Their memories were packed with bentrok (clashes with army or police), Molotovs, beatings, shootings, and kidnappings they endured and administered. Torture begat counter-torture, and kidnappings of students caused counter-kidnappings of army or police. Activists speaking of the mass demonstrations of 1998 and 1999 would shake their heads, saying edan appreciatively, to mean "wild," "mad"; that was to say, they were the ones who were wild and mad. The specters of the New Order state could be found in the various stories activists told me about infiltration, contamination, and provocation in demonstrations that turned violent for no apparent reason or, at least, outside the design of student activist strategists. However, the same informants also made it apparent that student counterviolence was a form of demo strategy, or what I have called manajemen aksi (action management) in chapter 2, and a means of fulfillment that expressed the student movement's internal logics of revenge, paranoia, and self-defense.

"Sweeping" (sapu bersih) was a term used by the army to describe how they cleansed society of communist elements.[24] Indonesians today continue to use the English term "sweeping" to refer to raids, arrests, and detentions, especially if they are mass arrests carried out in public.[25] The word carries a military and forceful connotation. In 1965–1966, the army swept through society using mass executions, imprisonment, and the dispossession of accused communists. In the mid-1990s, as the army tried to stir up anticommunist fears once again, they recycled the metaphor of maintaining a clean environment (bersih lingkungan), framing the nation as one's own neighborhood, requiring vigilance and care to sweep out the bad elements of latent communism (Honna 2001: 73). The term "bad elements" referred to student groups, such as the PRD and Forkot (City Forum), explicitly identifying them as part of a communist comeback.[26]

Instead of being swept away, Reformasi gave students and other groups the ability to "sweep" as well. The increased militancy of student groups and the rising level of bentrok (clashes) in the demos gave students the confidence to enact small-scale acts of vigilante justice. *Sweeping* was a common act of intimidation carried out by militant student groups, usually after a demo had already ended. Not content to go home after the dissolution of the demo, the riled-up activists climbed onto public buses and made antipolice or antiarmy statements to harass passengers who appeared to be members of the state security forces. They would "sweep" or physically remove these passengers off the buses and abuse these individual representatives of the army.[27] Such acts of ritual humiliation extended the verbal abuse that self-proclaimed "militant" (*militan*) activists would engage in during the demonstration in the hope of provoking a physical reaction from the police or army. Students felt justified in *sweeping* on public buses out of a sense of historical debt, for during the New Order soldiers rode the buses for free and intimidated and even beat students who dared to mouth back to them.[28] Now students were the ones riding for free. By intimidating soldiers and police unfortunate enough to be caught alone, students were exerting their power in a new society, where democracy would justify violent acts of civil disobedience as well as the spectacular use of force.[29] Benny Juliawan describes how the time of Reformasi was marked by "freedom and chaos [that] seemed to arrive at the same time," thus creating "an atmosphere of invincibility and bravado among certain elements of society, such as students and factory workers," that pushed them to demonstrate anytime, anywhere (2011: 355). Juliawan's research on labor mass mobilization in the post-Suharto eras captures the trace of student activists' *sweeping* techniques in the bullying tactics of striking workers: in preparation for a general strike, workers on motorcycles would sweep through a factory belt en masse, banging on the gates of factory compounds and revving their engines to intimidate the guards and management into letting out their workers to join the march (362). Through a simple reversal, the time of *demokrasi* meant that the rakyat were now the rulers, and student activists, as representatives of the rakyat, could channel the sovereign power of the rakyat on and off the demo field. *Sweeping* had to take place in public spaces as a rule, so that witnesses and spectators could see the reversal of power in action. But more generally, *sweeping* was an opportunistic act of physical retaliation against manageable targets that student activists identified. In more private and student-dominated settings, retaliatory and preemptive acts of counterviolence occurred with frequency at the height of Reformasi. From late 1998 to the end of 1999, students felt the most vulnerable (because of volatile national politics and increased surveillance), victimized (from the numerous tragedies that had befallen them), and powerful (able to fight back and expanding their organizations into national organizations). Their political senses were heightened to the point of paranoia, a condition that manifested in student counterviolence directed against the hidden intel (informants) in their midst.

Abdul told me about his experience confronting intel in his organization.[30] Each example he gave ended with the statement "That was during the Habibie era," inserting a temporal bookmark (1998–1999) that linked national politics to the turmoil in the student movement.

> It happened four or five times! Finding intel among us. We kept one guy for a month. We moved him from place to place every night. In cars, driving around at night, with one person holding him down on each side. He was always surrounded by us in the car. And one girl, we kept for a week. We told her to call her mother to let her know she was fine, and to say some made-up story about church activities to explain why she wasn't coming home. But she was so distraught she had a kind of breakdown on the phone to her mother, and I had to hang up the phone.

Abdul's words give us a taste of the dark suspicion of the times, driven by, as Veena Das might say, the "perlocutionary force of rumor," when one expects the worst to happen and moreover expects the state to be behind it (2007: 134). Activists would drive at night in borrowed cars, gripping the accused between them so he or she could not escape, to a rented *sekretariat* (headquarters) or to kost (rented rooms) that served as detention center, safe house, and headquarters all at once. Things were grim if a middle-class and religious girl could be cornered as intel with links to the army. Abdul told me that he was the most understanding person in his group, so he would let the intel go. He even went out to buy sanitary napkins for the young woman they caught. But others wanted revenge, so if intel were caught, they beat them. Once they placed an intel in an empty barrel and kicked it about. Even when Abdul had been angry at an intel, he could not make himself abuse him physically. As he told it to me, it seemed that he couldn't stomach enacting violence himself, especially when the accused intel acted afraid or pitiful. But Abdul was one of the few dissenting voices of his group.

When intel (intelligence officers or recruited informants) were discovered by activists, they were kidnapped, tortured, beaten, and punished in brutal ways, mirroring the interrogation techniques perfected by the state.[31] The students who participated in *sweeping* or "arresting" intel constituted themselves as moral subjects enacting justice and punishment. Intel accusations and discoveries fueled the political intrigue within and between student groups, as the accusations unmasked intimates who turned out to be in the employ of the army or other state intelligence units. Such acts of betrayal prompted a terrible anger in those betrayed, for the intel were often student-age peers or members of the rakyat who had also participated in the bonding experiences of hard times and violence. Intel discoveries and accusations happened in various organizations and provoked a range of sweeping measures and surveillance counter-measures on the part of students. Activists were wary about trusting outsiders and newcomers, even if those outsiders were from other student groups. An underlying fear regarding the vulnerability of activist groups to infiltration could be found in stories about unmasking enemies in the early 1990s. Students who had covertly rented houses or rooms (kost) in inconspicuous residential areas to use as their safe houses and meeting places would be "exposed" by intel who would often turn out to be the ubiquitous food vendor hanging around late at night. In one story, the undercover police agent was the fried-rice (*nasi goreng*) vendor who served the students every day. Oka, the activist who told me this story, was both admiring and indignant, for the nasi goreng vendor took copious notes on their meetings, down to the details of their outfits each night, providing the police with details he could not deny. After being released from police interrogation, the students were disinvited from the residential neighborhood, for the residents (*warga*) did not want further trouble from "politicals." When members of the PRD were kidnapped by the military, they faced their informers, who gamely announced their deep knowledge of activist movements. A former Forum for Student Action for Reformasi and Democracy leader ruefully described the unbending loyalty of a junior activist who followed him everywhere he went during the tense month of the First Semanggi Tragedy (November 1998), ostensibly to safeguard him. What the senior activist took as bravery and intense dedication was later revealed as the junior activist's effort to gather intelligence on the movements of key student activists.[32]

The particular markers used to identify suspicious behavior that led to intel accusations were blurry. From the stories recounted to me, it appeared that intel accusations were leveled at individuals whose backgrounds were unexceptional. Intel arose from the ranks of students and rakyat whom students were trying to recruit for their struggle. For all the populist radicalism that student groups espoused, there was an element of class anxiety about the motivations of activists culled from the rakyat who were different from middle-class students, such as food vendors, preman, buskers, and street children, who made their living and learning on the street rather than in the university. In other cases, student activists of similar middle-class backgrounds were singled out as intel. Activists described the physical and emotional toll of the demos as all-consuming. They only saw suspicious signs in hindsight, such as the fact that one intel owned a cell phone when everybody else was still using pagers. Precisely because there was no way of knowing for sure whether or not someone was intel, students established certainty by extracting confessions.[33] The authenticating force of the confession pushed student activists toward acts of violence, as they became intent on obtaining a confession by any means. A young woman who expressed too much enthusiasm on joining a student organization was deemed unnaturally curious, so the group "kidnapped" her in the middle of the night. Because she was so small, she was bundled up in a bag and thrown into a woven grain sack (*karung*) to be interrogated. "Do you confess? Confess!" Her peers yelled at her repeatedly while she was imprisoned in the grain sack. There was no "interrogation" beyond that. In another more startling act of counterviolence, a poor vegetable vendor who sold his wares from a pushcart was accused of being intel and assaulted by a hysterical student activist whose family had experienced harassment by the army and who had become "stressed" (*stres*), or mentally unstable, as a result. The student slashed the vendor's cheek with a razor blade, screaming at him to confess. Adi called these acts "paranoid" as he described them to me, disapproving of the violence but also laughing at the absurdity of some of the intel accusations he had witnessed in his organization.[34] "Society is not healthy," said Prio, for he explained that students had absorbed and were reenacting the "sadism" of the state. If violence could mark the body in particular ways, as Jim Siegel and Joshua Barker have argued separately, the marks produced on different types of bodies lend themselves to different narrative structures (see Barker 2001; Siegel 2006). The activist, when beaten (*digebuk*) by *aparat*,[35] receives proof that he is in fact, an innocent. It is the moment of his radicalization because he knows who he must become: an activist fighting for justice. The thief, when beaten by a mob (*dikeroyok massa*), experiences the outraged morality of the *massa* that beats him; similarly, the intel beaten by students must confess his or her transgressions and outsider status.[36] Confession reclaims the individual into the dominant moral framework but also reaffirms the identity of those making the accusation. By forcing others to confess, regardless of the truth of the confession produced under duress, the student activist was proving that he or she was not intel.

Intel accusations fed the paranoia of activists that they were under harmful surveillance, yet their feelings of revenge were limited in scope. Beyond the beatings students administered, there was no question of killing the accused. Even if they captured intel, they knew that intel were evidence of a higher-placed power they could not confront. Unable to get at the real perpetrators in the shadows, student activists participated in counterviolence that directed their anxiety at objects and individuals associated with power and security (cars, public property, lampposts, guard posts, uniformed men). Striking a blow against the invulnerable body of the state felt possible when the representative of the state was a person or an object that could and would react to abuse. Student politics had faded to a large extent a decade later, and intel accusations no longer took place. To close the arc of violence and counterviolence, I end this chapter by analyzing a series of demonstrations and retaliatory violence by students in Jakarta a full decade after the fall of Suharto, in May and June 2008.[37] My use of the term "retaliatory violence" conveys the long-term and ongoing nature of a feud, where one act of violence is always a response to prior acts of violence by an other, thus becoming mutually contextualizing even as the political meanings of the feud are contested. During the two months of May and June, several irruptions of bentrok between students, demonstrators, and right-wing forces took place, giving rise to an escalating atmosphere of revenge and punishment for student "tragedies" and state abuses of power. My final analysis shows how the balance has finally broken in the state's favor, as symbolic and stylized student resistance gives way to the image of demonstrations as "anarchic" and incomprehensible disorder. The demise of morally sanctioned and politically empowering counterviolence can be pinpointed to the rise of the depoliticizing and all-encompassing term *anarki*.

THE DISCIPLINARY STATE RETURNS

In the decade after Reform, student activist politics and civil society groups waxed and waned. Indeed, as Indonesia settled into a democratized yet more contentious atmosphere of identitarian (religious, ethnic, classed) and decentralized politics, student-led resistance gained an anachronistic character that was confirmed by their perceived attachment to violent behavior, manifested in "anarchic demonstrations." As the number of demonstrators dwindled each subsequent year, student clashes with the state security forces took on a different significance. No longer merely signs of resistance and bravery against army or police brutality, these semiorchestrated clashes (bentrokan) expressed an attitude of struggle (*perlawanan*) to keep student politics alive. Students were intent on reviving their claim to popular politics through displays of spectacular violence in their demonstrations, and were vulnerable to accusations by the state and the public that students were now a reactionary and destructive influence on Indonesian democracy. Nowhere was the accusation more damning and effective than in the charge of *anarki*, the Indonesian loanword that painted a broad picture of angry youth, asocial behavior, and material destruction in the media (*Kamus Besar Bahasa Indonesia* 2001). The Department of Education's comprehensive dictionary defines *anarki* as "1. that without government, laws, regulations, or order; 2. Disorder (within a country)." It is the second meaning (*kacau* in Indonesian) that has come to define *anarki* in its present usage. While the word *anarki* was already in circulation during the New Order to describe unwanted threats to national stability, it was not yet widely associated with youth politics and demonstrations in particular. As Reformasi became a distant political past, I observed the sharp increase in the use of the phrase *demo anarkis* (anarchic demonstrations) by media and government officials to cast doubt on activist actions. Reform-era repertoires of student counterviolence met their symbolic end at this juncture of state control and semantic control. After a full decade of street politics, student activist demonstrations were forcefully reclassified as provocative spaces of unlawful disorder rather than the natural expression of feeling (unjuk rasa) of civil discontent.

Anarki signals the temporal moment when the nation-state is under threat by malicious forces, validating strict censure or even eradication of the threat. Anarki consists of recognizable acts of spectacular violence from the student movement's repertoire, notably disrupting traffic, *sweeping*, bentrok, tire-burning, and car-burning. While these student activist techniques were once a common sight during Reformasi, they were greeted with irritation a decade later. The following reactions from the public indicate that state-led descriptions of student violence as spontaneous and irrational anarki have hit their mark. A radio show featured the following comments from listeners: "I used to be a student activist too, but before we used to demonstrate peacefully, not destructive like this."[38] Another person lamented: "Why are students so stupid . . . they are digging their own graves. When you graduate from university there will be no company or society who will accept you. Wake up and reflect now . . . or you will regret it . . . the people don't like [you] and hate the way you protest."[39] Why was *anarki* such a convincing name for student actions in the post-Reformasi era? Why did it generate disapproval rather than outright fear, as more conventionally propagandistic New Order terms such as "latent communism" might have done? In brief, the public's belief that students were behaving anarchically was shadowed by another, older belief: that student actions were being instrumentalized at the behest of others. This shift in perception reflects a growing level of distrust toward mass movements and disillusionment toward political transparency. By focusing on forms of resemblance between student demonstrations and anarki, such as *sweeping*, destruction of property, and mass arrests, statist definitions pointed out how far students had drifted from the moral movement framework of peaceful protest. The more spectacular and retaliatory student demonstrations became, the more they resembled the state's definition of *anarki*.

A DECADE LATER: SWEEPING THE STREETS IN 2008

The so-called UNAS Tragedy of May 23, 2008, saw one hundred student arrests and hundreds of injuries resulting from police action against a student demonstration. One student allegedly died from injuries sustained during his arrest. The violent event was a lesser tragedy when compared to the scale and brutality of previous tragedies of 1998 and 1999 and so did not spur national sentiment. However, the UNAS Tragedy worked at the local level to mobilize student solidarity in Jakarta and escalated the antagonism between demonstrators and the state security forces. The day began innocuously enough, with different student demonstrations against fuel price hikes occurring simultaneously across the city. In West Jakarta, student demonstrators from Christian University Indonesia attempted a symbolic act of counterviolence against the state by *sweeping* a car that drove past their campus gates, as the car's red license plates marked it as a civil servant's vehicle. The police who were monitoring their demonstration intervened, but students ignored the police and clambered onto the roof of the car and began attacking its body. Jefri Silalahi, a representative from the demonstration, stated that until the government heard their demands, they would "flood the streets" and halt the flow of traffic. When asked by a reporter whether they were aware that their actions had upset the people, Jefri challenged the reporter by asserting that their actions were sympathetic to and consistent with the feelings of the rakyat. He said, "It's the price hikes that upset the people, we just want to show our support and help the people. Let's see who's stronger, the rakyat or the government."[40]

On the same day, across the city, a hundred students were arrested at UNAS in East Jakarta after police stormed the campus, charging the gates and firing teargas and rubber bullets at demonstrators who had fled inside the campus. The student demonstration to protest the fuel price hikes had not been noticeably violent, but once students and police began arguing, the students threw rocks and other small objects at the police. That "provocation" (*provokasi*) was justification enough for the police to raid the campus, confiscating illegal drugs and alcohol that allegedly belonged to the students. The one hundred arrested UNAS students were taken back to the station, while 150 more claimed injuries as a result of police action. The contraband material was then used to charge more than thirty students with drug charges, while others were inspected for "anarchic behavior" that the police cited as causing the violence in the first place. The university buildings sustained US$60,000 worth of damage, and three campus security guards who had tried to protect the students were injured. By the end of the night the mood in the city ran hot, as twenty-six more arrests took place at demonstrations across Jakarta, and an incident of bentrok between students and police broke out in front of Christian University Indonesia. Student representatives protested the heavy-handed police methods used to quell their nonviolent demonstrations. "Our comrades have been silenced one by one today when they were in the midst of protesting the fuel price increase. The arrests were also accompanied by acts of terror and violence," said Naftali Jarin, central committee secretary of the Indonesian Christian Students Movement (Semiono 2008).

The UNAS Tragedy caused small ripples of solidarity demonstrations to form at the South Jakarta police station and the National Commission for Human Rights, attended by parents of the arrested students and student supporters from UNAS and other campuses. Maftuh Fauzi (age twenty-seven), one of the wounded students who had initially been arrested, died following his release from jail. The hospital where Maftuh had been treated for a head trauma and headaches, RS Pertamina, released a statement that he had died from HIV-related complications. His peers disputed the hospital's damaging assessment and brought a charge of wrongful death to the National Commission for Human Rights (Saputra 2008). In the coming days, students continued to hold their fuel-price-related demonstrations and referred to the UNAS Tragedy by aggressively calling the police "killers."[41]

In this atmosphere of protest and increased police surveillance, police and student reactions to the lingering effects of the UNAS protest were filled with mutually conflicting statements about the presence of agent provocateurs (provokator) and acts of provocation (provokasi) in student demonstrations. On the day of the UNAS Tragedy, the projectile the students threw at police was fixed upon as the opening act of provocation (provokasi) that escalated a tense situation and gave the police justification for raiding the campus. By *being* provocative, students deserved what violent treatment they got. The term *provokator*, however, implies a political conspiracy driving the action. Official responses by police to anarki formalized the validity of the provokator explanation. A police spokesperson suggested a typology based on levels of purity to classify the student actions of 2008: "We've analyzed three types of student actions. There are the pure ones, those that have been infiltrated or manipulated, and the third, actions based on the orders of specific interests" (Sugiyarto 2008a). I take up the explanatory potential of the provokator to demonstrate why the mere suggestion of provokator by authority figures worked to disempower and depoliticize student demonstrations so effectively.

PROVOKATOR

When anarki happens, who is responsible? Not "you," not "I," but a third person: the agent provocateur (provokator).[42] The provokator, like the ninja or other shadowy figures linked to New Order methods of causing civil unrest, is the person who starts the physical violence by inciting the masses around him, acting as an ignition point and accelerant, before slipping away into the crowd.[43] Victims of violence in the student movement and in civil society believe in the provokator's presence as much as their detractors do. Anthropologist Elizabeth Drexler indicates the reasons for the pervasiveness of the term *provokator* in New Order political discourse. "Provocations and *provokator* are explanations; they do not need to be explained. They are a type of public secret at the same time that they are a public threat. *Provokator* functions as an explanatory placeholder for an indeterminate threat and as a means of evading accountability for violence" (2008: 170). Public secrets, of course, can never truly be verified. Thus provokator accusations and denials were abundant in the violent demonstrations of May and June 2008, which reinscribed New Order techniques for creating diversions and evading accountability for political violence. The insertion of the explanatory provokator figure as the true cause of anarki amplified the public's disaffection with student demonstrations in Jakarta. Rather than critiquing students' increased use of counterviolence, Indonesians who cannot accept that middle-class, educated students are committing anarki for political ends alight on the explanation that the provokator has infiltrated and is manipulating the demo.

The provokator explanation framed the discussions for what would become the most "anarchic" street demonstrations of the season. On June 24, an activists' alliance named the Gathering of Activists Across Generations (Temu Aktivis Lintas Generasi), shortened to Tali Geni (Rope of Fire), demonstrated against the fuel price hikes in front of parliament.[44] The alliance, as the name indicates, was formed by both current students and former students under the activists' cross-generational banner but led by senior activists rather than currently enrolled university students. This detail concerning former students is important because of the ensuing suspicions regarding the identity and motivations of the demonstrators, considered by media reports and the police to be suspect. When the demonstrators burned tires and tried to bring down the tall iron gates by force, the police deployed water cannons. A clash (bentrok) with the police forces ensued. Truckloads of police officers herded hundreds of demonstrators away from the parliament building. Undeterred, the massa walked on foot to the nearby Atma Jaya University, an important site in student movement history where several tragedies and battles were fought in 1998 and 1999. Three of the police trucks that had followed the demonstrators to Atma Jaya University suddenly turned on the Tali Geni demonstrators, as police began throwing rocks at them and firing teargas into the campus. The demonstrators tried to escape by forcing their way into the university but were turned back. Police and demonstrators continued to fight (bentrok), and the demonstrators were enraged when a police car drove toward them and ran a student over, breaking his leg. The student's body was thrown a few feet into the air by the speed and impact of the police car, which then immediately drove away. The independent news website Indymedia cited this incident as the reason students began *sweeping* all cars that passed through in retaliation, hoping to get their hands on a police car. Two police cars were forcibly taken over by activists who shook and overturned them, setting fire to them as other demonstrators yelled out their encouragement. By the end of the night, more police had arrived on the scene and arrested sixteen activists ("Aksi Menolak Kenaikan BBM, Aktivis Bentrok dengan Polisi" 2008).

Instead of understanding the June 24 Tali Geni demonstration as a series of linked escalations of police abuse and activist retaliations, beginning with the bentrok (clash) at the parliament gates and ending with the violence at Atma Jaya University, the mainstream media, the police, and the public fixed on the final explosive act of the cars burning. The demo had disintegrated into anarki, sparking accusations by police that provokator were the real authors of the violence. Moreover, it was becoming difficult to isolate students from nonstudents in this crowd (Purnon 2008). The melting away of student attributes recognizable through clothing styles, age, or demo behavior created an anonymous crowd that appeared as a violent mob. When Tali Geni organizers were arrested the next day, mainstream newspapers called the leaders of the demonstration provokator. The revelation that two of them had already graduated and had therefore lost their claim to their privileged student identities led the police to frame their involvement in the demonstration as evidence of infiltration by outside interests.

"Students are intellectuals. If they hold demonstrations to convey their aspirations, they will do so with conviction and dignity. Not with anarchic methods like this. The anarchic actions happened because of other interests at play," said the police HQ public relations division head, Inspector-General Abubakar Nataprawira in a press conference at the Metropolitan

Police Headquarters on Tuesday (24/6) night. However Abubakar was reluctant to say who was suspected of manipulating the students' demonstration. The police were investigating whom and what interests would take advantage of the action. "We are going forward based on healthy logic. Students are an educated, intellectual group, and would not possibly carry out such destructive actions. We will find out who is using them," Abubakar declared. (Sugiyarto 2008b)

Once the police exempted the category of "student" from the violence, they were free to search for provokator and conspirators. The chief of the National Intelligence Agency, Syamsir Siregar, went even further in naming a member of the House of Representatives as the *dalang*, or puppet master, behind the students' demonstrations. Siregar hinted that the named representative was only one link up the vertical chain of command and that his interrogation would expose a high-level antigovernment conspiracy ("Lanjutan Kasus Ferry" 2008). He urged the police to arrest the suspected politician as the mastermind of the anarki, but the speaker of the house, Agung Laksono, immediately rebutted his claim. In a strongly worded and sarcastic reply to Siregar, Laksono said, "Prove it if there are really elected representatives who are puppet masters. As far as I know, out of the 550 members of the People's Representative Assembly, there are no puppeteers. There are doctors, engineers, legal experts, entertainers, and artists" ("Hentikan Tudingan Dalang Demo" June 2008).

In a disciplinary move reminiscent of depoliticizing actions against earlier generations of students to "go back to campus," students were increasingly urged to focus on their education, graduate quickly, and be orderly (*tertib*) in their political conduct. The minister of communications and information assured the public that the right to demonstrate was an inherent part of democracy and would not be revoked by the government. Demonstrations were allowed, as long as they were not "anarchic." However, he also urged "nonstudents" to stay out of student demonstrations to avoid heating up the situation (Setiyawan 2008). The minister's statement presented a double bind for students—the state would continue to protect students' (limited) right to protest but in doing so would isolate them from other members of society. Former students and other youth could no longer claim protection under the umbrella of a protected political identity, rendering their behavior criminal acts of anarki and their presence evidence of their provokator status. To keep their post as saviors of the nation and their reputation as a moral force, students and former students who still wanted to assert their right to protest had to give up counterviolence in exchange for a largely symbolic and historical claim to pemuda identity.

Student demonstrations are disciplined through various means, from physical alterations to the urban landscape (as seen in chapter 2's discussion of renovations and enclosure of public spaces) to the neoliberal reform of higher education and the media's amplification of public disaffection with student interruptions of the pace of normal life. Since demonstrations are now thought of as no more than a symptom of violent disorder, rather than a critical and contingent response to the state, their efficacy is diminished. Student counterviolence has been evicted from Indonesia's lexicon of political action. Yet student counterviolence cannot be fully resolved by disciplinary techniques or shifts in explanatory frameworks that criminalize student actions. Post-Suharto regimes have failed to secure a system of accountability and transparency in Indonesia, further reinforcing the epistemological distance between korban and perpetrators, civil society and the state. As I have argued in this chapter, student counterviolence captures the full range of political expressions by disenfranchised subjects who identify the state as the true source of violence. Student acts of counterviolence are moral claims against state violence as well as enactments of self-arbitrated justice and self-defense. It is consistent with pemuda fever's love of nation that this moral code draws deeply on a darker history of pemuda sacrifice and violence in the name of the People. Fever and passion, grief and paranoia, witnessing and contagion, the Molotov and the cell phone; these political sentiments and weapons mingle and mix in symbolic lines of flight and in utopic wish-images of the future. Generation 98 forged the model for high-stakes student resistance, and far from expiring, student counterviolence sticks like a shadow to their image.

Chapter 5 | HOME

Where might the activist feel at home, if not on the street? Where does an activist spend most of his or her time? Where do activists dwell, rest, and repair? The answer lies in the kost (rented room, lodgings), the sekretariat (*sekret*, secretariat), the basekemp (base camp or organizational headquarters), and the emergency posko (*pos komando*, command post, or pos komunikasi, communications post). All are spaces attuned to activist temporality, from the pop-up posko and the shared workspace of the sekretariat to the tiny rented room, the kost. As spaces that are always temporary, makeshift, ephemeral, and grounded in contestations and subversions of authority, activist structures abound with the energy of *camping out* and *playing house*. These two modes of occupation foreground the translation of interior space into politically charged spaces that renew and instruct community. They are also, to borrow Susan Stewart's phrase, spaces of "intense socialization" that concretize the fraternal bonds and kin-like relations between senior and junior activists, comrades, boyfriends and girlfriends (1993: 167). My focus on the structures of "home" is intended as a companion piece to chapter 2, where I discuss how activists have come to be at home on the street since Reformasi. I analyze activist spaces and dwellings as an extension of the outside in and the inside out, blurring the boundaries of spatially bound sociality and intimacy. This chapter is therefore not about the demarcations of private life. It is an attempt to show the same disposition of occupation, adaptation, and collective solidarity at work in the spaces of both the street and the home. I examine where and how the activists of Generation 98 felt at home, made their homes, and occupied space in prolonged pursuit of their activism. Neither "domesticity" nor "interiority" are adequate terms to convey the spatial and romantic effects of these borrowed and rented spaces, where political bonds are forged through the idiom of friendship and unending talk and where sociality is predicated on a certain loosening of social norms and an aesthetic of joyful disorder. Activist dwellings break away from the conventional notion of home as a place of safety and return by opening up "home" to the contingencies and transience of youth.

In high contrast to the ordered natal home, activists practice "domiciliation" rather than domesticity. Domiciliation is the act of making one's address. A domicile can be a house, that is, a place to live, without necessarily becoming a home. I use the term "domiciliation" to call attention to two movements: the first is a displacement of origin from the natal home to a spatial arrangement (the kost or rented room) that reveals the flexibility and freedom of movement a young man or woman enjoys; the second refers to the act of worlding that activists undertake when they inhabit such spaces. Activist spaces are not commensurate replacements for the New Order family home, yet the interior spaces made by activists are no mere rest stops. They have enduring impacts for activist relations, for providing a set of common experiences for youth from different class backgrounds and from different parts of the archipelago, and as a reflection of activist youth subjectivity. Activist interiors organize the feeling of communitas into a generalized disposition and grant a sense of play to the more mundane and obligatory aspects of political life. It is the site of the nostalgic, for it is the site of belonging, even if the street and the demonstration take narrative precedence as the eventful origin of activist memories. Activist interiors offer a holistic presence of what Heidegger calls dwelling, and what I understand as the act of being and inhabiting sites that become the proper home for the work of rest, imagination, and play (Heidegger [1971] 2001a: 141–159). As Bachelard reminds us, dwellings shelter dreamers, and "all really inhabited space bears the essence of the notion of home" (1994 [1964]: 5). Activist interiors require illumination to reveal how and where dissident dreams respond to activist imaginaries, as well as bear trace effects of what others have termed the politics of (middle-class) domesticity. In so doing, we contend with the conditions and functions of interiority that challenge and refract the legacy of the New Order family.

PEMUDA DOMICILIATION

In Indonesia, *domisili* is the Dutch loanword used on official forms to refer to a legally recognized address. It is the chosen residence that the act of naming as residence authorizes, yet it is an unbound and anonymous place. *Domisili* allows for impermanence and mobile understandings of the self. This is a phase, and I can move often. Locality is as fragile as where one lays down one's body to sleep (Appadurai 2000). The bureaucratic and legal understanding of place properly describes the conditions most activists find themselves in: they stay somewhere rather than living there. It is the difference between saying "Saya tinggal di Cikini" (I live in Cikini) and "Aku ngekost di Cikini" (I rent a room in Cikini). Activist domisili can be as impersonal as a bedsit or as permanent as a large house rented on a two-year contract. Moreover, domisili is a place of business, even though a laxity over professional standards prevails; activists rent houses for their organizational headquarters, where the filing cabinets may hold papers as well as bedding that appears after hours for sleep or relaxation. Yet domiciliation also describes a right to place and a voluntary and agentive mode of inhabiting. We can understand domiciliation as a process of emplacement and transplantation without necessarily evoking the emotional and material ballast of taking root.

Derrida's use of "domiciliation" is instructive here in enabling us to think through a more stable understanding of activist spatial practices as linked. In *Archive Fever*, Derrida describes the archon's role as guardian of the archive, the one who gathers the contents and arranges the domicile of knowledge *under house arrest* and establishes the parameters of public access to the archive. "*Consignation* aims to coordinate a single corpus, in a system or a synchrony in which all the elements articulate the unity of an ideal configuration" (1998: 3). The archive can therefore be considered the resting place or holding cell for a certain political legacy, a system of mass assembly, a gathering of signs that travel together and become an assemblage. To extend the logic of the archive, the different types of activist spaces are consigned together in this chapter as a series that bespeaks the "ideal configuration" of antiauthoritarian community. In the case of the student activist, domiciliation links the cell of the prison to the camping / staging grounds of the emergency shelter (posko) and the rented room (in de kost). Home-making, when done in contrapuntal fashion to the middle-class household and gender roles, becomes a reflection of the activist's marginal position and exposure to forms of insecurity (Said 1994). Why and how might community be strengthened under such conditions of impermanent domiciliation? In the section "Playing House," I describe the hierarchy that governed the domestic sphere, the living conditions of the kost, and the New Order institutions that facilitated an opening for political awareness to grow out of the bonds of friendship. "Playing house" suggests that youth have always had one foot out the door yet are drawn back in when they are subjected to the pressures of institutionalized authority. In "Camping Out," the different camps and encampments of posko and basekemp are featured. I analyze the mobile function of the posko as a symbolic encampment that plants the flag of activist occupation in political and public space, and I end with the specter of authority that becomes uncomfortably present and potentially divisive in the "home" base of the basekemp.

Domicile contains a trace of guardianship that is difficult to dispel; it bears an origin point rather than a destination, a belonging to someplace or someone proper, even as we proclaim for its referent a physical location for the present-day self that domiciliation has produced intentionally. There are still the father, the home, and social class as anchors of youth identity. It is in this tension between youth-as-activist and the New Order youth-as-ward that we find the act of worlding so potent. The interior spaces of the kost and the basekemp effect a different temporality, one before-the-demo and after-the-demo. We imagine the activist, in enacting a domicile by choice, feeling at home on the street and remaining an activist even in times of play and pleasure. We imagine home and return as the day's end, the winding down of the demo's micropolitics. Politically dissident and radical leftist activists ventured far away from their natal homes, and activist spaces reinforced the distance between the agentive self and the inscribed self. Activists referred to their "live-in" practices of embedding themselves for months among factory workers, living with them according to their minimal lifestyles and wages in shabby (kumuh) dormitories as a form of "class suicide" (bunuh diri kelas), revealing university students' ambivalence about their origins and their socially engineered destinies. Live-in ruined their health, they joked, as they talked about the damage to their lungs from damp, to their digestive systems from eating bad food, and the bouts of typhus and dengue they endured.

Students who self-identify as distinctly apolitical subjects (as was par for the course on the depoliticized university campuses of the 1980s and 1990s) present a false contrast to the politicized activist, for their expressions of youth culture nonetheless bear traces of the nationalist imagining of youth as appropriate and ideal national subjects. Such a cultural disposition to the world was simultaneously cosmopolitan, invested in making middle-class spaces mobile, and engaged in transforming the operating logic of the domestic into the national. In Friction, Anna Tsing writes about the activities of the Mahasiswa Pecinta Alam (Nature Lovers Club) university student groups who take to the great outdoors to be at one with nature and to emphasize the consolidating power of nature trips in forming lifelong generational attachments (2004: 131–132). There, the mobile university enabled urban youth to encounter nature as sublime and to view rural subjects as traditional and nostalgic others. Camping was a natural activity for university students who saw the great outdoors as *national* space and who subscribed to universal notions of the environment as a site of wild and free frontiers. While Tsing's nature-loving youth were not political activists for causes that directly challenged state authority, nonetheless the modes of sociality that Mahasiswa Pecinta Alam members enacted were similar to the socialization techniques that activists used to recruit others to their cause. There was no contradiction between the intense sociality youth experienced in the leisure act of hiking in the wild and the indoctrination retreats that activists ran to induct new members into the radical project of secular-leftist nationalism. Both political and apolitical groups enable a "home away from home" as they experience "the possibilities of a new social and cultural world" through the peer group (126).

PLAYING HOUSE

When space becomes technology, that is, a technique for expressing lifeworlds shaped by urban and "*concentrated* modernity" (Mrázek 2009: 290) we start to view the home differently as a factory of social types, in this case, of middle-class and activist youth. There are additional ways that spatial configurations provide an intimate portrait of individual aspirations and desires. In chapter 2, I analyzed the public life and the performative aspects of the student movement's demo culture, where motion and occupation of public space signified the vitality of student movement politics. Here I examine the movement's place of rest—the interiors and structures of the student movement that activists build, inhabit, and ultimately depart from. The most commonly associated activist structures are those of the posko, sekretariat, and basekemp. Posko are an emergency shelter or designated location for supplies and volunteer forces put up in the event of a crisis or natural disaster; sekretariat are the buildings students use for work related to their organizations; and basekemp are the more informal headquarters that house the core members of an organization, combining the facilities of home and work. These three spatial arrangements elaborate activism's ideal political configuration of collective spaces governed by democratic friendship, yet the quintessential space that expresses the initial freedom of youth is far more ubiquitous a domain for students, the working classes, and white-collar workers: the kost (rented room). The kost is the first step that takes youth out of the family home and removes them from the habitus of middle-class domesticity. To understand the significance of this departure, we must first look at the domestic bliss the ideal New Order family experienced.

Saya Shiraishi's ethnography *Young Heroes* provides a snapshot of the structures of feeling that infused the New Order family home. As Shiraishi (1997) describes it, family was a space of coziness and familiarity exemplified by the sociality of the courtyard, the most inner sanctum of shared spaces. The New Order family enfolded fictive kin into relations that were woven into the deep interiority of the house. The ritual of antar-jemput (to send off and fetch home) ensured that family members were always embraced in a protective zone of control by being kept in sight. All this was contingent on the authority of the *bapak* (father) as patriarch and guarantor of security and comfort. While Shiraishi describes the bapak as mainly an absentee figure in the New Order family home, his authority was nonetheless pervasive and foundational, constituting an unspoken law unto the relations of domesticity that guaranteed the comfort of the family and indexed the hierarchical position of its dependents. The homology between home and nation-as-household was manifested in Suharto's sought-after presence at social events. Bapak Suharto was the ultimate father figure in this regard, giving blessings to those who shook his hand or bowed over it with appropriate reverence. Appearing in person at elite wedding receptions, state ceremonies, and occasional propaganda-generating trips to rural areas and the provinces, Suharto was an accessible dictator (see Calvino 2003) who distributed his personal touch through the New Order photographic souvenirs that families and businessmen displayed in their homes and offices of Suharto shaking their hands at these privately public events.

The Asian Crisis and Reformasi destabilized the relationship between state-led prosperity and paternalistic authority, inside and outside. In post–Asian Crisis Indonesia, middleclassness trembled under the assault of political and economic crises, stripping the family of the luxuries that had defined their experience of modernity. The middle-class reaction was to turn the house into a fortress, replete with guards, fences, and locks. Abidin Kusno observes the correspondence between threat perceptions and architectural changes to the built environment. In this regard, Chinese Indonesian and middle-class neighborhoods were the most likely to build guard posts and high fences and take other security measures to turn their neighborhoods into gated communities (Kusno 2010: 239). Lizzie van Leeuwen's ethnography of life in the middle-class suburbs of Jakarta before and after the Asian Crisis dwells on domestic anxieties and small interior signs of fracture under new regimes of austerity, political insecurity, and social crisis. In one poignant example of thinning class membranes, van Leeuwen writes about her Auntie Annie's crisis response as part of the logic of the emerging "New Poor." The need to have clean white tissues inside cars, offices, purses and in every corner of the house was a pervasive middle-class practice that revealed the fear of staining and contamination from the outside world. During krismon, tissues became a dear luxury item that housewives could not justify purchasing, even though they still felt their cultural and psychological necessity keenly. Thus Auntie Annie continued to display frilly tissue boxes in her house, albeit ones that stood empty (van Leeuwen 2011: 144–145).

The transgressions of youth who lived outside the home, especially those middle-class youth whose consumer habits and appearances met the standard for popular representations of student identity across Indonesia, must be seen in this context of rebellion against the middle-class home. Playing house and setting up camp required imagination, partially because middle-class youth living in the kost lacked housekeeping and bookkeeping skills. They would be most familiar with the domestic comforts of a household where *ibu* (mother) and the servants tended to their needs. If they went home periodically from their kost, their laundry would be washed and favorite foods cooked for them. Even after university, very few activists cooked their own meals. The posko, sekretariat, and basekemp appeared to be the antithesis of the New Order home. They were often chaotic, unclean, mixed-gender spaces, with the barest furnishings gleaned from donations. In these houses, no one loved to help ibu cook or clean. The only presence of an ibu was often a maid hired to clean and do laundry once a week, if the group could afford it. What binds students to one another is their shared mobility and their freedom from the hours that work and family life would have imposed on them. The energy of collective life is made nervous by the fact that activist community is contingent on their status as youth, and in the case of students, a particular category of modern, middle-class privilege. This contingency is reflected back in the posko, sekretariat, and basekemp. Despite the language of equality, fraternity, and solidarity that activist organizations proclaimed, the fragility of activist inhabitation revealed the conditions of their ambiguous social status as "children" (anak).

"IN DE KOST"

The narrative of the student movement of the 1990s traces its origins to the informal study groups that were formed in the 1980s. Barred from politics on campus with the 1978 implementation of the Campus Normalization Act, students organized themselves in underground study groups, which they described as smoke-filled and theory-minded associations. The study groups discussed national and local politics, the grievances of the rakyat, and leftist perspectives that were not taught on campus, and took turns honing their writing and debating skills. Occasionally they published journals. Some study groups took to radical literature, reading "works by Paolo Freire and Franz Fanon, Islamic radicals like Ali Shariati, the Frankfurt school, classical Marxism, liberation theology, and publications of radical groups in South Korea and the Philippines" (Aspinall 2005: 121). Former Democratic Indonesian Students Solidarity activist Nezar, who taught himself Gramsci, recalled the pleasure of debating with other study groups and showing off his theoretical skills by winning these debates.

Several of these study groups coalesced into activist organizations that moved toward more direct forms of action. By the early to mid-1990s, student groups had found more stable homes in rented sekretariat that were better suited for their organizational work. The sekretariat, housed in a simple one-story house (*rumah kontrakan*), shielded the students from the prying eyes of campus authorities or other students in the kost. It was here that the most intense discussions took place and activist materials (banned books, leaflets, and posters being made) were assembled. These off-campus spaces had the added advantage of having a reputation of student slovenliness. No one would automatically deduce that the young men milling about in each other's rooms were organizing underground politics, in addition to doing what all normal students did, that is, hanging out, singing songs, and reading books. Pijar in Jakarta, for example, hosted several foreign journalists who were beginning to cover the connection between dissident student politics and labor issues. Students also hosted representatives from other campuses across the country for national-level meetings or, more informally, visitors who were testing the waters of intergroup alliance. The kost contained the overflow from the sekretariat, as students opened up their rooms to house out-of-town guests. These encounters match the culture-clash stories that describe the journey of a country mouse to the big city, as the margins met the center of Jakarta's activist culture. An example: "You wouldn't believe how naive M. was. He had just arrived from Solo, and you know how in Jakarta everybody calls you *coy*.[1] After a few days of greeting everybody politely, M. said, 'Why is every Jakarta activist named Coy?'"[2] An appellation from Jakarta slang that displays a degree of relaxed informality, *coy* is usually used among young men and is best translated as the American vernacular "bro" or "dude," as in the phrases "Nyantai aja coy!" (Relax dude!) or, in agreement, "Yo'i coy" (That's right bro). Coy is also an actual name, hence the out-of-towner's confusion. "Relax dude!" aptly sums up the belligerent and subcultural affect of activists on and off Indonesia's elite campuses.

While students privilege a biography that traces the intellectual genealogy of their organizations,[3] such as the evolution from informal study groups to more sophisticated and formalized organizations, these are not the only structures to pay heed to. Their physical structures reveal a great deal about how student worldviews and practices functioned. For instance, to be a student, one often had to be a boarder. These two identities went hand in hand, especially for students from the *daerah* (provinces) who did not have relatives in the city. *Kost* comes from the Dutch *in de kost*. The Dutch loanword *kost* literally means the cost of something, or renting a room in a pension or hotel. Transmuted into Indonesian it has come to mean "room and board," or just "room," appearing in the dictionary without mention of its Dutch origins. The practice of students paying room and board arose with the founding of colonial institutes of higher education in Java in the early twentieth century. Previously, kost was associated with young, European white-collar workers stationed in the Indies who lived in hotels or pensions. Kost for indigenous Indonesian students had different arrangements. Either students of a specific ethnic group, for example the North Sumatrans, would board together in the same dormitory, or a student would board with a family already acculturated in Dutch ways.

Urban Java did not engender the sense of anomie that characterized the young, single, white-collar city-dwellers of twentieth-century Europe.[4] Benedict Anderson's analysis of the 1945 pemuda generation emphasizes the significance of the dormitory (asrama) to youth politics; it was not the pemuda's covert actions against the Dutch and the Japanese that defined the underground resistance movement but their assembly in shared spaces that provided the opportunity for talk, learning, and identity-formation (1972: 39). The three most prominent pemuda underground groups in revolutionary-era Jakarta met regularly in dorms (asrama) that provided the "institutional base" that shielded students from the demands of their families, where they could conduct the "intense and reasonably private discussions" that contributed to their feeling of solidarity (39). The Medical Faculty's dormitory at Prapatan No. 10, which served a group of elite, Dutch-speaking students, was an important gathering place for the Western-oriented pemuda who were wary of collaboration with the Japanese occupying forces. Lecture series and gatherings were held at Prapatan No. 10 to prepare the younger generation of Indonesians for the nationalist struggle (41–44). These asrama proved to be enduring addresses in the nationalist memory. The asrama at Menteng 31, where older nationalists and pemuda gathered, became the site of the present Museum of Struggle (Gedung Djoang).[5]

Unlike the pre-Independence-era students, students in the 1990s did not tend to live in university housing or asrama that pooled all of them together in one building. Instead, they lived in kos-kosan.[6] In its current incarnation, kost (kos-kosan in the plural), refers to a boardinghouse primarily for students, a rented house (rumah kontrakan / rumah petak), or a single rented room. The practice of kost, that is, youth living independently of family, in proximity with other youth, is no longer associated with the privileged few. With the growth of universities from the 1970s to the present, the number of kost has increased as well.[7] The industrialization of the economy and the intensification of agriculture enabled enough capital accumulation by rural and working-class families for them to send their sons and daughters to university. Those who live in kost have diverse backgrounds, including students from previously exclusive communities, such as students who were primarily educated in religious institutions (Islamic boarding schools / pesantren or Catholic seminaries). S., who came from a pesantren background in East Java, first attended university in Yogyakarta and then moved to Jakarta in the mid-1990s to attend the Catholic Driyarkara School of Philosophy. The tale of his trajectory was punctuated with his recollection of how cheap his first kost was. In Yogyakarta you could live and eat for a whole year for under 300,000 rupiah, and a simple meal only cost 500 rupiah.[8] S. could pay his living expenses with the money he earned writing articles and editorials for newspapers. Many students lived in standard "women only" or "men only" kos-kosan, often single-family residences that had extra rooms let out to renters (see fig. 5.1). These rooms were usually located in the back of the house or in a separate building away from the main house. In university areas, such as the lanes and neighborhoods near the UI campus in Depok, single-sex boardinghouses were common, with shared bathrooms and some laundry or cleaning services included.[9]

The services provided indicated the class origins of the kost's clientele. While fairly basic in appearance and upkeep, students' kost conditions were far better and more hygienic than those of the working class and urban poor. Often friends would stay over (menginap) without prior planning, if the night was getting late. Early in my fieldwork I was puzzled by how often the women I knew menginap (stayed overnight) in their offices, secretariats, or other people's kost without a moment's deliberation. I wondered where their families were, knowing that many of these activists hailed from the greater Jakarta area. Farah, a human rights activist who worked in Central Jakarta, would stay over almost every weekend in South Jakarta with her younger girlfriend Abel, who still lived at home. During the week Farah would sleep over at the office if there were reports to write and deadlines looming or simply if her colleagues

FIGURE 5.1 A typical kost establishment in Depok, West Java, near the University of Indonesia campus. The two-story buildings and courtyard structure indicate that this is a specialized kost rather than an add-on to a house. Depok, June 2011. PHOTO BY AUTHOR.

had decided to do so as well. On these evenings they would stock up on a variety of fried snacks, Marlboro menthol cigarettes (the preferred brand of many women activists), bootleg DVDs and take advantage of the office's Internet subscription to play a constant stream of music from the computer terminal as they worked. The only indication that Farah went home at all was when she came to the Ikatan Keluarga Orang Hilang (Network of Families of the Disappeared) sekretariat with fresh vegetables in her packed lunch. "Yummy," she said as she picked at boiled spinach leaves. "I'm on a diet. My mom made this for me," she explained. Evidently, as the kost had no kitchen.

TRANSGRESSIONS IN THE KOST

Kost defined one's particular station in life; instead of saying where one lived (*tinggal*), young women and men answered where they boarded (*nge-kost*). To say that one was living outside of the home, alone, also indicated what sorts of freedoms these newly liberated men and women had. If the ibu or bapak kost (landlady or landlord) proved annoying or overly attentive, that is, too much like a parent, the student would move in search of better kost conditions. The widespread and relatively unsupervised institution of kos-kosan presented both a normative aspect of urban life and an anxiety-provoking site of moral panic. In keeping with the shift in viewing youth as uncontrollable remaja (teenagers), life in the kos-kosan brought the sexual morals of unmarried youth to the fore. It is assumed that living in kost is an invitation to sin. The specter of premarital sex, either between promiscuous youth or in *kumpul kebo* (cohabitation, lit. "buffaloes mating") arrangements, prompted a young and fiercely devout Muslim proselytizer to write a book titled *Sex in the "Kost"* with precisely such anxieties in mind.[10] We do not know what scientific methods he used to arrive at his conclusions, but he claimed that 97.05 percent of young women living in kost had lost their virginity before marriage. He himself had moved kost six times due to the immoral actions of his pemuda neighbors in his kost.[11] The book is filled with what we can assume to be a fictionalized assembly of debauched characters who engage in premarital sex, alcohol consumption, and drug parties that involve prostitutes. Kost exposed the hypocrisy of even those moral students who claimed a religious identity, for rented rooms that served as sekretariat allowed senior activists a space to seduce young women. Yet there are few alternatives to kost, nor are there other institutional alternatives that would protect the virtue of young men and women. The nominal authority of the bapak or ibu kost, who is supposed to guard his or her charges by imposing 10 PM curfews and no overnight stays (let alone mixed-gender fraternizing), can be easily bought off. The bapak or ibu kost are often absentee landlords who leave the children to their own devices.

The kost is a small space that suits the activist for practical and personal reasons. Its modest scale reflects the roundness of being that Michelet attributes to the fully inhabited nest, one shaped by the turning motion of the bird's own body (see Bachelard 1994 [1964]: 101). An activist I knew well, Elsa, had recently moved to her own kost after months of squatting here and there in the basekemp of the labor organization she belonged to. Elsa very proudly showed me a matching cup and saucer she had bought at the 5,000 rupiah store.[12] Spread on the bed was a batik cloth that doubled as a blanket. An English-language novel was face down on the bed. The room was otherwise bare, but Elsa felt it important to have her own place so that she was no longer reliant on the goodwill of other activists. A few weeks before, we had visited her younger sister's kost near Padjajaran University in Bandung where Elsa was from. That particular kost was tucked away in a warren of alleyways and narrow footbridges, suspended high and deep in a working-class residential neighborhood. It had been just as small as Elsa's but had many more items in use: a coverlet, books, drawings, even an extra mattress for guests. Clearly Elsa's sister had lived there much longer. But students move kost very often, so the fixings are usually inherited from the previous inhabitant. Taking this kost mentality with them, the houses that activist organizations found have the look of a kost with its contents spilled out. In these basekemp, one can drift from room to room freely, happening upon boys and girls watching TV on a shared mattress without an intrusive ibu kost disapproving the easy sociality of young men and women. Here are the objects that would complete a comfortable kost for youth:

For sale items for kos-kosan
For Quick Sale . . . I'm Broke [Butuh Uang] . . .
1. 3 x 4 meter carpet for sale . . . cleaned of semen and other stains
2. book shelf for sale . . . good for book collectors, cassettes, CDs, VCDs, DVDs, also good for storing tools for BDSM [bondage domination sado masochism]
3. 15" computer monitor for sale, SPC brand
4. spring bed mattress for sale . . . firmness and springs all ok . . . guaranteed to rock
5. bedside lamp for sale, antique circa the 70s[13]

There are probably less inflammatory ways of describing essential kost items, but the sexual innuendos that embellish some of the items add to our picture of the youthful interior. The rooms are generally small, not much more than the three-by-four-meter-square carpet listed. One Forkot activist's kost in Cawang, West Jakarta, was so small that it fit only a single mattress on the floor, a small dresser, and a desk with a computer terminal. I was given the seat of honor on the mattress with my knees drawn up as another activist sat adjacent and two others sat outside on the landing and chatted with us through the open doorway. The rent of 500,000 rupiah a month (approximately US$60) was pretty cheap for Jakarta and had not been increased in two years. The ibu kost was understanding when Roni, who worked for a meager salary at a community radio NGO, didn't have the rent for months on end.

The ad lists the luxuries of student life: a bookshelf to hold one's various media collections, a computer monitor to do work or watch movies on, a springbed, and a decorative antique lamp. The carpet hides dirt and warms up the cool tile floors. It becomes another surface for friends to sleep on should they menginap (stay over). This is a catalogue of items that are useful and quickly disposed of. "For quick sale" has the impatience of someone on the move. These heavy things must be left behind, while the small disposables (CDs, VCDs, and DVDs) are carted away as personal valuables. The ad is frank about a common problem for students, evident in the cry "I need money!" (Butuh uang!) Naomi Klein has marveled at the ingenuity of the global justice activists in the United States who are able to run the bulk of their operations from inside one tiny apartment, equipped only with a computer terminal and fax machine (see Klein 2002). Similarly, the sekretariat, in which each room might resemble an individual kost, are furnished with a surprisingly complete set of electronics; computers, printers, a land line for phone service, a television, a cheap DVD player, bookshelves. The rooms of the basekemp and sekretariat are adorned with the fixtures of current pemuda politics. Books by Pramoedya Ananta Toer or other leftist icons, like Marx and Lenin, pictures of Che Guevara, red stars, and organizational emblems all function the way film posters and photos of pop stars might for remaja (teenagers) still living in New Order households.

Once enough activists had coalesced as a group, they would leave their individual kost to invest in larger buildings to house their sekretariat or basekemp, where the core activists lived. Student activists rented large houses or humbler ones for basekemp, depending on their collective resources. Location and spatial orientation were important, and often I had to be safely delivered (diantar) by an activist who knew the way to the doorstep of an organization's new basekemp, for its nondescript address (for example, Orchid Flower Lane Street III, block V, no. 35a) only made sense within the deep locality of the housing complex or the immediate neighborhood. Once there I would marvel at their skill in discovering houses for rent in dense residential alleyways that looked peripheral but were only minutes away from a main road or a train station, or decent-sized houses next to a bustling marketplace with plenty of public transport available. The best base camp or secretariat locations, close to university areas or NGO offices, near busway stations and major landmarks, became the preferred gathering places, even if the building itself was slightly shabby. Activists turned these houses into a mixed space: a place for community, somewhere between the public and the private, and a place for work and play detached from bourgeois standards of cleanliness and comfort. It was because some of these social norms were broken that parental authority began to be replaced with a permanent state of fluid boundaries. Somewhere in the basekemp someone was always drinking coffee, smoking, working, or watching football on TV, sometimes simultaneously. I grew to associate activist spaces with the thick dark taste of Kapal Api brand coffee served in clear glasses and the smell of djisamsoe kretek (clove) cigarettes. In times of leisure we sat on the floors of these bare rooms, lying on our sides or stomachs or leaning against a wall. Domestic arrangements and comfort did not have to depend, as it did in the New Order middle-class home, on the supposition of a dangerous world outside, the world of the street.

CHOOSING FRIENDS OVER FAMILY

"Jakartans keep knitting and expanding their networks along whatever lines are available to them so long as they suit their interests, needs, tastes, and convenience. The way to expand the network is simple. One is introduced by someone to someone else. Antar-jemput, in which [the] pengantar takes his/her friends to the house of their would-be-acquaintance (kenalan), is the ritual of creating the tie" (Shiraishi 1997: 32).

For activists, ideal political community (*komunitas*) replaced the patrimonial frame of the New Order family, but more specifically, friendship defined community. Friendship delivered youth into politics, and thus in a reciprocal fashion politics became an expression of friendship. Friendships between young men, and sometimes between young men and women, trumped romantic love or other ties. These relations appear in the discourse of friendship, mapped by the words *fren, kawan, sahabat, teman, anak-anak,* all of which mean friend, comrade, or peer. *Kawan* is most salient because it offers an Indonesian translation of the leftist-sounding "comrade." Because these community or friendship ties are not articulated as family ties, one could be misled into thinking that they are not as emotive or as long-lasting as family bonds. Yet these friendship ties implicitly enable political solidarity and organizational work, such that the conflicts between friends can rupture political alliances as starkly as a divorce can rupture a family.

Communities form around the active members of youth organizations, and how these individual members arrive there reminds us of the omnipresence of antar-jemput as a mode of socialization and integration. You are introduced into the group by a friend, as he might bring a nonmember of the family into the fold by taking him home. This friend recruits you because he sees a potential affinity in you for (his) politics. If the friendship is reciprocated, it is understood that your politics are aligned with his. An activist's experience of political awakening (kesadaran) resonates with and replicates that of his friend. An older activist is simply one who arrived earlier. If the metaphor for politics is the path (jalan) or flow (*arus*), then those friends are walking together on it. Hence the frequent explanation of politics as an intersection where friends can meet (*bisa ketemu*) and walk together (*jalan bareng*). The journey is premised on maintaining these affinities between friends, whose experiences are in a sense always collective, always shared. As komunitas replaces the family, walking together and hanging out (*nongkrong*) after the demo promotes both self-discovery and a way to strengthen the bonds between activists.[14]

Reminiscing fondly about the past and an acquaintance he no longer saw, Anto said, "In the past I used to like walking together with X" (Dulu gue suka jalan bareng dia). There was also the inquisitive and slightly accusatory question that made me feel defensive: "I saw you walking with X the other day?" (Kemarin lu jalan bareng dia?) Jalan bareng is an act that carries several connotations of distance and proximity for activist youth. Much like antar-jemput, it is a relational category of interior life rather than a spatial orientation to the outside, for jalan bareng could be taking place in a mall as easily as at a roadside drinking beer together. In the memories of the early years, it tells the story of two like-minded comrades who walked the same political path and shared good times together. It might even signal more formal affiliations, such as membership in the same study group or organization. For men and women "stepping out," it foregrounded the romantic possibilities in activist circles and was a discreet way to acknowledge a romantic relationship. Or it could be a question that confronts the ethnographer, at once innocuous and potentially rife with implications, when one activist questions your closeness to a member of a rival group he saw you with at the demo site. Mostly, jalan bareng takes place off-site and after hours; it is perhaps the most intimate and unmonitored use of activist time and space; it describes the tempo of leisure rather than the intensity of the demonstration; it implies deep talk. In Victor Turner's terms, walking together is a ritual process that produces communitas among peers and, moreover, feels good to recount because of its natural rhythms and emotional profundity. If the teasing question "Were you out (walking) with him?" implies too much ideological or romantic closeness than could be justified, an activist would exclaim defensively, "You're crazy! When did I ever?"

The insistence on friendship (pertemanan) and comradeship (perkawanan) among students and between politically divergent groups provided a sharp contrast to the New Order regime's cruel (kejam) treatment of state enemies. Not long after the violence of the First Semanggi Tragedy (November 13, 1998) broke out, a reporter for the popular web periodical Detik.com interviewed Taufan Hunneman, the "general" of Togetherness Forum (Forum Bersama; Wawancara ([1998]). The legitimacy of Suharto's appointed successor, B. J. Habibie, was a matter of ferocious debate that had split student groups. Taufan's Togetherness Forum was on one side of the divide, calling for new elections and the removal of Suharto's sphere of influence. On the other side were the more conservative student groups, including those linked to political parties, that supported Habibie's presidency. The reporter's questions convey the sense that there is something questionable about demo culture. Why are students insistent (ngotot) on demonstrating during Ramadhan, a month of rest and reduced activities? Why are they interested in demonstrating? Perhaps there is something irresistible drawing them to the street, she suggests. At first Taufan's answers are serious, providing a *kronologi* of how each group came to be. "A lot of groups want to get in on the game [bermain, lit. play]." Those groups are opportunistic, whereas the student groups Taufan cites are in the same lane (*jalur*), and stand by their views.[15] "How are the personal relations between these two groups?" Taufan stresses that "being friends with people across the line is not a problem for us. But from a political standpoint, we are still different from them." The reporter follows this description of amicable collaboration across differences with a flippant "Apa sih enaknya demonstrasi?" (approximately: "What's so fun about demonstrating anyway?") *Sih*, a particle used for emphasis, is out of place in a conversation about politics. It is unclear whether *sih* implies skepticism or naïveté. Taufan brightens and gives an answer that titillates the reporter. He says,

> There is a lot of artistry in demos, outside of a political context, OK. First, demos contribute to more relations, a lot of friends. If before our associations were limited to the local university, Jayabaya for example [his university], now we can know [kenal] friends from other universities. The campus jackets only function as a sign of which university you belong to, but we feel that as Indonesian students we are all the same. Second, in aksi love stories also appear. During the Semanggi Tragedy on November 13, there was even an acronym, CBSA, Cinta Bersemi Saat Aksi (Spring Love during an Aksi).[16] Some friends were so mixed up [saking bingungnya] that they became attracted to some girls, and they've dated until now. Third, the demo builds solidarity. If one person is hungry, everybody is hungry. If the logistik [supplies] comes, then we eat together. If there is barely enough logistik, then we have to find ways so that everyone [semua teman, lit. "all friends"] gets to eat. Solidarity grows when our friends are arrested or beaten. This happens until some of us cry, want revenge, scream and yell, to show our solidarity with the victims.

The reporter is interested only in the salacious details of the second point. She asks, "Were there a lot of CBSA cases?" (Banyakkah kasus CBSA?) Then comes the moment of disclosure. Taufan answers, "There were a lot, including me, ha ha ha . . ." Spring love (*cinta bersemi*) buds in the season of demonstrations; it is like spring fever, hard to resist.

Embedded in the discourse of amity is the possibility of other passions: the uncontrolled mingling of young men and women, the intensity of their shared hunger and violence, their collective euphoria.[17] The demo universalizes Indonesian student identity, rendering distinctions as definitive as one's alma mater irrelevant. In the confusion, one can even fall in love. Pemuda fever and spring fever become interchangeable conditions. The reporter concludes with a question that reminds us of just how young these demonstrators are: "Your parents don't mind?" Taufan answers, "It depends on the parents . . . In the beginning my parents did mind. Especially as demos were still rare . . . But now my parents can accept it because truth and victory are in the hands of students. One girl's parents didn't want to pay her tuition because they didn't want her to go to demos [ikut-ikutan demo]. But slowly the student's parents will become aware, and will even be ready to let their child die. It is just a matter of time that will make a parent not mind their child's actions." In Taufan's story here, the parents have gone so far as to withhold their daughter's tuition so that she cannot attend classes. If she does not go to campus, they know that she cannot go to demonstrations. She would not have the relations with other anak (children, activists) that the university provided. The link between middle-class youth and politics would be broken. Even if the student indeed went to class and stayed there, her parents know that there is an irresistible force that makes all students turun ke jalan (go to the street). It is there that the most relevant relationships for youth are formed. Students are able to cultivate their own friends, lovers, and choices in places where parental authority is suppressed. As Taufan claims, parents inevitably come to terms with the nation's claim on their child once they recognize a higher power: that of pemuda history. Taufan's steadfast belief that over time authority figures will align with student desires presents a series of escalating student victories.[18] Here is one last proof of activism's committed refusal of domestic comfort: in 1998 activists who occupied the streets of urban Indonesia slept on cardboard boxes laid flat on the ground, reminiscent of the homeless and the shantytown. This was the first encampment, before the posko was built.

CAMPING OUT

When the cataclysmic tsunami struck Aceh on December 26, 2004, I had already done a year of fieldwork. By that point I found the rhythms of street politics to be fairly predictable; but suddenly, because of the tsunami, the tempo changed. All the activist groups I knew, from human rights organizations, women's NGOs, urban poor networks, the staid executive student bodies on campus, and alumni networks to more militant student groups, sprang into action. The disaster had overwhelmed state capacities to offer effective disaster relief, and the private sector's response soon overshadowed the larger organizations encumbered by red tape, such as the Red Cross. The popular television station Metro TV, owned by Acehnese businessman Suryo Paloh, drummed up sympathy by repeatedly playing *Indonesia Weeps*, a program that showed graphic images of destruction, including a shot of children's corpses laid out in rows, as if in slumber. Everywhere, in every neighborhood, sekretariat, and campus, banners proclaiming solidarity fund-raising efforts for the victims of the tsunami were hung up high and fronted buildings and gates. Activists organized emergency sites for posko that became collection and distribution points for supplies and people.[19]

A former NGO activist named Dian and her boyfriend, Irfan, got in touch with me to tell me about the Humanitarian Volunteer Team (Tim Relawan Kemanusiaan; TRK), led by the Catholic priest Romo Sandyawan, who was preparing to deploy emergency aid to Aceh as soon as possible. I spent the next few hours with Dian and Irfan driving in South Jakarta's Blok M area in heavy traffic in their beat-up old Toyota Corolla, scouring individual pharmacies to buy medical supplies to donate to TRK. Supplies were running low because so many concerned citizens had thought to do the same. When we had bought a decent amount, we drove toward the TRK headquarters, located an hour away in East Jakarta, near the Taman Mini theme park. When we got there, a meeting was in session, and a volunteer gestured toward a table of food for us new arrivals to eat from before we joined the others. My personal donation of a couple of hundred dollars' worth of bandages and medicines joined a massive tower of bundled-up supplies, which must have cost tens of millions of rupiah. A young woman wrote me a receipt for the medicines I had donated. "We need clothes. Warm long-sleeve shirts. We need sanitary pads. We need infant formula. More tarps." Urgent and practical statements such as these drifted over from the meeting circle. The two-story house was not TRK's formal sekretariat; it belonged to the Institute of Social History, whose members consisted of researchers, scholars, and former PRD activists who were close to TRK.[20] TRK's posko had overtaken the everyday functions of the Institute, and indeed, everyone present was behaving in an excited and serious manner befitting a state of national emergency. The first batch of volunteers were about to be dispatched, some of them young men who wore outdoor gear that made it seem like they were about to go camping. Over the next few weeks I volunteered my help to translate press statements, editorials, and funding proposals for TRK and other groups from Indonesian into English, all related to tsunami relief efforts. The posko atmosphere made activist labor seem more organized and concrete than it had been in months.

THE ACTIVIST POSKO

What draws so many people to the posko? Why is the posko so effective at marshaling and distributing material resources and energy? These two questions point to the monadic and symbolic function of the posko, as a crystallization of crisis-generated needs and civic responses that enable a momentary glimmer of another politics to shine through. *Posko* is the abbreviated name for the structure that is alternately known as the *pos komando* (command post) or *pos komunikasi* (communication post). Activists privilege the "command post" definition for their posko, in keeping with the assertive, organized, and militaristic register of their battle speech, where one can find the imperative (if not the sense of urgency) replicated in terms such as "command vehicles" (mobil komando) and "field generals" (jeneral lapangan or jenlap). But activists also assume the communicative function of the posko as an integral part of the structure. The posko is an exemplary Reformasi structure that has evolved from the security functions of the guard post to the communicative and public functions of oppositional political structures, as Abidin Kusno analyzes in his discussion of the PDI-P posko that flourished in urban areas across Indonesia (2010: 228). Yet grassroots activist posko are motivated by distinctly different temporalities and modes of occupation from the territorializing claims of semipermanent posko that political parties and paramilitaries impose on the neighborhoods they claim to be under their "sphere of influence" (231).

The posko claims to provide immediate relief, whether the need is medical, informational, or emotional. Much as the unique distress code of the bat signal works to conjure comic superhero Batman in Gotham's time of need, the call-and-response of the posko is a channel open only to the activist and the rakyat. The state's corrupt patronage system is cut out entirely, and if other authorities, such as the bapak RT (neighborhood chief), hope to intervene, they can only appear as outsiders looking in. Even when the posko is swarming with strangers, activists operate freely because antar-jemput is still the primary mechanism to integrate people into the posko, as my entry through Dian and Irfan's introduction proved. Only community members enter the zone; or rather, once inside one is part of community and quickly absorbed into the action of the posko. The posko is expected to be open and accessible twenty-four hours a day. It is thus a zone of encampment where boundaries are strongly felt and enacted through heightened temporality and constant occupation, even though outsiders view such dissident spaces as lawless and undisciplined (Hoffman 2011). Scholars have written about the Occupy movement in

FIGURE 5.2 Inside a posko supporting a workers' strike. Signs of domiciliation include the clothes hanging from nails and cooking equipment in a corner. The walls are made from tarps. PHOTO IN AUTHOR'S COLLECTION.

the United States and Tahrir Square in Egypt as political movements that are discursively represented by the image of the tent city and the mass occupation of public spaces (Mitchell 2012; Winegar 2012). The sustained occupation of Zuccotti Park in New York City by activists through the early winter months made their eventual eviction doubly expressive of state and structural violence against protestors. The tent as symbolic site of struggle is yet another example of what John Berger states as the demonstration's raison d'être: to demonstrate proof of power asymmetries between the state and its people in stark and representative ways (2001 [1968]). Images of flimsy tarps, tent cities, and small posko that stick out of the urban landscape are serially and semiotically linked to images of martyrdom and suffering: refugees, brave souls protesting military rule, unarmed student activists under siege, a "sea of humanity" (Malkki 1996). Images of "the suffering of others" affectively secure our reactions of empathy and outrage, yet for the casual spectator a formal distance is maintained in the act of viewing (Sontag 1977). For Indonesian activists the posko evokes memories of activist power, defiance, and sacrifice. It is a sight that swells.

Camping out has a frontier spirit to it, an expeditious side. It moves the act of domiciliation to even more precarious and fragmented settings outside the middle-class family home. Even when posko are set up in a sekretariat or basekemp, that is, in activists' own home territory, setting them up is a public act that invites the outside in, keeping the gates open. The temporal shift in the operations of daily life is visibly marked by the prominent cloth banner (spanduk) installed over the gates or the doorway of the secretariat that advertises the posko's existence. The leisurely secretariat becomes warehouse, communications center, and meeting point all in one. A steady flow of visitors enters the fold, and the interior space accommodates the public functions of press conferences and volunteer committees. The popularity of posko in times of national emergency harkens back to the connections forged between activists and ordinary people (*masyarakat*) during the Reformasi era, when political support for students materialized in the form of food and monetary donations dropped off by well-wishers at the posko. The posko thus became a powerful and emblematic structure of Reformasi.[21]

In its barest form, the posko resembles the traditional Javanese *pondok* (shelter).[22] Consisting of a tarp pitched on four aluminum posts or bamboo lashed together into a sheltered platform, the rudimentary posko is the first sign that a sympathetic outside presence is galvanizing the community into a unified force. It mediates between outsiders and the rakyat, yet student-run posko are not quite autochthonous presences; they remain borrowed spaces contingent upon activity and occupation. The student activist alliance City Forum defined the posko this way: "Posko are used to distribute information to the public, and to keep records of participants, as well as for meeting places for the surrounding rakyat near the posko's location. Posko are built on campus communities, as well as non-campus gerakan [movement] communities in various areas. The function of the posko is to strengthen the rakyat constituency near the posko for the purposes of mass demonstrations."[23] The multiple functions of the activist posko culminate in one essential purpose: to mobilize the masses for demonstrations. But "strengthening the constituency" also indicates an ethics of care and nourishment as part of activists' political program. The posko stakes a claim over territory and its surrounding people (imagined as the urban poor who then mobilize as massa) in order to quickly command resources and troops (pasukan) for the movement.

In 2004, I visited the ruin of a magnificent posko on the campus of UKI-Cawang, the Indonesian Christian University in West Jakarta. In a wide grassy field at the rear of the campus where a brick wall separated the university from the surrounding kampung, the outlines of a large, four-roomed structure with brick floors were clearly visible. Across the field lay similar houses the university had built. City Forum had commandeered one of these buildings for their operational headquarters in 1998. "Look," said Roni, pointing: "That was our documents room, that was the legal aid office, that room there was for logistik, and there was a lot of that! And the back room for sleeping at night." Roni said the posko had been burned down by the army and by the campus militia (*menwa*) in an ambush in 2000.[24] They had fled helter-skelter into the kampung, unable to save anything from the documents room, a loss he deeply regretted. When we walked away from the field, Roni's tour continued. "Here is a new gate," he said, "and here too. This was never walled off before. This campus was open twenty-four hours. We would stay here, sleep here, bathe in the rector's office." From Roni's description we can see that the posko had become the central command of student politics on campus, and in effect the entire university had functioned as an enlarged basekemp, accessible but safely under student control.

There were other stories of eviction I heard, and they too had the ring of a brave last stand. It wasn't until places were burnt down or activists forcibly and violently displaced that people gave up their posko. Activists faced down the threat of eviction with a high degree of confidence in their right to long-term occupation, supported by the majority of students and surrounding kampung residents drawn to Reformasi's reversal of fortunes. The case of the City Forum posko on UKI-Cawang's campus, where even the rectorate accommodated their prolonged two-year stay, suggests a political landscape that made the campus impenetrable. Other posko on more conservative campuses, for example the UI, fought more contested battles against eviction. The UI posko lasted only three months, despite financial support from outsiders ("Posko Salemba dibubarkan" 1998), while activists who wanted to build posko or sought shelter from attackers found Atma Jaya Catholic University to be a reliable campus with a sympathetic (or intimidated) administration. I have argued for the posko to be thought of as an encampment in line with other forms of intentional encroachment that contradict common uses of private or public property, such as those communal spaces built by social movements, yet the term "encampment" and its corresponding practice of temporary camping out threaten to neutralize the politics of occupation by displacing attention onto the territorial form of settlement rather than its political function as camp.

Agamben's formulation (1995) of the camp as "the nomos of the modern" is a chilling and by now much-discussed idea that situates the camp as the disciplinary and extralegal site of state impunity over biopower. In a productive amendment to Agamben's camp, Danny Hoffman proposes the use of "barracks" as the organizing principle of West African urban postmodernity. In his ethnography on militant youth in West Africa, Hoffman describes the barracks as a "spatial arrangement by which violence is alternately contained and deployed. . . . At its most effective, the barracks makes the speed of movement a weapon" (2011: 169). Specifically, the barracks enables circulation of bodies in and out of the encampment, and it is this mobility and concentration of resources (of reserve labor of young male combatants, weapons, and potential violence) that makes the barracks such an ambivalent site in the city. The "double status" of the barracks, where "no one paid rent . . . and the city's provision of electricity was free of charge" (178) resounds with the tension of the activist posko, where those who were most exalted because of Reformasi politics were also disliked and demonized by the authorities. One can see the beginnings of eviction in this double bind.[25] The university could not condone forever the siphoning of its resources for an anti-university that made such audacious claims of belonging. Since Reformasi began, students had become morally unimpeachable in the eyes of the public and therefore difficult to summarily expel from the university. Instead, eviction of the extracurricular posko served the purposes of expulsion and reminded students of their duty to attend to their studies instead of living in a state of disorder. When the last bit of activist presence had been swept from the campus grounds, activists founded new homes for their organizations in basekemp that celebrated their freedoms and cemented their autonomy. Having their own work space conferred political as well as social legitimacy on the group. This was the address on their *kops surat* (letterhead) that went out to the world. This was where they could gather, talk, organize, and play without restraint, much as organizing demonstrations and keeping abreast of political changes required intense sociality during the early days of Reformasi. But behind the joys of friendship and komunitas in the basekemp lurked a number of logistical problems that cut straight to the heart of the student activist economy and lifestyle.

Activists carried over a spatial politics from the posko that had been legitimate when they were squatting to make a moral claim on someone else's land, as the campus posko or the street occupations demonstrate, but in a different economy of private property and rental obligations, resistance did not beget spatial rights. Now that activists had set up camp off campus, their antiauthoritarian attitudes created other long-lasting conflicts that became internalized as organizational and generational weaknesses. Living in a state of permanent attention, or as Hoffman describes, a waiting for deployment, required an aptitude for temporariness even when a fixed abode was available. In general, activists were resourceful at making ends meet, by finding freelance jobs and short-term projects, and at finding places to stay. In addition, their material needs were modest. As we have seen in chapter 3, the activist aesthetic was less about distinction than reproducing group identity and solidarity. Still, the microeconomy of the individual activist was subsidized by the group's collective home. The basekemp was valuable because it was a safe haven to return to whenever activists were between jobs, towns, and demonstrations. However, activists struggled to pay for such a shared privilege. On the positive side, the off-campus site fostered social freedoms and intra-organizational relationships as the basekemp became the gathering place for old and young activists and their respective friends and networks. On the other hand the problem could be summed up thus: who was going to pay the basekemp's rent?

WHO PAYS FOR THE BASE CAMP?

"Anak-anak lagi dimana?" "Lagi ngumpul di basekemp." A typical conversation begins: "Where is everyone?" (lit.: Where are the children?) Answer: "They're gathered at the basekemp."

Maintaining a secretariat or a basekemp was hard work. An activist document in my possession, dated 1999, contains a handwritten list of *piket* (rotation) household chores from a basekemp. The list of activities includes mopping, sweeping, and cleaning the whole house in one day and was written in a way that suggests that chores were intended as punishment for a group member's wrongdoing. The stresses of the domestic labor required for the upkeep of these spaces had the potential to erode the activist promise of friendship and equality. At times these fractures were buried deep in the camaraderie of social life, and at other times hierarchy returned to the activist fold in a prominent fashion, particularly when political and financial claims became entangled. Founding members had proprietary claim to the group's name and identity, especially those activists who belonged to the original 1998 generation. In the activist community, activists were divided into the self-regulating identities of *junior* and *senior*. In some groups, senior members were even addressed as Abang (Older Brother).[26] *Junior* and *senior* were English loanwords that had made their way into the Indonesian student vocabulary to indicate the difference in age and status between students, but these words also pointed to the ties between them. Seniors were responsible for the juniors they recruited, and juniors were bound to their senior role models. Despite the autonomy that activists so valued in their regular and political lives, junior activists still needed their senior, particularly when the rent was due. Their financial dependency became clear then; unlike the monthly payments for a kost, the annual rent for a house had to be paid in one lump sum, an amount beyond any student's means.[27] Similarly, when large events like national congresses had to be arranged students went to their seniors, who then turned to their own patrons for funds. The time that older activists spent cultivating ties and networks with NGOs, politicians, journalists, and even society matrons bore fruit in these times of need.

The junior-senior relationship between activists were often genial and joking relationships, much like sibling relations that were close but unequal. When groups went out to eat lunch or ordered food at the basekemp from passing street vendors, junior would take advantage of their senior to order a full meal, drinks, and occasionally the more expensive cigarettes, as the senior sighed and paid up without comment. A childish and gleeful cry of entitlement "Asyik, ada yang traktir!" ("Yay! Someone's paying!") would ring out. In June 2011, when I was traveling with my research assistant to Yogyakarta to carry out research on street art (see Lee 2013), I ran into a former FPPI activist at the airport. He invited us to share a taxi and then to lunch afterward. We were joined by two more FPPI members at the airport, both of whom were younger than Johan and hence junior. After a simple lunch of *gado-gado* (peanut salad) at a cheap restaurant frequented by students, the elder Johan paid for the whole table, including the anthropologist and her assistant. Johan lamented in mock self-pity, "I used to think things would change, but years later, it's still the same people who are paying. We've been paying since 1998!" Johan's lament was humorous since he had felt equal to his peers in 1998 and was junior then, but over the years his senior status had accrued like a pyramid scheme, such that he could never be replaced by junior coming up in the ranks. In fact he fully expected to pay for lunch and refused my money, but it was also telling that the junior activists looked away or wandered away from the table as if they were already impatient to get to the next activity.

And so it was that senior activists became *abang* (older brothers) and patrons of the gerakan. Occasionally dropping by the basekemp after work to drink coffee and reminisce about the events of 1998, seniors would text or call each other to say, "Lagi ngapain? Ayo main ke basekemp" (Whatcha doin'? Let's meet at the base camp). As the day wore on, more and more seniors would walk in and be welcomed by other seniors already present, while the younger activists stayed in the offices and resumed working on their computers. It would be nightfall before anyone headed home to his kost, his wife, or his children.

CLOSING THE GAP

The need to address questions of leadership and life beyond the student activist framework had become pressing. From 1997 to 1999, the frequency of groups splitting over alleged political issues highlighted the conflicts that arose in the student activist community itself. Dominant members in a group did not like their authority challenged, and "coup" attempts periodically occurred, justified by political rhetoric about ideological differences.[28] City Forum was a case in point; once the largest alliance in the Jakarta student movement, by late 1998 it had rapidly disintegrated, sending splinters of former members into the rest of the leftist radical student organizations or into the NGO sector. In another common pattern of the movement, former leaders would found new groups once their tenure as secretary-general (sekjen) or chair (ketua) ended. As new generations of leaders took charge by getting elected to positions of authority, whole generations of activists, even founding members, were displaced or even expelled.[29] But even in groups that experienced no overt signs of conflict, there were still tensions over whose authority mattered most. Senior activists felt it correct to be replaced by newcomers and welcomed a more informal mentoring role in the group, but the younger activists continued to regard them as basekemp whose approval they periodically sought or bypassed as they saw fit. Older activists began to feel uneasy about their place in the movement, which increasingly relegated to them the role of living witnesses or actors (pelaku) of Reformasi while denying them direct involvement in the organizations they had outgrown.

In 2004 I was invited to Semarang to observe an FPPI reunion for older and former members of the group, whom the still active senior members Savic and Ardi called "poststudents." Savic explained, "It's just a gathering, to reaffirm what we already know and think." The Jakarta contingent had specific goals to rejuvenate the organization and provide a financial safety net for the precarious junior members of the organization, especially those who were from urban poor backgrounds. The "National Consolidation" meeting would seek to strengthen the ties of FPPI alumni, especially those with a secure income. The lodge they had chosen for the meeting was on the campus of an educational institute, set in the cool hills of the colonial town of Semarang. In the large white meeting room, which had a semicircular formation of tables set up, three men sat at the head of the central committee table to moderate the discussion. Twenty men were seated at the remaining tables, including two who were active in local politics, one as a legislative council member and the other as a member of a political party. The room was silent as everyone waited for someone else to break the ice and inaugurate the proceedings. Savic took the lead and began to list the problems they had been thinking about in Jakarta, to do with older "nonstructural," "poststudent" members. Savic asked a series of rhetorical and self-referential questions:

What can be done to hold those members, since so many have become professionals and have graduated a long time ago? How should we consolidate
our ranks so that we are not merely regarded as a source of funding that
younger members collect dues from?[30] I have spoken to many older members who are willing to contribute dues (*iuran*) but beyond that, what can
we contribute in terms of resources and energy? . . . FPPI has concentrated
on its campus *basis* for so long it has been identified with that, but we are
no longer in that framework. We need a different framework.

He continued in this vein, asking, "What is our next task? [Tugasnya apa?]
What kind of politics should we practice, because our dreams [mimpi] may
not be the same across [us], and may not be the same as FPPI in other provinces." While drawing attention to local differences and divergent interests in
the organization, Savic's critique toward the systematic failure of students to
maintain familial ties within their own organization was a pointed one, a condition he called "a lack of culture." According to Savic—and perhaps in agreement with several of the older activists there who, like him, had Nadhlatul
Ulama backgrounds, where traditional and communal life in the village was
tightly bound up in religion—only a politics of culture could build sustainable
extended families (*keluarga besar*) such as those of Nadhlatul Ulama.[31] Since
1998, political changes had happened in spite of the student movement rather
than because of it, Savic said. There appeared to be something inherently
wrong with the gerakan model that resulted in the present-day estrangement
between one generation of activists and the next. Another member quipped,
"Well, what do we do now? As an in-between group, we can no longer be students, but we don't peddle students to the elite either. Either because we won't
be *brokers* [sic], or because we can't! [atau mungkin juga kita tidak sanggup!])."
Laughter broke out at the self-mockery of the would-be broker, but the at-
tendees could not deny the concerns hidden behind the banner of "National
Consolidation." The youthful activist family was caught at a crossroads, disin-
tegrating from its own internal friction between its needs to both reproduce
itself and disperse power within itself.

When the moderator took over, Savic went to the whiteboard and began
drawing boxes to illustrate his ideas. First, he drew two neat boxes:

STUDENT	POST-STUDENT

Underneath each category, he wrote some words that branched outward.
Under "Student" he wrote the names of some of the large and active student

groups, such as the National Students Front, and then the words "Gerakan Mahasiswa" (student movement). Underneath "Post-student" he drew more lines, writing "journalists, NGOs, lawyers, professionals." He explained his diagram this way:

> This line of great distance has emerged between us, consciously or not, but it is there. Mostly because of work, we have entered into another world which takes up time and energy. Some of us are married, have families, other obligations. While the students still concentrate on getting new recruits [kader baru] on campus and elsewhere, they feel that they have no authority over us. We have dismissed our politburo, but in effect, they (the national council) still come to us for advice, and are afraid to exercise their claims over us. . . . This is a problem that has never been spoken of or tackled before [belum pernah ditangkap]. Seniority in our structure—who responds to whom? There is a lack of coordination. For example when the aksi among the farmers in Central Java happened and we didn't even know of it at the center [pusat]! This is because we have never left the model of the Gerakan Mahasiswa!

His presentation over, Savic sat down again, while the moderator resumed his task of summarizing the meeting and putting forth a resolution that those present could agree on. It appeared that some kind of "consolidation plan" had already been discussed prior to the meeting, perhaps at the informal gathering the night before or even prior to that. The moderator's formal reading of the plan received no protest. The FPPI members ended the meeting with an agreement to have the FPPI East Java chapter act as the national coordinating body (koordinator nasional) for the poststudent group, to put post- and current students in communication, as well as between the daerah. Yet another formal body, a national coordinator board, was elected to act as mediator between groups. In effect, the appointment of the council reinserted post-students back into the group on a formal level without subjecting them to the bylaws of the annual national congress. While Savic's idea had been to form an alternative politics of culture so that "family" might feel more organic as a natural outcome of everyday practice, the solution the poststudents arrived at pointed to the mechanisms that separated work from play. The organization decreed that any formal decision required the validation of a representative council, so the solution the post-students arrived at was to form yet another link in the chain of decision-making. While the East Java chapter of FPPI was singled out as a liaison and granted authority over the senior members, these moves to formalize the authority of junior activists obscured the fact that activists elected to head the ostensibly powerful national council (*dewan nasional*) did not feel empowered to articulate commands to those they considered senior. They needed close and senior intermediaries, such as Savic, to convey those messages. For instance, in another complaint Savic and Ardi voiced, when junior met face-to-face with much more senior activists, the social distance they experienced hindered them from collecting the financial contributions (*iuran*) that all parties had already agreed upon.

This social distance had political consequences that frustrated the older activists who remained active in their organizations, like Ardi and Savic. They remembered the immediacy of the social experiments of Reformasi, where being a prominent activist had not automatically given them any rigid bapak-style authority. Indeed, to guard against envy among their peers or the consolidation of power and resources in the hands of one (male) leader, the positions of field commander, media representative, and organizer of legal matters, security, and logistics, were rotated daily, perplexing the outsiders who tried to identify the missing heads of this student movement. In essence prefiguring the multitude Hardt and Negri describe as a headless body of flesh, the student movement maintained the carnivalesque elements of protest and strategic dissemblage for far longer than they received credit for. In the space of seven years, however, it was becoming clear the "gerakan model" of anti-authority had given birth to its own structural dilemmas, exemplified by the post-students' ambiguous position of holding and withholding authority. Savic and Ardi expressed a sense of deep concern, but the other members present were politely distant from the problems of the student movement. They had moved on to jobs and formal electoral politics, and the imperative of present time, the "now" that had moved student activists to act on the historical burden they carried as pemuda, had left them.

CONCLUSION

As I argued at the beginning of this chapter, domiciliation provides a new framework for assessing student politics and ideological comforts away from the street, in interior spaces that were rarely represented in the media or in public activist discourse. Domiciliation thus acts as an "enframing" in the sense that Heidegger proposes, as a challenging and revealing assembling that brings forth the meaning of the series of posko, sekretariat, basekemp, and kost (Heidegger [1971] 2001b: 62). These structures are homes away from home, a second or third home in a series that for activists reinscribes their sense of belonging to the nation yet produces unsettling feelings—that such a temporary lifestyle could be permanent.

Leaving the family home was both exhilarating and laden with personal risk for students. From their experiences in prison and on the street, we know that students continued to struggle with defending their actions as the greater good in the service of the nation. Looking inside the open structures of student interiors, we might think that their sparseness reflected an ease in lifestyle, a certain mobility and dislocation of urban, middle-class youth. Marching "forward" (*maju*) on the streets, and moving from kost to kost, sekretariat to basekemp at yet another rented house, students were constantly unmoored. As the student movement remained abreast of political developments by issuing statements and building posko, these swift reactions that anticipated the voice of the rakyat also affected activist solidarity. Their ties to community shifted constantly in the reactive politics of the student movement. And perhaps the most disturbing dislocation (disturbing for being so smooth in some cases) occurred when students, identified for so long as the moral voice of Indonesian history, found themselves grown up, moving along the path to becoming fathers (bapak) and mothers (ibu). The distance between senior activists and junior activists, contoured by the myth of 1998, made intergenerational conflicts a common if unmarked occurrence. Even student activists, we learn, outgrow the promise of their youth. As they became expert in the tactics and strategies of street politics, the radical possibilities of their community life began to resemble the structures of authority they had fled. Regulated by the processes of legitimation that upheld student activist authority, the interiors of the student movement ceased to liberate youth from the structures of everyday life and instead came to reflect the ambivalent comforts of the family home as the principal structure of youth politics.

The transformation of Generation 98 into senior activists exacted a price. In many cases, despite their unchanged living conditions (dwelling in kost and subsisting on the small salaries from their work with NGOs, human rights organizations, and other civil society groups), their accrued seniority gave them honorary status but also enforced a distance from the youth politics that had introduced them to the world of activism in the first place. Generation 98 thus felt the push from the political elite and from their established peers to accept their past pemuda status and move on by capitalizing on their pemuda identity. The only venue for political participation left for senior activists to pursue was the realm of formal politics. The next chapter describes how the 2004 elections became a rite of passage that tested activist resolve to transform the system from within and galvanized new political formations for those who chose to remain outside the system.

Chapter 6 | **DEMOCRACY**

The 2004 legislative and presidential elections were billed as the first truly democratic elections held in Indonesia in more than five decades. Even though the 1999 elections had a more properly historical claim to this title, the crucial five years in between elections had allowed democratic institutions to strengthen, activist experiments to settle, and new political party configurations to arise, such that national political conditions looked very different to activists. This chapter tracks Generation 98 in the grip of election fever, as activists sought to renew their representation of the People on the streets and from within the system. However, their enthusiasm was tempered by the continued presence of New Order–style "democracy festivals" and the monied politics and strong-arm techniques of the military and the elite. The time gap between 1998 and 2004 had also sharpened the political differences and judgments between activist groups and individuals. By focusing on discourses of corruption, individuation, and social difference that emerged during the elections, I convey pemuda identity's uneven integration into post-Suharto Indonesia. In this chapter I argue that the transition to institutionalized democracy, the codification of Reformasi narratives, and the temporal distance from 1998 made activist futures more insecure than ever. Generation 98's reappearance on the national stage during the 2004 national elections, under the banner of a recognized and named generational identity, masked the fractures that propelled activists together and forced them apart again.

It is inevitable at the close of this book that pemuda fever must at last contend with its own temporally bound contradictions, for it has proclaimed the pull of its dominant logic long enough. Pemuda fever's slow retreat into obscurity and its domestication by conservative and elite forces have haunted activism from the very beginning, for ongoing revolutions take a toll. Individual activists faced difficult choices to remain in politics several years after Reformasi broke. Many of them had burned out, left the country to pursue an education, struggled for relevance, or exposed themselves to backlash and condemnation when they joined political parties. The 2004 election forced the following questions to arise: Could Generation 98's legacy be monetized and materialized into mobile forms of political capital, or was it inalienable property, held in common? Are political trajectories still entangled with economic conditions in the post-Suharto era, and how do we forecast this future? The first question produced conflicting answers from activists, which I address in this chapter. The second question is far more complex, so I will share an insight from a New Order critic. In 2004, an activist from the 1980s generation took me on a pilgrimage to meet an old socialist in South Jakarta. The elderly man lived in a small and modest home, hidden in one of Jakarta's residential lanes right off a busy thoroughfare. He was a Dutch-educated socialist, and in my estimation, in his late seventies. I was in my twenties, and my friend was in his thirties. Oom Jaap seemed at ease with receiving youngsters in his home to talk about the history of Indonesian politics. I was charmed by his educated and otherworldly voice; his Indonesian sounded *klasik* and intellectual. Oom Jaap carefully repeated for me what he thought the difference was between Sukarno's time, the Old Order, and Suharto's New Order. Under Sukarno, politics was the commander ("politik adalah panglima"), while under Suharto, money was the commander ("Wang adalah panglima!"). He repeated this phrase again so that I heard his old-fashioned articulation of the Malay word *wang* (money) instead of the modern-day *uang*, and through that articulation also heard his elegant scorning of New Order Indonesia's evacuation from politics, leaving only money. A person from the Old Order could remember the dynamic world of politics from the 1950s, Before Suharto, but what about After Suharto? What next?

SIGNS OF CHANGE: FROM PEMUDA TO *TOKOH*

In the twilight hour of a demonstration in front of the Istana, the Presidential Palace, I sat in the shade of the large trees that bordered the National Monument and faced the palace.[1] Under these trees were the remnants of the massa, now drinking bottled water and buying cut fruit from the itinerant food vendors assembled under the trees. The police were still milling about but were not paying any attention to the demonstrators, who were preparing to disperse. Between the hours of 4 and 5 PM, most demonstrations would already have ended. The command truck with the borrowed sound system and speakers had driven away.

In the corner of my eye, and to the side of the palace vista, I glimpsed about a dozen young students from Bung Karno University, a small university named after Soekarno in Central Jakarta, and recognizable by their maroon university blazers (jaket kampus). They had arrived late to the demonstration and had not participated as part of the massa gathered in front of the Istana, demonstrating for workers' rights and fair wages. These students assembled in a row with their backs facing the palace. In front of them stood a foreign newsman holding a microphone, whom I guessed to be German from the insignia on his equipment, and behind him a small news crew of local cameramen. I understood what was to happen. In the next few minutes, these students, some with bandanas and school ties tied low on their foreheads, raised their left fists and lustily recited the youth pledge (Sumpah Pemuda) in its entirety. It began: "We, the sons and daughters of Indonesia, pledge to uphold one nation, one homeland, one language." It ended, as recitations of the Sumpah Pemuda usually did in demonstrations, with the exhortation "Long live the Students! Long Live the Rakyat!"

Lit up on a television screen and framed as a daily news story, the shot of maroon-jacketed students with the Istana and its fluttering flags as a white, regal, and imposing backdrop might have given the imagined global viewer the impression that Indonesian youth and their protests were still central figures in Indonesian democracy. Closer to the epicenter, the stunt might be interpreted as continuous to the demonstration just prior, a ritualized ending that served as a pledge that tomorrow, students would still be united in their resistance against the political elite and capitalist interests. Instead, I was struck by the students' theatrical recitation of the Sumpah Pemuda's iconic words, staged for the benefit of a foreign viewer in contravention to the laws of demo culture. In all my observations thus far, demonstrators did not turn their backs on those symbols of power and monuments of statehood that they were demonstrating against. They faced them head on for a more direct and communicative performance of encounter and courage. Hunger strikes yes, amateur performance art yes, silent demonstrations yes, even masked demonstrations;[2] but never with one's back turned for dramatic effect. Activists had in the past engaged different media forms in creative ways, and some were more aware than others of the instrumental role television played in the representation of the student movement as a vibrant mass movement.[3] Would viewers for a European television station be able to tell that twilight was fast approaching and that the Bung Karno University students had missed the main demonstration, creating their own short performance piece of nationalist youth spirit for the camera instead? And did such considerations matter in the spectacle the students were creating?

The ritual enactment of the Sumpah Pemuda did indeed mark another process of commodification and differentiation within demo space itself. Demo space had become a ritual site where political performances of increasingly instrumental images of pemuda rebellion were transacted between students and journalists, between the student movement and their presumed public audience, and between demonstrators and elite politics. The recitation by the Bung Karno University students was simultaneously detached from the demonstration that had just ended and parasitically feeding off its residue. The youth pledge was a statement by the students that their social and political roles were one and the same, and indeed, their politics depended on the perpetuity of this conflation. The Sumpah Pemuda's generative power was in this instance a reproductive mechanism—the ideological underpinnings of sameness and uniformity that was best expressed through appearance. The Bung Karno University students had come to the Presidential Palace dressed as a corporate unit in the fashions of pemuda style from 1998 (the jackets and bandanas), even though they were themselves too young to have been active that year. Stylistic conformity indicated their moral unanimity, while differences in tone and appearance signaled potential deviation from the group. Yet the possibility that political, economic, and even personal differences would fragment the student movement was quite real, given that the common enemy, Suharto, had galvanized much of the unifying energy of Reformasi and that in his absence activists had to work harder to articulate the relevance of their actions and preferred political methods. The anxiety among activists about their continuing role as mediators between the state and civil society, and between those hierarchically positioned in relation to them, grew in proportion to the increasing value of further individuation within Generation 98.

Difference was most closely linked to the murky acquisition of money and status by activists and was regarded by many activists as a betrayal of the collective effort to change entrenched modes of political practice in elite political culture. Read another way, the "fragmentation," "decline," and "failures" of the student movement were symptomatic of the political development of youth into figures who would assume authority on more institutionalized or authorizing grounds of power.[4] These figures, known as tokoh, assumed an ambivalent position. *Tokoh*, literally meaning "form" or "shape," and in its more common and relevant meaning of "character" (in a play) or "personage," is a word that implies an elevated degree of social polish and accomplishment. The tokoh is an admired and networked person who is socially influential and politically significant, whether overtly so or behind the scenes, a figure one aspires to emulate.[5] Tokoh are leaders, either born of well-respected families or naturally possessing charismatic qualities. In Weber's description: "Charismatic authority, in its genuine form, is of a character specifically foreign to everyday routine. Social relationships subject to it are of a strictly personal nature and play an important role in the validity of charismatic personal qualities and their confirmation" (1994: 37). Weber's emphasis on the "personal nature" of ties and power coheres with a long-standing debate on the corrupting and enduring influence of "informal" patronage and clientelism in the formalized realms of Southeast Asian politics and bureaucracy (Scott 1972; Sidel 1999; Khan 1998). However, the Weberian definition of personalized and individual charismatic power did not apply to the mechanisms that enabled Generation 98 activists to transform into full-fledged young politicians during Indonesia's democratic transition. When activists sought to become recognized tokoh, their parameters were determined by the wider reputation that Generation 98 held as a loosely imagined, generational entity in the public domain. Activists could not simply assert themselves as autonomous and isolated individuals, as their very presence signaled a link to mass politics. They were truly representatives of their generation. No longer under the direction of the New Order theater of appearances, the Tokoh 98 (the prominent figures of 1998) sought to prolong the political longevity of pemuda and take activism to new heights of institutionalized legitimacy.

The word *tokohisme* emerged as a neologism that described the token modes of behavior and thought that exemplified tokoh. A more dishonorable meaning given to tokohisme describes a trickster who puts on airs or a self-proclaimed big man who uses his political persona to fool and exploit others. The tokoh-as-trickster image alluded to the persistent sense that the center and its colluding local elite in the provinces were contributing to the spread of illicit practices that scholars of clientelism have termed "patronage democracy" (Simandjuntak 2012). In one of the allegorical "Letters from Palmerah" columns authored by the writer Seno Gumira Ajidarma, which ran in the popular magazine *Jakarta Jakarta*, an ordinary member of the rakyat meets a representative of the rakyat (*wakil rakyat*).[6] The representative of the rakyat turns out to not be particularly political or idealistic, as he has never even seen the constituency he claims to represent. It is revealed in chat that he is only pretending to be for the people ("saya cuma pura-pura merakyat"). Seno dreams up this scene between the two: a member of the rakyat asks, "Are you an important person [tokoh]?" The representative of the people replies: "Nope, I'm just a fake tokoh [tokoh gombal]." "What kind of fake?" "I'm just a small-fry politician, always trying to get a leg up, always thinking about my career, whatever can be a stepping stone, I use. Basically I just think of myself." "But you are a representative of the People right?" "*Yeah, actually* [*sic*], I just represent myself" (Ajidarma 2002: 184).[7] The common man strips away the tokoh's layers, but instead of shame and revelation, we are presented with the representative's disarming honesty. In the end, the tokoh acknowledges that his relationship with the rakyat is simply an instrument, a political tool to help the bogus politician get ahead. Furthermore, Ajidarma's skit portrays the tokoh as utterly without distinction. He does not read, does not engage in persuasive rituals of oratory; he decries the intellectuals and considers himself an ordinary person who agreed to be a member of parliament (wakil rakyat) because he was directed (by someone higher up?) to do so. The tokoh is revealed to be a fraud, but an honest fraud at that; he openly proclaims his intentions that he is only there to represent himself. The ordinary rakyat who engages with the tokoh is so impressed with the politician's honesty that he feels no offense; instead he congratulates the representative for being so impressive, a true oracle of the people!

The push to identify as individual tokoh was not a process open to all activists. Only a few activists had achieved name recognition during Reformasi and afterward. The most famous activist was perhaps Budiman Sudjatmiko, a charismatic PRD leader who emerged from prison a bona fide Reformasi hero and succeeded in becoming a PDI-P legislative candidate. The majority of student activists still active in 2004 formed the anonymous troops of the student movement. They kept the spectacle of youth spirit alive and in the news. Senior activists worked behind the scenes organizing NGO events and demonstrations and attended demonstrations equipped with protest T-shirts and speeches, while their younger counterparts were more flamboyantly dressed and precariously placed on the tops of metromini buses as they arrived or left a demonstration. Pemuda identity retained a powerful pull on students who had seen the explosive events and tragedies of 1998 and 1999 and who felt it an essential part of their role as students to contribute to history. The spectacular action of the Bung Karno University students at the Presidential Palace reveals the multiple referents that are tied to public articulations of pemuda fever—superficially, the students represented a narrow set of group and university interests when they appeared as a corporate body in a specific time and place, but in choosing to perform the Sumpah Pemuda they positioned themselves as wakil rakyat, representatives of the people. One last citation matters here: the Sumpah Pemuda as a well-known nationalist ritual linking youth to nation and rakyat owed its efficacy to the New Order state's control over pemuda history's nationalist power.

RALLY YOUTH SPIRIT: NEW ORDER RITUALS OF DEMOCRACY

During the New Order years, the Sumpah Pemuda had become a vehicle for the controlled production of the spirit (semangat) of youth. In election years, youth were corralled alongside other sectors of society to ensure the success (*mensukseskan*) of the election, with the explicit aim of keeping the ruling party, Golongan Karya (Functional Categories; Golkar), victorious. Under the management of the Ministry of Youth and Sports, the Sumpah Pemuda provided the occasion for a ceremony that gathered and channeled the physical energies of youth into sports and their spiritual energies toward the goals of national development plans. In annual ceremonies that solemnly repeated New Order propaganda about the central role of youth in national development, the Ministry of Youth and Sports celebrated the Day of the Youth Pledge (Hari Sumpah Pemuda) in a series of nationalist activities and athletic meets that directly referred to government policies and plans for development.

Each year, the Ministry of Youth and Sports produced a small commemorative booklet that enumerated the anniversary of the Youth Pledge. These booklets' jackets were emblazoned with the national colors, red and white, and cartoon symbols of the raised fist, with titles such as "Youth Pledge Day / The 58th Anniversary," or "Youth Pledge Day / The 64th Pemuda Day," counting backward to the first Sumpah Pemuda of 1928.[8] The didactic inscriptions on the flyleaf made clear the prescribed annual goals of the Youth Pledge day. In 1986, the theme was "With the spirit of the Youth Pledge we will make the 1987 election a success and the 1986 / 1996 decade of pemuda will increase the participation of Indonesia's pemuda." The subtheme that followed in the paragraph below was equally terse: "Increase real work as an embodiment of the responsibility and maturity of Pemuda in applying the Pancasila."[9] Youth spirit had been commandeered to uphold statist objectives, supplanting the nation and pemuda identity as the natural objects of pemuda interest. Compare this to an earlier era of pemuda zeal that still contained the revolutionary vocabulary of power and historical consciousness. A manifesto produced by a nationalist association a few years after the 1945 revolution reads: "The existence of pemuda is a necessary precondition for the continuation of human life and of a new society, in meaning and in essence: Pemuda are the new human beings, youthful in spirit, thought, and soul. Be aware that you must fight for your fate and the fate of the People of Indonesia. Historical destiny is in your own hands. Recognize your own power!!!"[10]

If the left fist raised in protest mirrors the right fist raised in approbation, and if we take into account the use of pemuda symbolism in heavily controlled ritual events (*upacara*) during the New Order, how might we differentiate between the mediatic rituals of the student movement, performed by the Bung Karno University students outside the Istana, and those that took place inside institutions of power? Joel C. Kuipers approaches a similar problem of performative citizenship on the marginalized island of Sumba during the New Order years, when citizenship was less an institution of membership in the nation-state than an "*activity*, something people *do* as they participate in social life" (2003: 163). Ritual, Kuipers argues, does not produce new political meanings but is itself a condition for its reception. The New Order dependence on the correctness of ceremony to ensure the proper outcome of political rituals such as elections had the determined air of a foregone conclusion, which anthropologists such as John Pemberton have translated as "democracy festivals," from the Indonesian *pesta demokrasi*. The guests are spectators, while the real event has already occurred elsewhere, offstage. Kuipers explains political ritual as a "formal event that the state is staging for the benefit of the citizens, an act of generosity and munificence, not an empowering institution by which the people get to select their own leadership and representation" (188–189). Following Kuipers's explanation, ritual is the site for both the production and reception of political meaning.

Political rituals that reaffirmed the Reformasi credentials of Generation 98 became a site of convergence that sharpened the significance of maintaining egalitarian attitudes and appearances and the emerging politics of difference arising from the corps of activists who had been marked as potential prominent figures (tokoh). Political gain and money were suspected outcomes of the "patronage democracy" practiced by the political elite to maintain activist ties to youth and, by extension, to the rakyat the activists controlled. The marketing of activists as individual personalities rather than as organizational spokespersons was intensified by the 2004 general elections. Nearly all the major political parties recruited former activists to run as legislative candidates in the 2004 election, thus sparking the trend that would crystallize in the 2009 and 2014 elections when activists joined their former enemies in military-dominated and New Order bastions such as the political parties Golkar and Gerindra (see Mietzner 2013). Former activists were integrated as clean young politicians who had come of age outside political institutions and whose history of resistance spoke well of their penchant for honesty and integrity. Political parties banked on these candidates' reputations as populist and ethical persons and recognized their special roles as Tokoh 98. It was difficult to not see the selection of legislative candidates as a reward system that benefited select activists who were predisposed to elite connections and institutional roles. Activists also joined the campaign and mobilizing work of *tim sukses* (success teams) for political parties and specific presidential candidates, acting as public relations managers, campaign organizers, or liaisons with interested parties from the ranks of intellectuals, civil society, and the rakyat. At the same time, former student activists who remained outside the agenda of the political parties had aspirations to form their own political bloc to resist the status quo that electoral politics maintained (a conclusion evinced by the military backgrounds of several candidates running for office in 2004). These nonpartisan activists formed various alliances, signing their names as individuals whose names had currency in civil society and among the press who had stayed abreast of their actions since 1998. In their preparations to regroup as a powerful force in civil society, nonpartisan activists consciously invoked the pemuda legacy to legitimate their position as the true representatives of the rakyat.

In the sections that follow I look at two idioms of difference, money and representational power (tokohisme), which were the most prominent and were in fact interdependent modes of activist critique and speech in the six months prior to the 2004 election. Money and the Tokoh 98 formed poles at which anxious political speech gathered. The language of pemuda politics remained an important expression of the democratic ideas of the Tokoh 98 on both sides of the election divide. The uneasy reactions to the differential claims made by activists on the collective lineage of Generation 98, and their widely divergent material outcomes, caused fundamental changes in the way that solidarity actions were framed. Many activists who felt secure in their positions as civil society actors in the capital realized that they had neither the means nor the nationwide support of massa to act in a national framework of electoral politics. The financial costs of setting up a recognized and independent political party were far beyond their reach, and the PRD's failed effort to launch as a mass political party in 1999 was often cited as an overly optimistic and rash political decision that belonged to the early Reformasi era. Activists thus returned to older ways of organizing, forming alliances and networks between activist groups, NGOs, labor unions, peasant groups, and select oppositional politicians to congregate and reassemble the massa around a "new" power formation. Alliances consisted of tentative relationships that were from the outset designed to be fragile, thus preserving political pride and the appearance of a high moral threshold if activists discovered that they could not collaborate with their new allies for unspecified, and often personal, reasons. Actors began to fight over what each considered his or her superior claim to the events of 1998. Groups of activists formed, positioning themselves in one way or another as the Generation of 98 (Generasi 98), as evinced in the names of the following alliances: the Circle of 1998 (Lingkar 98), the 1998 Forum (Forum 98), the Exponents of 1998 (Exponen 98), and—a quasi-institutional name—the 1998 Center (Center 98).[11] The last drew snickers from activists who punned on the Indonesian homonym *senter*, which means "flashlight."[12] Some of these groups overlapped with the campaign actions of the presidential candidates who had activists on their tim sukses. Every grouping was unhappily exclusive of every other, each one consisting of fractious former activists who claimed to act with the true voice of Generation 98. The branding of Generation 98 accelerated in the months before the July ballots were cast, as those entering electoral politics played up their Reformasi activist past.

MONEY AND DIFFERENCE

In a leaderless political movement that celebrates the conjoined rakyat-massa as the ideal form of collective solidarity, being exceptional or exhibiting signs of difference can arouse suspicion, discomfort, and resentment. But first let us look again at the production of the ideal massa in the demonstration. To assemble the massa in the first place requires care and preparation, promises to the rakyat, and recruitment of more youth. The demonstration has a carefully orchestrated effect of solidity and sameness. *We are many we are one.* But, as Deasy Simandjuntak describes in her study of local election campaigns in North Sumatra that were rife with *money politics*, the look of a few thousand supportive massa decked in flags, hats, umbrellas, stickers, pins, key chains, and T-shirts did not run cheap (2012). Money in the student movement had to come from somewhere, and often it could not come at a more opportune time.

The affective capacity of money to enhance feelings of social cohesion and status difference is something I have already noted in chapter 5, where I discussed obligatory gift relations between "patron" senior activists and their "client" junior activists. The symbolic properties of money exceed the form itself. Money is often more than just money. It is salve and worry; it mystifies and reveals. Activists creatively made money and sourced it to fund demonstrations, rent, and travel, yet money was often not a transparent thing. Its source is considered both suspect and an issue largely immaterial (thus deferred) to the pragmatic problems of feeding fellow demonstrators or paying this year's rent. Money is thought of as coming from others and from elsewhere rather than as a reliable outcome of activist labor. Yet money is, as Truitt explains, an "expression of moral economies" and a way of "creating and maintaining socially sanctioned forms of indebtedness" (2013: 103). Given the freelance, moral, and ideological nature of activist work, their efforts cannot be easily slotted into the exploitative economy of wage labor and remuneration. But it would be more apt to say that activists often resist the binding ties of salaried, hourly work. Activist organizations that were successful at acquiring *funding* (the English term is used) from foreign donors or funding agencies that supported broad principles of human rights and democracy were prime examples of how activists could successfully learn the value of networks, good governance, and technocratic approaches to political work while gaining access to multiyear streams of money. Moreover, grantee organizations achieved recognition and elevated status from accessing transparent sources of money, a fact that visitors, readers, and event participants were reminded of each time the logos of the respective funding agencies appeared on their print and digital materials. More commonly, senior activists would access their own patronage ties "above" to the elite they knew and disburse the funds they managed to mobilize to the junior activists below. The circulation of money in the early Reformasi years is described by lay activists as a wondrous manifestation of fateful generosity. It is positive magic, a gift to save the day. When money appears, it could well mean a spontaneous and sincere gift from the masyarakat (society). The masyarakat is urban, and we can deduce, also educated and middle class. The students can take from the masyarakat what they cannot take from the poorer rakyat—the gift of financial support and commodities (logistik) bought in bulk, such as bottled water, food, clothes, and other necessary provisions. Since bulk goods were often bought through members-only clubs or wholesale stores that had become popular with wealthier and cost-saving families, or at more upscale and costly *hypermart* (large, modern supermarkets), the scale of donations reflected the class position of the giver. The gift of money and commodities has as its greatest attribute the affirmative sense that the masyarakat, from which the political classes originate, recognize and legitimate the students. Hence, the "spontaneous actions" that followed the Trisakti and Semanggi tragedies were an example of how Reformasi mobilized the sentiments of the middle- and upper-classes, albeit in limited and symbolic ways. The educated and urbane citizens who comprise the masyarakat do not bear any resemblance to the poor and authentic rakyat, such that their moral compulsion to aid the students can only come in the form of releasing their money. Money pours forth from the middle and upper classes in limitless largesse, but behind their generosity activists can easily imagine exploited others in their households and in their factories. Money is one of the defining characteristics of elite figures and political aspirants, who are envied and admired in Indonesia.[13] How would traditional notions of leadership, as springing from social and economic capital combined, affect activists' efforts to enter the realm of post-Reformasi power circles? And why then did their activist expertise and mediating role toward the rakyat generate suspicion and distrust among their own circles?

ELECTION YEAR: BROKERAGE AND LEADERSHIP

Activists succumbed willingly to election fever in 2004, a year that felt distant enough from 1998 that most activists had begun to condemn the student movement to failure (as did many Indonesian and foreign scholars I spoke to). The 2004 national elections rekindled the energies and determined search for that magical amalgamation of chance and political opening, the *moment* (using the English word) of political change. Student activists were once again "looking for momentum" (*mencari momentum*) rather than waiting patiently for it, and this switch to an active search reflected important changes in their options for self-renewal. The discourse of failure pointed to political as well as moral failures on the part of the students. Even though scholars of Indonesian democracy point to crucial democratic gains evinced by a minority presence of elected reformist activists, who may not be dominant in politics but are significant nonetheless (Mietzner 2013), student activists were keenly aware that the democracy that Generation 98 had hoped for had not resulted in greater social and economic justice for the rakyat. The state and the army had not even been held accountable for past violations against citizens, among which the Trisakti and Semanggi tragedies were of the most pressing concern to the student movement (see fig. 6.1). More and more, activists told me stories about missing money, patronage relationships between activists and questionable politicians, even between students and the army, in an attempt to locate where things had gone wrong for them. These stories were inevitably framed as a colorful set of gossip stories that were common knowledge in the movement. So-and-so had embezzled money meant for mass demonstrations, so-and-so was always reporting back to the elite who engineered the demonstrations and the clashes (bentrok) for their own ends. In short, economically successful activists were suspected of long ago betraying the movement by stealthily becoming *brokers*. The English word "broker" was widely used and was more common than the Dutch-derived term *makelaar*, which had a more frank commercial meaning and therefore less of a political valence (and in-

FIGURE 6.1 Antimilitarism flyer by activist groups reminding the public of the Semanggi tragedies in 1998–1999. Anonymous, c. 2004 election campaign period. Top: front and back covers. Front cover has the title "Be Careful, Don't Let Militarism Return"; the hand-painted flag reads "ABRI [army] = I Massacre Indonesian People." Bottom: composite images inside the flyer represent army violence against students, including ID photos of four victims. AUTHOR'S PERSONAL COLLECTION.

deed in the Netherlands the term refers most often to real estate agents). Now activists-turned-brokers were more open about the nature of their political work. The proof was in the material possessions of senior activists, who owned cars and houses without ever having worked steady jobs in traditionally lucrative fields.[14]

During a demonstration that began with the massa gathering in the public gardens of the former Danamon building in the central business district of Jakarta, the name of a reputed broker and former UI activist came up. The activist in question now owned a successful cellular phone business and still socialized regularly with his former colleagues in the NGO scene but did not hide his elite connections to one of the leading political parties. Even as a student activist his sartorial sense had been well known. Now he wore natty batik shirts and smelled strongly of expensive cologne, resembling in appearance the minor politicians and brokers who could be spotted networking in hotel lobbies and late-night cafes.[15] In fact, I often saw this man visiting friends day and night at the shabby activist workspaces of the Legal Aid Institute extension building, so much so that I began to wonder what was the secret of his flexible schedule. He in turn still talked about Indonesian democracy and about his ties to his alma mater, inviting me to meet with student study groups he knew well, implying his sponsorship and mentorship of the students. At the demonstration, a young woman who was an NGO worker spoke of him: "It's amazing, but terrible! He runs with Wiranto [former general and commander-in-chief in 1998 whom activists held responsible for Reformasi's violence and who was running for president in 2004], with this, with that, with whomever, just to get a job. What happened to him?" Her question carried some distress, and Sinyo, an older activist, added fuel to the fire, saying, "He has a fancy new BMW, and who knows where that came from?"[16] Similar suspicions emerged when I visited Lampung and contacted a former PRD activist living there. Despite his history as a provincial activist who had developed his intellectual and political capital with one of the most radical leftist student groups in Indonesia, he was now open about his need to network and broker demonstrations. In fact, I had the distinct sense that he was boasting about his capacity for organizing the massa in a preparatory manner, so that Lampung, a small city that had less political competition and sophistication, might serve as a rehearsal stage for a grander political stage. When I returned to Jakarta I met with Sugeng, the activist who had recommended that I speak to his dear friend in Lampung. Sugeng admitted that the man had gone astray and had a reputation for freelancing.

The implication was that these rogue activists (also called *ronin*, a Japanese word for freelance warriors without fealty whom activists picked up from the translated samurai novels that were popular at the time) had become political brokers who elicited scorn from activists still on the straight and narrow path. Rogue activists were no longer bound to any groups, but many of them had the reputed skill of being able to contact student groups or urban poor massa to facilitate paid demonstrations. Activists had something of monetary value, that is, their access and hold over the massa. If a senior activist succumbed to temptation and allied with political elites from the parties and the military, then the demonstrations they were associated with became suspect. *Brokers* sold their massa to the political elite for sums of money that they then pocketed.[17] *Brokers* might have been depicted by their detractors as socially unmoored mercenaries, but they were also in the service of political elites and likely to accumulate favors in their ascent up the political ladder.

The literature on the term *broker* in Indonesian studies reflects the fluid and ambiguous moral economy of brokerage, even in received public opinion. Clifford Geertz first brought attention to the mobilizing potential of the term "culture broker" in his analysis of the changing roles of the Javanese *kyai*, the traditional Islamic scholar-teacher, in newly independent Indonesia. Writing in the decolonizing 1950s, Geertz identified an enormous social and ideological gap between the secular national elite in the center and the traditional communities in rural and marginalized areas that had been transformed into citizens. The kyai emerged as the most effective bridges between the secular aims of the modern nation-state and the idioms and social structures of traditional society (Geertz 1960). Brokerage, in Geertz's view, was a necessary service of *translation* that reflected the hybrid and dynamic arrangements that best served the interests of the collective in a time of political transformation. The more recent literature on brokerage has focused attention on the mainly predatory and volatile aspects of political brokerage, even going as far as to identify different categories and intentions of brokering as political practice. Activist brokers, as Aspinall classifies them, "are defined by a political, ethnic, religious, or some other loyalty to the candidate that motivates them independently of patronage calculations." Meanwhile, "clientelist brokers and opportunist brokers, by contrast, are primarily motivated by material benefits, but while the former have an eye to the long-term relationships they might build with the candidate, the latter are more interested in reaping immediate payoffs" (2014b: 548). Aspinall's categories result from his recent study of regional election campaigns in post-Reformasi Indonesia and depict the steep learning curve that activists and brokers have experienced in the democratic transition. In the course of a few national and regional elections, certain forms of brokerage have become more predatory and more visible to the naked eye.

Brokerage touched on sensitive and congenital failures in the student movement, particularly with regard to finances. Many of the leftist and radical student groups had experimented with communal life, living in sekretariat and basekemp, as I discussed in the previous chapter. To fund their expenses for food and lodging as well as political activities, students had tried a system of dues-collection (iuran) and some form of business activity. The iuran proved less than reliable, mainly because student activists were on the whole unemployed and unemployable for work other than intellectual, organizational or journalistic tasks such as writing, reporting, translation work, or organizing workshops for their NGO patrons. Their business activities also reflected their "idealism." Determined to put into practice a sustainable model of equitable cooperative, students sold their journals, often at inflated prices or—in the late 1990s, when *distros* (distribution outlets) of alternative fashion were popular— sold T-shirts and other items of "politically subversive" value.[18] The National Student League for Democracy publication, for instance, lists forty branches and distribution outlets for its publication "Supel" ("Suara Pelopor" [Pioneering voices]) in cities across Indonesia. The price of this publication was a mere 1,500 rupiah (15 US cents), advertised as its "solidarity price" (*harga solidaritas*).[19] Solidarity price extended to the rakyat and the workers, but as I found out, for middle-class solidarity mongers, paying the stated cost of the publication was a terrible faux pas. An activist who sold me one of his organization's pamphlets was disappointed when I handed him the 5,000 rupiah (US$0.50) price printed on the cover. "What, so little?" he exclaimed loudly. I duly exchanged the bill for a much larger denomination.

The staggered value system that used social class to determine the price of the product expressed common social understandings of obligation between social superiors and their *anak buah* (protégées; lit. children). If patrons were expected to neutralize the potentially disturbing effect of their own social advantages by paying more for an otherwise standardized good or service, their payment fixed the hierarchy in place while dissipating the social envy the lower classes exhibited toward the middle and upper classes. Such value systems created a chaotic mode of production and distribution for activist moneymaking enterprises. Each activist was given a stack of publications of intrinsic value, that is, a collection of saleable objects that required deploying the personal relation between the seller and the buyer to determine a fair monetary outcome. Thus the student had to make all the indexical decisions required to express the value of political solidarity whereby the rich paid more in support while the poor paid less, if anything at all. Thus each student tasked with selling his quota did not have a fixed revenue quota. Rather, he was given a minimal amount to achieve and went unpunished if the quota was not met.

The monetary value of the product was an additional value, a "gift," as it were, to the person who bought it. When the cooperatives involved more ambitious means of production, involving multicity cooperation between branches of the same organization, funds often disappeared into local expenses rather than returning to the national headquarters' cashbox. After the tumult of 1998, junior activists had become more skilled at hawking T-shirts, journals, and VCDs of amateur film documentaries, while senior activists had the experience and reputation to serve as paid guest speakers or organizers of political events, book launchings, and discussions that they had once participated in as audience members. Their lack of business acumen was an integral part of their anticapitalist persona. Since activists had strong romantic visions of realizing a proletarian or, at the very least, a prorakyat society in which the relations between labor and commodities were demystified, it made sense that one could not be too good at managing business interests if one was "for the people." Furthermore, one could be accused of being Chinese, or like the Chinese with their trickery and ability to make money.[20]

Student activists' claim to a greater transparency and their dedication to transcending the capitalist system, marked by the New Order systems of patronage and exploitation of labor, was frustrated by the fact that the "production" of money was simultaneously reviled and necessary. Circulation of money stopped within the student movement, leading to tales of corruption, embezzlement, or plainly amusing ineptitude. Where these moneyed relations became sources of organizational strain was in the revelation that the branches of local offices opened by student organizations, the cabang (branches) in the daerah (provinces/localities), were operating independently of the "national vision" put forth by the pusat, the leadership, who were most often located in the university-dense cities of Jakarta, Bandung, and Yogyakarta. In the previous chapter I cited the senior FPPI activist Savic articulating the fragmented relationship between the various generations (angkatan) of FPPI members by way of analogy; he gave the example of a demonstration that activists in the daerah had organized that the pusat (center) had no knowledge of. Could such an unauthorized demonstration be manipulated or corrupted from within? Was money a contaminant that obfuscated the political relations between peers in the same organization? Who was truly in charge? The tension between the national leadership and its branches in the daerah reveals the worry of corruption in the student movement, particularly after the exponential growth in student organizing and untraceable financial support after May 1998. Support from the masyarakat (society) poured forth, not only taking the form of logistik (supplies, cell phones, and cash funds) but also facilitating connections between the leadership of student organizations and political elites. Corruption was a central worry that permeated activists' stories of financial woes, for financial windfalls, or even the appearance of economic stability, summoned the anxiety that student activists were beholden to competing sources of authority that carried grave moral and financial consequences.[21]

PUBLIC FACES

Activists who had come of age in 1998 were now preparing to use the social and political capital they had accumulated from their part in Reformasi to enter the 2004 electoral race as *calon legislatif* (legislative candidates), or *caleg* for short. The National Election Commission released its data on the candidacies of several young candidates. Of the fifty-one former activists listed, twenty-nine hailed from Java, with the next largest number from Sumatra. The *caleg muda* (young legislative candidates), as they were called, were roughly split into two camps, between the "nationalist" and the "religious" (Muslim) parties. Twenty of those candidates had chosen to join two modernist Muslim parties widely identified with Reformasi ideals of transparency and social justice: the Justice Welfare Party (Partai Keadilan Sejahtera) and the National Mandate Party, led by the Reformasi tokoh Dr. Amien Rais (Adi 2004). The first half of the nationwide election on April 5, 2004, gave voters the chance to elect their representatives at the local district or city levels and at provincial and national levels. Despite the confusing new system, where voters could elect independent candidates at the district and provincial levels for the first time, and reportedly low voter-education rates, enthusiasts called it the most free and fair election since 1955.[22] The caleg muda were adamant that entering the race was the only logical and ethical consequence of their prior idealism. In their statements to the media, they refuted the charge that entering the most corrupt ring of all, elite politics in Indonesia, was a betrayal of their youthful activist ideals.

Rama Pratama, the poster child for the caleg muda phenomenon, was regarded as the most promising, virtuous, and reliable (*konsisten*) candidate.[23] In an interview with the newspaper daily *Kompas* on February 7, 2004, Rama clarified his perception of his responsibilities toward the public, given his stature as a moral student activist in 1998. He explained his choice this way: "When I decided to become a legislative candidate [caleg], I was aware that the question of my integrity was a greater burden compared to the question of my competency for the job. A lot of clever people who are exceptional in their field often run into trouble when it comes to integrity."[24] As a former president of the student senate at UI, Rama had been a prominent figure among the most elite of the student groups. In publicity photographs and on television programs, Rama looked the part, dressed neatly in a button-down dress shirt and slacks, with short hair and glasses. He was tall and solidly built, with the shade of fair skin (*putih bersih*) considered attractive in Indonesia. In February 2004, the private television station SCTV ran a late-night talk show with three caleg muda as the featured guests. Rama looked the most "clean" and appealing, dressed in the urban professional's uniform of a long sleeved V-neck pullover over a button-down shirt. Compared to Rama, Lutfi, the former Forkot member who had shockingly "gone over" to Golkar, the New Order stalwarts' party, looked thin, dark, and shifty. Their divergent appearances fit the class-image stereotypes of what modern politicians look like and reflected audience dispositions toward caleg muda in general. Lutfi was placed on the spot several times by the talk show host, who openly questioned why Lutfi had joined the enemy. Without an adequate response, Lutfi retreated into uncomfortable silence; he was at a disadvantage next to the eloquent Rama, who managed to repeat the political platform of his party (the Justice Welfare Party, a modernist Islamic party) without hesitation. Not even a hint of long hair and lower-class pemuda style for Rama. Indeed, Rama was elected to an office in the Justice Welfare Party and became active in its public events. Ironically, just one year prior to his election, *Tempo* had run a short article on him, titled "Normal Life," in which he claimed that he was now leading a thoroughly regular, nonpolitical life. The article contrasted the chaos of 1998 to the calm of the present and implied that Rama greatly preferred his current job at a prestigious accounting firm to politics. But if politics needed him again, Rama would descend (*terjun*) into the world of politics. However, he denied that he would ever "sell his name as a former activist" ("menjual namanya sebagai bekas aktivis"). That, he said, he was really reluctant to do ("Rama Pratama" 2003).

Other former activists joined the ubiquitous tim sukses that catered to and planned each presidential candidate's image, public statements, and campaign. The tim sukses was a newly invigorated phenomenon in Indonesian politics, resembling the interest lobbies and professionalized and grassroots campaigns of European and North American politicians that are headed by professional team leaders and rely heavily on media to advertise the candidate. The members of the tim sukses acted as liaisons between the candidate and the grassroots constituencies they hoped to gain, lending their expertise to staging appearances, manufacturing the locality of campaigns, and updating politicians on the fast-moving political landscape occupied by a range of post-Reform interests and demands. The incumbent, Megawati Soekarnoputri, was running such a complicated campaign for reelection that it was rumored that she had three tim sukses vying for supremacy within the party and competing for her attention.

The lessons the student movement brought to the table were mobilized by the establishment's political party machinery to run a "clean" and grassroots-centric campaign, a few years behind the "transparency and fairness" trend set by new parties in the 1999 elections, such as the Islamic Justice Welfare Party, which appealed to educated, middle-class Muslims. Former activists who joined tim sukses claimed direct knowledge of constituencies that had been sufficiently transformed by Reformasi to be political voters rather than bought constituents but who nonetheless would still be compelled by activists' skilled moral guidance and charisma. Activist members of tim sukses could promise votes in a clean and politically modern manner, unlike the entrenched elites who populated the political party machinery. Political parties that were trying to present a more democratic image gained immediate benefits from institutionalizing activist networks and expertise, but such benefits were balanced by the uncomfortable charge that activists had become collaborators with power. On the surface, the 2004 election campaigns were enlivened by the integration of familiar activist elements, seen in the number of seemingly autonomous public discussions, seminars, and press conferences held by the youth and progressive elements of the party to launch this and that *social contract*. But the uncomfortable fact remained that prodemocratic activists had joined forces with the very figures of authority they had once opposed. The activists who joined tim sukses, including those of military candidates such as General Wiranto, Agum Gumelar (Megawati's running mate), and former general Susilo Bambang Yudhoyono ("SBY"), were mocked by their former comrades, amid gossip about exactly how much funding they now had access to as aides to their military bosses. Joining tim sukses was a step up from freelance brokering but was not an assured path to financial stability either.

In the months of December 2003–March 2004, secret meetings between activists took place to determine the positions and stakes of friends and foes in the movement. Who would join tim sukses, and who would be the face of the Tokoh 98? The discussions pointed to a division of labor in the movement that more optimistic activists saw as a win-win solution that would disperse activists throughout the political system, formally and informally. But disappointments were rife. Lured by promises of the social programs they could accomplish and plentiful funds if they joined a political party, even if they did so informally through volunteer and patronage networks, activists found that they did not rise to prominence in the party once the election was over.

The choice over which role to take seemed partly determined by the technical requirements of party candidacy. The fifty-one former activists who were listed as legislative candidates (caleg muda) had by and large graduated with their Sarjana (bachelor's) degrees in hand. Some of the more prominent caleg also had strong organizational backgrounds in student senates (*Badan Eksekutif Mahasiswa,* or BEM) or in Islamic groups, which were highly structured, with ties to existing parties. Meanwhile, the majority of activists in civil society groups were automatically disqualified, for many were *mahasiswa abadi* (eternal students) and dropouts whose intense involvement in the student movement had nullified their chances to finish their skripsi (thesis) requirements for graduation. In addition, several of those elected to caleg status were members of national student organizations that had close ties to political parties, including religious organizations such as the popular HMI and KAMMI, as observers pointed out. A. Prasetioantoko predicted that the religious groups would progress and form collaborative relationships more quickly than nationalist groups because, "culturally, the first is more homogenous, calm, and rational, while the other is more heterogenous and emotional."[25] The claim that the religious-based student groups, such as Himpunan Mahasiswa Islam and Kesatuan Aksi Mahasiswa Muslim Indonesia, were better suited to formal politics was a widespread opinion held by many so-called nationalist groups in the student movement. The fragmented nationalist-leftist groups admired and resented the disciplined way that religious groups recruited cadres, won seats in student senate bodies, and maintained a presence on campus through their own disciplined efforts. The supremacy of faith-based groups on campus, and at times on the street, reinforced the talk of failure in the student movement, in part due to its own exuberance. In Islamic rhetoric, reason governed passion, while the student movement, with its passionate speeches, violent clashes, and dramatic display of moral righteousness, was driven by emosi (feelings). The political alignments between disciplined and homogenous groups and aspirational political parties supported the rise of neatly attired, "clean-looking" activists who were not especially close to the rakyat. The caleg muda phenomenon proved that the appearances of the street were not desirable. The face of formal democracy required cleanliness and smoothness, and young politicians with legitimate student senate experiences, like Rama Pratama, provided that sense of discipline and order.

It is only too obvious that the destiny of the revolution is linked solely to the interest of the dominated and exploited masses. But it is the nature of this link that poses the real problem, as either a determined causal link or a different sort of connection. It is a question of knowing how a revolutionary potential is realized, in its very relationship with the exploited masses or the "weakest links" of a given system. Do these masses of links act in their own place, within the order of causes and aims that promote a new socius, or are they on the contrary the place and the agent of a sudden and unexpected irruption, an irruption of desire that breaks with causes and overturns the socius, revealing its other side?

—GILLES DELEUZE AND FELIX GUATTARI, *ANTI-OEDIPUS: CAPITALISM AND SCHIZOPHRENIA* (1983: 377)

The activist event of 2004 was without doubt the "May Movement Alliance," a meeting between former student activists held at the National Library, in the Salemba area (see fig. 6.2).

The meeting was sponsored by a number of human rights NGOs and organizations, and the event itself generated a great deal of excitement from activists and from victims' groups, as well as researchers and journalists. I was told multiple times about this upcoming event on April 21, 2004, at the National Library. "Datang ya" (You're coming right?), activists pressed. The confusion over the time of the event indicated the scale and sheer number of actors involved in the meeting. First an activist named Teddy from Forkot (City Forum) called to tell me that the event would start at 9 AM. Forkot was heavily involved in the preparations and in the negotiating that succeeded in getting everyone to the table. Then Lukman, a member of TRK whom I did not personally know, called to inform me that the meeting would start at 10. Soon afterward, an older gentleman from the Korban 65 group called to correct the previous caller's information; the event was at 1 PM. A friend who was recording the whole thing on video for a documentary she was making had also given the time as 1 PM. Based on that majority information, I decided to go at 1. I had just settled down to write some notes when an activist named Ucok, whom I also did not know, called at 9:32 AM on behalf of someone else I knew to confirm the 10 AM time. I immediately sped to the National Library in a taxi and arrived to a vibrant and crowded scene outside the main hall. Young men and women served at reception tables on which leftist books (published by Hastra Mitra and Resist presses) were displayed for sale. A donation box was prominently displayed next to the guest book, and after we had signed in, the volunteers encouraged us to give bills of no less than 20,000 rupiah (US$2.20).

6 Tahoen jatuhnya sang Tirani SOEHARTO

PERNYATAAN SIKAP ALIANSI MEI BERGERAK

Tanggal 21 mei 2004 Hari ini genap sudah 6 tahoen SOEHARTO turun dari kekaisarannya yang sangat Tiran yang hampir 33 tahun lamanya SOEHARTO berkuasa .setelah sekian lama dan tahun berlalu,dan baru saja hiruk pikuk Pemilu sudah selesai dan kita telah 4 kali berganti Presiden dan juga bongkar pasang Kabinet ,perubahan apa yang didapat dan dirasakan oleh rakyat? Apakah harga-harga menjadi murah?apakah upah buruh menjadi sejahtera dan hidupnya lebih baik? Tidak!!tidak! tidak ada yang berubah.tetap saja konflik ditiap daerah sampai sampai saat ini tetap ada contohnya adalah Aceh tetap saja bergolak,kerusuhan ambon juga tetap terjadi yang semuanya Rakyat menjadi Korban terus menerus.dilain sisi juga sampai saat ini petani juga tidak mendapatkan haknya atas tanah yang selama ini dirampas.para jenderal yang seharusnya juga bertanggung jawab terhadap berbagai pembantaian jutaan Rakyat Indonesia sampai detik ini juga tidak bisa diseret dan diadili kepengadilan dan mendapatkan hukuman yang pantas salah satunya adalah Jendral SOEHARTO penjahat kemanusiaan terbesar abad ini yang juga tidak disentuh oleh hukum terlebih juga pada KORUPTOR yang membuat puluhan juta rakyat indonesia menjadi miskin kini juga tidak ditangkap dan diadili.

Militer yang membunuh mahasiswa serta yang membunuh Marsinah membunuh kawan-kawan di trisakti,dilampung dan disemanggi juga tidak dapat diseret dan adiadili.ternyata memang tidak ada perubahan tidak ada perubahan.para jenderal itu tetap saja bebas dan tetap saja bebas menembaki dan membunuh siapa saja bahkan kini jenderal yang penuh berlumuran darah tersebut menjadi Calon CAPRES yang dalam hitungan tidak lama lagi akan berkuasa dan memimpin bangsa ini.Pertanyaannya buat kita adalah apakah kita rela kalau saja para jenderal yang harus bertanggung jawab terhadap berbagai kasus-kasus pelanggaran Ham yang terjadi dibangsa ini.jawabannya adalah tentu TIDAK! TIDAK! TIDAK.biar bagaimanapun tidak dapat dipisahkan bahwa SOEHARTO,WIRANTO,SBY,AGUM GUMELAR adalah Militer yang punya karateristik FASIS dan MILITERISTIK.karena berkuasanya militer pada hakekatnya adalah matinya nilai-nilai DEMOKRASI SIPIL untuk iitulah maka kami dari ALIANSI MEI BERGERAK menyerukan kepada seluruh kekuatan PRODEMOKRASI tugas kita adalah menyelamatkan DEMOKRASI.

Adalah janji kita untuk mempertahankan sampai TITIK DARAH TERAKHIR untuk menegakkan SUPREMASI SIPIL di REPUBLIK INDONESIA sebab KEDAMAIAN tanpa KEADILAN adalah TIRANI.

Jakarta 21 Mei 2004

ALIANSI MEI BERGERAK

FIGURE 6.2 Flyer for the City Forum (Forkot)–driven "May Movement Alliance." The flyer is also a press statement on the national situation "6 years after the fall of Soeharto's tyranny." The last line in bold reads: "We promise to fight to the last drop of our blood to uphold civil supremacy in the Republic of Indonesia because peace without justice is still tyranny." Jakarta, May 21, 2004. AUTHOR'S PERSONAL COLLECTION.

It felt like a hefty solidarity price, but I was told by a smiling young woman that the money would go toward paying the expenses for the rental hall.

Inside the large white room, tables dressed in formal folds of cloth formed a U-shape, at the head of which stood the moderator's table. A number of microphones were available for the speakers at the tables, and two were propped on stands for the audience members, who sat in concentric rows around the tables. A banner (spanduk) naming the alliance was slung up on the small raised stage behind the conference area. Some of us opted to stand at the doorway or sit on the floor. A number of TV crews were there, as well as journalists and photographers, in addition to the documentarians from each student activist group. A street children's music group, sponsored by the large NGOs as part of their community development programs, prepared their songs for their performance later in the day. As the Tokoh 98 milled about, greeting each other jovially, the energy was palpable. Even those activists who normally went out of their way to tease me ignored my presence as they talked, shook hands, and hugged men they had sworn never to "meet" (ketemu) again. The moderator of the event, M. Fadjroel Rachman, a TV and radio personality, poet, columnist, former imprisoned student activist in the 1980s, and ardent socialist, was dressed in a splendid gold batik dress shirt and was busy fluttering about. He greeted people like a gracious celebrity, and later an audience member quipped that he was the best moderator around because he had presided over several generations of activists, from the 1980s to the present. Before the start of the event, Fadjroel performed an act of kindness and introduced me to several former activists who would be useful for my research.

Soon we were ushered to our seats, and a Forkot member acted as the opening master of ceremonies, introducing the respected and senior Fadjroel. There were twenty men at the table, and Fadjroel stood in the center, joined by Ibu Wawan, the mother of a student who was shot dead in the Trisakti Tragedy of May 12, 1998.

Fadjroel introduced Ibu Wawan, an elegant grey-haired woman who spoke simply and without emotion. She gave a long statement, recounting a chronology of events that led to the shooting of students, the death of her son, and the struggle to bring the perpetrators to justice. It was her hope, she said, that the day's event would reunite the tokoh seated in front of her and aid the victims in bringing their children's killers to justice.[26] She addressed the young men seated at the table directly, stressing their responsibility to the memory of her son and those like him, all of them bound by the memory of 1998. Two other mothers followed her speech, repeating the same heartfelt wish but in more maternal tones, expressing their gratitude to the activists for agreeing to the meeting. The tragedy that had taken their children remained unresolved, and there was still, seven years later, no recourse for justice. Would the students help them?

Fadjroel summarized the proceedings and reminded the participants that "we need concrete decisions and an outcome today." Each activist then given fewer than ten minutes to speak his mind and make suggestions, but most of them exceeded the allotted time. The first two, who spoke politely, pointed out various obstacles in their path to regrouping but expressed the vague hope that they could do something concrete in the near future. As the microphone was passed down the table, the speeches became even more heated and "honest," as activists began to allude to past events that had driven them apart instead of sticking to the script of harmony and cooperation. The next day, Ridwan, who had been seated at the table, assured me that there had been a lot of doublespeak and that had it not been for the presence of the mothers, they would all have come to blows. "It was really unhealthy," he said. Nobody had come forth with what sounded like a "concrete suggestion," that is, a political plan to answer the mothers' requests. One activist, artsy-looking with long hair and glasses, even read a poem he had written to express his feelings. The event lasted four hours, and the audience was restless but also curious about the unusual congregation of activists who were looking to revive the movement in a way that would recapture the unity in difference of 1998.

As I listened to the recording I made of the meeting of Tokoh 98, the combined din of audience laughter and the unclear sounds of the speeches made listening to the actual words difficult. The audience cheered and laughed and interacted with the speakers as they would while watching a play. Only when the tones grew strident and accusing, and clearly angry at the "thirty-two years of tyranny" the rakyat had suffered under Suharto, did the audience grow silent. Otherwise, laughter lightened the mood, expressed audience participation and appreciation for activists' speaking skills, and kept us rooted for the four hours the meeting took to finish. Each activist approached his moment on the floor with an assured oratory, listing problems and grievances rather than solutions. It became clear from the litany of problems that each person was indicating his politically inflexible stance. No alliance would be formed that day.

When there was a break for lunch, there was a mad rush to the side door toward the buffet laid out at the back. The food and water disappeared quickly, and an informal air came over us again, as activist groups sat on the flowersills and tiled floors, ate their lunches, and smoked kretek (clove) cigarettes. A group of us lingered, but the library staff gave signs that we had overstayed our welcome. The chairs were being stacked, the table cloths taken off the tables, and the lights dimmed. We were ushered out by the cleaners, and finally the door was shut upon us. "Diusir!" (Thrown out!) Fadjroel laughed at the unceremonious ending of the anticipated day. What I heard and observed in person was a great deal of goodwill and spontaneous laughter, for the underlying tensions had been well hidden. Fadjroel, the moderator, admitted his nervousness. "I was afraid," he said in English. Why? "Because there were so many factions there," he said. I said that he had been smart to remind the activists of their moral obligation and their deep primordial connection to the mothers of the victims. He said, "We'll see. This is just the beginning. With luck we'll have more meetings like this one."

THE DAY AFTER

The next day I met with Ridwan. He shook his head as he recalled the assembly. The poor mothers would have their hopes crushed if any movement forward depended on the student activists, he said. Echoing Fadjroel's unease, Ridwan repeated that Generation 98 were still deeply connected with one another but in a destructive way. They remembered betrayals rather than friendships, and they were okay meeting as regular people, but would not and could not get over their past "trauma." As I puzzled over the different actors who all called themselves by the name of Generation 98 and the nature of the betrayals between them, Ridwan took my notebook from me and grew animated as he explained Indonesian politics in general and yesterday's politics in particular.

"I'm very fond of drawing boxes," he said. He proceeded to cover five sheets of my field notebook in words, lines, squiggles, circles, and boxes. I can no longer read many of these boxes, but I can make out key words that punctuated our discussion. NGOs, the State, the Military, Industry, Culture, and one box filled with the words "State Nation Country" in the upper right corner. This last cluster looked especially dynamic, with lines drawn and redrawn thickly. Essentially, Ridwan's drawings were classification schemes that ordered the relations between state and civil society actors. He placed "us" prodemocratic actors in the middle and "them," the state, on top. State and society are naturally at odds, with no means of reaching a common understanding. He wanted to build this middle ground of middle actors as a "class" (not in the Marxist sense of creating class awareness, he explained) to advocate the demands of each and the other. In other words, civil society actors were mediators between the state and the rakyat. The drawing I like best is the one he drew in the shape of a tree. At the roots of the tree is the word "Problem," and flanking the branches is a list of words under the heading "Existensi" (in its more common spelling, *eksistensi*, meaning status and identity problems).[27] The tree, I deduced, was an organism that best described the set of relationships and cross-purposes Generation 98 found themselves in.

While the image of the tree made it appear that the problems that pervaded the student movement had a natural genetic structure directing its growth, from a central trunk to its widespread branches, it also made sense that the potent symbol of the wide-canopied banyan tree described the systemic conflict and ties that bound Generation 98 together. The banyan (*beringin*) tree had for years been the symbol of Golkar, Suharto's political party and the institutionalized mechanism that bound the various levels of functionaries, civil servants, and voters in the provinces to the center. Golkar's banyan tree was coeval with the development-era image of patronage politics itself. In return, the patronage system was replenished by bought votes during election years and by the obligatory membership of all civil servants and their families in government-sponsored unions, associations, and foundations. Ridwan's activist tree image recalled the warnings about *momok Suharto*, Suharto's ghosts, that plagued Reformasi politics with the specters of patronage and *money politics*.

Next to the tree was a diagram of overlapping boxes and circles that I had taken for a primitive television set peppered with dials but Ridwan had explained was a seating diagram of the event the day before. Ridwan had drawn lines that crossed from one person to another and crossed out some of them. Connecting these circles of people, as well as illustrating the concrete line of discord between them, the lines between these actors presented a complex view of how one activist's words and actions hurt another. The lines did not represent ties of solidarity but materialized the conflicts that made it next to impossible for the aktivis 98 to meet (ketemu) in a public forum to collaborate once again. Too many bridges burned. The problem, as Ridwan put it, was over *existensi*, a matter of identity and status issues where one had to constantly struggle to define oneself against the actions of others. *Existensi* is another name for the problem of individuation. Even if the gerakan sought to reassemble its former members, their past conflicts had personalized politics to such a degree that shared political goals were impossible to articulate.

GENERATION 98 SURVIVES

Two weeks after the high-profile congress at the National Library, a smaller alliance of several well-known individuals launched another short-lived alliance in a public event at the Legal Aid Institute. Some of them, including Ridwan, had been involved in the ill-fated National Library meeting. On May 11, GENBI, the New Indonesian Generation (Generasi Baru Indonesia), began the event with a big press conference in the Princen Room. The press statement contained a long list of seventy-three signatories, most of them activists from 1998 who were no longer a part of student organizations. Among these names were former PRD activists, former Famred members, and former National Student League for Democracy activists, all of whom were close friends and colleagues in human rights and labor organizing. Some of the names were more illustrious, including some prominent NGO leaders, and two female celebrities, who proved to be a big draw for entertainment journalists at the launch. The statement reiterated a universal humanist concern while warning against a narrow, corrupt politics reminiscent of the past. It culminated with this paragraph: "We emphasize our determination not to be trapped into the whirlwinds of corrupt, nepotistic, feudal, capitalist, discriminatory, and militaristic politics that belong in the past. Therefore, we are committed to and willing to continue our struggle to build a new Indonesian civilization. That is why we, the youth, have decided to come together in the New Indonesian Generation with a new spirit that is not limited by groupings of background, ethnicity, race, and religion. We, the New Indonesian Generation, ask all Indonesian youth to work together and fight for its realization."[28]

A new hope, or an old one? The statement put forth a new spirit (semangat) that echoed the Sumpah Pemuda in important ways, as a conscious effort to put aside identity markers and form a new generation. The sentiments of the statement were impeccably written, but skeptics were present in the room. An older journalist who cut a self-important figure got up to ask a question of the GENBI representatives. Mas Windoro, author of the *Kompas* article on former activists turned legislative candidates (caleg muda) that I cited earlier (Adi 2004), blasted the alliance with a series of provocative and antagonistic questions—"What are they going to do next? Why aren't all the Tokoh 98 present?" Outlining all the problems and fractures of the student movement, he wanted to know: *Why have the students failed to create anything in the last six years?* Instead, he concluded with the answer that the student movement had become a movement of troublemakers ("Gerakan Mahasiswa menjadi gerakan pengganggu").

The moderator looked grim at the insults. Addressing the room and the hostile detractor, he pointed to the diversity of the group as proof of their attempt to consolidate actors beyond the traditional sector of students. He mentioned the breadth of their agendas. GENBI signatories had a long-term, concrete platform that they would soon release in a future statement. They wanted to build a prodemocracy movement for everyone, not just an activists' circle. This was an early effort, he said, toward rebuilding a broader movement. Raising his voice, and asserting a more confident tone in the stylized mode of an orasi (demo speech), he said, "We are not going to give the elected government regime [rezim terpilih] a blank check any longer, but we are going to take control and hold people accountable!" It struck the right note of futurity and challenge to authority that Generation 98 had mastered.

A few months later, GENBI disappeared. When I asked one of the signatories why it had dematerialized, he laughed and said that the computer at the

Legal Aid annex that had held all their statements and data had been password protected, and now he could no longer access it, even though he had set up the administrative account. Bad luck and data loss yet again? As it turned out, the dream for Generation 98 to become the best positioned generation of youth leaders in the 2004 elections could not be institutionalized. Instead, one of the most lasting and meaningful contributions of Generation 98 to public political culture can be found in the post-Reformasi activism that continues to thrive in "emergency" settings, returning to occupy political and public space whenever activists recognized crises in the making (Paramadhita 2014).

Conclusion | A RETURN TO FORM

To put Reformasi in the past, to consider it finished, runs the risk of discounting the role of popular politics in ensuring Indonesian democracy today. And yet a common critique toward Generation 98 advances the idea that activists are now passé. Critics, especially those who observed activists from the outside but who nonetheless felt a right to speak as former students or historical witnesses, have asked why students didn't do more, and why they chose to fade back into ordinary life, as if the revolution was over. This charge highlights political intervention as event rather than afterlife and assumes that the postpolitical reintegration into normal life was easy and seamless; yet there are signs, here in this book, that tell us the opposite. "Melawan Lupa" (Resisting Forgetting) remains a powerful activist slogan today. This is a case where the wisdom of hindsight about Reformasi's failures and student activist disappointments are no more than an elegant (and sophist?) proof of an optic that Foucault calls a history of the present, where the marks of the past on the present reveal how and of what political matter the present is composed (1977: 31).

"The past is a position," Trouillot writes, begetting forgetting and remembering as distinct *political* positions. John Roosa's and Katherine McGregor's work on the horrors of 1965–1966 show how forgetting can become both a state and civil society project, shared through a relation to hegemony and domination. It is easy to see why there are older generations who prefer to forget, since the political past is encased in trauma (Cribb, cited in Stoler 2002). Remembering one's discordant past or the nation's submerged past is disruptive work, for remembering mars the surface of normality, draws the attention of state instruments tasked with stability and order, and can make the survival of survivors that much harder. Yet there have been cases where remembering did take place at the center, and even surprised people with its forms of emergence. Thongchai Winichakul's moving essay on the troubled silences surrounding the 1976 student massacre in Bangkok shows an accounting for justice where it appears most impossible. He argues that resolution after collective trauma requires official and unofficial channels of recognition in order to overcome deep societal ambivalence toward dredging up unpleasant pasts (Thongchai 2002). Such spaces for commemoration can range from official monuments to cultural events and rites, literary depictions, and other cultural or religious ways to open up discussions about political traumas. Here Indonesia falls short. As Abidin Kusno has written, there are only charred ruins of shophouses left in place in old Batavia (Kota) to remind the public of the May Riots in 1998, and the violence against Chinese Indonesians. Trisakti University added a small plaque on its main gates to rename itself the Reform Heroes Campus (Kampus Pahlawan Reformasi), while narrow lanes here and there, rather than main thoroughfares, have been named Jalan Reformasi (Reformasi Street). No monuments and, as I wrote in chapter 1, no place in the state archives either. The student activists of Generation 98 remain linked to the Reformasi movement through their marginalization as living "historical ruins" or, in Gaston Gordillo's term, mere "rubble," not even a ruin (2014). A danger lies ahead, in this slight, even easy, slippage: a politicized generation of youth, former agents of history and carriers of pemuda fever, could go from being regarded as the decentralized, living remnants of a populist movement (rubble) to becoming the ungovernable and easily manipulated massa (rabble).

PEMUDA FEVER'S REVERBERATIONS

Post-Suharto Indonesia, and indeed we may call it post-Reform Indonesia, is marked by conflicting tendencies of progressive social change and conservative push-back toward the institutionalization and internalization of democratic norms. This book stands firmly on the side of the former, while remaining clear-eyed toward the latter. I have described the slow-motion spread of student activism from its campus-based, moral-force roots in the 1980s and 1990s to its social-movement climax in the years of Reformasi and finally to its diffuse form more than a decade later as a "repertoire" of masculinist poses, images, and mass political techniques that others have appropriated to serve the diverse needs of the public domain (Taylor 2003). Activism is no longer a strictly student concern. Instead, activism has transformed into a more diverse set of universal concerns that engage Indonesian youth, from environmentalism, indigeneous rights, press freedom, and corruption to religious freedom, LGBT rights, and health care access. In the last ten years, social media, rather than the power of civil society groups and NGOs, have played an increasingly important mobilizing role in getting the public to protest outrage and express dissent, as in the well-known case of the Facebook fund-raising campaign "Coins for Prita" or, in a more vindinctive bent, the hounding of average citizens for their perceived transgressions.

Life in Jakarta has changed to reflect the multitudinous growth of the public sphere. Indonesian democracy is fractious and murky, as exemplified in the polarized relations between political parties and the unsavory alliances and scandals that plague elite politicians. Conservative politics has thrived, in the form of reconsolidated political dynasties and oligarchies, as Jeffrey Winters and others have convincingly argued, in the rise of organized violence in the form of New Order–style paramilitary groups (Wilson 2015), in the vocal and often disruptive politics of hard line Islamists whose vision of the ummat is homogenizing rather than pan-Islamic (van Bruinessen 2013), and finally, in increased biopolitical intrusions in the moral life and labor practices of Indonesians at home and abroad (Ford 2009, Ford and Lyons 2012; Lindquist 2008). The short burst of sociopolitical experimentation that challenged New Order power structures and the inherent instability of Reformasi-era street politics have been "course-corrected" by the enduring inequalities that continue to mark political and economic opportunities for the rakyat. Under such conditions of compromised democracy, inequalities of income, status, authority, and legitimacy get channeled into what Martin van Bruinessen (2004) calls "bonded life"—an exclusivity of communal life that is evident in the rise of religious closed communities of Christian and Islamic faiths and a growing intolerance for difference. Religious tolerance and cultural freedoms associated with westernized lifestyles and human rights ideas have declined, as identity politics narrowly defines the precepts of what is acceptable for a moral life. There is concern that the disappearance of Reformasi politics shows the coercive appeal of forgetting in a society that still rewards state actors's abuses of power with impunity (Haberkorn 2013).

Yet Indonesians are on the whole far more optimistic, for they have seen a loosening of borders between power and the People. A growing number of former activists, intellectuals, former dissidents, and progressive politicians have entered formal politics, giving rise to a new charismatic politics that allows local leadership to shine. Examples of this crop of new leaders include successful entrepreneurial figures with middle-class backgrounds, such as the mayor of Surabaya (Risma), the technocratic mayor of Bandung (Ridwan

Kamil), and of course Joko Widodo, popularly known as Jokowi, the former mayor of Solo, the former governor of Jakarta, and Indonesia's current president.

AVERTING CRISIS

In 2014 a crisis of democracy loomed, for an outwardly undemocratic presidential candidate looked poised to win the elections based on elite background, capitalist power, and jingoistic nationalist rhetoric. Crisis, as Janet Roitman tells us, does a lot of conceptual work, from giving us "a way to think history" through extraordinary time to marking "a moment of truth" that compels judgment and action (see Roitman n.d.). The actions of Generation 98 and of ordinary people galvanized to action in the months prior to the July 2014 presidential elections can only be read thus, as the acts of a political public that formed in response to a familiar and growing sense of crisis about Indonesian democracy. The 2014 presidential elections revealed crisscrossing conflicts between elites and commoners, between urbanites in the center and the complex electoral landscape of the provinces, and intergenerational differences of opinion that ranged from nostalgia for Suharto's time to a staunch Reformasi-era appreciation for Indonesian democracy.

Was Suharto's ghost (*momok Suharto*, a name activists liked to use as shorthand for the living remnants of New Order rule) back in town? Momok Suharto showed up after his death in true Father of Development style, smiling against a field of ripened paddy. T-shirts that said "How are ya? My time was better, wasn't it?" (Piye Kabare, Enakkan Jamanku Toh?) were sold in Yogyakarta's Malioboro markets and Internet memes featuring the same image and caption circulated online, while Suharto-era cronies and loyalists put up his beatified face alongside theirs on massive election banners.[1] A real New Order specter showed up in the 2014 elections in the returning figure of Prabowo Subianto, former son-in-law of Suharto, former commander of the Rose Team and the special forces, self-exiled to Jordan and now back in a cloud of marketing glory.[2] His face had aged and thickened, and his overall image had undergone a complete ideological transformation from that of a privileged member at the center of the former regime's power structure into a populist leader of the rakyat. No longer resting on the laurels of his troubled military past, Prabowo polished his family's nationalist history till it gleamed.[3] His brother Hasyim Djojohadikoesoemo, one of the wealthiest men in Indonesia, had already bankrolled the production of the nationalist film trilogy Merah-Putih (Red-White), which used Hollywood production values and foreign talent to reintroduce the Indonesian 1945 revolution to the public. Prabowo entered into an intense image war with Jokowi. "Polls showed that upper-middle-class voters backed Prabowo because they viewed him as more experienced, self-confident, and sophisticated than the down-to-earth and rather crude Jokowi, whose strong appeal among the rural masses irritated many urbanites" (Mietzner, 2013: 115). For the campaign trail, Prabowo wore pure white clothes and a black *peci* (hat) in the exact style of the nation's founding father, Soekarno. He took to riding his favorite horse in ceremonial fashion. On March 23, 2014, Prabowo inaugurated his Gerindra campaign launch at the Senayan stadium by arriving on horseback. Newspapers revealed that the steed was worth 3 billion rupiah, or US$300,000. The acting chair of Gerindra explained that Prabowo's entrance on horseback had a policy implication and was intended to encourage the rakyat to increase their efforts in farming and animal husbandry ("Pesan ekonomi kerakyatan Prabowo dari atas kuda seharga rp. 3 miliar" 2014). But the image of Prabowo nuzzling his horse triggered ridicule rather than awe among more critical Jakartans. Even as Prabowo's masculinist, heroic image circulated in sophisticated media campaigns, detractors focused on his elite and autocratic character. At the other end of the class spectrum, Jokowi, the populist candidate and former mayor of Solo, wore a mass-produced (and affordable) uniform of checked shirts and Converse sneakers that endeared him to his middle-class and poor constituents. Soon, supporters took to wearing Jokowi-style checked shirts, so that urban cafés were awash with young professionals, activists, and ordinary people of all ages in this new look.

In 2014, I was back in Jakarta for a few months to research a new wave of cultural and youth-oriented movements among artists and socially engaged youth, who were distinctly post-Reformasi in style and attitude. My experience in the field in 2014 reflected what anthropologist Alexei Yurchak has written (2005) about the post-Soviet generation in Russia: that their world had changed and suddenly what was forever was no more (2005). These new youth (aged eighteen to thirty) were not at all drawn to narrowly ideological frameworks and missions, for they enjoyed an entitlement to express individual thoughts regarding anything and everything (see Lee 2013). I moved between new and old research circles and marveled at the difference between Generation 98's experiences and how far Jakarta's youth had come. The post-Reformasi youth whom I met in Jakarta and elsewhere did not live in a divisive and uncomfortable political world; they lived in a post-Suharto world without mystery. They had bypassed the stages of discomfiting "transition" that regime change inflicted on the firsthand witnesses of "transitology" (Berdahl 1999). In sharp contrast to the new youth without generation or crisis, my old informants and friends from Generation 98 who still populated NGOs,

INGOs, media structures, and legal aid offices renewed their affiliation to a tenuous Indonesian democracy by becoming, each in his or her own way, enraptured with futurist possibilities for a new era of grassroots democracy through the figure of Jokowi. The months of April and May 2014 were dynamic with news and propaganda battles between the conservative nationalist and oligarchic candidates (former general Prabowo Subianto and scandal-ridden capitalist Aburizal Bakrie) and the People's favored candidate, Joko Widodo. The senior editorial staff of the Bakrie-owned online news agency Viva News, which included former PRD activist Nezar Patria, staged a collective resignation over the Bakrie family's attempt to enforce corporate loyalty toward Aburizal Bakrie's candidacy while blocking news, ads, and images of the Jokowi campaign ("Pimpred dan sejumlah redaktur vivanews mundur gara-gara iklan Jokowi" 2014). Activists went to planning meetings with graphic designers and advertising agency creatives who had been drafted to modernize tim sukses campaigns with slickly packaged and professional graphics and slogans, only to discover that the urbane and cosmopolitan imaginations of the private sector were fundamentally at odds with the grassroots tastes and expressions of the rakyat, the former actively provincializing the latter.

How did activists once again aim at building a national grassroots campaign? Marcus Mietzner's observation (2013) that in the post-Reformasi era former activists and progressive politicians remain close to civil society rang true, especially in the outcropping of pro-Jokowi campaigns in Jakarta that were spontaneous, loosely interconnected, and in close conversation with the official Jokowi tim sukses. Jokowi himself heralded the role of these *relawan* (volunteers), who became the foot soldiers of his campaign. Activists claimed insider knowledge of the campaign and gave frequent social media updates (complete with group photos of women and men at pro-Jokowi events, and at times self-portraits with the governor) that proved Jokowi's accessibility and receptivity to their opinions, overtures, and enthusiasm. In sharp contrast, Jokowi's own party, the PDI-P, remained closemouthed about their endorsement of his candidacy, even while the clock was ticking on the need to roll out a national campaign to counter the lavish spending of the Prabowo campaign. The PDI-P coffers remained closed to Jokowi, and the party elite replicated chair and former president Megawati Seokarnoputri's cold response to Jokowi, an elite "wait and see" attitude that only heightened the activists' awareness that they were necessary to make a difference. The scale of media and citizen involvement in the 2014 election differentiated it from the 2004 election. Polling, quick counts, citizen watch campaigns, image wars, exclusive television coverage were all immediately quantified, informatized, and interpreted for the public. By May 2014, just a few months before the vote was to take place in July, Jokowi's lead over Prabowo dropped to a few percentage points. Although Jokowi went on to win the election, the margin was decidedly slim. Crisis provided a familiar momentum for activists to gather, discuss, and strategize around the Jokowi campaign. What follows is only one example of several election "emergency activism" (Paramaditha 2014) stories I heard about and witnessed.

On May 22 I reunited with some old friends in time to observe their voluntary intervention in the Jokowi campaign. Present were Savic (an activist discussed in chapter 5) and Edhison Situmorang, a PDI-P politician and a former activist.[4] We met at Savic's online magazine office in Central Jakarta and were joined by Yacobus, a former FPPI member from Sumatra who was working with Edhison, and Heru, a Jakarta-based graphic designer who arrived at the office with one hundred Jokowi T-shirts individually wrapped in plastic that he had transported on his Vespa.

I had known Edhison for a decade now, and he looked radically different from his activist street years, when he wore dark T-shirts and jeans and had wild curly hair that made him stand out. Now he wore glasses and button-down shirts, and his hair was cropped short. The moment he saw the stack of Jokowi T-shirts, he immediately put one on and began posing for pictures in different corners of the office. Yacobus used his phone to take pictures that could be posted to social media. Edhison leaned for casual shots against a bookcase, against a wall, and then a desk. "Lagi narsis" (I'm being narcissistic), he said, grinning. Since becoming a politician he had evidently perfected his ideal friendly pose, for he gave the same big toothy smile over and over again. The four men debated whether the campaign T-shirts, which showed Jokowi's face rendered in colorful graphic pop art style, needed text, such as a slogan about the *kaum muda* (youth community) supporting Jokowi, or the logo of Relawan Perjuangan Demokrasi (Volunteers for Democratic Struggle) for provenance. Heru said the screen printing was done by hand, so each shirt would have to be individually screened to add the text. Edhison spent the remainder of the afternoon mulling over T-shirt and postcard designs for their Jokowi campaign, which they planned to launch a week hence at Relawan Perjuangan Demokrasi's Cikini secretariat.

Savic moved to the white board and started writing over an old meeting agenda that had over time become indelible. He moved quickly, writing in bullet points ideas for networking, campaign strategies, periodic progress reports, and campaign monitoring in the provinces they had selected as their targets. Savic thought that blasting SMS (short messaging system) messages through the sms Gateway (he pronounced it "getaway") machine would be most effective. The sms Gateway machine was a sim platform bulk messaging device (commonly used for mobile marketing or corporate messaging) that could reach tens of thousands of phone numbers at once, and the tactic could be repeated until you ran out of pulsa (phone credit). "At most we'd need 5 million rupiah for pulsa," Savic estimated. A momentary hiccup occurred when he miscalculated the cost of the machine—at first he thought it cost 1 million rupiah (US$100), but when he called a friend to inquire about the machine, he learned that it was in fact priced at 17 million rupiah (US$1,700). Silence followed this announcement. There was no money in the kitty. "Jangan dikesankan kita miskin sekali" (Don't give the impression that we're so poor), Edhison objected jokingly when he saw Savic's quiet disappointment. And even if we are, don't ruin our political image! his joke implied.

The discussion of costs spilled over into their next agenda item. Where and when would they hold the expected media events to announce their initiative, given that they had no budget for such events? The spaces for political events in Cikini that progressive politicians and activists favored were attractive tempo doeloe cafes or restaurants in colonial Dutch houses. Places with names such as Bumbu Desa (Village Spice) or Warung Daun (Leafy Foodstall) cost upward of 7 million rupiah (US$700) to rent. Even though it was cost-free, Relawan Perjuangan Demokrasi's secretariat was too small, Savic argued, and not optimal for reporters, who would have to fight among themselves to get a good camera angle at the doorway. It couldn't be held at night, either, as the press didn't attend events after 6 PM. Edhison was reluctant to organize yet another diskusi (discussion session) event, although the others seemed to think it necessary political work. He objected, saying, "Sudah ada banyak" (There've been a lot), emphasizing the need for novelty in these times. His friend opined that grassroots visibility was most important and was also what they were good at, for example giving stickers and posters to tukang bajaj (auto-rickshaw drivers) who could adorn their vehicles with campaign paraphernalia and spread the message on their voyages through the city. It was how Edhison had successfully canvassed his constituency in Central Jakarta. "Kerjaan kita cuman gitu gitu doang. Tenang aja. Gampang" (That's the work we [know how to] do. Just relax. It's easy), Edhison said. The statements were deliberately lighthearted, but they also rang true. Certain political strategies *were* easier to carry out by this experienced team of Generation 98 veterans.

Despite the material differences in the lifestyles of the senior activists and the transformations (and complications) of aging, the familiarity of activist actions in 2014 was an urgent reminder of how post-Reformasi Jakarta constitutes an ethical landscape, one that is only visible to the rest of the nation in times of crisis. Savic, Edhison, and other former activists like them wielded their expertise in mobilizing the masses without hesitation when faced with a vulnerable democracy. The material and visual economy of populism, its images and technical expertise, had stayed stable and close to hand. Whether or not these more recent returns to activism by Generation 98 still constitute pemuda fever is a less relevant issue. Sociologically speaking, the conditions of political, economic, and human rights crises that formed Generation 98 are no longer present as a shared national condition; the memories about the New Order have ebbed even as their specters live on. We must accept that the feats and rhetoric of Generation 98 are no longer in style, to be taken up by today's youth, who have their own concerns, styles, and visions for the nation. Generation 98 is aging, perhaps not very gracefully. They refuse to let go of their past selves. There is something good in that.

INTRODUCTION

1. On May 12, 1998, demonstrators were shot at with live ammunition by the security forces. The death of six students sparked popular outrage, which was further compounded by the spontaneous and organized looting and raping that claimed hundreds more lives in the May 13–14 riots in Jakarta.

2. Arbi Sanit is a well-known senior political scientist and professor at the University of Indonesia. Rudi has spelled his name "Arby Sanit" in his diary.

3. D. Rudi Haryanto, unpublished diary, 1997–1998, personal collection of Doreen Lee.

4. Thus I use these terms with some interchangeability in this book, while issuing a reminder here that "youth" or pemuda presents a sociological and historically situated category of analysis, whereas "activist" ushers us into a political lexicon of seemingly global significance.

5. See Ian Wilson's essay (2014) on the vigilante actions of organizations that foment violence, such as the extremist Islamic Defenders Front.

6. Dedicated collections at North American and Dutch institutions that have traditionally hosted centers for Southeast Asian or Indonesian studies provide a wealth of Indonesian-language resources outside Indonesia. In the politically repressive New Order years, librarians and researchers paid special attention to media sources and political ephemera that would otherwise have been lost. I have consulted Cornell University's collections at the Kroch Library, the IISG's unique collections on 1980s–1990s Indonesian activism in the Netherlands, and my own acquired collections in the writing of this book.

7. Anthropologist Katherine Verdery's epistemological analysis of her own *securitate* (secret police) file builds on Ann Stoler's work on the Dutch colonial archives to situate the archive as the site of categorical alignments that capture the anxieties and articulations of power.

8. See Strassler (2010), chap. 5, "Witnessing History."

9. Numbers from the 2010 census give us approximately 82 million between the ages of fifteen and thirty-four, out of a total of 237 million. See the United Nations Statistic Division's Demographic Statistics for Indonesia, at data.un.org, accessed September 1, 2015.

10. The 1978 Campus Normalization Act dissolved student councils, broke student autonomy, and enabled a military presence on campus.

11. See Ryter (1998), Siegel (1998b), and Wilson (2011) for a detailed discussion on how the state cultivated the criminality of underclass youth to turn them into the "left hand of the state," such that the term *pemuda* came to mean *preman*, "underclass gangster," during the New Order.

12. See Barker and van Klinken (2009) and Aspinall and Fealy (2010) for examples of recent scholarship in Indonesian studies that interrogates the primacy of state-centric analysis and reassesses the role of New Order political institutions.

13. See Miftahuddin's biography of Faisol Reza (2004), 101–107.

14. Growing interest in political Islam in Indonesia as an object of study in US, Australian, and European academies has created in Indonesian studies a huge subfield of Islamic and political Islam studies. These changes follow the opening up of religious politics in the post-Suharto years and touch on global preoccupations with the War on Terror and the presumably vexed relationship between Islam and democracy. In my experience, it is most often international scholars rather than Indonesians who ask me questions about the role of Islam in my work and who remain dissatisfied with my answer that for the most part, entrenched secular-nationalist ideas and class-based discourses linking labor, agrarian, and urban sectors supersede the claims made by the religious right in an admittedly complex and religiously inflected post-Reformasi world.

15. The national organization Himpunan Mahasiswa Islam is an exception. It split into two factions with the birth of the splinter group Himpunan Mahasiswa Islam-Majelis Penyelamat Organisasi (HMI-MPO) in the 1980s over the issue of accepting Pancasila as the sole ideological doctrine, a decision that resulted from state intrusion in the organization.

16. The People's Democratic Party, its predecessor, Democratic Indonesian Students Solidarity, and Pijar predate 1998, while the City Forum, City Front, Students Action Front for Reform and Democracy (Forum Aksi Mahasiswa Untuk Reformasi), Indonesian Youth Struggle Front (Front Perjuangan Pemuda Indonesia), National Democratic Students League, and National Students Front later emerged as actors in the post-1998 Jakarta-based student movement.

17. See the opinion column in the student publication POLITIKA, titled "Ekspresi: Pemuda dan Kegairahan Politik" (1987).

18. Abbreviations and slang were important markers of "cool" but also were strategic choices for activists, who were always chronically short of *pulsa*, prepaid phone credit on their cell phones. See Hefner-Smith (2007).

19. Rumors about me took on a local cast. For example, in one rumor I was a relative of Kwik Kian Gie, a rare ethnic Chinese politician in the Indonesian Democratic Party of Struggle and economist who had been an outspoken member of Megawati's cabinet. In another rumor, someone had heard somewhere that I had ties to Baperki, the defunct political association founded by ethnic Chinese in the 1950s.

CHAPTER 1: ARCHIVE

1. "Bandel" means "naughty" or "rebellious." One can also translate the name as "King of Mischief" or "Bandit King." The name appears in a four-page demonstration planning meeting report, undated (c. July 1989), Indonesian Student Protest Movement Collection, IISG. Better known by his nickname, Beathor, Bambang Suryadi continued to be an activist in increasingly formal political organizations, participating in progressive networks such as the election-monitoring body KOMITE INDEPENDEN PEMANTAU PEMILU in the 1997 election and, after Reformasi, in Relawan Perjuangan Demokrasi (Volunteers for the Democratic Struggle), the political organization started by former student activists that became enfolded into the Indonesian Democratic Party of Struggle. He has since climbed high in the ranks of that party's leadership. In March 2014 the party officially elected him speaker of the house in Indonesia's parliament; his predecessor in this office, Taufik Kiemas, Megawati Soekarnoputri's husband, had died of a heart attack in June 2013.

2. *Bergema* literally means "resound" or "reverberate" but is also a play on the commonly known term Gema, short for gerakan mahasiswa (student movement). Thus the leaflet title implies that the university campus is defiantly breaking out in waves of student movements.

3. The reference to Pancasila, or the Five Principles, is a coded way to refer to Suharto's crackdown on Islamic groups in the 1980s. Suharto forced all religious groups to declare allegiance to the "one true principle" of Pancasila, thereby asserting the power of the secular state over Muslim communities with strong religious affiliations whose religious identities provided forms of autonomous, potentially political expression. Affected groups included the student group Himpunan Mahasiswa Islam, which experienced an internal split as a result of the decree, and other Islamic mass organizations. "Tanjung Priok Tragedy" refers to the mass violence that took place at the port of Tanjung Priok, North Jakarta, in September 1984 between soldiers and a Muslim congregation. The civilian death toll remains unclear, ranging from dozens to hundreds reported dead.

4. From documents related to Bambang Beathor Suryadi's subversion trial, Stanley's archive, Indonesian Student Protest Movement Collection, IISG, 4 pp., 1–2. My translation.

5. Beathor's poem precedes Wiji Thukul's famous poem "Resist" but is evocative of it in style and tone. A more similar poetic source might be W. S. Rendra's famous dissident poem "Poem of an Angry Person," closely linked to the mass student mobilizations of the 1970s. An excerpt: "Because we are silenced, and you never stop nagging . . . Because we are threatened and you use violence against us . . . So we say to you NO." Translated by Max Lane; cited in Lane (2008: 89).

6. Social text in the sense that Geertz uses to describe culture as text, and to evoke textuality in the Derridean sense, to enter the field of the text as domain.

7. "The contemporary is the person who perceives the darkness of his time as something that concerns him, as something that never ceases to engage him. Darkness is something that—more than any light—turns directly and singularly toward him. The contemporary is the one whose eyes are struck by the beam of darkness that comes from his own time" (Agamben 2009: 45).

8. See Siegel (1997, 1998b). Siegel's work approaches the problem of recognition and interiority in postcolonial Indonesia through language and mass mediation. For an analysis of how channels of communication are broadened, intensified, and delimited by crowds, i.e., mass publics in the age of the world picture, see Mazzarella 2013.

9. Generation 1978 marked the last nationwide and well-organized student movement against Suharto, involving coordination by student councils across the country.

10. I thank Henk Schulte Nordholt for his observation that activist documentary practices are performances that place more importance on the performativity of production (being able to do activist tasks) than on ensuring a readership. Personal communication, March 4, 2014.

11. In 1989, there were mass expulsions of students who had dared to demonstrate against the visit of a state minister to the Bandung Institute of Technology. Nine of those students were imprisoned. In the same year, students in Yogyakarta who protested in solidarity outside the courthouse where two youth were being tried for subversion experienced mass arrests and violence at the hands of the army. To give a sense of escalating dissent in the 1990s, a human rights report by Bimo Nugroho lists thirteen cases of human rights violations in violence against student protests and solidarity actions in 1994, spread out across the country. *Catatan Keadaan Hak Asasi Manusia 1994* (1995). Mass arrests, physical violence, and even death occurred at the hands of state security forces.

12. Human Rights Watch (1998a) provides a comprehensive view of the university as an ideological field dominated by New Order institutions and structures that kept students in line.

13. On the classed and criminal implications of the term *pemuda* during the New Order, see the work of Loren Ryter (1998) on the criminal organizations, such as the Pemuda Pancasila, that acted as the "left hand" (i.e., the illicit arm) of the state, as well as the documentary film *The Act of Killing* (2012). For a more recent treatment of lower-class urban and peri-urban youth mobilized into ethnic, religious, and criminal gangs, see Wilson (2012a, 2012b).

14. Cibodas Charter, 1989, Indonesian Protest Movement Collection, IISG.

15. Of these six, I have met two former prisoners. Fadjroel Rachman continues to be a vocal opposition activist and media figure in the present and was involved with Reformasi politics and student organizations at the time of my fieldwork (2003–2005). Enin Supriyanto has become a prominent figure in Indonesian contemporary art, working as an art critic, writer, and curator nationally and internationally.

16. Arief Budiman was a dissident lecturer, a former '66 activist, and the brother of deceased '66 activist Soe Hok Gie (see chapter 3). Budiman had a conflicted relationship with the administration of Satya Wacana Christian University in Salatiga, Java, where he taught from 1981 until his contested dismissal in 1994. Arief had frequently exposed questionable practices at the university and was isolated as a result. In 1987, the conflict between Arief and the rector, Willi Toisuta, escalated, and student activists took up Arief's cause by distributing widely photocopies of a letter, addressed to "Dear Willi" (Willi yang baik), that he had written to the rector. The student press also reprinted the letter in an issue of the student magazine *Imbas* and distributed the publication at the Dies Natalis event at the university. See Andreas Harsono's (2002) account in his blog post. The Indonesian Student Protest Movement archive at the IISG also contains several handwritten letters and documents detailing this case and its related activism, as Stanley, the archive's founder, was a student at Satya Wacana Christian University.

17. "Pers mahasiswa tidak boleh kritis. Tidak boleh bicara politik, dia harus mendekam dibalik dinding-dinding kampus saja. Siapa bilang begitu? Gejolak mudanya usia, latar belakang keilmuan yang dimiliki serta kepekaan sosialnya, justru menuntut pers mahasiswa 'tampil lain' dari pers umum lainnya." "Pers Mahasiswa, Anarkhis-Oposisionil? (1985), 1.

18. A move nowhere more evident than in the perceived rise of the "Berkeley mafia"—economists and engineers whose pet projects were designed to be friendly to foreign investors.

19. Keterbukaan ended abruptly when three popular news magazines, *DeTik*, *Tempo*, and *Editor*, had their publishing permits revoked in 1994.

20. Hannah Arendt's analysis of the efficacy and strategy of using propaganda to influence the masses in *The Origins of Totalitarianism* contains this useful comment on the extent of manipulation of truth by power: "Totalitarian propaganda can outrageously insult common sense only where common sense has lost its validity" (1958, 352).

21. Jeffrey Winters comes to a sobering conclusion about the lack of democracy in post-Suharto Indonesia in his book *Oligarchy* (2011), in which he describes the reinstatement of elite power through oligarchic arrangements in the political and economic spheres. This bleak view is echoed by George Aditjondro's controversial banned publication *Membongkar Gurita Cikeas* (Uncovering the Cikeas tentacles, 2009) on political dynasties and state abetted corruption under the SBY administration. For a contrasting view, see Max Lane on the emancipatory potential of

mass movements in Indonesia in his book *Unfinished Nation: Indonesia before and after Suharto* (2008).

22. See the *Critical Inquiry* article cluster on Occupy and the Arab Spring, in particular Taussig (2012).

23. I borrow Benedict Anderson's title from his essay on East Timor, "Gravel in Jakarta's Shoes" (1998a).

24. At the IISG, I consulted four different collections over 2008–2009, and most recently in 2013. These were the People's Democratic Party Collection, the Wilson Bin Nurtiyas Papers, the Indonesian Protest Movement Collection, collected by Stanley, and the Jaap Erkelens Collection.

25. In a pragmatic blow to the movement's talk of independence, the post-Suharto era saw former activists who entered or founded NGOs that had received donor funding fulfilling "output" promises at the end of each budget cycle, often in the form of not-for-profit publications.

26. A former PRD activist revealed this change in talking about the disappeared role of the demonstration's chronicler (*kronolog*), whose job was to prepare a historical document that could be circulated and used for press releases or for legal defense should activists be arrested. The kronolog would have been, in the early 1990s, known for their writing and rhetorical skills, as well as a dedication to the craft of writing.

27. A common question posed to me by nonparticipants, including foreign scholars and political observers, captures this sense of analytical predetermination. I was often confronted with the "challenge" of how to analyze a failed movement, with the assumption that the failure lay in the students' inability to take formal power or take over the government, even though that objective was nowhere in the activists agenda. Activists demanded social change and governmental reform, but, as a surviving quirk of New Order youth policies and nationalist historiography, did not see themselves at the apex of presidential or dynastic power.

28. For a comprehensive analysis of the student movement's group identities and alliances and a list of the demonstrations held in the 1990s, see the Indonesian Institute of Sciences report by Widjojo et al. (1999). Regarding group names, it was and remains a common naming practice to use different names with catchy acronyms for each demonstration as a way to mark new alliances, but more often to mark the specificity of the issue and the name of the group as a retort to the issue under protest.

29. "Laporan Hasil Dialog-Diskusi Dengan Mahasiswa Ujung Pandang Agustus 1989" [Report on dialogues—discussions with Ujung Pandang students August 1989], document marked secret, Indonesian Protest Movement Collection, IISG.

30. The IISG holds a collection simply titled the Indonesian Protest Movement Collection, spanning the 1980s to early 1990s, which contains a small pamphlet consisting of an Indonesian translation of Lenin's 1920 address to youth, "Tasks of the Youth Leagues," published by Amanah Ra'jat.

31. Hadiz and Dhakidae's study of the history of the social sciences in Indonesia describes the close relationship between institutes of higher learning and the state as the "embedding of academia in bureaucracy" (2005: 7). It is therefore not unusual that student dissidents practiced literary forms that replicated the code of bureaucracy, since every aspect of their organizational life would have been governed by the supplication and authority that forms and signatures instill.

32. Rudolf Mrázek (2010) describes with touching detail the material deterioration of an elderly Indonesian's typed, curling, stapled, and restapled memoirs.

33. The postcolonial relation with the Netherlands is of interest here. Home to a large Indonesian community of exiles, students, academics, and politically concerned individuals, the Netherlands has been an important outpost of the Indonesian student movement. Hill's history of the Indonesian student press reveals how in the 1980s–1990s, to avoid censorship, students would write pieces in Indonesia and in Indonesian and send them to the Netherlands for printing. The print copy would be sent back to Indonesia as a "foreign" journal, exempt from censorship. See Hill (2006).

34. The extent of state violence and repression, murder, and torture of citizens as a matter of policy has often come to light decades after the fact through the excavation or declassification of archives belonging to the state apparatus, for example in Argentina's dirty wars and Cambodia's genocide. Colonial regimes, too, had a practice of documenting their killings, photographing individuals bound for execution, such as the Japanese colonial government in Korea at the turn of the century and the French in Indochina. More recently, the capacity of states to collect information and archive everything under the sign of security has established a spectacular digital threshold for metadata, creating exceptional and illegally obtained stores of information, as the WikiLeaks scandal and Edward Snowden's whistleblowing on the National Security Agency have brought to light.

35. See Bradley Simpson's ongoing project, the National Security Archive housed at George Washington University, to declassify documents related to US-Indonesia relations during the Suharto years and in particular to Indonesia's US-approved invasion of East Timor. Accessed August 17, 2015, http://www2.gwu.edu/~nsarchiv/.

36. Untitled document, 6 page meeting report. The Indonesian Protest Movement Collection, IISG. Translation mine; emphasis added.

37. "Laporan Hasil Dialog-Diskusi Dengan Mahasiswa Ujung Pandang Agustus 1989" (Report on the Dialogues-Discussions with Ujung Pandang Students August 1989). The Indonesian Protest Movement Collection, IISG.

38. The mention of several different faculties (*fakultas*) shows the strength of student support in Ujung Pandang. Rivalries between high schools are strong in Indonesia and can escalate into public and deadly brawls called *tawuran*. See Nilan et al. (2011). At the college level, students I spoke to reported historic feuds between different disciplines, often displayed in territorial "battles" and displays of bravado on campus.

39. See Tausig and Haberkorn (2012), tracing the recent political turmoil of Thailand through everyday objects.

40. An informant who was a former PRD member shared a "secret" military report from 1994 that likened the radical PRD to the Indonesian Communist Party. I was unable to verify its veracity, but the clumsy comparisons the author of the report made between the PRD and the PKI fits the simplistic tone of New Order anticommunist propaganda. The report indicates that the state, in its paternal capacity, could not imagine its children (*anak*) engaging in communist activities or leftist ideology out of their own conscious volition. Hence the writer concludes that the PRD's similarity to the Indonesian Communist Party's discourse and organizational structure is actually proof that the PRD were naïve youth who were being manipulated by sinister forces.

41. Berkas Perkara (Case File), Wilson Bin Nurtiyas Papers, box 2, IISG.

42. This activist tradition has a long and illustrious precedent in founding father Soekarno's own colonial-era defense speech, titled "Indonesia Accuses" (Indonesia menggugat), at his 1930 trial. Sukarno's pledoi was published as a book with the same title and has provided inspiration for nationalist and dissident texts; particularly relevant is its rhetorical mixing of political analysis interspersed with moments of direct address to the judge (Hakim) and by extension the reader (Soekarno 2001). See also Ratna Sarumpaet's 1997 play *Marsinah* (Marsinah menggugat), a one-woman monologue about murdered labor activist Marsinah (Sarumpaet 1997).

43. The East Timorese freedom fighter Xanana Gusmao never had a chance to assemble a legal team with proper notice, nor was he allowed to read a pledoi. The denial of his legal rights and his unfair treatment by the courts prompted human rights organizations to protest the trial's illegitimacy.

44. Oka's defense team included a group of activists operating under the acronym KADO (Komite Aksi Demokrasi untuk Oka; Committee of Democratic Actions for Oka), which puns on the Indonesian word for "gift" (from Dutch *kado* or French *cadeau*).

45. *Eksepsi* by Oka Dwi Candra, 2–3.

46. *Eksepsi* by Oka Dwi Candra, 6. Italics mine.

47. Just a year before Oka's arrest, another Pijar activist, Triagus "TASS" Susanto Siswomihardjo, had been arrested for his critical and satirical writings. Even his activist nickname was an insult to the state, since activists joked that TASS stood for "Tri Agus Makes Suharto Suffer" (Triagus susahin Suharto). The East Timor Action Network volume of documents from 1995 provides a number of translated articles from Pijar supporters, such as Goenawan Mohamad; news articles covering arrest and trial; Pijar's own statements; and Triagus's statement to the court (cited as *demurrer*). See *East Timor Documents*, 1995.

48. Emile Schwidder, e-mail to author, June 2, 2010. Emphasis added.

CHAPTER 2: STREET

1. Food, water, and transport costs were glossed as logistik, or logistical matters, but *logistik* often became activist code for funding or money, carrying with it a nuance of corruption or undue political influence.

2. See Erik Harms (2011) on how urban Vietnamese articulate the tensions of modernity through urban / rural dichotomies of moral and "cultural" practice, especially with regard to the perceived lack of order and hygiene of the village other.

3. Most famously, the student movement's iconic three-day occupation of parliament in the days leading up to Suharto's resignation on May 21, 1998, was criticized in the press and by reactionary figures for precisely this reason. After the students left the building, rumors circulated about the drink bottles, trash, and used condoms found in the sacred halls of parliament. Such rumors about the loose morals and slovenly behavior of students persisted in the years afterward as a means to denigrate and dismiss student activism.

4. This is considered to be an old-fashioned practice that occurs in both rural and urban settings. In the late afternoon, fires and smoke plumes dot the city, smoky with wet leaves and acrid with plastic bags burning in the same pile. Burning the day's rubbish was famously associated with the dissident novelist Pramoedya Ananta Toer, who would go out to take care of the day's trash in this "traditional" manner.

5. Wilson was a former PRD member who was imprisoned in Cipinang Prison along with several other leading PRD figures. Famous as a historian and blessed with an impressive memory, he was sought after by researchers for the most accurate version of gerakan history, or even by his friends who wanted to verify their own memories. In 2005 he published a book based on his experiences at Cipinang. See Wilson (2005).

6. See *Public Culture* 19 (2007); much like "alternative modernities," "cultures of democracy" proved a usefully plural formulation for the diverse cases of social movements and popular uprisings in the global South.

7. See Abu-Lughod (1990: 42) for this line: "I want to suggest we use resistance as a diagnostic of power." Read in this way, Abu-Lughod's analysis of Bedouin women's Egyptian-style consumption produces complex readings of the intersecting power structures of patriarchy and nation that affect Bedouin life.

8. The fifth and sixth presidents of Indonesia, respectively.

9. For a thorough analysis of how stability and order are ritually achieved through the "festival of democracy" of New Order elections, see John Pemberton's introduction (1994).

10. Ajidarma (2004b: 13); translation mine.

11. For a short biography of Wiji Thukul, see Krishna Sen and David Hill's first chapter, "Books: Translations and Transgressions," on Indonesian literature under the New Order, in Hill and Sen ([2000] 2007: 42–45). For an extended biography of Thukul, see "Teka-Teki Wiji Thukul: Tragedi Seorang Penyair" (2013).

12. Thukul (1994); translation mine.

13. "Urban popular radicalism" is Abidin Kusno's term linking urban modernity to Indonesia's early nationalist movement in the 1920s. See Kusno (2010).

14. The Long March [sic] is a protest strategy that disappeared for three decades during the New Order and was only brought back by the student activists of Generation 98. It alludes to Mao's historic Long March through China, but the term has also gained a localized meaning through Reformasi's history of activist struggles on the street. A Long March in Indonesia might take all day or multiple days to conclude and marks a special degree of perseverance to carry out the march in the face of state repression and violence.

15. See essays by Allen (2006) and Hebbert (2005) and the volume edited by Leach (2002).

16. The street vendors who fill the sidewalks must rent space for their enterprise, paying protection money to gangs or police, until the time when they are evicted by law enforcement officers for illegal settlement and disturbance of public order. See Bijlmer (1985: 3), and Gibbings (2014).

17. For a description of an older urban kampung community, see Lea Jellinek's (1985) history of Kebun Kacang and more recent work on Jakarta's urbanism by Marco Kusumawijaya (2006) and Patrick Guinness (2009).

18. City beautification projects in large Asian cities such as Bangkok or Kuala Lumpur coincide with international diplomatic meetings or election years. Walls are built to shield the city from the sight of the slums, or temporary tin walls are put up, painted in bright colors. Poverty becomes invisible to the potential overseas investors seeing the sites. See Klima (2002) on this point. In Jakarta, beautification projects take place in the already vibrant and visible parts of Jakarta—the tourist attractions of monuments and museums and garden districts.

19. For a historical analysis of massa and violence in the turbulent history of late colonial nationalist history, see Colombijn and Lindblad (2002).

20. Demi Demokrasi, PRD Menolak Takluk (1999), 54. Translation mine.

21. See Prasetyantoko and Indriyo's discussion (2001: 80–83, 108–110) of the student movement's self-reflexive acknowledgment of the tension between their aims for a "solid," united, and fully conscious crowd of demonstrators and the field reality of leading an unpredictably "liquid" (cair), temporary, and uncontrolled crowd.

22. See Jim Siegel (1998a: 95), for an analysis of middle-class fears of the street and the massa.

23. There have been noticeable changes to the middle class's views on outdoor public space, which anthropologist Lizzie van Leeuwen traces back to the kafe tenda, or tent café austerity chic, that began with Reformasi and continues today in malls, upscale cafés, convenience stores, and parks that provide a trendy "green" and al fresco lifestyle in major Indonesian cities. The provision of free wifi in many of these commercial establishments adds to their allure as middle-class sanitized spaces. See van Leeuwen (2011).

24. Activists theoretically have to register with the police all the details of a demonstration, including its stated intention, the number of organizations and participants, the routes used, and any equipment used, twenty-four hours in advance of a demonstration, but the activists I talked to ranged from conscientious to uncaring when it came to registering their demonstrations. The National Police website lists the requisite procedures for obtaining permits related to public displays: http://www.polri.go.id/pro/tpsp/pages/3. Labor movements have benefited from the shift toward allowing peaceful demonstrations by holding vast May Day demonstrations, while religious groups regularly mobilize vast congregations on the streets for weekly prayers.

25. The term used by Indonesian activists for performance art in the context of the demonstrations.

26. In the post-Reform era, the paid massa showed their political and entrepreneurial acumen by publicly admitting on television and in print media that they were indiscriminately for hire by political parties in exchange for cash and goods (T-shirts and other paraphernalia), while insisting that their votes remained free and inviolate.

27. See the foreword to de Certeau (1988), vi.

28. During the months of Ramadhan, activists' self-discipline and foresight in timing the demo are paramount to ensure that demonstrators can maintain their fast and still march and chant in the demo.

29. This is iced tea, a popular bottled drink.

30. In 2006 Tomy Winata was ranked 35 on Forbes's list of the 40 Richest Indonesians, with an estimated fortune of US$110 million.

31. Tomy Winata supporters surrounded and violently attacked the Tempo office and journalists on March 8, 2003. Nobody was convicted for any part in the assault. See Taufik's (2003) eyewitness account and chronology.

32. "Ada Tomy di Tenabang?" (2003).

33. Thukul, translation mine.

34. See Keane (2003).

CHAPTER 3: STYLE

1. "Mereka Pun Meliput Kita" (1998). Translation mine.

2. "Mereka Pun Meliput Kita" (1998). Translation mine.

3. On this point, see the articles by Kees van Dijk, Rudolf Mrázek, and others in the edited volume Schulte-Nordholt (1997), as well as Siegel (1997). These authors demonstrate the important place that appearance has in modern Indonesian politics in charting transformations from the traditional to the European-modern, and the ethnic to the Western-universal, as well as the concentration of identity effects on dressed bodies in Indonesia.

4. See the feature films Kutunggu di Sudut Semanggi (2005), Gie (2005), and Rumah Maida (2009) and the documentaries Student Movement in Indonesia (The Army

Forced Them to Be Violent) (2002) and *Setelah 15 Tahun* (2013), both directed by Tino Saroengallo.

5. Most recently, see the controversy generated by a photo of beauty queen Anindya Kusuma Putri, Miss Indonesia 2015, on the social media site Instagram. In February 2015, an old photo surfaced of Anindya as a student, sporting a bright red T-shirt with yellow hammer and sickle symbols and the caption in English "I am so Vietnam today!" Anindya later explained it as a gift exchange with a Vietnamese counterpart during an inter-ASEAN community service program. She had given a shirt with a Pancasila symbol on it and in return wore the Vietnamese *national* symbols of hammer and sickle without concern. Within hours her Instagram account was besieged by negative comments from the public about her un-Indonesian and unworthy (*tidak pantas*) behavior, while conservative Muslim clerics opined that Anindya should be stripped of her title and investigated by the police and military for her implied communist associations. Ilandra, 2015.

6. For a discussion of how the history of 1965–1966 was actively obscured and images of student purity and New Order propaganda about PKI violence were substituted for such history, see Strassler (2010: 235–242).

7. Loyal Soekarnoists were also silenced; however, they remained a powerful support base for Soekarno's daughter, Megawati Soekarnoputri, and her opposition party, the PDI, in the 1990s. Several activists I worked with claimed that student activism could be explained by their upbringing in the politically dissenting atmosphere of a Soekarnoist family background, or even whole neighborhoods or villages that voted PDI in New Order elections.

8. On July 27, 1996, the headquarters OF the opposition party, PDI, in Jakarta was attacked and burned by pro-Suharto groups. The radical student party PRD, which supported the PDI leader, Megawati Soekarnoputri, against a hostile leadership takeover by a pro-Suharto candidate, was blamed by the New Order state for the ensuing "riot" that resulted in dozens dead, hundreds injured, and more than a hundred PDI supporters and activists arrested.

9. In the 1980s and early 1990s media outlets were subject to censorship by the powerful Ministry of Information and practiced self-censorship that ensured a media blackout on demonstrations, workers' strikes, land struggles, and peasant rebellions. University student presses were also shut down by university administrators or by order of local military commands when they appeared too critical of New Order authority.

10. See McGregor (2009) on the attempts of Muslim youth activists who attempted reconciliation between the families of the former PKI and of the Nadhlatul Ulama, the Muslim organization whose youth wing, ANSOR, had carried out communist killings in 1965/66.

11. Each university campus had its own specific colored blazer, so the identities of students were easily identifiable on the streets. The distinction the campus blazer gave to student activists was especially important during the May 1998 occupation of the parliament compound, when the security forces forbade nonstudents

from entering it. The jackets of Trisakti University, which yielded the first martyrs of May 12, 1998, were blue, the UI yellow, the University of Bung Karno burgundy, and UNAS green.

12. This word is used by historian Rudolf Mrázek to describe the double presence of language in the "broken English" that circulates in everyday speech among Indonesia's cosmopolitan subjects. Globalish is that mode of English that is neither grammatically correct nor perfectly spelled, but with the slightest effort, the astute reader discerns what the author is trying to express in both English and Indonesian. See Mrázek (2006).

13. See Jeremy Menchik's photo essay (2009) for a look at the spectacle and pageantry of rallies, motorcades, and election memorabilia that political parties produced during the 2009 election campaigns.

14. The word *rakyat*, usually translated as "the People" in English, contains these nuances: nation, ordinary people. In the usage of Generation 98, *rakyat* referred to workers, farmers, peasants, artists, and the urban poor.

15. See Frederick (1997). A severe textile crisis during the war, as well as regional and political differences, influenced the range of styles expressed by competing youth groups and militias.

16. Goenawan Mohamad writes that the activists of 1998 were emulating Generation 66, who also sported bandanas with their campus jackets (Mohammad 2009). Certainly there was a consensus on the look of Reformasi activists, even though Generation 98 did not agree with what they considered the right-wing politics of Generation 66.

17. See Ryter (1998) on New Order pemuda and the evolution of *pemuda* into the criminal *preman*.

18. "Sebagai seorang pejuang muda (Yosef menolak dirinya disebut sebagai aktivis mahasiswa) dia tidak bisa berdiam diri dengan berbagai persoalan yang sedang dihadapi oleh bangsa ini." *BOMB (2004)*, no. 2, Tahun 1, Januari.

19. The epigraph to this section is from Hobsbawm (2003: 1).

20. As a point of comparison, during my fieldwork I saw no images of Marx displayed, even among committed leftist groups who collected banned literature.

21. In 2003–2007, the opposite was in effect. The "Che-ification" of local figures began to happen, where the faces were rendered in three-quarter profile or simply in graphic outline with dark shadows, much like the iconic image of Che looking upward, wearing a cap with a red star. The populist effect of such images made a clear association between the politics of local heroes, like the assassinated human rights lawyer Munir, and the populism of social movements associated with Che.

22. Recall Edward Said's final lines in his introduction to *Orientalism*, where he quotes Raymond Williams. The task of criticism and awareness is to unlearn the "inherent dominative mode" of knowledge (Said 1994 [1978]: 28).

23. Even groups that have agreed to march together in the same demonstration patrol and discipline their own "masses." Activist groups maintain boundaries through

visual markers such as T-shirts, headgear, colored campus jackets for students, large flags with the group insignia, and even rope cordons.

24. The juxtaposition of these images might be read as an uninformed "pastiche" of "Eastern" and "Western" cultures, a leveling or a flattening of both context and meaning for each historical figure portrayed. However, such an argument lies beyond the interests and the scope of this book. What I wish to point out is the fact that such images of youth culture were fairly standard on university campuses and in the small no-brand stalls where young people shopped, a presence that indicates both the global media flows that urban Indonesians are exposed to on a daily basis and the reconfiguration of the political and the popular in post-1998 public culture in Indonesia.

25. The cost of 50,000 rupiah (US$5) per shirt pointed to urban middle-class standards of consumption. Even though former student activists, as educated middle-class subjects, had access to permanent or flexible employment in the NGO sector, their earned income did not often exceed a range of $100–$500 per month. At the lowest end of the scale, 50,000 rupiah in cash represented a significant portion of disposable income given, the high cost of living in the capital city of Jakarta. Journalism, another sector that proved extremely popular with former student activists, provides a comparable wage structure to the NGO sector. In 2008, the Alliance for Independent Journalists estimated a living wage for entry-level journalists at approximately US$400 per month, while in practice entry-level or freelance journalists could be paid as little as US$100 per month, the same amount that a factory worker would earn in the Greater Jakarta area.

26. Gie's older brother, Arief Budiman (Soe Hok Djin), is a respected dissident scholar who earned his Ph.D. in sociology at Harvard University and currently teaches Indonesian studies at the University of Melbourne. Like Gie, Arief Budiman was also an activist who belonged to Generation 66. However, unlike the well-documented life of his younger brother, Arief Budiman's personal story and political trajectory did not serve as an equally inspirational template for Generation 98.

27. *Tionghoa*, the vernacular term for "Chinese," is regarded as the respectful and politically correct term for indicating a person of Chinese descent. Its usage reflects an attempt by the state to correct the New Order practice of openly using the term *cina* (chink).

28. This acronym stood for *suku, agama, ras, antar golongan*: "ethnicity," "religion," "race," and "intergroup relations." Under the New Order, it was forbidden to evoke the social, cultural, and religious differences that SARA stood for, for fear that that the mere mention of such issues would provoke violence in a society ridden with social inequalities and conflicts.

29. On arriving home after days of demonstrating on the streets, Soe writes that his mother greeted him with these words: "You look old now; filthy, smelly, and black with dirt." In response, Soe only smiles. "Ibuku menyambut kedatanganku dengan kata-kata 'Kau kelihatan tua sekarang; kotor, bau dan degil.' Aku hanya senyum saja." Gie (2005: 150); translation mine.

30. Nicholas did not look at all ethnically Chinese and was famous for playing the heartthrob role in a blockbuster teen movie, *Ada Apa dengan Cinta?* (What's up with love?). But Nico (Nicholas's nickname) in the role of Gie would clearly make "Gie" admirable as a dashing figure rather than as an intellectual, in the same way that the image of Che Guevara was acknowledged to be "handsome" (*cakep*) by new students on campus familiarizing themselves with the signs of protest culture.

31. During my fieldwork, bookstores selling leftist publications were attacked by "concerned citizens" who formed anti-PKI groups to vandalize property and intimidate gatherings that right-wing and Islamist groups considered communist. This pattern of intimidation continues today. In June 2010, the mobile clinics sponsored by the opposition PDI-P politician Ribka Tjiptaning, the daughter of a former communist, were forcibly disbanded by local thugs who questioned the legality of the free clinics and, by virtue of Dr. Tjiptaning's involvement, the "PKI" intentions behind them. As recently as August 2015, militant Islamist groups have intimidated local gatherings of korban 65 (victims of 1965) and prevented them from holding an annual closed door meeting with other victims' groups and human rights bodies in Java.

32. The joke referred to two things—to the pride the activists had that in the past they managed to organize large-scale demonstrations, especially given their left-leaning politics, but also to the widespread belief that crowds could be manipulated and bought by those in power, a political legacy from the New Order years.

33. Following Reformasi, the concept and practices of oral history gained a large following among politically conscious academics, students, and activists engaged in the larger project of historical revision of the New Order era. Film and documentary circles were also engaged in the idea of using oral history to tell new and previously unvoiced stories.

CHAPTER 4: VIOLENCE

1. Galuh is a pseudonym for a Jakarta activist interviewed by the author in 2004.
2. Galuh is referring to a bomb plot that he likens to the PRD Tanah Tinggi bomb case discussed in this chapter. The PRD were never proven to be behind building the Tanah Tinggi bomb, and high-ranking PRD members I interviewed refuted the accusation.
3. One of the largest luxury malls in Jakarta.
4. Erroneous detail; the primitive explosive device went off in a low-income housing flat in Tanah Tinggi, Jakarta.
5. Tawuran are street brawls involving high school students from rival schools. They are at times highly organized and public fights, where one gang attacks another in retaliation for a perceived offense. Salemba Street, which housed several universities in one long strip, would often be barricaded by police due to tawuran. The Generation 98 activists expressed worries to me that the younger activists (2003–2005) were recruits with a tawuran background who were therefore more interested in engaging in organized shows of violence on and off campus. See "Ospek

Mahasiswa Tiru Pola Militeristik" (1999), "Premanisme Kampus dan Akal-akalan Mahasiswa" (2003), and "Ospek Tumbuhkan Peradaban Primitif" (2003).

6. These figures that I cite from 1995–1998 are from the published research conducted by the research team headed by Muridan S. Widjojo (1999).

7. This understanding of a fundamentally violent massa finds an interesting correspondence with nineteenth-century European crowd theory, particularly in the destructive possibilities of a revolutionary crowd. Canetti's influential work "Crowds and Power," speculating on why and how crowds are susceptible to suggestion toward both positive and negative outcomes is a broader lens through which to view the culturally specific massa (McClelland 1989).

8. On the May Riots of May 13–14, 1998, see the findings of the special investigative team set up by the National Commission for Human Rights. Laporan Akhir Tim Gabungan Pencari Fakta, 1998.

9. Tragedi Ujung Pandang (1996), Tragedi Makassar (1996), Tragedi Trisakti (Jakarta, 1998), Tragedi Semanggi I (Jakarta, 1998), Tragedi Juli (Jakarta, 1999), and so on. The student press, mailing lists, Internet, pagers, and cell phone technologies were crucial in circulating information about aksi and their aftermath almost instantaneously.

10. In an essay remembering the disappeared student activist Suyat, an anonymous former comrade of his recounts how Suyat initially did not understand the goals of demonstration, being a new member to the movement. But through his experience of being beaten by police and preman, Suyat became emboldened and "radicalized." "Suyat: Biar tidak sia-sia pengorbanannya" (2004).

11. See the experience of activist Dhyta Caturani, who suffered a serious injury to her head and face after being shot at point-blank range with a rubber bullet on July 1, 1999. The incident was soon afterward called the "Tragedi Juli" (July Tragedy). Green Left Australia (1999).

12. Online column by Mugiyanto (2005), former student activist and current director of IKOHI—the Network of Families of the Disappeared.

13. See the official court statement (pledoi) of Benny Sumardi, the older brother of Romo Sandyawan, a well-known Catholic priest who had often helped PRD activists. After July 27, 1996, Benny Sumardi provided shelter for Romo Sandyawan and three PRD activists on the run. Published in Belajar dari Mistik Perjuangan Korban (1998).

14. The number of kidnappings in 1997–1998 totaled twenty-three victims, with nine released, one found dead, and thirteen still missing. These thirteen disappeared are Yani Afri alias Rian, Noval al Katiri, Dedy Umar alias Hamdun, Ismail, Herman Hendrawan, Petrus Bima Anugerah, Suyat, Yadin Muhidin, Hendra Hambali, Ucok M Siahaan, M. Yusuf alias Yusuf, Sonny, and Wiji Thukul. Leonardus "Gilang" Nugroho's body was discovered abandoned at the edge of a forest near Magetan, East Java, on May 23, 1998. A few of the kidnappings occurred in the period prior to the general elections of 1997; the bulk of the 1998 kidnappings were con-

nected to the state's targeting of the PRD and its affiliates. See *Mereka yang Hilang dan Mereka yang Ditinggalkan* (2004).

15. "Sepanjang malam itu sampai dengan subuh kami tetap terus disetrum dan diteror dengan suara alarm yang sangat memekakkan (bunyinya mirip dengan alarm mobil). AC dihidupkan dengan sangat kencang, sehingga tubuh saya yang setengah telanjang menggigil. Lalu seorang petugas datang mendekat memeriksa tubuh saya (kelihatannya tenaga medis) dan lewat suaranya samar-samar saya dengar bahwa ia melarang untuk menyetrum daerah perut dan dada. Lalu saya dan kawan-kawan dipakaikan kembali celana panjang kami. Kami tak bisa tidur sampai pagi hari, sampai para petugas penjaga berganti regu. Karena mata tertutup kami sepertinya kehilangan orientasi waktu. Petugas yang baru masuk juga mengulangi pertanyaan seperti regu sebelumnya. Siksaan terus kami alami sepanjang hari." Nezar Patria (testimony dated June 7, 1998), in Margiyono and Yunanto (2007: 127).

16. This last extraordinary detail of torture by ice was told by Raharjo Waluyo Djati, in Margiyono and Yunanto (2007: 136).

17. Fieldnotes, March 26, 2004.

18. A Human Rights Watch report (1996) details his ten months of imprisonment in 1993 for "insulting the President" and his kidnapping in 1996 by uniformed men and men in plainclothes when he attended a court hearing against Soerjadi after the July 27 Incident.

19. Pius Lustrilanang and Desmond Mahesa are exceptions to this group of PRD activists, as they were never a part of the radical left. It is interesting to note that among this group of kidnap victims, Pius and Desmond were the first to be co-opted by proestablishment political parties, such as Golkar (Suharto's party) and Gerindra, the party founded by their former kidnapper, Prabowo.

20. The haatzaai artikelen were colonial-era laws used to contain political dissidence by censoring political action and writing. The accusation of "sowing hatred" could be used to great effect by defining any actions and words as possible crimes of provocation. During Megawati's presidency (2001–2004), the haatzaai artikelen generated debate and alarm among activists when the laws were used to prosecute student activists who critiqued the state.

21. Fieldnotes, June 28, 2004.

22. Andi Arief, Democratic Indonesian Students Solidarity activist, came to this conclusion during his abduction and detention. One of the kidnappers would embrace him, have long chats with him, and even openly talk about his own family. Arief heard him call his daughter on the phone, "Hi, this is Papa in Jakarta. Don't stay out in the sun too much, or you'll be ugly." Arief wrote, "It was no wonder if you thought this was a split personality." Margiyono and Yunanto (2007: 148).

23. The July 27 Incident was the state's violent response to grassroots support for Megawati Soekarnoputri, politician and daughter of Sukarno, who had become a challenger to Suharto. The regime forcibly deposed Megawati from the leadership

of her own political party in a staged congress in Medan, in June 1996. On July 27, the PDI headquarters in Central Jakarta were attacked and sacked by soldiers and hired preman, resulting in 210 arrested, 149 wounded, between two and five reported dead, and twenty-three reported missing. These numbers combine figures from *Kronologi Demonstrasi Mahasiswa 1989–1998* (Widjojo 1999), a report written by the 98 Student Movement Research Team (Tim Peneliti Gerakan Mahasiswa 98), led by Muridan S. Widjojo, and from Wessel (2001: 67), who cites *Peristiwa 27 Juli* (1997), published by AJI (Alliance of Indonesian Journalists) and ISAI (The Institute for the Study of Information Flow).

24. See Kusno (2006: 109). For a detailed account of the events of the September 30 Movement and its aftermath, see Roosa (2006).

25. The term *sweeping* has been italicized throughout to indicate Indonesian speakers' use of the English word.

26. Internal reports by army intelligence that tried to link the PRD to the PKI were prepared after the July 27 Incident: "Mewaspadai Bangkitnya Kembali Gerakan Komunis di Indonesia" (Markas besar Angkatan Bersenjata Republik Indonesia Pusat Penerangan, Jakarta, August 7, 1996), Report in author's personal collection. In 1998, army officers claimed another communist link between Forkot and the PKI, citing as evidence the "communist orientation" of the group. Honna (2001: 87–88).

27. *Sweeping* refers to a practice used by students, militias, and police, where they search in groups for "guilty" individuals to abuse or capture them. Media reports have also given *sweeping* an Indonesian translation as *sisir*, literally, to "comb through" (hair). "Combing through" and "weeding out" are apt translations of *sweeping*, which often involves searching out those intended for capture in traffic or in a crowd (Sugiyarto 2008b).

28. Interview, Forkot activist, February 2004.

29. The media has reported various cases of retaliatory *sweeping* by students. More recently, in 2004, in response to a bentrok between students and police on a university campus, students from the Muslim University and Universiti 45 in Makassar constructed a roadblock and blockaded a road for two days, making all passengers step out of their vehicles, until they had isolated four students of the Police Academy. These Police Academy students were beaten severely and had to be hospitalized. See "Blokir Jalan di Makassar, 'Sweeping' Polisi di Kendari" (2004).

30. Interview, June 1, 2004.

31. One of the techniques activists named was dousing the prisoner repeatedly with cold water. Another was administering electroshocks. These are both techniques cited by kidnapped activists as part of their torture by police and army. The mildest form of treating intel was by using restraints, tying up their hands, or being accompanied at all times by other activists.

32. Fieldnotes, June 2004.

33. The procurement of confession and its inherent instability form a problematic that is familiar to scholars of witchcraft and, in genocide studies, reminiscent of what Alex Hinton calls "manufacturing difference" (Hinton 2004).

34. Interview, former PRD member, December 18, 2004.

35. *Aparat* is the all-encapsulating term for the various grades of army, navy, police, mobile brigades, KOPKAMTIB (Operational Command for the Restoration of Security and Order), etc.

36. Common words to describe this act of student violence would be *menghantam* or *menghajar*, both of which connote a righteousness, an act of teaching a lesson. *Digebuk*, meanwhile, usually implies the beating of demonstrators with a heavy, blunt object, either fists or a police truncheon.

37. The months of May and June are traditionally popular protest months, with national holidays, such as May Day (May 1) and Pancasila Day (June 10), and Reformasi commemorations, such as the Trisakti Killings (May 12), May Riots (May 13–14), and Suharto's resignation (May 21). In addition, a government announcement regarding severe cuts to fuel subsidies sparked mass protest.

38. From the announcement text for a televised discussion forum, *Violence and the Student Movement*, held by the Indonesia Institute station (TVRI), June 30, 2008.

39. "Muhasyim," online comment published at kompas.com, accessed June 25, 2008, http://kompas.com/read/xml/2008/06/25/04513256/polisi.aksi.demonstrasi .ditunggangi.

40. "Mahasiswa UKI 'Sweeping' Mobil Plat Merah" (2008). Jefri Silalahi was arrested a month later on June 25 as a provokator *aksi* (an instigator of the action).

41. Students put up posters outside their campus walls showing Maftuh Fauzi's face and spray-painted graffiti with the words "Polisi Pembunuh" (The Police Are Murderers).

42. This logic was particularly powerful in explaining the extraordinary violence of the May Riots and mass rapes of ethnic Chinese women in 1998, and in attempts to implicate the military in student movement deaths in 1998–1999.

43. An essay by Fadjar Thufail (2005) analyzes the "*ninja* killings" in East Java in 1998–1999 as a case of nationally inflected local violence that claimed hundreds of lives, linked to but not fully explained by the social breakdown generated by Reformasi. Thufail addresses the connection between unofficial explanations for violence in narratives such as rumors about the identities of the victims and the perpetrators, said to be dressed in black like ninjas, and existing New Order frameworks for interpreting mysterious outbreaks of violence as signs of state intervention, most commonly seen in the propensity of political observers and scholars to hypothesize the role of provokator.

44. Tali Geni, "Rope of Fire," refers to the wick on a bomb or possibly a stick of dynamite. In student movement discourse, this "rope" could very well be the rope that ignites their common symbol, the Molotovok cocktail. My thanks to Ben Anderson for providing me with this translation and its implications—that the catchy acronym preceded the name of (convenience for) the group.

CHAPTER 5: HOME

1. The masculine effect of *coy* is similar to calling someone "comrade" or (a male) "friend" and facilitates the narration of comic stories, so that men who were comfortable with my presence or had met me in the context of their sekretariat would sometimes refer to me as *coy* in order to maintain the narrative flow of their story or conversation.

2. Wilson, personal communication, June 2012.

3. See Miftahuddin (2004), which is organized by the biographies of individual activists and narrates their political comings-of-age.

4. See Siegfried Kracauer's (1995) scathing piece on the "little shopgirls" of jazz-age Berlin and Simmel (1997a).

5. Gedung Djoang was a popular venue that activists booked for public meetings, meet-the-press events, political party or group launches, book launchings, and so forth during the runup to the 2004 election. In addition to its historical significance, its central location, immaculate white façade, and graceful *tempo doeloe* (old times) architecture were attractive features for opposition politicians and the prodemocracy movement. However, these meetings actually took place in the unremarkable dark glass and air-conditioned meeting hall built during the New Order period behind the museum, so that the nationalist atmosphere ended with the glass display case of Sukarno's car in the courtyard outside.

6. An alternate spelling is *kos*.

7. In 1950 there were only ten universities in Indonesia. In 1970 there were 450 institutions of higher education, both private and state-run. In 1990, this figure had doubled to 900, with a total of 1,486,000 students registered. Yet rates of attrition remained very high, with few finishing their degrees in the three to four years allotted, mainly because of thesis (*skripsi*) requirements (Frederick and Worden 1993). The numbers of buildings used as kost are difficult to ascertain, and any published research about them is difficult to find, as the system of kos-kosan is such a ubiquitous part of everyday life in large cities. References are most often made in the media about anak kost, youth who live in kost, or about the moral dangers of living in kost. My thanks to Freek Colombijn and Ben Abel for enlightening me with the historical information of the Dutch origins of the term *in de kost*, which verified the general sense of how kost operates that I observed in my own fieldwork.

8. Using the exchange rates of the mid-1990s, 300,000 rupiah was equivalent to about US$135; 500 rupiah was about 22 US cents.

9. From my own observation in dense kos-kosan areas near the UI in Depok, various multistory boardinghouses abutted residential housing that was also rented to students. A study on the urbanization of Depok indicates that the rental market has been an important factor in the expansion of Depok's economy, particularly with the presence of two universities, the UI and Gunadarma University. Their study also suggests that the highest degree of movement occurs in the urban kampung

areas of Depok, with the highest density in population and the smallest spaces, with house sizes averaging smaller than one hundred square meters. These are perhaps where kost operations are most prolific. See *Growing Metropolitan Suburbia* (2004), chap. 3.

10. Wijayanto (2003) speculates that the word *kost* might have been borrowed from the English language. His explanation bears repeating: kos-kosan came from the word "cost," meaning the process of bargaining over rent prices before moving in; from the word "choice," that is, to choose which place to live; or from "house," a house to live in. The etymology is mistaken, but the idea of choice over where to live is clearly important.

11. The author intends *pemuda* to mean *preman*, youth who engage in criminal and amoral activities quite the opposite of the virtuous scholar-student, i.e., himself.

12. In 2003–2005, a chain of 5,000 rupiah (about 60 US cents) stores opened in Indonesia, targeting low-income mall shoppers. Equivalent to the dollar stores in the US, these stores mainly sold cheap household items and toys that were most likely made in China.

13. Online ad posted on Ruangrupa.org/forum, September 10, 2006:

DIJUAL CEPAT . . . BUTUH UANG . . .

1. jual karpet 3 x 4 meter . . . bersih dari sisa sisa peju dan lain sebagainya
2. jual lemari buku . . . cocok buat kolektor buku, kaset, cd, vcd, dvd, cocok juga buat nyimpen alat alat BDSM
3. jual monitor komputer 15" merk SPC
4. jual kasur spring bed . . . pantulan dan goyangannya masih oke . . . dijamin greng
5. jual lampu tidur antik ala taon 70

Dijual barang-barang kos-kosan, accessed, http://ruangrupa.org/forum, September 10, 2006. VCDs were video CDs with images of low quality that could be easily mass-produced on a computer with replication software.

14. The dominance of "friend" in activist discourse provides a useful framework to explain how individual actors and their decisions reflect broader patterns in Indonesian civil society, and to argue against theorizing activist relations through network theory. While activist groups and organizations in the NGO sector do carry out international campaigns and national alliances that fully utilize or even expand their network base, the historicized social and political links between individual activists matter as much as the functionalist explanation of strategy and politics.

15. The groups listed are the Togetherness Forum, made up mainly of students from the Law Faculty at Jayabaya University; Komrad, a radical student group that was the precursor of the National Democratic Students League; the Greater Family of the UI, the same posko activists I discuss later in this chapter; Alarm; Gempur, the Pancasila University Students for Reformation (Gerakan Mahasiswa Universitas Pancasila untuk Reformasi; in 2004 I visited the secretariat of an organiza-

tion of the same name in Pasar Burung, where there were several senior activists and junior activists linked to UNAS, so it was unclear if it was the same Gempur mentioned in 1998); the All-Jakarta Communication Forum of Student Senates, a leading coalition force in early 1998; Front Jakarta and Famred were both Forkot splinter groups; and Forkot itself.

16. The acronym is a pun on the Indonesian elementary school textbook *Cara Belajar Siswa Aktif* (The study method for active students; CBSA). Shiraishi (1997: 132).

17. I am referring to Durkheim's notion of collective effervescence as much as to activist descriptions of 1998 demonstrations as having an atmosphere of *eforia* (euphoria), in particular when Suharto resigned.

18. Taufan's description of a cascade of positive political effects resulting from state repression and violence resembles Franz Fanon's description of the galvanized masses in *Wretched of the Earth*, where the violent methods of the colonial state apparatus fail to work and instead produce more resistance and radicalization.

19. An alternate meaning of *posko* is *pos komunikasi*, "communication post." Both meanings are implied by activist usage, but the military-sounding "command post" is privileged because of its militant appearance and action-oriented goals.

20. After the May Riots in 1998, TRK was one of the first volunteer task forces on the ground, operating as a quasi–Red Cross organization that dispatched aid, medics, and even food and clothing supplies to distressed communities. Volunteer TRK medics were present at some of the largest protests in 1998–1999. Their high-profile documentation and investigative work with rape victims from the riots and victims of state violence gave them an impeccable reputation. Many activists had in one way or another worked with or knew Romo Sandyawan Sumardi by reputation during Reformasi, hence the good relations between TRK and other civil society organizations.

21. In 1998, the PDI-P built hundreds of posko all over Indonesia to galvanize their supporters into voting for Megawati in the upcoming election. The posko were semipermanent structures, painted red, and often had the flag of the paramilitary youth (*satgas*) flying alongside the PDI-P paraphernalia. More recently, paramilitary groups linked to security and intimidation work, such as the Forum Betawi Rempug, have built small but elaborate posko in alleyways, unused sites, or on the main streets, with their organization's emblems and flags openly displayed to passersby on the street.

22. The posko has been likened to the colonial *gardu*, a guardhouse built at the entrance of a compound or a village. The proliferation of neighborhood watch systems, known as *siskamling* (*sistem keamanan lingkungan*), in the late 1990s reflected the insecurity urban communities felt. See Kusno (2006).

23. "Mahkamah Rakyat: Benteng Terakhir Kebeneran, Keadilan dan Kedaulatan Rakyat," Forkot Research and Development Division, internal document, author's collection.

24. Fieldnotes, March 24, 2004.

25. The best-known case of Reformasi eviction is the forced dismissal of student activists from the parliament compound on May 22, 1998, following three days of occupation. The image of students in their campus jackets and tie-bandanas sitting on the convex twin roofs of the parliament building remains an iconic image of victory. Thousands of students had stormed the gate, but they were also required to verify their student identities by going through ID checks at the exit points by the army. The convoy of buses that sent the students "home" under the protection of the navy were allowed only one stop: back to campus.

26. *Abang* is also a term for "husband" among Sumatran and other non-Javanese ethnic groups. Hence the deference implied refers to the household unit.

27. In 2004–2006, several groups I knew were trying to figure out ways to pay their annual rent, which in Jakarta ranged from 20 to 30 million rupiah (about US$2,000–3,500) a year on average. When a contract ended, student groups moved, trying to match their former basekemp (secretariat) location and price. In Tebet, a popular area for leftist groups, rental prices were rising. The only way to get a cheaper basekemp was if a patron or friend had a house they could rent out cheaply, or even let for free for a limited time.

28. Several of the former Forkot activists I interviewed who had been important in the organization in 1998 cited conflict with Adian Napitupulu, the long-reigning leader and abang of Forkot, as the reason for their split.

29. The founding members of National League of Democratic Students and the former sekjen of the National Students Front merged to found the Association of the Nation of Workers in 2004, after leaving their organizations.

30. By 2005, many of the FPPI activists had moved on to more comfortable middle-class lifestyles, becoming *mapan* (established, with a secure job). If twenty people could each afford to contribute at least 100,000 rupiah on a single meeting, not including travel costs to Semarang, it gives an idea of the income these former students now have.

31. Nadhlatul Ulama, the largest Muslim organization in Indonesia, led by the famously idiosyncratic cleric Abdurrahman Wahid. Not coincidentally, Savic himself is of Nadhlatul Ulama background and pesantren-educated.

CHAPTER 6: DEMOCRACY

1. The Monumen Nasional, or Monas, was built on the grounds of the former Dutch Koningsplein (King's Square).

2. In December 2005, the December 10 Alliance (Alliansi 10 Desember), consisting of prominent human rights groups, such as Ikatan Keluarga Orang Hilang, and KONTRAS, along with workers' and students' groups held a demonstration on International Human Rights Day in memory of the murdered human rights lawyer Munir. Masks with mimeographed copies of Munir's face were passed out to demonstrators, with the eyes cut out, and with rubber bands to attach these masks to the ears. But the mouth was left whole, Munir's mouth, so that those who wore

the mask demonstrated in peaceful silence, as Munir himself was silenced. On the posters was the slogan "Who has silenced him?" (Siapa membungkam dia?).

3. Chris Brown writes about the lively way the mass demonstrations of 1998 included performance pieces by students involving fake microphones and video cameras fashioned out of cardboard and plastic. Brown's analysis of the performance piece emphasizes the mobility of the viewer and the "object" of the camera. The dangling plastic microphone moved as much as the activist in front of it did, capturing the crowds and, perhaps intentionally, mimicking the reporters who were gathered there to make the evening news. See Brown (1999: 58).

4. The words "fragmentation," "decline," and "failure" often surfaced in discussions and analyses of the student movement by political activists themselves, as well as by the press and political observers. The trope of failure described a chronological series of events that tracked the fission of the large alliances in 1998, notably with the rise of Forkot and its unraveling, as well as the breakup of groups in large cities that directly affected the alliances between groups in smaller branch cities. It is difficult to find a satisfying explanation in the student movement literature for the fission, beyond the vilification of individual student leaders or the often-cited but vague "ideological reasons."

5. Echols and Shadily define *tokoh* in this way, as "shape, form, personage, prominent" but also, in its secondary meaning, to "cheat and deceive." Echols and Shadily (1989).

6. The term *wakil rakyat* implies that the tokoh in question is a member of parliament. See Ajidarma (2002: 184–185).

7. The word *gombal* is often used to describe an insincere or exaggerated person or speech.

8. Some of the publications published by the Ministry of Information (Departemen Penerangan) that I consulted for this chapter are the commemorative booklets for 1981, 1986, 1991, 1992, and 1994. These materials are located in the John M. Echols Collection on Southeast Asia at the Kroch Library, Cornell University.

9. *28 Oktober 1986, Hari Sumpah* pemuda */Hari Pemuda ke-58* (np: Direktorat Publikasi / Direktorat Jenderal PPG / Departemen Penerangan RI, Percetakan Negara RI, 1986). In the John M. Echols Collection on Southeast Asia, Kroch Library, Cornell University.

10. "Adanja *pemudapemuda* adalah sjarat mutlak bagi kelangsungan hidup manusia dan masjarakat baru, dalam arti dan istillah: Pemuda adalah manusia baru, manusia muda dalam semangat, fikiran dan djiwanja. Sedarlah bahwa engkau harus berdjuang untuk nasibmu dan nasib Rakjat Murba Indonesia. Nasib sedjarahmu terletak ditanganmu sendiri. Sadarlah akan kekuatanmu!!!" Pemuda Republik Rakjat Indonesia (1952: 24). In the John M. Echols Collection on Southeast Asia, Kroch Library, Cornell University.

11. On February 15, 2005, a few months after Susilo Bambang Yudhoyono of the Democratic Party had won the election, the Lingkar 98 activists continued to be active, organizing a seminar in the Sahid Jaya Hotel in Central Jakarta, a hotel

popular for political seminars, discussions, and launchings. The theme of the day's seminar was "Is it true that there is discord between SBY [former general Susilo Bambang Yudhoyono] and his cabinet?" (Antar SBY dan kabinetnya, benarkah tidak se-visi?). Fieldnotes, February 15, 2005.

12. It became evident when I followed a few activists around to newly launched centers and meetings as they sought funding for political and research centers that these activists were in fact imagining setting up posko rather than formal research or policy institutions.

13. Before 1997, the wealthy ethnically Chinese conglomerates like Liem Sioe Liong, Bob Hasan, and Ciputra, who were closely linked to Suharto, were consistently listed in polls as some of the most important tokoh in Indonesia. In post-Reformasi Indonesia, the political rise of *pribumi* Indonesian conglomerates, such as the current vice president, Jusuf Kalla, and Golkar politician and media owner Surya Paloh, indicate that tokohisme has not ceased.

14. Fadli, an activist and potential caleg in 2004, named one well-known senior activist as a fraud, "pretending to be poor" (pura-pura miskin).

15. To view such specimens in Jakarta, visit any of the Café Phoenam locations and twenty-four-hour cafés, such as Café Oh-La-La.

16. Fieldnotes, May 11, 2004.

17. Personal technology aided these "sales." Most activists who narrated their experience of meeting brokers, or who had friends who had become political brokers, told me that all the proof that the political elite needed that they had gotten what they paid for was a photograph of any demonstration taken on a mobile phone camera. These stories exposed the immorality of brokers, but also expressed admiration for activists' ingenuity at scamming money out of political elite who read the language of demonstrations in the field so differently, as signs of *their* influence.

18. Gifting was another practice students partook in. Many organizations were remarkably generous with their printed materials, giving me extra copies of books and journals and refusing payment for them. They wanted to help me in my research, and indeed they might have also realized that some of these pamphlets and journals were past their sale date. The activists' indifference to the operational costs of producing the pamphlets pointed to other systems of exchange and economy that served to keep the student movement afloat. Magical sums of money would often appear when they needed it, either from one-time jobs or from donors or friends who had some cash to spare.

19. Konsentrasi Gerakan Mahasiswa (Concentration of the Student Movement; KGM), another student group, sold their journal, which was about the size of a letter-sized page folded in half, for a more affordable 500 rupiah (5 US cents).

20. EE, a former PRD activist of ethnic Chinese descent, albeit from a very poor working-class background, was accused of hoarding money because he was Chinese. Even when some of these accusations were practical jokes, EE discovered that several of his "indigenous" Indonesian comrades believed them.

21. Marcus Mietzner has written extensively, and with cautious hope, on the contested nature of post-Reform democratic movements in Indonesia. Mietzner argues against the corruption and co-optation framework for analyzing activists-turned-politicians, showing instead that the strong links between civil society and progressive politicians have enabled a democratic agenda to slowly encroach on Indonesia's patronage democracy. However, Mietzner also discusses two key figures, Desmond Junandi Mahesa and Pius Lustrilanang, two former kidnapping victims in 1998 who a few years later had joined their former enemy (Prabowo's party, Gerindra) and appeared to profit from lucrative posts in the political party machinery. The most dramatic case of activists-turned-corruptors has taken place in the elite ranks of the Justice Welfare Party, an Islamic party that has been plagued by spectacular scandals over the last few years. See Mietzner (2013: 28–50).

22. The last year when multiparty constitutional democracy was practiced in Indonesia was 1955. Soon afterward, Soekarno installed "Guided Democracy" and put into place increasingly restrictive political and security measures, including banning various political parties.

23. A Generation 98 activist called to ask me what I thought of the caleg muda and to remark with great irony that most of the well-known caleg muda like Rama Pratama, had been a real "mama's boy" (*anak mama*) and had not been particularly heroic in the battlefield. Rama, he said, was one of the elite students who was being groomed for leadership but was not treated with great respect by the more rakyat-based student groups. In other words, he was a tokoh but not a hero.

24. "Ketika saya memutuskan menjadi caleg, saya sadar, saya akan membawa beban integritas lebih besar dibanding kompetensi. Banyak orang pandai dan terampil di bidangnya mengalamai banyak persoalan karena terbentur soal integritas." Rama Pratama, quoted in Adi (2004).

25. "Melihat penyeberan dan konfigurasi caleg mantan aktivis di dua kubu tersebut, penulis buku Gerakan Mahasiswa dan Demokrasi di Indonesia A. Prasetioantoko memperkirakan, kelompok agamis akan lebih cepat mengalami kemajuan dalam membangun platform dan semangat yang sama dibandingkan kelompok nasionalis. 'Secara cultural, yang pertama lebih homogen, tenang, dan rasional, sementara yang lain lebih heterogen dan emosional,' katanya menjelaskan." "Mantan Aktivis Jadi Caleg" (2004).

26. Ibu Wawan (lit. "Wawan's mother"), also known by her own name, Ibu Sumarsih, became an important vocal critic of state violence after the death of her son, speaking out at human rights events, demonstrations, and other civil society–related actions. Ibu Wawan stood out from other korban, as she became well versed in the workings of the judicial process and always stressed the need for the rule of law as the mechanism for justice. She won the Yap Thiam Hien Award in 2005, which she dedicated to her son.

27. Here Ridwan wrote *existensi* to more closely resemble its English origin "existence," but most Indonesians will spell it *eksistensi*. The word means the state of existing, or simply put, *being*, in an existentialist framework. In movement poli-

tics, activists understand their political *eksistensi* as a fragile state of being, one that has to be constantly proven and defended in a hostile political environment, so that presence or being is never a neutral state of existence. *Eksistensi* is always relational and confrontational. If one's *eksistensi* is threatened, one has to vanquish the threat or reassert dominance over it. Hence one way that activists dismissed or explained conflict was to categorize those problems as problems arising from individual activists' narcissistic concerns over *eksistensi*, prompting individuals to act in unwise ways because they felt threatened and insecure.

28. Deklarasi Generasi Baru Indonesia "Bekerja dan Berjuang untuk Indonesia," Jakarta, May 11, 2004. Flyer in author's personal collection.

CONCLUSION

1. See Rofiuddin (2013), on a Hanura politician's campaign tactic in Pati, Central Java. Sunarwi, a local Pati politician, paid for over a hundred large banners (*baliho*) featuring Suharto's face, the phrase "Piye Kabare" (How Are You?), the faces of party leaders Wiranto and Harry Tanoesudibyo, and Sunarwi's own image to be erected.

2. Prabowo had already tried to enter national politics in 2009 as Megawati's running mate. Both were defeated by the incumbent, Susilo Bambang Yudhoyono.

3. Gerindra's campaign strategy included a rather unsubtle propaganda film on the life and times of Prabowo, *Sang Patriot: Prabowo Subianto* (The patriot: Prabowo Subianto), which crafted a noble nationalist genealogy for this modern-day leader and fighter by focusing on the anticolonial battles fought by his nineteenth-century ancestor Prince Diponegoro and the contributions of his father Soemitro, chief economist during the New Order. The thirty-three-minute film, available on YouTube on the Gerindra party channel, was produced by Media Desa Indonesia, a production company owned by Prabowo's brother Hashim. The propaganda value of the film was boosted by the appearance in the film of Peter Carey, famed Oxford historian and author of a biography of Prince Diponegoro. See Ed Aspinall and Peter Carey's debate: Aspinall (2014a).

4. Edhison had won his parliamentary seat in 2014 on a "Caleg Bersih" (Clean Candidate) campaign. His constituency included Central Jakarta, where his organization, Relawan Perjuangan Demokrasi (Volunteers for Democratic Struggle), affiliated with the PDI-P, was located; South Jakarta; and overseas voters.

BIBLIOGRAPHY

Abdullah, Taufik. 1980. "Nationalism and Social Structure: A Problem in Indonesian Historiography." S.I: sn.

Abeyasekere, Susan. 1985. "Overview of the History of Jakarta, 1930s to 1970s." In *From Batavia to Jakarta: Indonesia's Capital 1930s to 1980s,* edited by Susan Abeyasekere. Victoria, Australia: Monash University, 1–28.

Abinales, Patricio N. 2012. "The Philippines: Students, Activists, and Communists in Movement Politics." In *Student Activism in Asia: Between Protest and Powerlessness,* edited by Meredith L. Weiss and Edward Aspinall. Minneapolis: University of Minnesota Press, 259–280.

Abrams, Philip. 1988 [1977]. "Notes on the Difficulty of Studying the State." *Journal of Historical Sociology* 1, no. 1: 58–89.

Abu-Lughod, Lila. 1990. "The Romance of Resistance: Tracing Transformations of Power through Bedouin Women." *American Ethnologist* 17, no. 1: 41–55.

The Act of Killing. 2012. Film directed by Joshua Oppenheimer, Anonymous, and Christine Cynn. Denmark: Final Cut for Real.

Adam, Asvi Warman. 2004. *Pelurusan Sejarah Indonesia.* Yogyakarta: Tride.

Adam, Asvi Warman. 2005. "History, Nationalism, Power." In *Social Science and Power in Indonesia,* edited by Vedi R. Hadiz and Daniel Dhakidae. Jakarta: Equinox Press.

Adam, Asvi Warman. 2009. *Membongkar Manipulasi Sejarah: Kontroversi Pelaku dan Peristiwa.* Jakarta: Penerbit Buku Kompas.

Adam, Asvi Warman. 2010. *Menguak Misteri Sejarah.* Jakarta: Penerbit Buku Kompas.

"Ada Tomy di Tenabang?" 2003. Edisi Senin. *Tempo,* 3 March.

Adi, Windoro. 2004. "Pemilihan Umum 2004." *Kompas,* 7 February.

Aditjondro, George. 1993."The Media as Development 'Textbook': A Case Study on Information Distortion in the Debate about the Social Impact of an Indonesian Dam." Ph.D. diss., Cornell University.

Aditjondro, George. 2009. *Membongkar Gurita Cikeas*. Jakarta: PT Galang Press.

Agamben, Giorgio. 1995. *Idea of Prose*. Albany: State University of New York Press.

Agamben, Giorgio. 2009. "What Is the Contemporary?" In *What Is an Apparatus?" and Other Essays*, translated by David Kishik and Stefan Pedatella. Meridian: Crossing Aesthetics Series. Stanford, CA: Stanford University Press, 39–54.

Ajidarma, Seno Gumira. 2002. "Wakil Rakyat." In *Surat dari Palmerah, Indonesia dalam Politik Mehong: 1996–1999*. Jakarta: Kepustakaan Populer Gramedia, 184–185.

Ajidarma, Seno Gumira. 2004a. *Affair: Obrolan Tentang Jakarta*. Yogyakarta: Buku Baik.

Ajidarma, Seno Gumira. 2004b. "Berhala Jakarta, Semoga Sukses!" In *Affair: Obrolan Tentang Jakarta*. Yogyakarta: Buku Baik.

"Aksi Menolak Kenaikan BBM, Aktivis Bentrok dengan Polisi." 2008. *Jakarta Indymedia*. 25 June. Accessed April 21, 2014. http://jakarta.indymedia.org/newswire.php?story_id=1879.

Allen, John. 2006. "Ambient Power: Berlin's Potsdamer Platz and the Seductive Logic of Public Spaces." *Urban Studies* 43, no. 2: 441–455.

Anderson, Benedict R. O'G. 1972. *Java in a Time of Revolution: Occupation and Resistance 1944–1946*. Ithaca, NY: Cornell University Press.

Anderson, Benedict R. 1990a. "Cartoons and Monuments." In *Language and Power: Exploring Political Cultures in Indonesia*. Ithaca, NY: Cornell University Press, 152–193.

Anderson, Benedict R. O'G. 1990b. "Sembah-Sumpah: The Politics of Language and Javanese Culture." In *Language and Power*. Ithaca, NY: Cornell University Press, 194–237.

Anderson, Benedict R. O'G. 1990c. "A Time of Darkness and a Time of Light: Transposition in Early Indonesian Nationalist Thought." In *Language and Power: Exploring Political Cultures in Indonesia*. Ithaca, NY: Cornell University Press, 241–270.

Anderson, Benedict R. O'G. 1998a. "Gravel in Jakarta's Shoes." In *The Spectre of Comparisons*. London: Verso.

Anderson, Benedict R. O'G. 1998b. "Nationalism, Identity, and the Logic of Seriality." In *The Spectre of Comparisons*. London: Verso, 29–45.

Anderson, Benedict R. O'G., ed. 2001. *Violence and the State in Suharto's New Order*. Ithaca, NY: SEAP.

Anderson, Benedict R. O'G. 2014. "Impunity and Reenactment: Reflections on the 1965 Massacre in Indonesia and Its Legacy." *Asia Pacific Journal* 11, 15, no. 4.

Antlov, Hans. 1999. "The New Rich and Cultural Tensions in Rural Indonesia." In *Culture and Privilege in Capitalist Asia*, edited by Michael Pinches. London: Routledge, 188–207.

Appadurai, Arjun, ed. 1986. *The Social Life of Things: Commodities in Cultural Perspective*. Cambridge: Cambridge University Press.

Appadurai, Arjun. 1996. *Modernity at Large*. Minneapolis: University of Minnesota Press.

Appadurai, Arjun. 2000. "Spectral Housing and Urban Cleansing: Notes on Millennial Mumbai." *Public Culture* 12, no. 3: 627–651.

Appadurai, Arjun. 2002. "Deep Democracy: Urban Governmentality and the Horizon of Politics." *Public Culture* 14, no. 1: 21–47.

Appadurai, Arjun. 2007. "Hope and Democracy." *Public Culture* 19, no. 1: 29–34.

Appadurai, Arjun, and Carol Breckenridge. 1988. "Debates and Controversies: Why Public Culture?" *Public Culture Bulletin* 1, no. 1 (fall): 5–9.

Appel, Hannah. 2014. "Occupy Wall Street and the Economic Imagination." *Cultural Anthropology* 29 (4): 602–625.

Arendt, Hannah. 1970. *On Violence*. Orlando, FL: Harcourt.

Arendt, Hannah. 1958. *The Origins of Totalitarianism*. Cleveland: Meridian Books.

Arismunandar, Satrio. 2012. "Sejarah dan Fenomena Pers Mahasiswa." Unpublished paper. Jakarta.

Aryono. 2009. "Jalan Mendaki Menuju Reformasi: Gerakan Mahasiswa di Semarang Tahun 1990–1998." Thesis, Fakultas Ilmu Budaya Universitas Diponegoro Semarang.

Aspinall, Edward. 2005. *Opposing Soeharto: Compromise, Resistance, and Regime Change in Indonesia*. Stanford, CA: Stanford University Press.

Aspinall, Edward. 2012. "Indonesia: Moral Force Politics and the Struggle against Authoritarianism." In *Student Activism in Asia*, edited by Meredith Weiss and Edward Aspinall. Minneapolis: University of Minnesota Press, 153–180.

Aspinall, Edward. 2014a. "A Lesson for Researchers." *New Mandala*, 16 May. Accessed March 4, 2015. http://asiapacific.anu.edu.au/newmandala/2014/05/16/a-lesson-for-researchers/.

Aspinall, Edward. 2014b. "When Brokers Betray: Clientelism, Social Networks, and Electoral Politics in Indonesia." *Critical Asian Studies* 46, no. 4: 545–570.

Aspinall, Edward, and Greg Fealy, eds. 2010. *Soeharto's New Order and Its Legacy: Essays in Honour of Harold Crouch*. Canberra: Australia National University EPress.

Bach, Jonathan. 2002. "'The Taste Remains': Consumption, (N)ostalgia, and the Production of East Germany." *Public Culture* 14, no. 3: 545–556.

Bach, Jonathan. 2010. "'They Come in Peasants and Leave Citizens': Urban Villages and the Making of Shenzhen, China." *Cultural Anthropology* 25, no. 3: 421–458.

Bachelard, Gaston. 1994 [1964]. *The Poetics of Space*. Boston: Beacon Press.

Banning, Jan. *Traces of War: Survivors of the Burma and Sumatra Railways*. London: Trolley. 2005.

Barker, Joshua. 2001. "State of Fear: Controlling the Criminal Contagion in Suharto's New Order." In *Violence and the State in Suharto's Indonesia*. Ithaca, NY: SEAP, 20–53.

Barker, Joshua, and Gerry van Klinken, eds. 2009. *State of Authority: State in Society in Indonesia*. Ithaca, NY: SEAP.

B.A.T.A.M. 2005. Film by Johan Lindquist, Per Erik Eriksson, and Liam Dalzell.

Bayat, Asef. 2013a. "The Arab Spring and its Surprises." *Development and Change Forum 2013* 44, no. 3: 587–601.

Bayat, Asef. 2013b. *Life as Politics: How Ordinary People Change the Middle East.* Second edition. Palo Alto: Stanford University Press.

Belajar dari Mistik Perjuangan Korban: Pertangungjawaban Moral Terhadap Suaka Kemanusiaan Korban Insiden Berdarah 27 Juli 1996. 1998. Jakarta: Tim Relawan.

Benjamin, Walter. 1968a. "On Some Motifs in Baudelaire." In *Illuminations.* New York: Schocken Books, 155–200.

Benjamin, Walter. 1968b. "The Storyteller: Reflections on the Works of Nikolai Leskov." In *Illuminations.* New York: Schocken Books, 83–110.

Benjamin, Walter. 1968c. "Theses on a Philosophy of History." In *Illuminations.* New York: Schocken Books, 253–264.

Berdahl, Daphne. 1999. *Where the World Ended: Re-unification and Identity in a German Borderland.* Berkeley: University of California Press.

Berger, John. 2001. "The Nature of Mass Demonstrations." In *Selected Essays: John Berger*, edited by Geoff Dyer. New York: Pantheon Books, 246–249.

Bhabha, Homi. 1997. "Of Mimicry and Men." In *Tensions of Empire: Colonial Cultures in a Bourgeois World*, edited by Frederick Cooper and Ann Laura Stoler. Berkeley: University of California Press, 152–160.

Bijlmer, Joep. 1985. "The Ambulatory Street Economy of Surabaya." Urban Research Working Papers. Amsterdam: Free University.

Blanchot, Maurice. 1993. *The Infinite Conversation.* Minneapolis: University of Minnesota Press.

Blanchot, Maurice. 1995. *The Writing of the Disaster.* Translated by Ann Smock. Lincoln: University of Nebraska Press.

Bloembergen, Marieke. 2007. "The Dirty Work of Empire: Modern Policing and Public Order in Surabaya, 1911–1919." *INDONESIA* 83: 119–150.

Bloembergen, Marieke. 2011. "The Perfect Policeman: Colonial Policing, Modernity and Conscience on Sumatra's West Coast in the Early 1930s." *INDONESIA* 91: 165–193.

"Blokir Jalan di Makassar, 'Sweeping' Polisi di Kendari." 2004. *Kompas*, 4 May.

Bourdieu, Pierre. 1977. *Outline of a Theory of Practice.* New York: Cambridge University Press.

Brenner, Neil, and Nik Theodore. 2002. "Cities and the Geographies of 'Actually Existing Neoliberalism.'" *Antipode* 34, no. 3: 349–379.

Brown, S. Cristopher. 1999. "Blood in the Streets." *Inside Indonesia* 58 (April–June): 8–9.

Brown, S. Cristopher. 2010. "Pointy Fences." In "Streets and Children in Surabaya." Ph.D. diss., University of Washington.

Brown, Wendy. 2001. "Specters and Angels: Benjamin and Derrida." In *Politics out of History*. Princeton, NJ: Princeton University Press, 138–173.

Bruinessen, Martin van. 2004. "Post Suharto Muslim Engagements with Civil Society and Democracy." In *Indonesia in Transition: Rethinking "Civil Society," "Region" and

"*Crisis,*" edited by Hanneman Samuel and Henk Schulte Nordholt. Yogyakarta: Pustaka Pelajar, 37–66.

Bruinessen, Martin van, ed. 2013. *Contemporary Developments in Indonesian Islam: Explaining the "Conservative Turn."* Singapore: ISEAS.

Buck-Morss, Susan. 1991. *The Dialectics of Seeing: Walter Benjamin and the Arcades Project.* Cambridge, MA: MIT Press.

Budianta, Melani. 2003. *Menembus Tirai Asap: Kesaksian Tahanan Politik 1965.* Jakarta: Amanah/Lontar.

Burton, Antoinette, ed. 2006. *Archive Stories: Facts, Fictions, and the Writing of History.* Durham, NC: Duke University Press.

Calvino, Italo. 2003. "Il Duce's Portraits: Living with Mussolini." *The New Yorker,* January 6, 34–39.

Calvino, Italo. 1997. "Continuous Cities 4." In *Invisible Cities.* New York: Vintage, 146–147.

Caruth, Cathy. 1996. *Unclaimed Experience: Trauma, Narrative, and History.* Baltimore: Johns Hopkins University Press.

Catatan Keadaan Hak Asasi Manusia 1994. 1995. Jakarta: YLBHI.

Catatan Si Boy. 1987. Film directed by Nasri Cheppy. Jakarta: Bola Dunia Film.

Chakrabarty, Dipesh. 2007. "'In the Name of Politics': Democracy and the Power of the Multitude in India." *Public Culture* 19, no. 1: 35–57.

Christanty, Linda. 2004. "Makam Keempat." In *Kuda Terbang Maria Pinto.* Jakarta: KataKita, 123–134.

Cohen, Paul A. 1998. *History in Three Keys: The Boxers as Event, Experience, and Myth.* New York: Columbia University Press.

Colombijn, Freek. 2002. "Maling, Maling!" In *Roots of Violence in Indonesia,* edited by Freek Colombijn and J. Thomas Lindblad. Leiden: KITLV Press, 299–329.

Colombijn, Freek, Martine Barwegen, Purnawan Basundoro, and Johny Alfian Khusyairi, eds. 2005. *Kota Lama, Kota Baru: Sejarah Kota-Kota di Indonesia.* Indonesia Across Orders Research Programme. Jogjakarta: Ombak Press.

Colombijn, Freek, and J. Thomas Lindblad. 2002. *Roots of Violence in Indonesia.* Leiden: KITLV Press.

Comaroff, Jean, and John L. Comaroff. 2006. "Reflections on Youth, From the Past to the Postcolony." In *Frontiers of Capital: Ethnographic Reflections on the New Economy,* edited by Greg Downey and Melissa S. Fisher. Durham, NC: Duke University Press, 267–281.

Cooper, Frederick. 2005. *Colonialism in Question: Theory, Knowledge, History.* Berkeley: University of California Press.

Cooper, Frederick, and Ann Laura Stoler, eds. 1997. *Tensions of Empire: Colonial Cultures in a Bourgeois World.* Berkeley: University of California Press.

Coté, Joost, and Loes Westerbeek, eds. 2005. *Recalling the Indies: Colonial Culture and Postcolonial Identities.* Amsterdam: Aksant.

Crary, Jonathan. 1991. *Techniques of the Observer: On Vision and Modernity in the Nineteenth Century.* Cambridge, MA: MIT Press.

"Daftar Korban 'Semanggi Berdarah' 14 Nov. 1998, Dari KB-UI dan Daftar Pasien di RSCM." http://indoprotest.tripod.com/111701.htm.

Daniel, E. Valentine. 1996. *Charred Lullabies: Chapters in an Anthropology of Violence*. Princeton, NJ: Princeton University Press.

Das, Veena. 2007. *Life and Words: Violence and the Descent into the Ordinary*. Berkeley: University of California Press.

Data Statistik Indonesia. 2005. http://www.datastatistik-indonesia.com.

Davis, Mike. 2004. "The Urbanization of Empire: Megacities and the Laws of Chaos." *Social Text* 22, no. 81: 9–15.

Davis, Mike. 2006. *Planets of Slums*. London: Verso.

de Certeau, Michel. 1988. *The Practice of Everyday Life*. Berkeley: University of California Press.

Deleuze, Gilles, and Felix Guattari. 1983. *Anti-Oedipus: Capitalism and Schizophrenia*. Minneapolis: University of Minnesota Press.

Derrida, Jacques. 1978. "Structure, Sign, and Play." In *Writing and Difference*. Chicago: University of Chicago Press, 278–294.

Derrida, Jacques. 1998. *Archive Fever: A Freudian Impression*. Translated by Eric Prenowitz. Chicago: University of Chicago Press.

de Vries, Hent, and Samuel Weber, eds. 1997. *Violence, Identity, and Self-Determination*. Stanford, CA: Stanford University Press.

Di Batas Panggung. 2005. Film directed by Lexy Junior Rambadeta. Offstream.

Dick, H. W. 1990. "Further Reflections on the Middle Class." In *The Politics of Middle Class Indonesia*, edited by Richard Tanter and Kenneth Young. Victoria, Australia: Centre of Southeast Asian Studies, Monash University.

Drexler, Elizabeth. 2008. *Aceh, Indonesia: Securing the Insecure State*. Philadelphia: University of Pennsylvania Press, 2008.

"Dying Alone in the Heat Wave: An Interview with Eric Klinenberg." 2002. Accessed March 20, 2015. http://www.press.uchicago.edu/Misc/Chicago/443213in.html.

East Timor Documents. Vol. 39. *June 28–August 31, 1995*. East Timor Action Network. Accessed March 12, 2015. http://www.etan.org/etanpdf/timordocs/timmas39%2095–08–31.pdf.

"Ekspresi: Pemuda dan Kegairahan Politik" [Expression: Youth and political dynamism]. 1987. *Politika*, February–April.

Echols, John M., and Hassan Shadily. 1989. *An Indonesian-English Dictionary*. 3rd ed. Edited by John U. Wolff and James T. Collins. Ithaca, NY: Cornell University Press.

Enwezor, Okwui. 2008. *Archive Fever: Uses of the Document in Contemporary Art*. Göttingen: Steidl/ICP.

Farge, Arlette. 2013 [1989]. *The Allure of the Archives*. Translated by Thomas Scott-Railton. New Haven, CT: Yale University Press.

Ford, Michele. 2009. *Workers and Intellectuals: NGOs, Trade Unions, and the Indonesian Labour Movement*. Honolulu: University of Hawaii Press.

Ford, Michele, and Lenore Lyons. 2012. *Men and Masculinities in Southeast Asia*. London: Routledge.

Foster, Susan Leigh. 2003. "Choreographies of Protest." *Theater Journal* 55, no. 3: 395–412.

Foucault, Michel. 1972. *The Archaeology of Knowledge and the Discourse of Language*. New York: Pantheon Books.

Foucault, Michel. 1977. *Discipline and Punish: The Birth of the Prison*. New York: Pantheon Books.

Foulcher, Keith. 2000. "*Sumpah Pemuda*: The Making and Meaning of a Symbol of Indonesian Nationhood." *Asian Studies Review* 24, no. 3 (September): 377–410.

Frederick, William H. 1989. *Visions and Heat: The Making of the Indonesian Revolution*. Athens: Ohio University Press.

Frederick, William H. 1997. "The Appearance of Revolution." In *Outward Appearances: Dressing State and Society in Indonesia*, edited by Henk Schulte-Nordholt. Leiden: KITLV Press, 199–248.

Frederick, William H., and Robert L. Worden, eds. 1993. *Indonesia: A Country Study*. 5th ed. Washington, DC: Federal Research Division, Library of Congress.

Furnivall, John Sydenham. 1948. *Colonial Policy and Practice: A Comparative Study of Burma and Netherlands India*. Cambridge: Cambridge University Press.

Gaonkar, Dilip. 2007. "On Cultures of Democracy." *Public Culture* 19, no. 1: 1–22.

Geertz, Clifford. 1960: "The Javanese Kijaji: The Changing Role of a Cultural Broker." *Comparative Studies in Society and History* 2, no. 2: 228–249.

Geertz, Clifford. 1977. "Afterword: The Politics of Meaning." In *Culture and Politics in Indonesia*. Ithaca, NY: Cornell University Press, 319–335.

Gibbings, Sherri Lynn. 2014. "Street Vendor." In *Figures of Southeast Asian Modernity*, edited by Joshua Barker, Erik Harms, and Johan Lindquist. Honolulu: University of Hawaii Press, 156–159.

Gie. 2005. Film directed by Riri Reza. Mira Lesmana, Jakarta.

"*Gie* meminjam wajah Nicholas." 2005. *Gatra* 33, 27 July.

Goldstein, Daniel. 2004. *The Spectacular City: Violence and Performance in Urban Bolivia*. Durham, NC: Duke University Press.

Goldstein, Donna. 2003. *Laughter out of Place*. Berkeley: University of California Press.

Gordillo, Gaston. 2014. *Rubble: The Afterlife of Destruction*. Durham, NC: Duke University Press.

Gordimer, Nadine. 1995a. "Hanging on a Sunrise: Testimony and Imagination in Revolutionary Writings." In *Writing and Being*. Cambridge, MA: Harvard University Press, 20–42.

Gordimer, Nadine. 1995b. *Writing and Being*. Cambridge, MA: Harvard University Press.

Greenberg, Jessica. 2014. *After the Revolution: Youth, Democracy, and the Politics of Disappointment in Serbia*. Stanford, CA: Stanford University Press.

Green Left Australia. 1999. "Dhyta Caturani: 'Nothing Has Changed' in Indonesia." 4 August. Accessed June 2, 2015. https://www.greenleft.org.au/node/19165.

Growing Metropolitan Suburbia: A Comparative Sociological Study on Tokyo and Jakarta. 2004. Jakarta: Yayasan Obor Indonesia.

Guinness, Patrick. 2009. *Kampung, Islam, and State in Urban Java*. Singapore: NUS Press.

Gupta, Akhil. 2012. *Red Tape: Bureacracy, Structural Violence, and Poverty in India*. Durham, NC: Duke University Press.

Gupta, Akhil, and James Ferguson, eds. 1997. *Anthropological Locations: Boundaries and Grounds of a Field Science*. Berkeley: University of California Press.

Haberkorn, Tyrell. 2011. *Revolution Interrupted: Farmers, Students, Law, and Violence in Northern Thailand*. Madison: University of Wisconsin Press.

Haberkorn, Tyrell. 2013. "Getting Away with Murder in Thailand: State Violence and Impunity in Phattalung." In *State Violence in East Asia*, edited by N. Ganesan and Sung Chull Kim. Lexington: University Press of Kentucky, 185–208.

Habermas, Jürgen. 1991. *The Structural Transformation of the Public Sphere: An Inquiry into a Category of Bourgeois Society*. Translated by Thomas Burger. Cambridge, MA: MIT Press.

Hadikoemoro, ed. 1999. *Tragedi Trisakti 12 Mei 1998*. Jakarta: Penerbit Universitas Trisakti.

Hadiz, Vedi, and Daniel Dhakidae. 2005. Introduction to *Social Science and Power in Indonesia*, edited by Vedi Hadiz and Daniel Dhakidae. Singapore: Equinox Press, 1–30.

Han, Clara. 2012. *Life in Debt: Times of Care and Violence in Neoliberal Chile*. Berkeley: University of California Press.

Hanna, Joel M., and Daniel E. Brown. 1983. "Human Heat Tolerance: An Anthropological Perspective." In *Annual Reviews of Anthropology* 12: 259–284.

Hardt, Michael, and Antonio Negri. 2004. *Multitude: War and Democracy in the Age of Empire*. New York: Penguin Press.

Harms, Erik. 2011. *Saigon's Edge: On the Margins of Ho Chi Minh City*. Minneapolis: University of Minnesota Press.

Harsono, Andreas. 2002. "Kemelut Universitas Kristen Satya." Blog entry, December 7, 2002. Accessed January 30, 2014. http://www.andreasharsono.net/2002/12/kemelut -universitas-kristen-satya.html.

Harvey, Barbara. 2002. *Permesta: Half a Rebellion*. Cornell Modern Indonesia Project Monograph Series. Ithaca, NY: SEAP.

Harvey, David. 2012. *Rebel Cities: From the Right to the City to the Urban Revolution*. London: Verso Press.

Havelaar, Ruth. 1991. *Quartering: A Story of Marriage in Indonesia during the Eighties*. Edited by David Hill. Monash Papers on Southeast Asia, no. 24. Victoria, Australia: Monash University

Hayashi, Sharon, and Anne McKnight. 2005. "Goodbye Kitty, Hello War: The Tactics of Spectacle and New Youth Movements in Urban Japan." *positions* 13, no. 1: 87–113.

Hebbert, Michael. 2005. "The Street as Locus of Collective Memory." *Environment and Planning D: Society and Space* 23: 581–596.

Hedman, Eva-Lotta E. 2003. "The Dialectics of 'EDSA Dos': Urban Space, Collective Memory, and the Spectacle of Compromise." In *Southeast Asia over Three Generations: Essays Presented to Benedict R. O'G. Anderson*. Ithaca, NY: SEAP, 283–302.

Hefner-Smith, Nancy. 2007. "Youth Language, *Gaul* Sociability, and the New Indonesian Middle Class." *Journal of Linguistic Anthropology* 17: 1184–1203.

Heidegger, Martin. [1971] 2001a. "Building Dwelling Thinking." In *Poetry, Language, Thought,* trans. Albert Hofstadter. New York: HarperCollins, 141–159.

Heidegger, Martin. [1971] 2001b. "The Origin of the Work of Art." In *Poetry, Language, Thought,* trans. Albert Hofstadter. New York: HarperCollins, 15–86.

Heidegger, Martin. 1977. "The Question Concerning Technology." In *The Question Concerning Technology, and Other Essays.* New York: Harper and Row, 3–35.

"Hentikan Tudingan Dalang Demo." 2008. *Suara Pembaruan,* 27 June.

Heryanto, Ariel. 2010. "Entertainment, Domestication, and Dispersal: Street Politics as Popular Culture." In *Problems of Democratisation in Indonesia: Elections, Institutions and Society,* edited by Edward Aspinall and Marcus Mietzner. Singapore: Institute of Southeast Asian Studies, 181–198.

Hill, David T. 2006. *The Press in New Order Indonesia.* Jakarta: Equinox.

Hill, David T., and Krishna Sen. 2005. *The Internet in Indonesia's New Democracy.* New York: Routledge.

Hill, David T., and Krishna Sen. [2000] 2007. *Media, Culture, and Politics in Indonesia.* Jakarta: Equinox.

Hinton, Alexander Laban. 2004. *Why Did They Kill: Cambodia in the Shadow of Genocide.* Berkeley: University of California Press.

Hinton, Alexander Laba. 2005. *Why Did They Kill? Cambodia in the Shadow of Genocide.* Berkeley: University of California Press.

Hobsbawm, Eric. 2003. "Introduction: Inventing Traditions." In *The Invention of Tradition,* edited by E. Hobsbawm and T. Ranger, 11th ed. Cambridge: Cambridge University Press, 1–14.

Hoffman, Danny. 2011. *The War Machines: Young Men and Violence in Sierra Leone and Liberia.* Durham, NC: Duke University Press.

Holston, James. 2009. "Insurgent Citizenship in an Era of Global Urban Peipheries." *City and Society* 21, no. 2 (December): 245–267.

Honna, Jun. 2001. "Military Ideology in Response to Democratic Pressure during the Late Suharto Era: Political and Institutional Contexts." In *Violence and the State in Suharto's Indonesia,* edited by Benedict R. O'G. Anderson. Ithaca, NY: SEAP, 54–89.

Hull, Matthew. 2012. *Government of Paper: The Materiality of Bureacracy in Urban Pakistan.* Berkeley: University of California Press.

Human Rights Watch. 1996. "Indonesia: Tough International Response Needed to Widening Crackdown." August. Accessed September 20, 2015. http://hrw.org /reports/1996/Indonesi2.htm.

Human Rights Watch. 1998a. "Academic Freedom in Indonesia: Dismantling Soeharto-Era Barriers." August. Accessed February 15, 2014. https://www.hrw.org /sites/default/files/reports/inacfr98.pdf.

Human Rights Watch. 1998b. "The Soeharto Legacy on Campus: A Historical Overview." Accessed February 15, 2014. http://www.hrw.org/reports98/indonesia2 /Borneote-04.htm.

Human Rights Watch. 2003a. "A Return to the New Order? Political Prisoners in Megawati's Indonesia." Accessed March 17, 2014. http://www.hrw.org/reports/2003/indono703/.

Human Rights Watch. 2003b. "The Use of Colonial Legislation and Soeharto-Era Practices to Detain Political Activists." In "A Return to the New Order?: Political Prisoners in Megawati's Indonesia."

Human Rights Watch and Amnesty International. 1998. "Indonesia: Release Prisoners of Conscience Now!" Joint Human Rights Watch and Amnesty International Report on Indonesia. June. Accessed February 15, 2014. http:hrw.org/reports98/Indonesia/indo1-3.htm.

Ilandra, Aisyah. 2015. "Puteri Indonesia Pakai Baju Palu Arit untuk Hormati Vietnam." CNN Indonesia, 24 February. Accessed: 20 September 2015. http://www.cnnindonesia.com/gaya-hidup/20150224185537-277-34546/puteri-indonesia-pakai-baju-palu-arit-untuk-hormati-vietnam/.

Jain, Kajri. 2007. Gods in the Bazaar: The Economies of Indian Calendar Art. Durham, NC: Duke University Press.

Jakarta Crackdown. 1997. Jakarta: Institut Studi Arus Informasi/Alliansi Jurnalis Independen.

"Jakarta Membara." 1997. In Peristiwa 27 Juli. Jakarta: Institut Studi Arus Informasi/Alliansi Jurnalis Independen, 1.

Jellinek, Lea. 1985. "Underview: Memories of Kebun Kacang, 1930s to 1980s." In From Batavia to Jakarta, edited by Susan Abeyasekere. Victoria, Australia: Monash University, 25–90.

Jones, Carla. 2010. "Materializing Piety: Gendered Anxieties about Faithful Consumption in Contemporary Urban Indonesia." American Ethnologist 37, no. 4: 617–637.

Jordan, Jennifer. 2006. Structures of Memory. Palo Alto: Stanford University Press.

Juliawan, Benny. 2011. "Street-Level Politics: Labour Protests in Post-authoritarian Indonesia." Journal of Contemporary Asia 41, no. 3: 349–370.

Juris, Jeffrey. 2012. "Reflections on #Occupy Everywhere: Social Media, Public Space, and Emerging Logics of Aggregation." American Ethnologist 39, no. 2: 259–279.

"'Kampus Perjuangan Orde Baru' Tumbang Kampus UI 'Diduduki.'" 1998. Bergerak, 10–17 November.

Kamus Besar Bahasa Indonesia. 2001. 3rd ed. Jakarta: Balai Pustaka, Pusat Bahasa, Departemen Pendidikan Nasional.

Kasian Tejapira. 2001. Commodifying Marxism: The Formation of Modern Thai Radical Culture, 1927–1958. Kyoto Area Studies on Asia, Center for Southeast Asian Studies, Kyoto University, vol. 3. Kyoto: Kyoto University Press.

Keane, Webb. 1997. Signs of Recognition: Powers and Hazards of Representation in an Indonesian Society. Berkeley: University of California Press.

Keane, Webb. 2003. "Public Speaking: On Indonesian as the Language of the Nation." Public Culture 15, no. 3: 503–530.

Kepolisian Negara Republik Indonesia. "C. Perizininan Penyampaian Pendapat di Muka Umum." Accessed September 20, 2015. http://www.polri.go.id/layanan -keramaian.php.

Khan, Mushtaq H. 1998. "Patron-Client Networks and the Economic Effects of Corruption in Asia." *European Journal of Development Research* 10, no. 1: 15–39.

Klein, Naomi. 2000. *No Logo*. New York: Picador.

Klein, Naomi. 2002. *Fences and Windows: Dispatches from the Frontlines of the Globalization Debate*. Edited by Debra Ann Levy. New York: Picador.

Klima, Alan. 2002. *The Funeral Casino*. Princeton, NJ: Princeton University Press.

Klinenberg, Eric. 2002. *Heat Wave: A Social Autopsy of Disaster in Chicago*. Chicago: University of Chicago Press.

"Korban Penculikan Minta Presiden Berbicara." 2007. *Kompas*, 26 January.

Kracauer, Siegfried. 1995. "The Little Shopgirls Go to the Movies." In *The Mass Ornament: Weimar Essays*, translated and edited by Thomas Y. Levin. Cambridge, MA: Harvard University Press, 291–306.

Kuipers, Joel C. 2003. "Citizens as Spectators." In *Cultural Citizenship in Island Southeast Asia*, edited by Renato Rosaldo. Berkeley: University of California Press, 162–191.

Kusno, Abidin. 2000. *Behind the Postcolonial: Architecture, Urban Space, and Political Cultures*. London: Routledge.

Kusno, Abidin. 2006. "Guardian of Memories: *Gardu* in Urban Java." *Indonesia* 81 (April): 95–150.

Kusno, Abidin. 2010. *The Appearances of Memory: Mnemonic Practices of Architecture and Urban Form in Indonesia*. Durham, NC: Duke University Press.

Kusumawijaya, Marco. 2002. "Jakarta, Sang Metropolis." KALAM 19 *Ihwal Kota*: 5–34.

Kusumawijaya, Marco. 2004. "Jalan, Kaki-lima, Mall." In *Jakarta: Metropolis Tunggang-langgang*. Jakarta: Gagas Media.

Kusumawijaya, Marco. 2006. *Kota rumah kita*. Jakarta: Borneo.

Kutunggu di Sudut Semanggi. 2005. Film directed by Lukmantoro. Jakarta.

Laclau, Ernesto. 2005. *On Populist Reason*. London: Verso.

Laffan, Michael. 2003. *Islamic Nationhood and Colonial Indonesia: The Umma below the Winds*. New York: Routledge Curzon.

Lane, Max. 1999. "Interview and Speech by Pramoedya." In [INDONEWS] mailing list, posted by INDONEWS editors, 23 March.

Lane, Max. 2008. *Unfinished Nation: Indonesia before and after Suharto*. London: Verso.

"Lanjutan Kasus Ferry: Lapor, Komando Sudah Diambil Alih!" 2008. Berpolitik.com, 7 July. Accessed December 4, 2015.

Laporan Akhir Tim Gabungan Pencari Fakta (TGPF): Peristiwa tanggal 13–15 Mei, 1998: Jakarta, Solo, Palembang, Lampung, Surabaya dan Medan. 1998. Jakarta: TGPF.

Leach, Neil, ed. 2002. *The Hieroglyphics of Space: Reading and Experiencing the Modern Metropolis*. London: Routledge.

Lee, Doreen. 2003. "Boxed Memories." *Indonesia* 75 (April): 1–8.

Lee, Doreen. 2011. "Styling the Revolution: Masculinities, Youth, and Street Politics in Jakarta, Indonesia." *Journal of Urban History*: 933–951.

Lee, Doreen. 2012. "Aktivis, Activist." In *Figures of Southeast Asian Modernity*, edited by Joshua Barker, Johan Linquist, and Erik Harms. Honolulu: University of Hawaii Press, 143–145.

Lee, Doreen. 2013. "Anybody Can Do It: Aesthetic Empowerment, Urban Citizenship, and the Naturalization of Indonesian Graffiti and Street Art." *City and Society* 25, no. 3: 304–327.

Lee, Namhee. 2007. *The Making of Minjung: Democracy and the Politics of Representation in South Korea*. Ithaca, NY: Cornell University Press.

Lindquist, Johan. 2008. *The Anxieties of Mobility: Migration and Tourism in the Indonesian Borderlands*. Honolulu: University of Hawaii Press.

Locher-Scholten, Elsbeth. 2002. "State Violence and the Police in Colonial Indonesia." In *Roots of Violence in Indonesia*, edited by Freek Colombijn and J. Thomas Lindblad. Leiden: KITLV Press, 81–104.

Lombard, Denys. 1993. "Des images pour un développement: Les panneaux de la Place Merdeka (17 août 1983)." *Archipel* 46: 41–58.

Lomnitz, Claudio. 2007. "Foundations of the Latin American Left." *Public Culture* 19, no. 1: 23–27.

Luvaas, Brent. 2010. "Designer Vandalism: Indonesian Indie Fashion and the Cultural Practice of Cut 'n' Paste." *Visual Anthropology Review* 26, no. 1 (May): 1–16.

"Mahasiswa UKI 'Sweeping' Mobil Plat Merah." 2008. *Kompas*, 23 May.

Maier, Henk. 2004. *We Are Playing Relatives: A Survey of Malay Writing*. Leiden: KITLV.

Maier, Henk. 2005. "In Search of Memory: How Malay Tales Try to Shape History." In *Beginning to Remember: The Past in the Indonesian Present*, edited by Mary Zurbuchen. Singapore: Singapore University Press, 99–120.

Malkki, Liisa. 1996. "Speechless Emissaries: Refugees, Humanitarianism, and Dehistoricization." *Cultural Anthropology* 11, no. 3: 377–404.

Mandal, Sumit K. 2004. "For the Record: An Anti-war Protest in Jakarta Days before the Bali Bomb Attacks." *Kyoto Review of Southeast Asia* 5 (March). Accessed March 10, 2015. http://kyotoreview.cseas.kyoto-u.ac.jp/issue/issue4/index.html.

"Mantan Aktivis Jadi Caleg: Pertaruhan Integritas dan Kompetensi." 2004. Sabtu, *Kompas*, 7 February.

Margiyono and Kurnianan Tri Yunanto, eds. 2007. *Neraka Rezim Suharto: Misteri tempat penyiksaan Orde Baru*. Jakarta: Spasi & VHR Book.

"Masa Depan sebuah Masa Lalu." 2005. In *Memahami Kebebasan*. Jakarta: Oktagon.

Mauss, Marcel. 1935 [2006]. "Techniques of the Body." In *Techniques, Technology and Civilisation*. Edited by Nathan Schlanger. New York: Durkheim Press/Bergahn Books.

Mazzarella, William. 2013. *Censorium: Cinema and the Open Edge of Mass Publicity*. Durham, NC: Duke University Press.

McClelland, J. S. 1989. *The Crowd and the Mob: From Plato to Canetti*. London: Unwin Hyman.

McGregor, Katherine E. 2005. "Nugroho Notosusanto: The Legacy of a Historian in the Service of an Authoritarian Regime." In *Beginning to Remember: The Past in Indonesia's Present*, edited by M. S. Zurbuchen. Singapore: University of Singapore Press, 209–232.

McGregor, Katherine E. 2009. "Confronting the Past in Contemporary Indonesia: The Anticommunist Killings of 1965–66 and the Role of the Nahdlatul Ulama." *Critical Asian Studies* 41, no. 2: 195–224.

McGregor, Katherine E. 2013. "Fighting the Hellhounds: Pro-democracy Activists and Party Politics in Post-Suharto Indonesia." *Journal of Contemporary Asia* 43, no. 1: 28–50.

McGregor, Katherine E. 2014. "How Jokowi Won and Democracy Survived." *Journal of Democracy* 25, no. 4 (October): 111–125.

McRae, Dave. 2001. "The 1998 Indonesian Student Movement." Working Paper 110. Victoria, Australia: Centre of Southeast Asian Studies, Monash Asia Institute, Monash University.

Mehta, Uday. 1999. *Liberalism and Empire: A Study of Nineteenth-Century British Liberal Thought*. Chicago: University of Chicago Press.

"Meledak di Kandang Sendiri." 1998. *D&R* 48, no. 2 (30 January).

Menchik, Jeremy. 2009. "Symbols and Signs." *Inside Indonesia* (online magazine) 97 (July). Accessed May 8, 2014. http://www.insideindonesia.org/edition-97/symbols-and-signs.

"Mereka Pun Meliput Kita." 1998. *Bergerak*, 25 March.

Mereka yang Hilang dan Mereka yang Ditinggalkan: Potret Penghilangan Paksa di Indonesia. 2004. Jakarta: IKOHI.

Mietzner, Marcus. 2013. "Fighting the Hell Hounds: Pro-democracy Activists and Party Politics in Post-Suharto Indonesia." *Journal of Contemporary Asia* 43, no. 1: 28–50.

Miftahuddin. 2004. *Radikalisasi Pemuda: PRD Melawan Tirani*. Jakarta: Desantara.

Mitchell, Don. 2003. *The Right to the City: Social Justice and the Fight for Public Space*. New York: Guilford Press.

Mitchell, Don. 2012. "Tent City: Spaces of Homeless Survival and Organizing in the American City." In *Social Housing—Housing the Social: Art, Property and Spatial Justice*, edited by A. Phillips and F. Erdemci. Amsterdam: SKOR, 277–306.

Mohamad, Goenawan. 1989. "The 'Manikebu Affair': Literature and Politics in the 1960s." *Prisma* 46, LP3ES.

Mohamad, Goenawan. 1994. "City." In *Goenawan Mohamad, SIDELINES: Thought Pieces from TEMPO Magazine*. Translated by Jennifer Lindsay. Jakarta: Lontar Press, 28–29.

Mohamad, Goenawan. 2009. "Remembering the Left." 5 October. Accessed September 20, 2015. http://goenawanmohamad.com/2009/10/05/remembering-the-left/.

Mrázek, Rudolf. 2002. *Engineers of Happy Land: Technology and Nationalism in a Colony*. Princeton, NJ: Princeton University Press.

Mrázek, Rudolf. 2004. "Bypasses and Flyovers: Approaching the Metropolitan History of Indonesia." *Social History* 29, no. 4 (November): 425–443.

Mrázek, Rudolf. 2006. "Literature or Revolution." *Social Text* 86, 24, no. 1 (spring): 86–103.

Mrázek, Rudolf. 2009. "Boven Digoel and Terezín: Camps at the Time of Triumphant Technology." *East Asian Science, Technology and Society: An International Journal* 3: 287–314.

Mrázek, Rudolf. 2010. *A Certain Age: Colonial Jakarta through the Memories of Its Intellectuals.* Durham, NC: Duke University Press.

Mugiyanto. 2005. "Wiranto mengetahui 14 Korban Penculikan 1998: Mencari Jejak 14 Korban Penghilangan Paksa 1997–1998" [Wiranto knew about the 14 kidnap victims in 1998: Looking for the traces of the 14 victims of forced disappearances 1997–1998]. 18 July. Accessed November 22, 2013. http://mugiyanto.blogspot.com /2005/07/wiranto-mengetahui-14-korban.html.

Munir. 2001. "Indonesia, Violence and the Integration Problem." In *Violence in Indonesia*, edited by Ingrid Wessel and Georgia Wimhofer. Hamburg: Abera, 17–24.

Muryanto, Bambang. 2015. "Prosecutors Seek Suspended Sentence for Florence Sihombing." *Jakarta Post*, 16 March. Accessed March 17, 2015. http://www .thejakartapost.com/news/2015/03/16/prosecutors-seek-suspended-sentence -florence-sihombing.html.

Nas, Peter, and Pratiwo. 2003. "The Streets of Jakarta: Fear, Trust and Amnesia in Urban Development." In *Framing Indonesian Realities*, edited by Peter Nas, Gerard Persoon, and Rivke Jaffe. Leiden: KITLV Press, 275–294.

Niewenheuys, Rob. 1999. *Mirror of the Indies.* Singapore: Periplus Books.

Nilan, Pam, Argyo Demartoto, and Agung Wibowo. 2011. "Young Men and Peer Fighting in Solo, Indonesia." *Men and Masculinities* 14 (October): 470–490.

Nuttall, Sarah. 2003. "Stylizing the Self: The Y Generation in Rosebank, Johannesburg." *Public Culture* 16, no. 3: 430–452.

"Oase di Jalanan Jakarta." 1999. *Mahasiswa Indonesia*, 25 January.

Offstream and YAPPIKA. 2002. *Jalan Panjang Menuju Demokrasi: Buku Foto Gerakan Masyarakat Sipil di Indonesia, 1965–2001.* Jakarta: YAPPIKA.

"Organisasi Tanpa Ketua." 1999. *Mahasiswa Indonesia*, 25 January.

"Ospek Mahasiswa Tiru Pola Militeristik." 1999. *Kompas*, 27 August.

"Ospek Tumbuhkan Peradaban Primitif." 2003. *Kompas*, 8 September.

Pamuk, Orhan. 2010. *Museum of Innocence.* New York: Vintage International.

Pandey, Gyanendra. 2006. *Routine Violence: Nations, Fragments, Histories.* Stanford, CA: Stanford University Press.

Paramaditha, Intan. 2014. "Indonesia's Election and Emergency Activism." *Jakarta Post*, 14 August. Accessed March 1, 2015. http://m.thejakartapost.com/news/2014/08 /14/indonesia-s-election-and-emergency-activism.html.

Partai Rakyat Demokratik. 1999. *Demi Demokrasi, PRD Menolak Takluk.* Jakarta.

Patria, Nezar. 2003. "May 1998, the Razing of Jakarta." *Tempo* 26 (May).

Pavin Chachavalpongpun. 2014. " 'Good Coup Gone Bad': Thailand's Political Developments since Thaksin's Downfall." In *Good Coup Gone Bad: Thailand's Political Developments since Thaksin's Downfall*, edited by Pavin Chachavalpongpun. Singapore: ISEAS, 3–16.

Pemberton, John. 1994. *On the Subject of "Java."* Ithaca, NY: Cornell University Press.

Pemuda Republik Rakjat Indonesia. 1952. Manifesto P.R.R.I.

"Pers Mahasiswa, Anarkhis-Oposisionil?" 1985. *Politika* 8/9 (October/December): 1.

"Pesan ekonomi kerakyatan Prabowo dari atas kuda seharga rp. 3 miliar." 2014. *Detik. com*, 25 March. Accessed March 4, 2015. http://news.detik.com/read/2014/03/25 /160937/2536177/1562/pesan-ekonomi-kerakyatan-prabowo-dari-atas-kuda-seharga -rp-3-miliar.

Pijar Edisi Khusus. Majalah Mahasiswa Fakultas Filsafat UGM. September 1989.

"Pimpred dan sejumlah redaktur vivanews mundur gara-gara iklan Jokowi." 2014. *Mimbar Rakyat*, 11 April. Accessed April 20, 2014. http://mimbar-rakyat.com/detail /pimpred-dan-sejumlah-redaktur-vivanews-mundur-gara-gara-iklan-jokowi.

"Posko diminta pindah dari kampus Salemba." 1998. *Bergerak*, 10 June.

"Posko Salemba dibubarkan." 1998. *Bergerak*, 15 June.

Prasetyantoko, S. E. A., and Ignatius Wahyu Indriyo. 2001. *Gerakan Mahasiswa dan Demokrasi di Indonesia*. Jakarta: Yayasan Hak Asasi Manusia, Demokrasi dan Supremasi hukum.

"Premanisme Kampus dan Akal-akalan Mahasiswa." 2003. *Kompas*, 14 September.

Purnon, Kristianto. 2008. "Polisi Datang, Mahasiswa Bubar, Mobil Padam." *Kompas*, 24 June.

Rafael, Vince. 2003. "The Cell Phone and the Crowd: Messianic Politics in the Contemporary Philippines." *Public Culture* 15, no. 3: 399–425.

"Rama Pratama: Hidup Normal." 2003. Pokok & Tokoh, *Tempo* 32, no. 12 (19–25 May).

Raudal Tanjung Banua. *"In Memoriam Seorang Demonstran: Sebuah Sajak, Sepotong Pamflet, Sepenggal Buku Harian: Suatu Pertemuan Dengan M. Yusuf Rizal."* On/Off *17/11/2003.*

Rheingold, Howard. 2003. *Smart Mobs: The Next Social Revolution*. New York: Basic Books.

Robinson, Geoffrey. 1995. *The Dark Side of Paradise: Political Violence in Bali*. Ithaca, NY: Cornell University Press.

Rofiuddin. 2013. "Baliho Hanura: Harry Tanoe, Wiranto, dan Soeharto." *Tempo*, 2 June. Accessed March 3, 2015. http://www.tempo.co/read/news/2013/06/02 /078485120/Baliho-Hanura-Harry-Tanoe-Wiranto-dan-Soeharto.

Roitman, Janet. N.d. "Crisis." *Political Concepts*. Accessed April 14, 2015. http://www .politicalconcepts.org/issue1/crisis/.

Roosa, John. 2006. *Pretext for Mass Murder*. Madison: University of Wisconsin Press.

Roosa, John, A. Ratih, and H. Farid. 2004. *Tahun yang tak pernah berakhir: Memahami pengalaman korban '65: Esai-esai sejarah lisan*. Jakarta: Lembaga Studi dan Advokasi Masyarakat.

Rumah Maida. 2009. Film directed by Teddy Soeriaatmadja. Jakarta: Karuna Pictures and Lamp Pictures.

Rutherford, Danilyn. 1993. "Unpacking a National Heroine: Two Kartinis and Their People." *Indonesia* 55 (October): 23–40.

Rutherford, Danilyn. 2003. *Raiding the Land of the Foreigners: The Limits of the Nation on an Indonesian Frontier*. Princeton, NJ: Princeton University Press.

Ryter, Loren. 1998. "Pemuda Pancasila: The Last Loyalist Free Men of Suharto's Order?" *Indonesia* 66 (October): 44–73.

Said, Edward. 1993. *Culture and Imperialism*. New York: Vintage Books.

Said, Edward. 1994 [1978]. *Orientalism*. Twenty-fifth anniversary ed. New York: Random House.

Saputra, Hervin. 2008. "Komnas HAM Agar Bentuk Tim Dokter Alternatif." (6 July).

Sarumpaet, Ratna. 1997. *Marsinah: Nyanyian dari Bawah Tanah*. Yogyakarta, Indonesia: Yayasan Bentang Budaya.

Sassen, Saksia. 2008. *Territory, Authority, Rights: From Medieval to Global Assemblages*. Princeton, NJ: Princeton University Press.

Sastramidjaja, Yatun. 2006. "Memories of Protest, Students, History, Space, and the Loss of Agency in Post-Suharto, Jakarta." In *Indonesian Transitions*, edited by Henk Schulte-Nordholt and Ireen Hoogendoom. Yogyakarta: Pustaka Pelajar, 249–288.

Schulte-Nordholt, Henk. 1997. Introduction to *Outward Appearances: Dressing State and Society in Indonesia*, edited by Henk Schulte-Nordholt. Leiden: KITLV Press, 1–37.

Scott, James. 1972. "Patron-Client Politics and Political Change in Southeast Asia." *American Political Science Review* 66, no. 1: 91–113.

Scott, James. 1985. *Weapons of the Weak*. New Haven, CT: Yale University Press.

Scott, James. 1999. *Seeing Like a State: How Certain Schemes to Improve the Human Condition Have Failed*. New Haven, CT: Yale University Press.

Semiono, Ruht. 2008. "Polisi Serbu Kampus Unas, 126 Mahasiswa Ditangkap." *Suara Pembaruan*, 24 May.

Sen, Krishna. 1991. "Si Boy Looked at Johnny: Indonesian Screen at the Turn of the Decade." *Continuum* 4 (1): 136–151.

SenseCity. 2005. Jakarta: Goethe Institut Jakarta. December.

Setelah 15 Tahun. 2013. Film directed by Tino Saroengallo.

Setiyawan, Iwan. 2008. "Demo Mahasiswa Tidak Akan Dilarang." *Kompas*, 29 June.

Shiraishi, Saya. 1997. *Young Heroes: The Indonesian Family in Politics*. Ithaca, NY: SEAP.

Shiraishi, Takashi. 1990. *An Age in Motion: Popular Radicalism in Java, 1912–1926*. Ithaca, NY: Cornell University Press.

Sidel, John. 1998. "Macet Total: Logics of Circulation and Accumulation in the Demise of Indonesia's New Order." *Indonesia* 66 (October): 158–195.

Sidel, John. 1999. *Capital, Coercion, and Crime: Bossism in the Philippines*. Stanford, CA: Stanford University Press.

Sidel, John. 2001. "Riots, Church Burnings, Conspiracies: The Moral Economy of the Indonesian Crowd in the Late Twentieth Century." In *Violence in Indonesia*, edited by Ingrid Wessel and Georgia Wimhofer. Hamburg: Abera.

Sidel, John. 2006. *Riots, Pogroms, Jihad: Religious Violence in Indonesia*. Ithaca, NY: Cornell University Press.

Siegel, James T. 1986. *Solo in the New Order*. Princeton, NJ: Princeton University Press.

Siegel, James T. 1997. *Fetish, Recognition, Revolution*. Princeton, NJ: Princeton University Press.

Siegel, James T. 1998a. "Early Thoughts on the Violence of May 13 and 14, 1998." *Indonesia* 66 (October): 75–108.

Siegel, James T. 1998b. *A New Criminal Type in Jakarta*. Durham, NC: Duke University Press.

Siegel, James T. 2006. *Naming the Witch*. Palo Alto, CA: Stanford University Press.

Simandjuntak, Deasy. 2012. "Gifts and Promises: Patronage Democracy in a Decentralised Indonesia." *EJEAS* 11: 99–126.

Simmel, Georg. 1997a. "The Metropolis and Mental Life." In *Simmel on Culture: Selected Writings*, edited by David Frisby and Mike Featherstone. London: Sage, 174–185.

Simmel, Georg. 1997b. *Simmel on Culture: Selected Writings*. Edited by David Frisby and Mike Featherstone. London: Sage.

Simone, Abdoumaliq. 2014. *Jakarta: Drawing the City Near*. Minneapolis: University of Minnesota Press.

Slater, Dan. 2010. *Ordering Power: Contentious Politics and Authoritarian Leviathans in Southeast Asia*. Cambridge: Cambridge University Press.

Soe Hok Gie. 2005. *Catatan Seorang Demonstran*. Jakarta: Pustaka LP3ES.

Soekarno. 2001. *Indonesia Menggugat: Pidato Pembelaan Bung Karno di muka hakim kolonial*. Giwangan, Yogyakarta: Yayasan Untuk Indonesia.

Sontag, Susan. 1977. *On Photography*. New York: Macmillan.

Spyer, Patricia. 1998. "The Tooth of Time, or Taking a Look at the 'Look' of Clothing in Late Nineteenth-Century Aru." In *Border Fetishisms: Material Objects in Unstable Spaces*, edited by Patricia Spyer. New York: Routledge, 150–182.

Spyer, Patricia. 2000. *The Memory of Trade*. Durham, NC: Duke University Press.

Spyer, Patricia. 2008. "Blind Faith: Painting Christianity in Post-Conflict Ambon." *Social Text* 96 26, no. 3: 11–37.

Steele, Janet. 2005. *Wars Within: The Story of "Tempo," an Independent Magazine in Soeharto's Indonesia*. Jakarta: Equinox.

Steijlen, Fridus, ed. 2002. *Memories of "The East."* Leiden: KITLV Press.

Stewart, Kathleen. 1996. *A Space on the Side of the Road: Cultural Poetics in an "Other" America*. Princeton, NJ: Princeton University Press.

Stewart, Susan. 1993 [1984]. *On Longing: Narratives of the Miniature, the Gigantic, the Souvenir, the Collection*. Durham, NC: Duke University Press.

Stoler, Ann Laura. 2002. "On the Uses and Abuses of the Past in Indonesia: Beyond the Mass Killings of 1965." *Asian Survey* 42, no. 2: 642–650.

Stoler, Ann Laura. 2009. *Along the Archival Grain: Epistemic Anxieties and Colonial Common Sense*. Princeton, NJ: Princeton University Press.

Strassler, Karen. 2005. "Material Witnesses: Photographs and the Making of Reformasi Memory." In *Beginning to Remember: The Past in the Indonesian Present*, edited by Mary S. Zurbuchen. Singapore: Singapore University Press, 278–311.

Strassler, Karen. 2008. "Material Resources of the Historical Imagination: Documents and the Future of the Past in Post-Suharto Indonesia." In *Timely Assets: The Politics of Resources and Their Temporalities*, edited by Elizabeth Emma Ferry and Mandana E. Limbert. Santa Fe: SAR Press, 217–244.

Strassler, Karen. 2010. *Refracted Visions: Popular Photography and National Modernity in Java*. Durham, NC: Duke University Press.

Student Movement in Indonesia (The Army Forced Them to Be Violent). 2002. Film directed by Tino Saroengallo.

Sugiyarto. 2008a. "Mahasiswa Unas Merasa Ada yang Susupi Aksi Mereka." *Kompas*, 30 May.

Sugiyarto. 2008b. "Polisi: Aksi Demonstrasi Ditunggangi." *Kompas*, 25 June.

Sulistyo, Hermawan. 2002. *Lawan! Jejak-jejak di balik Kejatuhan Soeharto*. Jakarta: Pensil 324.

Supriyanto, Didik. 1998. *Perlawanan Pers Mahasiswa: Protes Sepanjang NKK/BKK*. Jakarta: Pustaka Sinar Harapan.

"Suyat: Biar tidak sia-sia pengorbanannya." 2004. Mailing List Nasional Indonesia—PPI—India, 14 April.

Tanter, Richard, and Kenneth Young, eds. 1990. *The Politics of Middle Class Indonesia*. Monash Papers on Southeast Asia, no. 19. Victoria, Australia: Centre of Southeast Asian Studies, Monash University.

Taufik, Ahmad. 2003. "Kronologis Penyerbuan Tomy Winata ke Tempo." 11 March. http://abdulmanan.blogspot.com/2003/03/kronologis-penyerbuan-tomy-winata-ke.html.

Taufiqurrahman, Mohammed. 2010. "Student Movement Close to Obsolescence." *Jakarta Post*, 14 March.

Tausig, Ben, and Tyrell Haberkorn, eds. 2012. "Unspeakable Things Special Collection." Special issue, *Sensate Journal*. Accessed November 10, 2013. http://sensatejournal.com/category/special-collections/unspeakable-things/.

Taussig, Michael. 1997. *The Magic of the State*. New York and London: Routledge.

Taussig, Michael. 2004. *My Cocaine Museum*. Chicago: University of Chicago Press.

Taussig, Michael. 2012. "I'm So Angry I Made a Sign." *Critical Inquiry* 39, no. 1: 56–88.

Taylor, Diana. 2003. *The Archive and the Repertoire: Performing Cultural Memory in the Americas*. Durham, NC: Duke University Press.

Taylor, Jean Gelman. 1983. *The Social World of Batavia*. London: University of Wisconsin Press.

"Teka-Teki Wiji Thukul: Tragedi Seorang Penyair." 2013. Edisi Khusus. *Tempo*, 12–19 May.

Thompson, Michael. 1979. *Rubbish Theory: The Creation and Destruction of Value*. Oxford: Oxford University Press.

Thongchai Winichakul. 2002. "Remembering/Silencing the Traumatic Past: The Ambivalent Memories of the October 1976 Massacre in Bangkok." In *Cultural Crisis and Social Memory: Modernity and Identity in Thailand and Laos*, edited by Shigeharu Tanabe and Charles Keyes. Honolulu: University of Hawaii Press, 243–286.

Thufail, Fadjar I. 2005. "Ninjas in Narratives of Local and National Violence in Post-Suharto Indonesia." In *Beginning to Remember: The Past in the Indonesian Present*, edited by Mary S. Zurbuchen. Singapore: Singapore University Press, 150–167.

Thukul, Wiji. 1994. "Sajak Kota." In *Mencari Tanah Lapang*. The Netherlands: Manus Amici.

Thukul, Wiji. 2000a. *Aku Ingin Jadi Peluru*. Magelang: IndonesiaTera.

Thukul, Wiji. 2000b. "Nyanyian Akar Rumput" [Songs of the grassroots]. In *Aku Ingin Jadi Peluru*. Magelang: IndonesiaTera, 6.

Tilly, Charles, and Sidney Tarrow. 2006. *Contentious Politics*. Boulder, CO: Paradigm.

Toer, Pramoedya Ananta. 1978. "Dendam" Translated as "Revenge" by B. R. O'G Anderson. *Indonesia* 26: 43–61.

Toer, Pramoedya Ananta. 1999a. "Houseboy + Maid." In *Tales from Djakarta: Caricatures of Circumstances and their Human Beings*, translated by Julie Shackford-Bradley. Ithaca, NY: SEAP, 17–26.

Toer, Pramoedya Ananta. 1999b. *The Mute's Soliloquy*. Translated by Willem Samuels. New York: Hyperion East.

Toer, Pramoedya Ananta. 1999c. "Pidato Pramoedya Ananta Toer dalam Pelantikan Sebagai Anggota PRD." Accessed September 21, 2015. https://sites.google.com/site /pramoedyasite/home/works-in-bahasa-indonesia/pidato-pramoedya-ananta-toer-dalam-pelantikan-sebagai-anggota-prd.

Trouillot, Michel-Rolph. 1995. *Silencing the Past: Power and the Production of History*. Boston: Beacon Press.

Truitt, Allison J. 2013. *Dreaming of Money in Ho Chi Minh City*. Seattle: University of Washington Press.

Tsing, Anna Lowenhaupt. 2004. *Friction: An Ethnography of Global Connection*. Princeton, NJ: Princeton University Press.

Turner, Victor. 1995. *The Ritual Process: Structure and Anti-Structure*. New Brunswick, NJ: Transaction.

Uhlin, Anders. 1995. "The Struggle for Democracy: An Actor-Structure Approach." *Scandinavian Political Studies* 18, no. 3: 133–158.

Uhlin, Anders. 1997. *Indonesia and the "Third Wave of Democratization."* New York: St. Martin's Press.

van Dijk, Kees. 2001. *A Country in Despair: Indonesia between 1997 and 2000*. Leiden: KITLV Press.

van Dijk, Kees. 2002a. "The Good, the Bad and the Ugly." In *Roots of Violence in Indonesia*, edited by Freek Colombijn and J. Thomas Lindblad. Leiden: KITLV Press, 277–297.

van Dijk, Kees. 2002b. "The Realms of Order and Disorder in Indonesian Life." In *Violence and Vengeance: Discontent and Conflict in New Order Indonesia*, edited by Frans Hüskens and Huub de Jonge, Nijmegen Studies in Development and Cultural Change, vol. 37. Saarbrücken: Verl. Für Entwicklungspolitik, 71–94.

van Klinken, Gerry, and Joshua Barker. 2009. "Reflections on the State in Indonesia." In *State of Authority: The State in Society in Indonesia*. Ithaca, NY: SEAP, 1–16.

van Leeuwen, Lizzy. 2011. *Lost in Mall: An Ethnography of Middle-Class Jakarta in the 1990s*. Leiden: KITLV Press.

Verdery, Katherine. 2014. *Secrets and Truths: Ethnography in the Archives of Romania's Secret Police. The Natalie Zemon Davis Annual Lecture Series, Vol. 7*. Central European University Press.

Wawancara. 1998. "Komentar Aktivis Forbes." *Detik.com*, 21 December. Accessed August 20, 2007. http://www.detik.com/wawancara/199812/19981221–1758.html.

"Wawancara: Riri Riza: Saya Dulu Makan Nasi Golkar." 2005. *Gatra* 36, 18 June.

Weber, Max. 1994. *Sociological Writings*. Edited by Wolf Heydebrand. New York: Continuum.

Weiss, Meredith L., and Edward Aspinall, eds. 2012. *Student Activism in Asia: Between Protest and Powerlessness*. Minneapolis: University of Minnesota Press.

Wessel, Ingrid. 2001. "The Politics of Violence in New Order Indonesia in the Last Decade of the 20th Century." In *Violence in Indonesia*, edited by Ingrid Wessel and Georgia Wimhofer. Hamburg: Abera Verlag Markus Voss, 64–81.

Widjojo, Muridan S. 1999. *Kronologi Demonstrasi Mahasiswa 1989–1998*. Jakarta: Yayasan Insan Politika.

Widjojo, Muridan S., et al. 1999. *Penakluk Rezim Orde Baru: Gerakan mahasiswa '98* [The conquerers of the New Order regime: The '98 student Movement]. Jakarta: Pustaka Sinar Harapan.

Wijayanto, Iip. 2003. *Sex in the "Kost": Realitas dan Moralitas Seks Kaum "Terpelajar."* Yogyakarta: Tinta.

Wilson. 2005. *Dunia dibalik Jeruji*. Yogyakarta: Resist Book.

Wilson, Ian. 2006. "Continuity and Change: The Changing Contours of Organized Violence in Post–New Order Indonesia." *Critical Asian Studies* 38, no. 2: 265–297.

Wilson, Ian. 2011. "Reconfiguring Rackets: Racket Regimes, Protection and the State in Post–New Order Jakarta." In *The State and Illegality in Indonesia*. Leiden: KITLV Press, 239–260.

Wilson, Ian. 2012a. "'The Biggest Cock': Masculinity, Violence and Authority amongst Jakarta's Gangs." In *Masculinities in Southeast Asia*, edited by Lenore Lyons and Michelle Ford. London: Routledge Press, 121–138.

Wilson, Ian. 2012b. "Testing the Boundaries of the State: Gangs, Militias, Vigilantes and Violent Entrepreneurs in Southeast Asia." In *Routledge Handbook of Southeast Asian Politics*, edited by Richard Robison. New York: Routledge, 288–301.

Wilson, Ian. 2014. "Morality Racketeering: Vigilantism and Populist Militancy in Indonesia." In *Between Dissent and Power: The Transformation of Islamic Politics in the Middle East and Asia*. New York: Palgrave Macmillan, 248–274.

Wilson, Ian. 2015. *The Politics of Protection Rackets in Post–New Order Indonesia: Coercive Capital, Authority and Street Politics.* New York: Routledge.

Wimhofer, Georgia. 2001. "Indonesian Students in 1998: Civil Society and the Effects of Violence." In *Violence in Indonesia*, edited by Ingrid Wessel and Georgia Wimhofer. Hamburg: Abera Verlag Markus Voss, 168–184.

Winegar, Jessica. 2012. "The Privilege of Revolution: Gender, Class, Space, and Affect in Egypt." *American Ethnologist* 39, no. 1: 67–70.

Winters, Jeffrey A. 2011. *Oligarchy.* Cambridge: Cambridge University Press.

Wolff, John U., and James T. Collins. 1989. *Kamus Indonesia-Inggris.* 3rd ed. Jakarta: Gramedia.

Wolfarth, Irving. 1986. "Etcetera? The Historian as Chiffonier." In *New German Critique* 39 (autumn), special issue on Walter Benjamin, 142–168.

Young, Ken. 1999. "Consumption, Social Differentiation and Self-Definition of the New Rich in Industrialising Southeast Asia." In *Culture and Privilege in Southeast Asia*, edited by Michael Pinches. London: Routledge, 57–86.

Yurchak, Alexei. 2005. *Everything Was Forever, Until It Was No More: The Last Soviet Generation.* Princeton, NJ: Princeton University Press.

Zinn, Howard. 1980. *A People's History of the United States: 1492–Present.* New York: Harper Perennial.

Zon, Fadli. 2004. *The Politics of the May 1998 Riots.* Jakarta: Solstice.

INDEX

Deleuze, Gilles, 200

democracy: activism and, 61–62, 71–74, 98–99, 225n31; citizenship discourses and, 71–74; crises of, 212–17; electoral politics and, 22–23, 179–80, 190–96, 243n13; history's relationship to, 37–41; Indonesia's transition to, ix, 60; Islam and, 219n14; New Order discourses of, 179–80, 184–88; pemuda's relation to, 3–5, 12–17; spatiality and, 60–65, 138–40; trash of, 40, 57–60; violence's justification and, 132–38. *See also* activists; demonstrations; election fever; Indonesia

demonstrations: aesthetics of, 85–87, 163–64; bodily techniques and, 74–80; commodification of, 180–85; disorder discourses and, 57–60, 74–78, 88–89, 98–99, 119–21, 133–34, 138–45; efficacy of, 71–74; expertise in, 71–84; media coverage of, 71, 74–78, 80, 82–84, 180–85, 196–97; paid protesters and, 76–78, 229n26; pemuda style and, 9–10; photos of, *58, 77, 81, 102*; spatial practices of, 5, 17–21, 59–71, 228n23, 229n24; temporality and, 5–7, 60–61, 150; violence and, 118–22, 132–40, 142–45. *See also* activists; class; massa; rakyat; spatiality

"The Demonstrator" (Haryanto), *92*

dependency theory, 99

Derrida, Jacques, 11–12, 149, 222n6

Detik, 27, 162

Diary of a Demonstrator (Gie), 8

Dien, Cut Nya, 128

disappearances, x, 21, 37, 42, 48, 90, 124–33, 224n26, 234n10, 234n14, 236n31, 244n21

Djati, Raharjo Waluyo, 127–28

Djejak Darah (film), 128

Djojohadikoesoemo, Hasyim, 212

domiciliation, 55–56, 147–53, 166–71, 176–77

Drexler, Elizabeth, 142

Dur, Gus, 4

Durkheim, Emile, 70, 240n17

dwelling, 148, 176–77

East Timor, 35–36, 226n43, 226n47

Editor, 27

Egypt, 4

eksepsi, 49–53

election fever, 179–80, 190–99

emosi, 84, 120, 122, 199

Enwezor, Okwui, 39

existensi, 204–5, 244n27

family ideology, 148, 151–53, 157–64, 174–75

Fanon, Franz, 154, 240n18

Farge, Arlette, 41

fashions. *See* style

Fauzi, Maftuh, 141

fevers: archive fever, 11–12; election fever, 179–80, 190–99; pemuda fever, 3, 11–12, 31–33, 38, 179–80, 210–12

First Semanggi tragedy, xi, 66–71, 123, 136, 162–63, 189–90, *191*

Forkot. *See* City Forum

Forum for Student Action for Reformasi and Democracy, 136, 220n16

Foster, Susan Leigh, 75

Foucault, Michel, 30

Foulcher, Keith, 42

FPPI (Front for Indonesian Youth Struggles), 39, 172–75, 195, 215, 241n30

Free Papua Movement, 90

Freire, Paolo, 154

Friction (Tsing), 150

G30S, 87–89

Gadjah Mada University, 8

Gathering of Activists Across Generations, 142–43

Gatra, 113

Geertz, Clifford, 193, 222n6

gender: activism's masculinity and, 6–7, 11–12, 96–99, 152–53, 213–17; activist kinship relationships and, 147–48, 171–77, 239n14; family ideology and, 152–53, 157–60; morality and, 22, 157–60, 163–64, 227n3; violence and, x, 30, 124

Generation 28, 14–15, 96

Generation 45, 95–96, 155. *See also* Indonesian Revolution of 1945

Generation 66, 7, 13, 73, 89, 112, 209, 231n16, 232n26

Generation 74, 7

Generation 78, 7, 222n9

Generation 98: commodification of, 180–85, 187–96; demonstrations of, 60–62; elections of 2004 and, 22, 179–80, 186–88, 196–99, 204–7; internal politics of, 200–205; May Riots and, x, 2, 19; memory and, 5, 8, 11–12, 76–77, 95–99; Soe Hok Gie and, 108–14; 2014 elections and, 212–17. *See also* activists; May Riots; memory; Reformasi; Suharto

Gerinda, 186–87, 213, 235n19, 245n2

Gie (Reza), 109, *109*, 111, 113–15

Gie, Kwik Kian, 221n19

Gie, Soe Hok, 8, 21, 89, 108–14, 223n16, 232n26, 232n29

globalish, 94, 231n12

globalization, 89–95, 101–8, 114–15, 231n21

Golkar, 85, 186–87, 205, 235n19, 243n13

Gordimer, Nadine, 131

Gramsci, Antonio, 154

Greenberg, Jessica, 3

Guattari, Félix, 200

Guevara, Che, 99–100, *100*, 101, 103–4, 110, 160, 231n21

Gumelar, Agum, 198

Gunadarma University, 238n9

Gusmao, Xanana, 226n43

Habibie, B. J., xi, 135, 162

Haiti, 89–90

Hambali, Hendra, 234n14

Hardt, Michael, 176

Harvey, David, 71

Haryanto, D. Rudi, 12–15, *16*, 92–93

heat, 78–80

Heat Wave (Klinenberg), 78

Heidegger, Martin, 30, 148, 176–77

Hendrawan, Herman, 234n14

Himpunan Mahasiswa Islam, 199, 219n15

Hinton, Alex, 236n33

Hobsbawm, Eric, 95, 98

Hoffman, Danny, 122–23, 169–70

Holston, Jim, 71

horizontal violence, 120, 132

Humanitarian Volunteer Team, 165

Human Rights Watch, 222n12, 235n18

Hunneman, Taufan, 162–63

IAIN Sunan Kaligaja, 8

ibu, 152–53, 157–59, 177, 202, 244n26

Ibu Wawan, 202, 244n26

IDP (Indonesian Democratic Party): July 27 Incident and, x

IISG (International Institute for Social History), 6, 25, 32–33, 38–39, 45, 55–56, 214n6, 221n1, 224n30

Ikatan Keluarga Orang Hiland, 157

Imagining Argentina (film), 127

Imbas, 223n16

Indonesia: Chinese ethnicity in, x–xi, 19, 152, 195, 210, 221n19, 232n27, 237n42, 243n20; democracy and, ix, 60; Dutch colonial legacies in, 6–10, 42, 48–53, 61–62, 69, 95–96, 112, 155–57, 222n8, 225n33; history's controversies and, 37–41; modernity in, 10, 33–34, 89–95, 169–70; religious diversity in, ix, 8–9, 72, 162–63, 174, 199, 211, 219n11, 221n3, 230n5. *See also* activists; democracy; New Order regime; pemuda; violence; *specific generations, people, and events*

"Indonesia Accuses" (Soekarno), 226n42

Indonesian Christian Students Movement, 141

Indonesian Revolution of 1945, 95–96, 155, 212

Indonesia Weeps (documentary), 165

Indymedia, 143

insurgent citizenship, 71–74

intel, 57, 84, 127, 130, 133, 135–38

Interaction Forum '66, 13

International Day of Solidarity for Victims of Torture, 128

patronage democracy, 183, 187–90, 212–17. *See also* brokers; money

PDI-P (Indonesian Democratic Party of Struggle), 47–52, 86, 124, 129, 184, 214, 220n16, 230nn7–8, 233n31, 240n21

Pemberton, John, 186

pemuda: activism and, 5–6, 95–99, 107–8, 210–12; aesthetics of, 9–10, 21–22, 85–87, 89–99, 183–84, 230n11, 231n16; definitions of, 7–12, 219n4, 239n11; domiciliation and, 148–51; fever, 3, 11–12, 38, 210–12; Indonesian Revolution and, 95–96; memory and, 7–17; morality discourses and, 6–7, 41–43, 157–60; New Order's uses of, 6–7, 12–17, 25–27, 184–88, 219n10, 222n13; post-Suharto politics and, 22–23, 176–77, 179–80; rakyat's relation to, 8–10, 63–64; Soe Hok Gie and, 108–14; university student identification and, 2, 95–99. *See also* activists; Sumpah Pemuda; university students

"Peringatan" (Thukul), 82–84

Petrus campaign, 26, 62–63

Philippines, 69, 118, 154

Pijar, 25–31, 53, 127, 220n16, 226n47

Pijar, 43

PKI (Indonesian Communist Party), 88, 90, 110–12, 132–33, 226n40, 230n10

pledoi, 48–53

"Poem of the Angry Person" (Rendra), 222n5

Politika, 35

posko, 22, 147–49, 151–53, 166–71, *167*, 176–77, 240nn21–22

Pramoedya, 9

Prasetioantoko, A., 199

Pratama, Rama, 196–99, 244n23

PDR (People's Democratic Party), 8, 38–39, 48, 54, 66, 100, 117–18, 127–36, 184, 205, 224n26, 226n40, 230n7, 235n19

"The Problem of Style" (Simmel), 98

propaganda, 20, 29, 36–40, 43, 47, 86–91, 112, 152, 185, 214, 223n20, 245n3

provokator, 141–45

Putri, Anindya Kusuma, 230n5

"The Question Concerning Technology" (Heidegger), 30

Rachman, M. Fadjroel, 202–4, 223n15

Rais, Amien, 196

rakyat: definitions of, 231n14; demonstrations and, 66–71, 82–83, 134–38; morality and, 59–60; as paid demonstrators, 76–78, 229n26; university students' relation to, 8–10, 17, 21, 63–64, 89, 122–24, 140–45, 153–54, 168–71, 180–85, 199, 203; violence by, 117–24. *See also* class; demonstrations; massa; university students

rape, x–xi, 30, 124, 237n42

Reformasi: archives of, 31–33, 37–41; definition of, 2; demonstration practices of, 60–62, 132–40; memory and, 5, 12–17, 60, 95–99, 209–10; morality and, 41–43; style of, 9–10, 19–20, 84–87, 90–95, 112–14; Suharto's downfall and, 11–12, 29–30. *See also* activists; demonstrations; Generation 98; memory; New Order regime; Suharto; *specific incidents and tragedies*

Reform Heroes Campus, 210

Refracted Visions (Strassler), 29

Relawan Perjuangan Demokrasi, 215–16, 221n1, 245n4

Rendra, W. S., 222n5

Revolutions in Islamic Thought (Wahib), 8

Reza, Faisol, 8

Reza, Riri, 111–13

Roitman, Janet, 212

Rose Team, 125–27, 132–33, 212

Rusdianto, Aan, 128

S21 La Machine de Mort Khmer Rouge (film), 128

Said, Edward, 231n22

"Sajak Kota" (Thukul), 63–64

TASS (Siswomihardjo, Triagus Susanto), 226n47
Taussig, Michael, 78
tawuran, 120, 225n38, 233n5
Taylor, Diana, 6
techne, 30–31
techniques of the body, 74–80
Tempo, 27, 80–81, 197, 229n31
temporality: activism and, 12–17, 161–64, 167–71, 176–77; archival gaps and, 8, 20–21; demonstrations and, 60–61, 150; domesticity and, 147–48; memory and, 5–7, 209–10; pemuda history and, 31–33; trash and, 40, 57–60. *See also* activists; archives; demonstrations; memory
Thailand, 4, 69, 210
Thufail, Fadjar, 237n43
Thukul, Wiji, 21, 41–42, *48*, 62–64, 82–84, 222n5, 234n14
tim suskes, 197–99
Tjiptaning, Ribka, 233n31
Toer, Pramoedya Ananta, 4, 160
Toisuta, Willi, 223n16
tokoh, 180–87, 196, 198–99, 202–4, 206–7, 242n5
Tomo, Bung, 83
torture, 48–53, 123, 125–35, 225n33, 236n31
translation, 35
trash, 40, 57–60, 227n4
trauma, 21, 48, 113–15, 123–32, 141, 204–5, 209–10
Trisakti tragedy, x, 1–2, 79, 123, 189–90, 202, 210, 237n37
Trouillot, Michel-Rolph, 89–90, 114–15, 209–10
Truitt, Allison J., 189
Truth and Reconciliation project (South Africa), 131
T-shirts, 21–22, 86–87, 89, 95, 99–102, *102*, 103–8, 184, 188, 212, 215
Tsing, Anna, 150–51
Turner, Victor, 162
Turn Left productions, 103, *104*

Ucok M Siahaan, M. Yusef, 234n14
Uhlin, Anders, 31
UKI-Cawang, 168–69
Umar, Dedy, 234n14
UNAS (National University), 35, 69, 140–42
UNAS Tragedy, 140–42
University of Indonesia, 13, 85–86, 111–12, 238n9
university students: aesthetics of, 9–10, 19–20, 84–87, 90–102, 112–15, 170–71, 182, 188, 230n11, 231n16, 241n25; class discourses and, 8–10, 17, 33–34, 63–64, 66–71, 89, 93–94, 96–104, 140–42, 152–56, 171–72, 174–77, 189–90, 232n25; counterviolence and, 132–38; internal politics of, 172–77; kost and, 147–64, 238n7, 239n10; morality of, 41–43, 119–21, 157–60, 163–64, 227n3; New Order's depoliticization of, 7–8, 59–61, 70–71, 141–42, 150, 222n9, 222n12; spatiality and, 60–62, 64–66, 228n23; subversion fears and, ix, 25–26, 28–33, 38, 46–56, 62; Suharto's downfall and, ix; violence against, x–xi, 1–2, 4, 119–22, 124–26, 233n5. *See also* class; demonstrations; New Order regime; pemuda; style
urban spaces, 60–74, 78–80, 91, 93–94
"Use if necessary" (Haryanto), 93

van Bruinessen, Martin, 211
van Leeuwen, Lizzie, 152, 228n23
Verdery, Katherine, 219n7
Videla, Jorge Rafael, 126
violence: activists and, 21, 30, 37, 42, 47–53, 107, 117–32, 140–45, 162, 253n23; anti-Communism's justification of, x, 1–2, 49–53, 111–12, 124–26, 129; Chinese ethnicity and, 19; gendered, x–xi, 30, 124, 237n42; media coverage of, 67–68; morality and, 21–22, 118–24, 137–38; New Order's militarism and, 21, 25–27, 66–71, 162, 234n14, 235n23; tawuran and, 120, 225n38, 233n5; techniques of